THE KENNEDYS
THE THIRD GENERATION

BOOK YOUR PLACE ON OUR WEBSITE AND MAKE THE READING CONNECTION!

We've created a customized website just for our very special readers, where you can get the inside scoop on everything that's going on with Zebra, Pinnacle and Kensington books.

When you come online, you'll have the exciting opportunity to:

- View covers of upcoming books
- Read sample chapters
- Learn about our future publishing schedule (listed by publication month *and author*)
- Find out when your favorite authors will be visiting a city near you
- Search for and order backlist books from our online catalog
- Check out author bios and background information
- Send e-mail to your favorite authors
- Meet the Kensington staff online
- Join us in weekly chats with authors, readers and other guests
- Get writing guidelines
- AND MUCH MORE!

**Visit our website at
http://www.pinnaclebooks.com**

THE KENNEDYS
THE THIRD GENERATION

**Barbara Gibson
with Ted Schwarz**

Pinnacle Books
Kensington Publishing Corp.
http://www.pinnaclebooks.com

PINNACLE BOOKS are published by

Kensington Publishing Corp.
850 Third Avenue
New York, NY 10022

Copyright © 1993, 1999 by Barbra Gibson and Ted Schwarz.

All rights reserved. No part of this book may be reproduced in any form or by any means without the prior written consent of the Publisher, excepting brief quotes used in reviews.

If you purchased this book without a cover you should be aware that this book is stolen property. It was reported as ''unsold and destroyed'' to the Publisher and neither the Author nor the Publisher has received any payment for this ''stripped book.''

Pinnacle and the P logo Reg. U.S. Pat. & TM Off.

First Printing: July, 1999
10 9 8 7 6 5 4 3 2

Printed in the United States of America

CONTENTS

CONTENTS

When the idea first came to me to write a book about the third generation of the Kennedy family and how they grew up, I knew it had to include the story of both the first and second generations as well. That the Kennedy children were growing up in the shadow of the two assassinations was more than incidental to the story. I thank Ted Schwarz for his hard work, faith, and tenacity in helping to bring this story to print.

This book is dedicated to all those children who grew up during the 1960s and 1970s, and who experienced the turbulence and stress that affected the third generation of the Kennedys.

PREFACE

Few Kennedy family intimates know more about the three generations than I do. For a decade, I lived in the midst of the family, secretary to Rose Kennedy, observing the children and grandchildren. I was present during several of the scandals, observing strategy sessions, emotional reactions, and coverups. I watched the third generation grow into young adulthood, witnessed their triumphs and tragedies. I was present for the sexual escapades, the drug abuse, great accomplishments, and needless deaths. I was a confidante of Rose Kennedy, hearing her most personal concerns. Sometimes this was in the capacity of friend, to the degree Rose would allow any employee that much intimacy. At other times Rose was dictating letters to close personal friends; the rich and powerful associates from her years as the wife of a leading figure in business, Hollywood, diplomacy, and politics; and to common people who had written to Rose, reaching out to what they perceived as a person of greatness.

I never intended to write a book on the family. I had the opportunity for a job more interesting than my previous work for the Federal Bureau of Investigation, and in a part of the country where the climate was more agreeable than in Washington, D.C. That was why I went to work for the Kennedys. Yet as I observed their comings and goings, as I listened to their in-fighting, learned their family secrets, I came to understand them perhaps better than any other individual who has come forth to talk about them. I saw how they had created a myth that enabled them to achieve wealth, power, and influence greater than almost any other twentieth-century American family.

I also amassed extensive documentation, from the never-before-revealed personal diaries of Rosemary Kennedy to interviews with some of those directly involved with the Kennedy "damage control" efforts relative to David Kennedy's death and Willie Smith's alleged rape (he was acquitted) of Patty Bowman. I had the trust of numerous family members and insiders. And I had extensive firsthand observations that gave me a unique awareness of the third generation of Kennedys as they began their move into twenty-first century positions of power, influence, exploitation, or self-destruction.

This book is the culmination of those years, coupled with extensive new research; previously unknown, overlooked, or hidden documents, many of them from the Kennedy Library; and many interviews with people who had firsthand knowledge of the Kennedy family.

INTRODUCTION

Kennedy. The name is freighted with romance and power. Some consider the family the royalty of America—a dynasty begun by Joseph Kennedy and Rose Fitzgerald, continuing through the Camelot of sons Jack and Bobby, the tainted Teddy, and thence to the grandchildren. Even the names of the children bespeak the Old World custom of primogeniture: Joseph Patrick Kennedy (the founder of the line), Joseph Patrick Kennedy Jr. (the oldest of the second generation), and Joseph Patrick Kennedy II (first son of Robert); John Kennedy and John Kennedy Jr.; Robert Kennedy and Robert Kennedy Jr.; Edward Kennedy and Edward Kennedy Jr.

To others, this famous American clan has been the bane of America. First there were the Brahmins of Boston who snubbed Joe and Rose for their immigrant Irish backgrounds. Then there were the people Joe bested in business deals while building the family fortune, and the enemies he made in political circles. Next were those that Jack and Bobby angered, betrayed, or disappointed during their time in power. For every Kennedy supporter, there seems to be someone who's ready to tear them down.

Through all the family's travels and travails, the Kennedy myth steadily grew. The fabulous wealth, the glamorous addresses, the rich-and-famous vacations, the political power obscured the real people behind the high walls of the compounds in Hyannis and Palm Beach. And as the myth became more elaborate, so did the efforts to maintain it—to keep out prying eyes, to keep others from seeing that the Kennedys are really closer to the average American than we can imagine.

The history of the clan is one that is seen often in other immigrant families. The ancestors arrive in America, intent on bare survival. They manage to move out of the tenements and provide a springboard for their children—the first generation born in their new country—to move ahead. A child shows great ambition and builds substantial wealth. Having money, the next step is to achieve power, often through politics. It falls to the second generation to fulfill the dreams of the first, sometimes in spite of the dreams of the children.

If the parents' ambition becomes the guiding light of the second generation, failures are as inevitable as successes. The faults as well as the good traits of the parents are magnified in the children; the hatreds as well as the friendships are passed on. Unless the parents' ultimate plans for the children are completely satisfied, the children, especially those in the media spotlight, are seen as having failed.

The family's fortunes and power crest in the second generation. The first generation, bitter at the reverses the family has suffered, is now dying or infirm. The second generation, for so long intent on fulfilling the dreams of the first, has neglected the third generation. These grandchildren, who seemed to start life with all the advantages, struggle to find their own way in the world. A few follow the life course set out by their predecessors. Others distance themselves from the family and try to create their own lives. And still others are destroyed.

There had always been the secrets—personal secrets, family secrets, secrets that could bring the police, secrets that could lead to public disgrace, secrets that caused pain from one generation to the next. And there had always been rage—against the social elite, the holders of power, the attitudes that made even the most successful Irish Catholic immigrants feel like second-class citizens.

Perhaps it was the rage that caused the need for control. Husband and wife were equally headstrong. He dominated through sex, repeatedly impregnating his wife until she would tolerate neither child nor intercourse. He enjoyed a string of mistresses, hiding some, flaunting others. There was the movie star—the most beautiful, brilliant, audacious, and ambitious woman in Hollywood in her day, and he had the nerve to bring her to the family estate. Her daughter went to school with one of his daughters, and both were teased by their classmates, who were too young to understand lustful adultery yet old enough to know something socially unacceptable was taking place in their schoolmates' lives.

Both husband and wife dominated their children through violence—she with wooden coat hangers wielded like make-shift whips, he with surgery. His children were to be obedient, respectful, aggressive achievers whose life's work would be determined by their father. They learned to be winners, having to triumph each day no matter how petty and meaningless the achievement. They learned to think solely of the end, and to seek it without regard to morality, ethics, or any of the restraints society believed appropriate for the average person.

When the children grew to adulthood, he would be the behind-the-scenes manipulator who would pull the strings that would make their lives. The children would be like a team of horses, and he would hold their reins like an Irish shanty team-ster driving a cart laden with the prohibition whiskey from which he profited. He would brook no rebellion, even if it meant virtual estrangement from one daughter for marriage to a Protestant and the lobotomization of another.

Without their family wealth—which ultimately grew to hundreds of millions of dollars—Joe and Rose Kennedy's destructive behavior might have netted them a place on the *New York*

Times annual list of the hundred neediest families. Corrupt, deceitful, bigoted, and constantly in fear of what others would say if they knew the truth, the Kennedys raised their children in an atmosphere so destructive, neither their sons nor their daughters were able to achieve lasting happiness. Alcohol, drugs, inability to commit to a relationship, inability to provide a healthy family environment for their children all shattered the moral fiber of men and women who might otherwise have helped lead America to greatness. Instead, they pulled together to create a myth, attempting to bribe, hide, or ruin anyone and anything that might rend the fragile fabric of their adult existence. They achieved the heights of power and influence, only to be destroyed by their own weaknesses. And in the end, the sins of the grandparents were passed on to the third generation of Kennedys, some of whom have triumphed, some of whom have barely survived, and some of whom have been destroyed.

This is the inside story of what has happened within the closed doors and high walls of the Kennedy clan. It reveals the reasons behind the triumphs and tragedies of the young men and women who share the wealth and the burden that has come from the sins of the grandparents.

1

JOSEPH KENNEDY II: THE STATE OF THE DYNASTY TODAY

An intriguing place to start a review of the third generation of Kennedys is with Joseph Kennedy II, the oldest son of the late Senator Robert F. Kennedy, and the current heir apparent to the great Kennedy legacy.

Of all the third-generation Kennedys, Joe comes closest to the mold of the previous generations. He had an essentially undisciplined childhood, with an often-absent father and a seemingly uncaring mother. He has chosen politics over business as a career. He seems to have trouble committing to one woman. He strives to keep the Kennedy myth alive. And his reputation is built as much on image as on substance.

When Joe II was eleven years old, his uncle Jack was assassinated on national television. For months, images of the shooting and the aftermath appeared throughout the media. Disturbing as this would have been for a child of that age, Joe had a heavier burden to carry—the Kennedy name. Arthur Schlesinger Jr., author of *Robert Kennedy and His Times,* quoted a letter Bob wrote to his son on November 24, 1963, only two days after Jack's assassination: "You are the oldest of all the male grandchildren. You have a special and particular responsibility now which I know you will fulfill. Remember all the things that Jack started—be kind to others that are less fortunate than we—and love our country.''

It was a difficult calling for a youth, especially one who was a cross between his namesake, the oldest of the second-generation males, whom he never knew, and his Uncle Ted. Like Ted, he was slow, heavy, and not particularly coordinated. Like Joe Jr., he was expected to be responsible for the younger children, helping them get ready for church or school when he was home. And also like Joe Jr., he was the family bully, chasing and punching the younger kids, punishing them in their touch football games.

Joe, those around him allege, is also not very bright. One associate talked off the record of Joe's delightful personality, his closeness to friends, and the extremely competent, loyal congressional staff assembled to help him with his work. However, he also said that, intellectually, Joe was "thick as a plank." And Rose told me this about Joe on one of our almost daily walks: ''It's a pity that he's not smart, him being the oldest boy.''

Joe was frustrated by the fact that his brother Robert Jr., born two years later, was tall, handsome, athletic, and smart. By contrast, Joe had to be tutored throughout school, and, especially after his father's assassination in 1968, he didn't care about schooling. He was in and out of several boarding schools, but none seemed to have the answer for him, and his grades dropped year after year. He did manage to graduate from Milton Academy, and he enrolled at MIT in 1972, his name as important a consideration for the admissions committee as his academic performance. However, the course work was too difficult for him, and he dropped out.

Family friends, including the noted Harvard psychiatrist Robert Coles, persuaded him to try his hand at the University of California at Berkeley. But he soon recognized that he was out of place there, too, and abruptly dropped any pretense of attending classes.

Joe also developed a quick temper while growing up. Perhaps

he got it from his mother, whose inappropriate rage I witnessed on a number of occasions. There were numerous battles between Joe and his mother after Bob died, and Ethel several times threw Joe out of her house, telling him never to come back. (Joe would usually seek refuge at his grandmother's house on those occasions, where he would stay until his mother forgot the battle.)

His temper would often flare at seemingly insignificant slights or injustices. For instance, there is a famous photograph of Rose Kennedy and all her grandchildren in which Joe appears in the back row, wearing an ill-fitting jacket and a sullen expression. Rose had ordered all twenty-nine of the grandchildren to be in her sunroom at one time for the photograph to be taken. In this instance, as in so many others through the years, Joe Gargan, a Kennedy cousin, was there to make certain her wishes were obeyed. Young Joe did not show up at the appointed time, so Gargan went looking for him.

Gargan discovered Joe trying to leave the compound. When Gargan pursued him, Joe shouted, "I'm not showing up for any fucking picture!" Gargan, a big man himself, rushed Joe, grabbed him by the collar, and told him, "Oh yes you are, or I'll knock the shit out of you." Gargan then dragged Joe into the house, gave him his own blazer, tie, and white shirt, and ordered him to pose.

There was some goodness in Joe, despite his reputation as a spoiled Kennedy. On one occasion, he invited the domestics from all the compound houses in Hyannis Port on an outing on a sailboat he had rented for the day. Being a Kennedy, he made certain that this was a staff day off, so they participated on their own time and no one was paid. But even this good work was doomed. After everyone was loaded on the boat and the party had sailed barely outside the harbor, the mast broke and the entire entourage had to return to land.

Joe's problems adjusting to life as a Kennedy were not all of his own doing, of course. His father, Bob, truly loved his kids, being the one second-generation Kennedy male who seemed to really want a family, to be a father. However, he had gotten started early in the intense world of politics—at twenty-one he helped his brother Jack win his first congressional seat in 1946—and his rising career kept him away from home. When Bob married Ethel Skakel in 1950, she was accepted into the family as one of the sisters, an accomplishment none of the other in-laws could achieve, for she was very much like the Kennedys. However, part of the similarity was a seeming lackadaisical attitude toward raising her children. (Although she would later be voted "Mother of the Year" in some popular polls, this seemed due more to the number of her children, eleven, rather than the quality of her parenting.)

Because of Bob's absences and Ethel's laxness, their children lacked discipline and guidance. For instance, unless all of the family had to be somewhere at the same time, they arose when they felt like it and ate when they felt like it. The cook at the family home in McLean, Virginia, was expected to serve as a short-order cook; if the children arose at eleven different times, then eleven different breakfasts were to be made. With such chaos, it was hard for Ethel to keep cooks. Secretaries also quit, blaming the undisciplined children, who would frequently go through the staff's belongings and take what they wanted with no thought to the consequences of their actions.

In other ways, Ethel set a bad example for her children. She had a reputation for not paying her bills, and Stephen Smith, Jean Kennedy's husband and the one second-generation male with business sense, often had to bail her out. During one Aspen vacation, Ethel threw a lavish party and then refused to pay the caterer. The caterer sued, and months later Ethel and Stephen flew back to Aspen to settle the matter in court. (She was ordered to pay the bill.) Although Ethel used the Skakel family jet, Stephen complained that she wouldn't let him fly with her.

Ethel would at times accuse the staff unjustly of stealing things. After leaving Hyannis at the end of one summer, she called from Virginia to say that she was missing some clothes. Assuming the staff had taken them, she threatened to call the police. The clothes were soon discovered—in one of her bags that had been misplaced when she got back to Virginia.

The major turning point for the family, of course, came in 1968, when Bob was killed. The oldest sons, Joe II (who was sixteen), Bobby Jr., and David, were seemingly the most affected by their father's death. They acted out in several ways, including rebelling at school, abusing drugs, and getting into scrapes with the law. Ethel, rather than becoming closer to her children in this time of tragedy, seemed to turn away from them, continually shipping them off to boarding schools, skiing vacations, other people's homes. She would refuse to talk about Bob's death, even though her children were floundering in their sadness, rage, fear, and grief.

The battles between Ethel and Joe (and the two other older boys) became fiercer. Joe would hide out in stables to avoid her. Joe's friend Chuck McDermott recalled that "almost anything could trigger a fight between them. She would scream at him for ten or fifteen minutes, without letting up, and tell him to leave, which he did. Later, it would be like it never happened."

Once when Ethel threw him out of the house at Hyannis, Rose gave him permission to live in the staff apartment over the garage. This was convenient for him, as it was a good place for him to bring the girls he picked up, away from his mother's disapproving eyes. He used the women mostly for casual sex, not trying to develop any lasting relationship. But in his uncaring way, he left the apartment a shambles. Rose was so annoyed that for months, whenever she met Joe, she gave him the "disdainful look." It was almost comical to see how the expression made the young man cower, even though he was more than a foot taller than Rose. Thereafter, Joe tiptoed around Rose's house during family gatherings, cautioning me to not let Rose know that he was there.

Joe II was the oldest of the third generation, and thus was the leader of the group that would redeem the Kennedy name. He had supposedly proven his skills during a crisis on his father's funeral train. He and Ethel walked among the people who filled the train, thanking them all for coming. He spoke with friends and dignitaries with ease and style. Purportedly, his mother watched with awe and mounting excitement, recognizing that Joe had the potential to achieve the pinnacle of power her husband could have reached.

At home, Joe had to sit in his father's chair at the dinner table, elevating him to the position of authority that assured he would go into politics. The oldest Kennedy male had a duty, not to the country, but to the Kennedy image whose high point was Jack's administration. Nothing could rend the fabric of Camelot in the family's mind, although they were blind to the fact that the cloth was already tattered and frayed. But this duty weighed too heavily on the sixteen-year-old boy, and he broke and ran.

He first ran to Spain, where he went with his friend McDermott. He visited a bullfight, rode a motorcycle, and cluttered his days with activities to avoid thinking too much about anything.

When he came home, he began to run away from things. He made less effort at school, and began taking drugs and being truant. He seemed torn by a role he did not understand yet knew he had to play. He was the heir apparent, anointed by his dead father, supported by his mother and aunts. He liked being fawned over, being considered special, yet he railed against not being allowed to discover himself.

In the few months he attended Berkeley in the 1972-73 school year, he was, incredibly, asked to sit on a University of California Regents' committee to help pick professors for the law school. The invitation was obviously made because of his name, and the grotesque fawning became obvious to Joe. He was a youth who bragged that he never read a book from cover to cover. He had no interest in academics, no interest in learning. His only concern seemed to be doing better than his brother Robert. His low point came when he tried out for the Berkeley rowing team, then overturned the boat on San Francisco Bay. Brother Bobby made the team at Harvard.

Ethel tried to help in her usual manner—avoiding the reality of the situation. (As William Plummer wrote in the May 14, 1984, issue of *People* magazine about her, ''Ethel is 100 percent or her children in some areas. But she doesn't understand them always, and what she doesn't understand, she doesn't want to hear about.'') When she realized that her oldest son was no longer bothering with college, she used her political influence with San Francisco Mayor Joseph Alioto. Soon Joe was the $750-a-month coordinator for federally funded programs in the city's Public Health Department. It took him three weeks to understand that he was being used. The job was a make-work position, and his value was only in whatever media attention his name would bring. He quit the job, friends and acquaintances saying that he was becoming alternately emotionally explosive and withdrawn. He seemed self-destructive, but the closest the family came to seeking help for him was in asking Robert Coles to talk with him. Coles, one of the most respected experts in the nation on children and family dynamics, was never asked outright to treat Joe. He acted as a learned friend, taking their calls or talking casually with them. The Kennedys could claim they sought the best, but the truth was they never truly utilized Coles's skills. The Kennedy troubles would remain within the family's walls.

In August 1973, Joe was back on the East Coast, meeting with his mother and uncle Ted on the Cape. Since Joe was the heir apparent to the Kennedy political dynasty, the older Kennedys wanted him to straighten out. And it seemed that Joe himself was ready to take on the responsibilities of being a Kennedy.

It was an exciting time for Joe. He was going to begin classes at the University of Massachusetts soon, and then he would go on to fulfill the destiny that his father seemed to have ordained for him after his uncle Jack was assassinated. This would mean going into politics, winning a seat in Congress, moving up to the Senate, and eventually running for the White House. Joe's life once again had direction, which had been missing ever since his father's death.

At the time, Joe's brother David was camping out in a small building called the ''Doll House'' on the Hyannis estate. In a rage, Ethel had forbidden David to see Pam Kelley, an old friend of the younger Kennedys to whom David had grown very close. Instead of obeying his mother's wishes, David snuck Pam into the Doll House to be with him. On Monday, August 13, Joe, David, Pam, Pam's sister Kim, and friends Patricia Powers, Mary Schlaff, and Francesca de Onis went swimming off Nantucket Island. Joe, David, and Pam had spent the night there, having held a cookout that lasted well past sunset. Joe borrowed a sport vehicle from Peter Van Dyke Emerson, a friend with whom he had been staying in nearby Siaconsett. He was going to drive himself, David, and the girls to where they could sail back to the mainland.

The car was somewhat unstable, having a short wheelbase and a high center of gravity. It was built for moderate speeds on rough terrain, not high-speed maneuvers. It did have a roll bar, which provided some protection for the occupants in case of a crash. But the seven kids who squeezed into the car overloaded it, and Pam and David were standing up in the back, with no protection at all. On the trip back, Joe was driving wildly through the woods in circles, careening on, off, and over the road.

He came back to the road one last time, but didn't see an approaching car until too late. He swerved violently to avoid a crash, but lost control of the car. It flipped over, and all seven occupants were tossed from the vehicle, which burrowed through the underbrush at the side of the road, then crashed into a tree.

Police and ambulances rushed to the scene. Joe, relatively unhurt, was issued a citation for "operating a vehicle negligently, so that the lives and safety of the public might be endangered." De Onis was badly bruised, Powers had injuries to her waist, neck, and back, Schlaff's pelvis and right leg were broken, and Kim Kelley had a small fracture in her right leg. David had shattered vertebrae, and he was in traction for weeks while his back healed. Pam Kelley, with major damage to her spine, was paralyzed from the waist down.

The Kennedy family knew it was in trouble. Joe had caused

a lifetime injury to Pam Kelley, and David was severely injured, too. There was no question that Joe was at fault for the way he had driven the car, though he pleaded not guilty in Nantucket District Court on August 20 before Judge George Anastas, who had been a college friend of Joe Kennedy Jr. The judge could have given him two years in jail and a $200 fine, but the family's name and connections saved him. Fining Joe $100, Judge Anastas commented, "You had a great father and have a great mother. Use your illustrious name as an asset instead of coming into court like this."

Joe appeared to take the judge's admonishment to heart. In 1976, he graduated from the University of Massachusetts without any further publicized incidents. He immediately began his training in politics, managing uncle Ted's Senate sure-thing reelection campaign in 1976. In 1979, he married Sheila Rauch, a city planner with degrees from Wheaton College and Harvard and the daughter of wealthy Philadelphia banker R. Stewart Rauch. According to Rauch, the two had known each other for nine years, and they took part in lengthy counseling with Catholic clergy before their marriage, since she is Episcopalian. The couple had twin sons, Joseph III and Matthew, in 1980.

In 1979, he became president of the Citizens Energy Corporation, the brainchild of family friend Richard Goodwin. (Goodwin was on Jack Kennedy's Senate staff, and then worked for him when he was president as a speech writer and policy adviser. After Jack's death, he went to work for Robert.) Although the project may have been motivated as a way to keep the Kennedy name in the papers and to give a young Kennedy experience doing "good works," a tactic that Joe Kennedy Sr. had used with his own sons, it was actually a productive organization, using the profits from its activities to provide the poor with low-cost heating oil.

The corporation was much more successful under the later leadership of brother Bobby and the businessman of the third-generation, brother Michael, although Joe ran it competently. But Joe's first interest was what he had been groomed for—politics. Bored with business, he ran for Congress from Boston in 1986, challenging for the seat vacated by Tip O'Neill. Joe spent $1,550,916 in this first campaign, which was far and away the most money ever spent in the district on a campaign up to that point. (The fifteen other original candidates for the seat together spent only $2.3 million, an average of about $150,000. Joe clearly bought the election, something the Kennedys had been doing for years.)

Joe has been reelected twice from his district, and Democrats as well as Republicans acknowledge that he can hold his seat forever if he desires. However, statewide positions and beyond seem out of his reach at the moment. The electorate has changed since the heyday of Kennedy power; as Ross Perot found out in the 1992 presidential election, it's not enough to spread some money around and try to get by on image alone. The media and the voters ask too many questions. And therein lies Joe's problem. He's not a detail person, leaving it up to his excellent staff to handle those matters. His opponents seem to have learned this, and they frequently challenge him on specifics in such a way to make him look foolish. And when he is made to look foolish, Joe reacts angrily, hurting his chances with those who aren't blinded by the Kennedy mystique. He doesn't seem to have yet mastered the down-and-dirty side of politics.

In Congress, Joe has not distinguished himself as a leader, although his seniority has given him the chance to chair subcommittees. He wrote a resolution to make October 8 National Children's Day. As he said when proposing the resolution, "It really came down to a little conversation between me and my boys a year or so ago, where they pointed out that there was a Mother's Day and a Father's Day, but lo and behold there was no Children's Day. And they thought that was kind of an outrage." Despite this sentiment, his family life came apart in 1990 when his wife, Sheila, separated from him and sued for divorce for reasons not made public. Joe never spent the time with his children that his father had—Bob used to have his kids come to the Justice Department to have dinner with him when he was working late—and the demands of a congress-man's schedule mean fourteen- and sixteen-hour days. He said the proper things when Sheila left him: "This has been a very painful day for me and my family. As a father, my principle obligation and deepest personal desire is to assist my children through the most difficult time in their lives." But this was in the context of announcing that he wouldn't run for Massachusetts governor in 1990, an election he had a good chance of losing.

Then, in 1993, he petitioned the Catholic Church for an annulment of his marriage so he could marry his staff scheduler, Anne Elizabeth Kelly. If the annulment were to be granted, it would mean that a sacramental bond never existed between Joe and Sheila. Such an action had precedent in the family. In 1992, Ted Kennedy, often considered a role model for the third generation, also sought an annulment so he could marry Victoria Reggie. And Rose Kennedy, although a devout Catholic, was more concerned with the ritual of the Church than with the true meaning of its preachings.

Joe started the annulment proceedings without consulting Sheila. As the *Boston Globe* reported on September 4, 1993, the first time that Sheila knew about it was when she received a notice in the mail from the Archdiocese of Boston. When they discussed the matter later, she said, "I told him I was opposed to it. He was very surprised and not very pleased."

In a letter to *Time* magazine published on September 6, 1993, Sheila wrote, "If our marriage were deemed never to have existed in the eyes of the church, then our children, like others of annulled marriages, would have been neither conceived in nor born to a sanctified union." And the *Boston Globe* quoted Sheila as saying, "I am not going to lie before God about the birth and conception of his kids, just so he can have a big church wedding." She also said that she found it hard to accept that Joe would feel that their marriage was never sanctified, and that she thought he was a good father. "The marriage did last almost 13 years. The breakup didn't just happen in the first few months."

Perhaps Joe's desire to effectively shut the door on his

relationship with Sheila is more understandable when considered against the backdrop of the Kennedy personality. Kennedy men have been marrying for convenience and career, and not necessarily for love, for years. This can be seen in the marriages to wealthy or well-bred women, and then continued affairs after marriage. Certainly, wedding vows were not taken seriously by the first and second generation—the affairs of Joe Sr., Jack, Bob, and Ted are well-known. It really should be no surprise that the third generation should have the same difficulties committing to one solid relationship.

Thus, Joe II's life is a reminder of the best and the worst of the Kennedy dynasty. He has done good works, he has reached for power, and he will probably be a force to reckon with, perhaps on a national scale, in years to come. But his image is tarnished—a troubled childhood, difficulty committing to relationships, an attempt to close the book on an unhappy time, and to move on unfettered by the past and without respect for others. This is the Kennedy legacy that has been passed down from generation to generation.

2

THE DYNASTY'S ROOTS: KENNEDYS AND FITZGERALDS

To understand the Kennedy legacy—the desire for money and power, the ultimately destructive need to win at everything—we must go back to the conditions that faced the Irish Catholics when they began coming to the United States in large numbers in the mid-1800s.

The ancestors of both Joseph and Rose came to America during the great wave of Irish immigration in the 1840s and 1850s, around the time of the potato famine. Hundreds of thousands of Irish were crowding into the booming American cities, and they suffered the hideous privations known by almost all mass immigrant groups.

The ships making the ocean crossing were quite diverse. Some were seaworthy, their captains experienced and honest. Others were in such disrepair that the passengers and crew had to work together to keep pumping the hold free of water. They worked around the clock in shifts so that the vessel would stay afloat.

Steerage was planned for maximum crowding and minimum comfort. Four travelers were assigned to each bunk. Eating, sleeping, and any other activities were confined to a space six feet long, two feet wide, and two-and-a-half feet high. Food provided by the captain was served by the steward who moved among the passengers, ladling out portions into the passengers' tin plates.

Irish Catholic steerage passengers were seldom allowed on deck during good weather. During storms, the hatches were sealed, placing the passengers in total darkness. There was so little air that headaches were common.

Illness was inevitable on the voyages. Some of the passengers arrived in steerage already sick from diseases caused by malnutrition and starvation. The air was foul, the food often rotten, the water contaminated. With no access to sanitary facilities, the passengers lived in filth that bred bacteria, viruses, and disease. The death rate aboard such ships has been estimated at 10 percent, and in some years during this time as high as 20 percent.

Arrival in Boston and other cities brought short-lived hope. If the ship docked late at night, the new arrivals were forced to huddle together in the streets until sunrise. Then they tried to find places to live, often being helped by Irish who had arrived earlier. However, this help was not solely because of good feelings toward countryfolk. So many had already arrived, and competition for jobs and money was so intense, that a large number of the "helpers" were out to fleece those just off the boat. If their luggage and money weren't taken outright, they were often brought to boardinghouses where both the rates and the accommodations were outrageous (and from which the "helpers" got kickbacks of some sort). The new-comers often lost so much of their money that they had to live in tent cities until they could find jobs and make enough money to move inside.

The Irish who left their homes were escaping not only famine but also the poverty and oppression forced on them by their Protestant British rulers. However, those who came to America often found the same conditions, especially in predominantly Protestant New England. The prejudices of the Old World were carried over to the New World, and were intensified as more and more Irish came to the docks of Boston.

For example, although the United States had recently fought its second war with England, a Protestant nation, a number of American publications told of the danger from the Roman Catholic Church. The pope and his followers were considered to be the greatest enemies of the new nation. The Catholics planned to subvert the civil and religious liberties detailed in the Bill of Rights. Because the Irish openly promoted their Catholicism, they were not only victims of this hate, they also encountered malice from other American Catholics who wanted them to shut up and assimilate.

The jobs the Irish could find were limited for several reasons. One was discrimination. Classified ads of the time blatantly excluded the Irish: *"Wanted. A Cook or a Chambermaid. They must be American, Scotch, Swiss, or Africans—no Irish." "Wanted. A woman well qualified to take charge of the cooking and washing of a family—any one but a Catholic who can come well recommended, may call."* Another reason was that there were so many people coming to the New World. A third was that the immigrants, who mostly came from farming backgrounds, lacked skills marketable in an urban setting. Physical labor was usually all the work a man or woman could do.

The menial jobs were embraced as a way to avoid starvation and cursed for the way they limited the respect a person might receive. The Irish provided the muscle necessary to build roads and homes and to make steel. They served as porters, wagon drivers, police officers and firefighters, housemaids and cooks, and similar professions. Some of the labor was extremely dangerous, and the death rates were high. Others were mindless, back-breaking toil that wore a person down physically and mentally.

The Irish lifestyle was different from that of the Protestants. They hadn't had access to the arts and education in their homeland, so their entertainment tended to be boisterous, physical, and noisy. Even the uneducated Protestants in the cities where the Irish settled understood that they were to maintain a certain decorum in public. But the Irish men worked hard and liked to spend time in bars, drinking, arguing, and sometimes brawling when their work was over.

Ironically, when Joseph Kennedy was trying to become as respectable as the Protestant elite who snubbed him, his offspring frequently behaved like the early Irish immigrants. The police regularly chased the unruly Kennedy kids around Cape Cod, and few of their neighbors liked them. Joe regularly called Jack Dempsey, a state highway patrol officer, to cover for the children. (Years later, in retirement, he would hang around my office on the Cape, much to the disgust of Rose. She did not like to be reminded of the ways he had helped the family.) This pattern was followed with the third generation of Kennedys, who were even more wild and uncontrollable than their parents had been. When the grandchildren were arrested for various reasons, the Kennedys used their connections with the law and the media to cover up the incidents as much as possible.

Joe Gargan, a Kennedy cousin who handled many of the affairs of the family, told me how the young Jack used to strip to his underwear, get on the prow of his motorboat, and ride around the harbor in Cape Cod, drinking a beer and shouting obscenities. Senator Ted Kennedy's drinking and womanizing, and similar activities by other family members (including Willie Smith's treatment of Patty Bowman, for which she pressed rape charges, although he was acquitted), would have been the norm in the Irish Catholic Boston of the mid-1800s.

Because of prejudice against them, the Irish were shut out of the better schools, the government, and most areas of business. The community soon developed a sense of helplessness within the greater society, and a siege mentality developed. When large-scale organized crime groups evolved within major East Coast urban centers, the Irish offered a willing base for their operations. To the Irish, mainstream society was the enemy. They very often viewed the gangster element as the lesser of two evils compared with the police, or felt that they should protect their own, no matter how bad they were.

This is not to say that all Irish were gangsters in those early years. Most of the immigrants and their children were hard-working, intensely lawful citizens. But for the minority who turned to professional crime for all or part of their living, the experiences of the first generation Irish were such that it was understandable why their neighborhoods would be breeding grounds for antisocial behavior.

Ironically, among the families whose members were involved with organized crime in those early years, only the Kennedy family has maintained a highly destructive, self-enclosed, self-obsessed world. The first-generation isolation experienced by most immigrants was quickly shed by the second and third generations of almost all other families. They saw such fear of outsiders as unnecessary, and as a block to their continued development in the new society. They became willing to speak openly about the triumphs and scandals of one or another family member, recognizing that the actions of a grandparent, an uncle, or a cousin were unique to that person, and that any shame or glory produced by a relative was not theirs to shoulder. Yet while almost all of the nation's powerful families opened up in this way, the Kennedys have sustained their code of silence for three generations. Requests for interviews are granted or denied based on the activities of the most prominent family member of the moment. When Ted Kennedy, drunk and womanizing, caused the drowning of Mary Jo Kopechne, the family closed ranks to outsiders even though the death was only one member's responsibility. The same situation existed when David Kennedy died of a drug overdose, and when William Smith was charged with rape. (He was acquitted.) Guilty or innocent, if a family member gains negative headlines, all siblings, cousins, uncles, and aunts who had nothing to do with the event unite. For them, it is better to deny documented evidence of adultery, manslaughter, sexual violence, drug dealing, and other self-destructive or criminal behavior than to admit that a family member, no matter how disturbed and guilty, might be less than perfect.

The Kennedys of Ireland never wanted to come to America, and had the potato famine been somewhat less severe, they never would have needed to come. Patrick Joseph Kennedy was born in Ballynabola village, outside New Ross in County Wexford. The land escaped the early failure of the potato crop. His family had more land to work than most, and the bulk of his 80 acres were used for growing barley and raising beef cattle.

It has never been certain why the 26-year-old Patrick decided to leave for America in 1848 or 1849. Some researchers have said that it was to improve his lot in life, but this seems unlikely, for the only improvement for Irish immigrants was there was food to eat in America. His father, mother, brother, and sister remained in Ireland the rest of their lives. Another brother, John, had been killed fighting the British, though the Kennedys' hatred of the British did not seem to be a consideration in Patrick's decision to emigrate. Most likely, Patrick Kennedy was simply ambitious.

Patrick was more fortunate than most when he arrived at Noddle's Island in East Boston. He had not succumbed to serious illness on the ocean voyage. He could afford the high prices charged to immigrants buying food when they landed, at least long enough to find work. And he had fallen in love with Bridget Murphy, a fellow immigrant from County Wexford.

Success came almost immediately for Patrick. Gold had been discovered in California, and countless Easterners were going west to get rich digging in the ground. They needed Conestoga wagons and barrels to hold their supplies. In addition, Boston saloons were flourishing and whiskey barrels were in great demand. Someone had to make the barrel staves, yokes, and similar items, and Patrick was able to find a job as a cooper. It was a skilled position, rarely given to a man whose life had been spent working a farm.

Patrick's pay was lower than what an American-born worker could have earned for the same work, but it was high pay for an immigrant, and it allowed him to marry Bridget. They exchanged vows on September 26 and immediately began a family, quickly having Mary, Margaret, and Johanna, and on January 14, 1858, Patrick Joseph, who would be known all his life as P.J.

The joy of P.J.'s birth was short lived. A cholera epidemic struck Boston, and though Patrick had been a strong youth, fourteen-hour days as a cooper, the stress of a growing family, and all the other problems of life in Boston had weakened him. He contracted the disease and died on November 22, 1858. Ironically it was exactly 105 years later that his great-grandson, the president of the United States, would be assassinated.

Although Patrick had had ambivalent feelings toward his new country, Bridget Kennedy felt that she was an American first. Her family in Ireland had not been prosperous, and America meant the difference between survival and slow starvation. When Patrick died, the famine was over in Ireland and she could have returned to her family, but she never looked back. Determined to succeed on her own, she took a job in a notions shop, saved what money she could, and eventually bought the store from her employer.

It might be said that P.J. was the best and the brightest of the Kennedy dynasty he would be founding. He wanted to get ahead, and though he attended the parochial school run by the Sisters of Notre Dame, work was more important for him than an education. He helped his mother around the shop, then took a job as a dock laborer because it offered the highest pay he could earn with the skills he had gained. However, he maintained a humanitarian side to his actions, even as he sought wealth and power within the community.

P.J. Kennedy accepted two aspects of life for a Boston Irish Catholic. The first was that he would never be accepted in the community at large, no matter how well educated he was or what his skills might be. Unlike the son he would eventually have, P.J. seemed to feel no anger about the unfair situation.

He accepted life for what it was, determined to make his money within the community where he was welcome.

The second aspect was that he could exploit the Irish Catholic community in a positive way or a negative way.

In most of the major cities, the members of the immigrant ethnic groups tried to better one another's lives. When people fled tenements and could afford to buy better housing of their own, they might rent space to others from their community. They would move their friends or relatives from overcrowded, darkened rooms to apartments where rooms were no longer subdivided, windows provided sunlight, and the risk of death by fire and disease was greatly diminished.

Unlike the experiences elsewhere, including among the Irish Catholics in New York and other Eastern cities, success for some of the Boston immigrants came from exploiting newer arrivals. A man often considered himself to have succeeded when he went from living in an overcrowded deathtrap to living in a newer house and owning the deathtrap. He did not rehabilitate the facility, enlarge the quarters, improve the safety, or reduce overcrowding. Instead he exploited the new wave of immigrants as he had been exploited.

The same was true for some of the saloon owners. They recognized the growing problem of alcoholism and often were victimized by it in their own families. Yet they found success through buying those very same pubs, and encouraging the overindulgence of their fellow countrymen.

P.J. recognized that achieving wealth required him to become involved with businesses that were successful within the Boston Irish Catholic community. However, unlike the son he would eventually have, P.J. felt the need to provide genuine community service.

Alcoholic beverages were both the bane and the vehicle for socialization among his neighbors, and they formed the one business area where Irish Catholics were not excluded. P.J. saved his money and opened a lager beer business in 1881 when he was twenty-three. Three years later he bought a small saloon in Haymarket Square, quickly followed by an Elbow

Street liquor wholesale operation, along with a retail liquor business on Border Street. He thus was involved with all phases of selling liquor. His success would eventually impress his son, who would become one of the more successful New England bootleggers.

P.J. had one other important trait for a bar owner. He was a good listener.

Today there is the stereotyped image of the bartender as confidant of the poor soul needing to unburden a tale of woe. But in nineteenth-century Boston, a tavern owner who would truly listen to his customers gained far more critical knowledge. The bar was the center from which the concerns of the community could be determined and from which assistance could quietly be provided.

Was a family going hungry? P.J., along with other saloon owners who heard the whispers of the plight, would see that food was quietly delivered to where they were living, often saving them from starvation. In addition, P.J. would use his money or his friendships with area politicians using the bar to either stop or delay an eviction for such families. The caring saloon owner was a one-man social worker and relief agency, often preventing homelessness and starvation among the poor.

There were other services as well. Was someone suspected of a crime he did not commit? The saloon owner, through reasoning with the police, bribes, or identifying the guilty party, would frequently correct the injustice. If the accused was probably guilty, bail would be raised and representation found. When new immigrants arrived, a friendly saloon owner would help the families understand the necessary paperwork without charge. He and the politicians understood that such actions also engendered strong feelings of gratitude that could be tapped in the form of favors, such as voting in a manner requested of them. The compassionate, attentive saloon owner was a man who could exert strong political clout if he was so inclined.

These power centers marked the beginning of machine politics in Boston. New arrivals, indebted to these power brokers for jobs, food, and shelter, voted for whomever they were told.

As the brokers influenced more voters, they controlled more jobs, and their power grew. By 1900, Boston was being run by the so-called Board of Strategy, the four most powerful men in the city: "Smiling Jim" Donovan of the South End, Joseph Corbett of Charlestown, P.J. Kennedy of the East End, and John F. Fitzgerald of the North End. In 1906, Fitzgerald became the first of Irish descent to be elected mayor.

In 1885, P.J. decided that he wanted to experience life in the state legislature. He had been on the Ward Two Democratic Committee since 1884, and his popularity was evident to everyone. He ran and won, taking his seat in 1886 where he served five one-year terms before becoming a member of the Massachusetts Senate for 1892 and 1893.

P.J. enjoyed becoming chairman of the Ward Two committee, attending the Democratic National Convention that nominated Grover Cleveland for president, and eventually becoming chairman of the East Boston Democratic committee. But his interest was in his community, genuinely enjoying helping the Irish Catholics who lived there. There was no question that he profited from them, both with his saloon and liquor businesses and with the votes he controlled. Yet he was always available to the people of East Boston, always discrete in his actions, and genuinely caring about them.

It was 1887, during his early terms in the state legislature, that P.J. married Mary Augusta Hickey, whose background gave her full understanding of her husband's careers. Her father was a saloon owner and businessman prosperous enough to have sponsored an Irish girl who came to America to work as the family's housekeeper. Her brothers had chosen careers in medicine, police work, and undertaking, and one of them was also in politics in Brockton, Massachusetts. At least as intelligent as P.J., she was outgoing where he was withdrawn. She would delight everyone she met with her wit and friendliness while he would hold back, enjoying what was taking place, yet too shy to participate as Mary was. It was from this marriage that

Joseph Patrick Kennedy was born in 1888. And it was from this child, who inherited his father's business acumen and political savvy but not his compassion, his striving for success without his tempering morality, that a family of mythic importance would rise like Icarus to reach the sun before crashing in the harsh light of reality.

In radical contrast to P.J. Kennedy was a man five years his junior who delighted in politics for the sake of power and fame. John Francis Fitzgerald saw the city of Boston as one giant theater, and the rites of passage for the people formed the stages on which he performed. Baptisms, weddings, wakes, and funerals all experienced his presence. He went to picnics, church celebrations, and holiday festivities. He was the first to dance, the first to kiss, the first to sing, and the last to shut up when speeches were called for. His years in Massachusetts politics were filled with the cultivation of strangers, adultery, and an orating style friends and enemies alike dubbed "Fitz-blarney." Where P.J. Kennedy sought Massachusetts State Senate committees where he could do substantive work without publicity, Fitzgerald, who served during the same era, wanted head-lines. He selected the Committee on Election Laws and the Committee on Liquor Laws. Both were high profile, areas where power and influence could be exerted either subtly or by bribery and backroom deals. More important, the two committees would keep him one of the best-known state legislators in Boston.

John Fitzgerald—nicknamed "Fitzie" in his early days, "Honey Fitz" in his later years—was an exploiter and woman-izer, the opposite of P.J. Kennedy. He had known the grinding poverty that was typical of the immigrant's lot. Baptized the same day he was born (a common practice among immigrant Catholics, since their children too often died within days of birth), he was raised by Thomas and Rosanna Fitzgerald in a small tenement with a ground floor saloon and a series of tiny one- and two-room apartments into which thirty-seven adults and children were crowded. Straw served as beds, and tenants and saloon customers shared a single toilet. His father was a fish peddler, walking the streets with the day's catch to sell whatever he could convince other poverty-stricken Irish Catholics to buy.

Thomas was emotionally rooted in Irish farmland, having been raised on a tiny tenant plot in Ireland on which he expected to work all his life. Instead, the famine forced Thomas's family to emigrate in waves, each family member coming only when leaving was necessary for survival. Thomas stayed with the land as long as he could, eventually admitting the hopelessness of fighting whatever it was that was destroying the potatoes. He arrived in 1854, working as a farm laborer in Acton, twenty-five miles west of Boston, before coming to the city proper in 1857 in pursuit of a higher income. He found his opportunity in a partnership with his brother, James, a grocer who added liquor sales to his store.

Thomas and James profited. They were good businessmen, and took good care of their customers. And in the midst of all this was John Fitzgerald, delighting in being the center of attention to the steady stream of customers.

John Fitzgerald was three-and-a-half when his father became an exploiter among the Irish. He bought a brick tenement building at 435 Hanover Street. There was a grocery store on the ground floor, the profits of which went to Fitzgerald. The family had two bedrooms, one for the parents, the other, with dormitory-style beds, for the children. The family had a parlor and kitchen, large windows, fire escape, lighted hallway, and safe stairs. They also had their own toilet. However, the quarters for the tenants remained the hell it was in every tenement building, with small rooms, little light, and communal toilets.

John Fitzgerald had the misfortune of being the smallest of nine brothers. Bullied by the others in the same manner that his grandson and namesake, John Fitzgerald Kennedy, would be bullied by his brother Joe Jr., Fitzgerald tried desperately to increase his body strength. When endless calisthenics failed to help, he used his natural endurance to become a long distance runner. Fitzgerald had the endurance to become a champion at distances of a half mile or longer, though he also had both the drive and the natural athletic ability to achieve occasional wins in competitions of 120 to 150 yards.

There were two aspects of young Fitzgerald's character that would have an impact on the lives of the generations to follow. One was his competitiveness, very often used to prove himself equal or better than his brothers. This competitive spirit would be passed on to his children, especially his daughter Rose, who learned to delight in winning for the sake of triumph. She would later pass on to her children the idea that success mattered more than the way it was achieved, and that winning at anything was more important than the type of event in which you were competing.

The second aspect had to do with Fitzgerald's early sense of politics. Low-income city dwellers have always used the streets as their front yard. Crammed into tenements, urban dwellers would sit on curbs and stoops. The children darted among horses, wagons, and cars, playing their games in the midst of traffic.

The police tried to keep the order by breaking up the endless street games of poor children. They made the boys and girls stay off light poles and stop their curb-jumping contests, and otherwise frustrated their efforts to play like children in wealthier communities

Fitzgerald recognized that the police were only keeping him and the other children out of the street because they were paid to maintain order. Most of the patrolmen were sympathetic to the urge for summer fun in an area without formal recreation centers. Instead of battling them as his friends did, sneaking back to play in the same spots from which they had been moved, he negotiated with the officers. He convinced them to let the kids play on Union Wharf when local traffic was minimal. As a result, the children had a makeshift play area they could use for an hour or more a day without disturbance.

The situation made little difference in anyone's life, yet it revealed the young Fitzgerald's skills of observation and negotiation. Another solution revealed his cunning. As a result, when the wharf could not be used, he thought of a way to play relatively unharassed in the streets. Two children were stationed as lookouts. When they sighted approaching police, they would sing out, and the rest of the children would go to a different area or pretend to be busy in approved ways until the strolling officers passed through.

Being raised in a grocery store/saloon also had its influence on young Fitzgerald. He became comfortable with large numbers of people of all ages. He came to delight in any large gathering, seeking out celebrations of all types. He attended as many of the church pageants and festivals as he could.

John Fitzgerald grew to love the Catholic Church, though not for reasons of the spirit. The saloons formed the social center for men; the churches were where families could gather for music, picnics, or pageantry and splendor. Even the most solemn masses had an excitement to them for someone whose normal surroundings were the dark, drab, barren rooms of the tenements.

The choice of jobs the teenaged Fitzgerald pursued were in marked contrast to the work that P.J. Kennedy chose. P.J. had gone to work as a stevedore; Fitzgerald preferred the rough-and-tumble violence of a newsboy.

Newspaper boys in New York, Boston, Cleveland, and else-where were subject to extortion and violence at best, and were corrupted by the whorehouses and gambling joints at worst. But selling newspapers provided higher pay than many better-educated adults were able to earn, especially in the Irish Catholic, Italian, and Jewish ghettos of the various cities. In September 1877, when the fourteen-year-old Fitzgerald was licensed to sell newspapers, a high school graduate working as a clerk earned less than 50 cents a day. Newsboys usually averaged more than $2.50 a week. Selling papers at the end of the nineteenth century had the same appeal for low-income street kids seeking a fast dollar as drug sales would have for boys from similar backgrounds a century later.

In some cities, the newsboys were assigned a specific corner according to how strong they were and how long they had been selling. A newsboy could move up to a corner with greater profit by beating up another newsboy. In some cities, organized crime sold protection to all the boys, taking a percentage of their sales. But when Fitzgerald was beginning, a Boston newsboy had the freedom to walk the streets, selling wherever he could, and that was the approach with which he began.

Where the newsboys were not victimized by territorial violence, they were often corrupted into a life of crime. Prostitutes and the madams of brothels would arrange for nearby newsboys to steer men to them. Some of the boys aggressively pursued well-dressed men who looked like they could afford the prostitutes. The boys were given tips by the women and, at times, the customers.

Gambling establishments used the newsboys in the same way, having them guide men into the smoke shops and other businesses that had backroom gambling. The police were usually bribed to ignore all such activity, so everyone prospered in the subculture of hustlers.

Fitzgerald did not avail himself of opportunities to work for prostitutes or others. Instead, he analyzed city traffic during his wanderings, locating the best places for selling papers. He found that older boys, known as "hawks," had long before conducted their own analyses. The hawks rarely bothered to sell papers. Instead, they arrived near the best locations about the time the newsboys had sold all their papers. Then they would mug the carriers, taking the day's receipts. Since the money earned by the newsboys both paid for the next day's papers and was the difference between food on the table and hunger, such muggings were a serious concern to the newsboys. The hawks knew just how often to steal, eventually giving the carriers the chance to pay only a percentage of their day's profits.

In 1878, when Fitzgerald had advanced to better sales areas, he began organizing the younger newsboys into groups. They would meet after selling their papers, but before the hawks could stage their attacks. Then they would walk home together so they would outnumber the extortionists in the area. It was an ingenious solution and it earned him the respect of the other boys.

Fitzgerald gained more than money and organizing skills from his days as a newsboy. He was able to observe other areas of Boston, not just the Irish Catholic ghetto. He was fascinated by the fine clothes, the elegant homes, and the expensive possessions of the Brahmins. He wanted power and respect, and to be able to live in the grand style of the Protestant elite. He was willing to work for it, to study hard, and to find a way to combine the long hours and difficult life of the newsboy with the diligence needed for success in school. He was eventually sent by his father to the prestigious Boston Latin high school, and from there to medical school at Harvard University. However, his father's death his first year forced him to leave his classes.

It was not until 1889 that John married, having first prepared himself for business and politics. He worked for a ward boss, obtained a job in the Boston Custom House, and then began selling insurance. He was ambitious enough to want to play polo, a game that was generally reserved for wealthy Protestants, and was soon wealthy enough to afford his own pony. He joined a polo team and competed throughout the state, one of the few Irish Catholics to do so. Then, with success already achieved, he looked for a wife, marrying his second cousin, twenty-three-year-old Mary Josephine Hannon.

John Fitzgerald had an intense power drive, but he was smart enough to know that the higher the position he achieved in politics, the more diluted would be his influence. He held both state and public office, serving in the State Senate starting in 1892, followed by a term in Congress. But such races only served to give him the experience he needed to take the position he felt was the ultimate achievement for any Irishman. In 1906, he ran for and won the position of mayor of Boston, the first Irishman to achieve that office.

The achievement was a dramatic one as well as a moment that proved Fitzgerald's true power. He used his constituents from the North End to help him, but other politicians, including rivals such as P.J. Kennedy, discovered that Fitzgerald had done his homework in unexpected ways. To Kennedy's amazement, his rival on the Board of Strategy was more familiar with the people of Ward Two than he was. As a result, when the new mayor offered his hand in friendship, Kennedy accepted. Both men realized that the Irish takeover of city hall represented a new era for the country. The immigrants had seized power from the entrenched, wealthy establishment, and nothing would be the same again. It was a feat that would inspire similar takeovers in other cities throughout the United States, a triumph of ethnic machine politicians who would maintain their hold in some areas for at least three-quarters of a century.

Although it was seldom discussed at the time, there was a dark side to John Fitzgerald that he would pass on to his daughter, Rose. This was the need to win any competition, regardless of the cost, provided victory helped you maintain or increase your power. Rose would ultimately apply the idea with her own family, creating for her children a competitive environment so intense that her oldest son committed suicide and her oldest daughter violently rebelled.

John Fitzgerald's intensity was limited to the political arena. However, his actions went beyond merely stuffing the ballot box.

The ballot was not secret when Fitzgerald got his political training. The United States was a representative democracy from the start, and voters were protected from abuse prior to casting their ballots. However, the idea of a totally secret ballot had not been introduced into U.S. elections. In Fitzgerald's day, only the casting of the ballot was a private matter. Once you marked your ballot, election workers had a variety of ways to learn what you had done before you placed the paper in the ballot box.

Party bosses sent two types of observers to the polls to assure that people voted as ordered. The first were known as "checkers," and their job was to stay with the voter from the time he took a ballot until he was ready to put it in the box. The checker would be able to tell if a man voted as he had been told by the ward boss, or if he had gone against orders.

The voters who cast their votes under orders were usually men whose jobs were secure only for so long as they supported the party boss. The party in power controlled 14,000 patronage jobs in turn-of-the-century Boston, and these jobs often were supervisory positions. The underlings knew that their jobs were only as secure as their immediate supervisors, so a worker quickly learned to vote for any man his boss voted for, and the checkers had the job of making certain no one tried to act independently.

The second type of observer was the "ward heeler," men like John Fitzgerald who handled anything the ward boss desired. The ward heeler frequently had to be a strong-arm bully who would wait outside the polling place, watching the checker to see which men deviated from the requested vote. Those who made a "mistake" were handled according to the importance of the candidate they defied. If the candidate was the party choice but not critical to the boss, then the miscreant would be beaten as a warning to others. If the candidate was important to the boss's future and the errant voter held a patronage job, the heeler would fire him instantly. For those who did not hold patronage jobs, the heeler would pressure their employers to fire them. No one escaped punishment, a fact that kept most voters in line.

By 1888, Fitzgerald had proven himself as a heeler. In addition to a willingness to fire or hurt anyone who had not voted correctly, Fitzgerald had gained a reputation for being more effective with vote fraud than any other young heeler in the North End.

The 1888 election was an important one for Matthew Keany, Fitgerald's ward boss. Keany's candidate for Common Council was not popular among the workers. They found him arrogant and abusive, and there was rumor of a mutiny among the voters.

It was Fitzgerald's job to be certain that each rebel voter was fired, an action that ultimately cost the job of the uncle of a youth who had been John's best friend. The uncle was known to be the sole support of a needy family, but Fitzgerald preferred destroying him to bucking the system. He knew that ultimately he would be rewarded by the system, and his election to mayor simply reinforced that decision seventeen years later. The end justified the means.

On July 22, 1890, Mary Hannon Fitzgerald, known as Josie to her friends, gave birth to their first child, a girl they named Rose. The child filled the couple with hope for a better future, though for radically different reasons. Josie was an intensely private person, as withdrawn and uncomfortable in groups as her husband was outgoing and gregarious. During the courtship they would take long walks together, sharing private time of great intensity. However, instead of being a portent of their life to come, John was merely doing what he had always done. He wanted to win Josie, not share a life with her as the center of his concerns. She was another prize, no different from his races for political office or even the work for Keany. He would do whatever was necessary to achieve that prize, and if that meant acting for a while in the manner Josie desired, so be it.

Because he was away from home most of each day, Fitzgerald decided that it would be most convenient to continue living in the family home at 465 Hanover Street. Six of his brothers were living there, so he assumed that Josie would have plenty of company to keep her happy. She would have preferred a country place, solitude, a chance to walk the quiet roads, treasuring their time together and so not minding their time apart. She wanted a life with John as the center, not a life where she was at the tail end of an extended family. She was shocked to discover that he wanted a life actively in the midst of the Irish Catholics of Boston.

There was no convincing John to move at first. However,

when Josie became pregnant, John agreed to find a separate house. The couple moved to their own house, though in typical Fitzgerald fashion it was owned by his family.

Rose Elizabeth Fitzgerald was her father's treasure, a fact that would further estrange him from his wife. Shortly after her birth, he decided to run for office, starting the climb that took him to the mayor's office. He was away from home more than ever, and when he was at home, so much of his attention was centered on Rose that Josie's jealousy increased. She hated sharing him with the public, with his brothers, and with the politicians. Had he at least shared their new daughter, the stress would have been less. But John Fitzgerald adored his little girl, and except for sexual relations, there was little intimacy with Josie.

The sex was productive. Agnes was born two years after Rose, and then came Thomas. In 1897 the couple moved to the country home Josie had always desired, even though the decision was politically risky because it gave Fitzgerald a primary residence outside his ward.

Rose thrived in the house in West Concord, which had a barn, a henhouse, and fairly extensive land just two blocks from Mary's brother's home. It was there that she grew from a girl of seven to a budding woman of thirteen. And since John Francis Fitzgerald and Eunice Fitzgerald were also born there, her mother left her alone much of the time, concentrating on the needs of the younger children. This delighted Rose, who became athletic, outgoing, self-reliant, and independent, traits that were in no way squelched when the family moved back to Boston.

It was in 1903, after Fitzgerald's three terms in Congress, that the family returned to Boston so he could make a run for mayor. They bought a mansion high atop a hill, a property so large as to provide isolation from the masses of Boston. Josie was able to experience the happiness she had once thought impossible in the city.

The mayor's race was a three-way battle among Republicans Louis Frothingham and Henry Dewey and Democrat Fitzgerald.

Because the Republican vote was split, Fitzgerald emerged victorious. On October 1, 1906, with Josie and five of his six children present (Fred was still an infant, too small to attend), Fitgerald became the first Irish Catholic mayor of Boston. And though Josie proudly stood by his side, it was fifteen-year-old Rose who would reap the benefits of her father's triumph.

3

JOE AND ROSE:
THE DYNASTY RISES

Joe Kennedy Sr. always wanted to be the hero in a Horatio Alger story. He delighted in tales of individuals coming from a lowly background, working hard, and gaining riches and power after an early life of poverty. But Joseph was never poor—he was a wealthy man's scion, albeit one raised in a community that was for many years excluded from the power centers of Protestant Boston. His family wealth and relative power made him an outsider to many of the Irish, as well. And at least in part as a result of this, he seemed to grow up with both unfocused anger and a striving for wealth regardless of the cost to anyone else. Money meant control, dominance, respect, and security. What would jokingly be said of his son Jack could honestly be said of Joe Sr.: he was so intensely ambitious that he looked upon the White House as a stepping stone to *real* power.

Joe's parents did little to nurture their child as he was growing up. His father may have been a strong machine politician, a man who understood that winning votes at all cost was critical to success, but he also felt that power brought unusual responsibility for others. He devoted his time to taking care of his constituents, frequently being absent from home, seldom giving time or attention to his son.

The guiding principals Joe adopted for his life were quite different from those of his father. He felt that to be a successful man was to be a winner in everything undertaken, no matter how meaningless the challenge, and he felt that accumulated wealth was the way to measure a man's worth. Public service was never an option, and though he intellectually understood why his father spent so much time helping people in the community, emotionally he scorned any form of public service or public charity unless there was a direct benefit for himself.

Whereas P.J. accepted the social caste system of the time, Joe wanted acceptance by the Brahmins. Thus, the social snubs that P.J. disregarded worked themselves under Joe's skin. Unlike his father, Joe wanted to be part of larger society, wanted the power that the Protestant Brahmins held. If he couldn't find acceptance by those who felt they were his betters, then he would damn them and gain so much wealth and power that they would have to accept him.

P.J. and Mary Kennedy liked the idea that Joe valued money, and they encouraged their son to take every job he could find so long as it did not prevent him from attending school. Education was important to them, not because it gave greater insight into the world, but because it made you the equal of the Boston Brahmins. The Cabots, the Lodges, and the other Protestant families who dominated Boston and Massachusetts were educated at expensive private schools, then attended colleges such as Harvard. A man could become a financial success, as P.J. had, without an extensive formal education. But a man could not become respected unless he received a Harvard education.

The drive for money led the tall, strong, freckle-faced youth into an endless series of odd jobs and money-making schemes. Joe worked as a stovelighter for Orthodox Jews, who could do no work on the Sabbath; a delivery boy for the makers of fine hats; a newspaper boy; and an errand boy for one of the banks in which P.J. had invested. In his spare time, he was an avid baseball player, playing first base as well as being coach and business manager for his neighborhood team.

Joe's attitude toward baseball was an odd foreshadowing of his children's obsession with touch football. He was never a well-rounded player, having skill at the bat but not much else. He was not a team player, never understanding the concept of sacrificing his glory for the success of the team. To him, winning meant Joe doing well, not necessarily the team. When his children played the touch football games the family was famous for, they were known for their aggressive enthusiasm and bruising style of play, not their running, passing, or catching skills.

His attitude toward baseball also foreshadowed how he would approach business, politics, and even personal relationships— all that mattered was that he got what he wanted. For instance, in Joe's senior year at Boston Latin School, the elite private school where his parents had sent him so he would have a better chance to achieve his ambitions, he batted .667, an extraordinary average even at the high school level. (He was given an award for the highest average by his father's political opponent, Mayor John Fitzgerald.) On the strength of his hitting, he made first string on the freshman team at Harvard and earned a starting varsity position at first base when he was a junior. But a better player took his position when Joe was a senior. Even his once legendary skill as a batter meant little against the superior college pitchers. Joe discovered that he was a legend only in his own mind.

The only way that Joe could get his letter in baseball was to play in a game in his senior year. Gaining his letter was important to Joe, because it symbolized respect that he had mostly been denied at Harvard. Joe's years there had been spent intensely studying history and economics, two areas that truly interested him, and barely passing his other courses. His main concern was creating an image of himself that would be acceptable to Protestant society. He lived in Harvard Yard with the sons of Brahmin families, rather than commuting to school as the other local Irish boys did. He also selected his roommates based on their success in athletics and family background. One such roommate, Bob Fisher, was a football All-American and a member of the Porcellian Club, which only the Protestant elite could join. Joe deliberately cultivated this friendship to assure an entree to important families who would have otherwise ignored him. He also had Fisher teach him the mores and manners of Brahmin society. Despite his efforts, however, Joe found through continued rejection that old money meant more than new money. New money Irish was probably the lowest form of humanity that could exist in the pecking order of Harvard, probably even lower than being Jewish, the other religious minority just beginning to be allowed to attend the school.

The respect Joe did gain was that which might be grudgingly given to a gifted family retainer whose success is within his place. He represented the best example of Irish Catholic success, and was considered a good role model for "his kind."

Thus, Joe felt that obtaining his letter in baseball would make him seem the equal of the boys who would never quite respect him. When the 1911 game against Yale, the last of the season, was to be played, Joe knew there was no legitimate way he would be in it. So he called on some ward heelers who were friends of his father. They went to the Harvard captain and pitcher, Charles "Chick" McLaughlin, to both bribe and blackmail him.

Joe knew that McLaughlin wanted to run movie theaters when he left school. Silent movies were becoming extremely popular, and McLaughlin, who had the capital and the site, wanted to get in on the ground floor. All he needed was a business license, and for that he had to go to a government office controlled by men who were beholden to P.J. Kennedy. The ward heelers made it clear that the success of McLaughlin's license application would be determined by whether or not Joe played against Yale.

McLaughlin disliked Kennedy, and hated him for the pressure. However, he agreed to the request and put Joe into the game when there was no chance of losing. Joe struck out in his turn at bat, but he made the last play of the game, tagging

out a Yale runner at first. Then, instead of giving the winning
ball to the pitcher as tradition demanded, Joe showed his contempt for the way he had been treated in the past by pocketing
the ball as a souvenir.

It was during the Harvard years that Joe came to admire
writers and the intellectual image they had. Poorer Irish Catholics, involved with neither higher education nor reading, valued
what they did not do, and Joe knew it would help him to have
a reputation as a writer. Here, too, he found a way to use
another person to gain credit for himself.

Joe's batting prowess won him a place on a team sponsored
by a resort in Bethlehem, New Hampshire, in the White Moun-
tains. (The pitchers in this league were considerably less skilled
than the ones he had faced at Harvard.) The area was popular
with the elite of Boston society. While being given room and
board in place of pay, Joe decided to take a part-time job as a
sports and society stringer for the *Boston Globe.*

Kennedy did not want to write. His skills were limited and
his interest did not extend beyond the chance to make money,
as the average stringer for the *Globe* made as much as $30 a
week, and the chance to promote the image of himself as a
writer. He arranged for the team manager, a would-be writer
named Henry O'Meara, to do all the work. (Many years later,
he would use this same technique to help his son Jack win
a Pulitzer Prize for the mostly ghostwritten book *Profiles in
Courage.*)

O'Meara was thrilled at the opportunity to improve his skills
and see if his work could succeed. Every article submitted was
written by O'Meara, but the byline was Joe's and Kennedy
pocketed the weekly check. The reporting was so good that at
the end of the summer, the editor offered Kennedy a full-time
job. He turned the job down, not out of shame, but because of
disinterest. Throughout his life, he never felt shame at decep-
tions that furthered his personal desires.

Many years later, Joe used this same technique to help his
son Jack gain a reputation as an intellectual and historian. Joe
paid to have Jack's senior thesis at Harvard published as *Why*

England Slept, and Jack's book *Profiles in Courage,* for which Jack won a tainted Pulitzer Prize (Joe influenced the selection committee) was mostly ghostwritten. These books served to enhance Jack's image in the minds of Americans, which furthered Jack's political career.

One other story told about Joe in this period illustrates his devious approach to business. He and close friend Joe Donovan spent about $600 to buy a bus they intended to use for sightseeing tours of historic Boston during the summer. They decided to get Mayor Fitzgerald to help them gain the most lucrative bus stand, South Station, as their base. Joe figured that the mayor would help him, since he was the son of one of the most powerful politicians in Boston. However, the South Station operator appealed to Police Commissioner Stephen O'Meara, an enemy of both Fitzgerald and Kennedy, who made it clear to Kennedy and Donovan that they would have to share the stand.

This was fine with Joe, who said he had already worked out schedules that guaranteed equal revenues for the rival sightseeing companies. When Commissioner O'Meara reviewed the schedules, he saw that Joe had kept the best times for himself. But playing along with Joe's contention of fairness, O'Meara said that, since the revenues would be equal, Joe wouldn't mind if the schedules were switched, and his competitor got Joe's schedule. Joe was caught, and had to go along with O'Meara's solution. He and Donovan lost thousands of dollars because Joe tried to pull strings to get the best deal for himself rather than work out an equitable deal with the competition.

Rose Fitzgerald was as interested in academics as Joe Kennedy was in money. Bright, personable, and outgoing, she graduated from high school with honors and wanted to attend prestigious Wellesley College. However, the school was Protestant, which troubled her father; he was concerned more with the politics of her education than its quality. As a result, Rose was forced to attend the Convent of the Sacred Heart and the New England

Conservatory of Music before being sent to complete her education at Blumenthal Academy of the Sacred Heart at Vaals, Holland, in 1908.

The subjects Rose studied were typical of the convent schools of the day. There was music, in addition to the intense piano studies she enjoyed at the conservatory; French and German, which she failed to master to the degree her immersion would indicate; and such matters as "domestic science." Her fellow students abroad were the daughters of the wealthy and socially prominent elite from many countries, and none were likely to ever have to do anything more strenuous than inherit and marry wealth. By contrast, the Wellesley curriculum would have exposed her to math, chemistry, physics, and political science, the background needed for careers such as law, medicine, education, and business. Wellesley also would have given her personal freedoms that, though not extensive when compared with contemporary schools, still provided greater independence than Sacred Heart.

Rose was well chaperoned at the convent schools, strictly disciplined (her mother had also been a harsh disciplinarian, who spanked her children for minor infractions), and forced to learn religious ritual to a degree seldom practiced outside the nunnery. For a young woman with Rose's temperament and abilities, her situation was like that of a wild mare, ready to run the prairies as an equal with the stallions, only to be corralled and broken so she would content herself with carrying children round and round a fenced ring.

Rose led a dual life while in Holland. She disciplined herself to gain the nuns' approval, arising fifteen minutes earlier than necessary and becoming so devoted to the ritual of the convent school that she ultimately achieved the title "Child of Mary," the highest honor a student could attain. The award was not for academic achievement, nor was it for involving herself in the community. It was for mastering all the rituals of prayer and religious worship, a mastery that was believed to result in piety.

Rose went to extremes with her pursuit of ritual, as though

putting the energy she had hoped to devote to the broader range of courses and activities at Wellesley into almost obsessive participation in the minutiae of the Church. Rose took comfort in the trappings of the Church, comfort that sustained her throughout her life. She never sought the Christian community outside the walls of the churches she attended; never participated in the Church's social outreach programs; never concerned herself with the issues of poverty, hunger, and education that became especially acute during the Depression. Her idea of being right with God was to perform all the rituals available to the laity, to do them longer, more obediently, and with greater mastery than anyone else. She used them as discipline, for comfort, and as an opiate she let dominate her life as thoroughly and almost as destructively for her family, as many of her children and grandchildren used alcohol and drugs.

At the same time that Rose was enduring the intense discipline of the school, she was secretly writing to the boy for whom she had felt growing affection. Rose and Joe Kennedy, casual friends since childhood despite their fathers' professional hostility to one another, were becoming sweethearts. Although Rose's mother wanted her to date a variety of young men, and though Joe never let his relationship with Rose interfere with other social doings, they were inseparable when they could be together. They stayed together even at formal dances, where the girls were given program cards onto which they were expected to place a different boy's name for all but the first and last dances. Joe simply filled Rose's card with a series of aliases so that her parents would think she mingled throughout the evening.

When Rose finished school, her religious activities diminished in favor of the life of Boston's surrogate first lady. Her mother wanted nothing to do with the world of politics, with the endless social involvements that came with campaigning, with having to hear the snide attacks, mostly justified, on her husband's moral character. Rose, by contrast, loved the excitement, the intrigue, the glamorous trappings, and the way in which her father was greeted by his adoring supporters. She ignored the stories of her father's infidelities, seeming to accept the idea that unfaithfulness was a natural part of manhood. Honey Fitz was good to her mother, good to her, a delightful little man who barreled through life in ways that made her feel a little like royalty probably felt when they let their hair down. And when he and her mother encouraged her to act as his hostess, she was thrilled.

Rose's social flings were as glamorous and raucous as the convent school had been sedate and colorless. Her society debut was attended by four hundred people, an acknowledgment of New York society's legendary "400," established by the Vanderbilts. Among the Fitzgerald 400 were all the Boston City Council members, the governor of Massachusetts, and two congressmen. The day was declared an official holiday in Rose's honor. And the event was the talk of Irish Catholic society for weeks following.

Normally, such a debutante was sought out for membership in one or more of the fashionable, almost exclusively Protestant, women's clubs. But because she was Catholic and the daughter of a controversial politician, no organization contacted Rose. She was hurt and angered by the snub. As retaliation, the strongheaded Rose founded her own exclusive social organization, the Ace of Clubs, which would become even more restrictive than the Brahmins' clubs.

While Rose was making the rounds of social functions, working with her father, who would soon be facing stiff opposition for reelection, Joe was making his first move into finance. He had little practical understanding of business, but he knew how to gain the knowledge he wanted. He became a state bank examiner in eastern Massachusetts, a job that required only basic awareness of accounting and banking laws. In this job he learned how loans were made, how businesses were investigated for soundness, and where predictable, avoidable mistakes had been made. He was also able to judge the relative value of the banks, and discovered that a bank could be a vehicle for wealth for the owner. It was a graduate-level course in business and finance.

Until well after the Depression, a common attitude amongst business leaders was that a corporation existed to make its owners money. The welfare of the workers and the development of a long-term industry were not considerations for most executives. Many a corporation was created and then destroyed so the owner could milk it for maximum profits. This was an idea to which Joe Kennedy subscribed and the way he frequently conducted business.

For example, his first business venture involved Old Colony Realty, in which he invested $1,000 and became treasurer. There is no indication that he provided substantive service to the business. But when the company was dissolved during the First World War, he claimed $25,000 in corporate assets.

This company deserves closer scrutiny because the nature of its business reflected an attitude toward making money that Kennedy would hold for the rest of his career. The firm specialized in taking the homes of low-income families who couldn't quite hold on to what was usually the first decent housing they had had. When the owners fell behind in their payments, Kennedy's firm bought their homes for a fraction of their worth. Then they rehabilitated the houses just enough to sell them at a substantial profit.

Perhaps there were alternatives to dispossessing the owners that were less onerous, but that is not the point. What is important is that the three real estate partners involved themselves only with such transactions. They made their money by preying on the weakest in society.

Despite his quick real estate profit, Kennedy realized that a better way to make a lot of money, as well as to gain power and respect, was to own a bank. This was especially true in a community with many immigrants who had experienced discrimination seeking loans and jobs. They wanted to deposit their money in institutions that would not only help them with their needs, but also hire them. Most banks refused to use the Irish for anything more meaningful than cleaning offices, and the few that did offer better opportunities limited them to dead-end jobs as tellers.

Columbia Trust was a bank in name only. As with similar institutions founded within the Boston Irish community, it was really the equivalent of a credit union. It had minimal assets (about $200,000) compared with the broader-based banks in the surrounding area, but it had the solid loyalty of the community. It was a modest success, not particularly profitable for the stockholders, yet making enough money so a larger bank could absorb it and profit from its market. And it was partially owned by P.J. Kennedy.

The Protestant-owned First Ward National Bank decided to acquire Columbia Trust. Their plans included making it part of a system from which the Irish were excluded at all management levels, which was anathema to the community. Joe realized that if he could raise enough money to prevent a takeover, he could use both his father's influence and the staff's gratitude to take control himself.

Joe was successful, borrowing $45,000 to manipulate stock and stop the First Ward takeover. To reward his efforts, Columbia Trust made him president, a position more impressive in title than in substance. It was not uncommon for young men, even younger than Joe, to head financial institutions of even greater size than Columbia, especially in the Southwest. Joe, at 25, may have been one of the youngest bank presidents in Massachusetts, but at Columbia Trust's level his age meant little. However, he claimed to be the youngest bank president in the United States, and was sometimes mentioned as living the Horatio Alger stories he so adored.

The greatest immediate value to Joe of this episode was winning Rose Fitzgerald as his wife. Honey Fitz had long been hostile to the Kennedys. In a city where social position was of great importance, there were rigid rules of marriage. P.J. Kennedy was a saloonkeeper and politician. John Fitzgerald was the mayor of Boston. No matter what else the men did, this difference made the Fitzgeralds more prominent than the Kennedys, a factor in Honey Fitz's longstanding refusal to encourage Rose's romance with Joe. He undoubtedly knew of the times she sneaked off to meet Joe, especially since she had the family chauffeur drive her to her trysts. Fitzgerald had sent her to Palm Springs and then to Europe to keep her from Joe's clutches. But once he could claim that his daughter's beau was a bank president, no matter the size of the bank, he was more comfortable with the liaison. The marriage was a quiet one in a small chapel on October 7, 1914. The only nod to the prominence of the families was that Cardinal O'Connell officiated.

It is impossible to be certain just what the couple's relationship was. Did Joe love Rose, or was the marriage just another step in the career course he had set for himself? Given the mistresses he accumulated later in his marriage, this speculation is a fair one. Certainly there came a point when he and his wife began leading separate lives. And though Rose continued to have intercourse with her husband, something she would not refuse given her Catholic teachings, even the friendship they sustained seemed to become strained.

The marriage excited Rose in the beginning. Joseph Patrick Jr. was born in 1915, and John Fitzgerald in 1917. Three other children followed quickly—Rosemary in 1918, Kathleen in 1920, and Eunice in 1921. Such frequent childbirth was the natural order of life for a Catholic family. Marriage was for procreation, and sex was not to be denied no matter what stresses existed within the family.

Most writers about the Kennedys like to speak of the close, loving family that produced men who took leadership roles in the nation. There is a tendency to overlook anything negative, even when the negative affected the family down to the third generation and altered the politics of the country.

Rose quickly tired of her "duty" as a Catholic wife. She missed the excitement of the world her father had provided. Joe was just as intense in his power drive as Honey Fitz, and as charismatic in his own way when necessary. But his was the work of a power broker, a mover behind the scenes. He was not someone who went to parties, whose success depended upon his public actions rather than his private ones. Rose was not part of Joe's backstage world, nor did he want her there.

She and Joe were living in suburban Brookline in a mostly Protestant neighborhood. Although the area was a good place to live, with shaded yards and room for children to play, there was no sense of community, no shared customs, no single church. People might know neighbors by sight without knowing their names. It was a radical change from the gregarious life in the inner city—the endless round of wakes, weddings, baptisms, fund-raisers, and dances that she had known with her father.

Rose busied herself with her children. At that time, there was no organized support to guide new mothers on how to raise their children. There were childrearing manuals, but many of these had been written to combat the ills of poor environment rather than to help children develop. For instance the advice to bathe children daily and to get them out-of-doors, rain or shine, was a reaction to the foul living conditions of city dwellers of the time. Such procedures were less critical for suburbanites.

Rose followed the childrearing books without exception, using them as she used the rituals of the Church. She turned childraising into a business, with file cards kept on every child marking the details of their lives. She did not seem to enjoy her children; rather, they were more like special responsibilities whom she was to raise according to strict standards and a set agenda from which any deviation was taken as a personal affront, as a failure to be overcome.

Joe was rarely at home, and he talked to her little about his life when he was. He felt she shared no interest in his ever-changing business deals, a conclusion that was probably accurate. He was a womanizer, so he couldn't talk about his social activities in any great depth. And he had entered the world of organized crime through the door of Prohibition whiskey, the first of the dirty family secrets that have almost been eliminated from public records through the sealing of some of Joe Kennedy's papers and the allegedly accidental loss of others.

In 1920, Rose was deeply saddened by what she sensed was the failure of her six-year-old marriage. She was hurt and isolated by her husband's refusal to make her part of his life, except when he came home to eat, sleep, and make more babies. For a time in that year she tried moving back with her parents in the house on Welles Avenue, even staying in the same bedroom she had shared with her sister Agnes as a girl. However, at thirty years of age, with three children and a fourth soon to be born, she was no longer a child, no longer the first lady of Boston's mayor, and no longer wanted by her parents, who had their own personal crises to handle. The visit lasted three weeks, after which she knew she could never return. She had to make her own life, and from then on she would move toward a relationship that would keep her separated from both her husband and her children as much as possible in the years ahead.

Soon after Joe and Rose were married, the United States was plunged into a national debate over whether to take part in World War I. Joe was against war and would be all his life. He was not a pacifist. Rather, his opposition to war was a practical one: it interfered with his making money, and making money was the driving force of Joe Kennedy's life.

When the United States declared war on Germany in 1917, Kennedy's fellow Harvard graduates joined the army, making disparaging remarks about any classmate who stayed home. Joe ignored the patriotic call. He got the job of general manager of the Bethlehem Steel Fore River shipyards in Quincy, Massachusetts. There were two thousand employees, and his salary was $20,000 a year, a staggering amount for someone so young. He never returned to the bank, his father taking over in his place. Yet he would always hold the title of banker in higher regard than the genuine respect he deserved for his accomplishments at the shipyards, where he truly proved his business skills.

No matter how dishonest or unethical he would prove to be in many of his endeavors, the work he did in the shipyards was remarkable. Among other accomplishments, he led the production of thirty-seven destroyers before the armistice, a larger number in a shorter time than anyone had thought possible.

Kennedy was not scandal-free, however. His job at the shipyard was not considered so important to the war effort that he could not be drafted. When he received a draft notice, he was expected to comply with it; Bethlehem Steel would have simply moved someone else into the management position. But he saw no money to be made in the army, and so he used political connections to keep from being drafted. Recognizing how bad his actions might look to others, he had his biography amended in later years to imply that he began working in the shipyards before the war, intimating that his work there was far too valuable to be interrupted.

Another arrangement showed the usual Kennedy willingness to push ethics to the limits. The shipyard lacked a place for the workers to eat, so Joe had a cafeteria built. The food was good and reasonably priced, and the lunchroom boosted morale. It made for shorter lunch breaks, since workers could stay on the premises to eat. And it also helped line Kennedy's pockets, as he managed to assure himself a percentage of the profits.

Following the war Joe again went into a new business. He became stock department manager of the Boston office of the investment banking firm Hayden, Stone and Company. His salary was half what he earned at the shipyard, and he had no way to make side profits. But he learned the stock market from the company's head, Galen Stone, one of the most successful men in the business. And the job was the last stage in what he considered the graduate education of a businessman.

By 1922, Joe had learned everything he felt he needed to know from others. He had mastered banking and finance, business management, the stock market, and investment. He understood the emotional nature of the stock market and how to manipulate prices. He participated in stock pools with his friends, manipulating just enough stock to cause other investors to buy in to a business and send the stock value soaring. Kennedy and his friends sold their shares and took their profits as the stock value plummeted back to its true value.

Kennedy also used inside information, years later considered a felony offense, to make himself a millionaire. For example, while still working with Galen Stone, he was told Henry Ford was buying the Pond Creek Coal Company, whose stock was selling for $16 a share. Knowing that the price would rise as the news became known, Kennedy borrowed enough to purchase 15,000 shares. He waited until the stock had almost tripled in value, then sold and pocketed $210,000.

The organized crime activities in which Joe Kennedy engaged beginning in the early 1920s reflected his eagerness to make money in any manner. Since his family knew the liquor business, when it appeared Prohibition would become reality, Joe made his first foray into organized crime. It is not known whether Kennedy, like many members of organized crime, actively supported passage of the Volstead Act, which many foresaw would increase the demand for liquor. At the very least, Kennedy recognized that the law would be good for farsighted businessmen like himself.

The market for illegal whiskey was limitless, and seemingly, so was the supply. Some of the supply came from caches of bottles laid aside by entrepreneurs, and some came from distilleries in Ireland, Canada, and other countries. Some bootleggers made their own, the quality varying from poisonous to mild to as good as what came from distilleries.

Kennedy teamed up with the Irish Mafia in New England to import liquor from Europe, apparently primarily from Ireland. This first came to light among his friends when he supplied the Scotch for the tenth reunion of his Harvard class in 1922. (This account was provided by one of Kennedy's classmates. It contradicts a statement by Helen Barron, a family member, to Doris Kearns Goodwin, author of *The Fitzgeralds and the*

Kennedys, that the liquor came from stock from P.J. Kennedy's retail store that had been stored in the basement of P.J.'s home.) Other liquor sales of the group went at least into the Chicago area, where Irish, Italian, and Jewish crime bosses were constantly at war for control of bootlegging and related activities.

Joe Kennedy entered the Chicago wars indirectly. The bootleggers working for the Irish Mafia sent truck convoys into Chicago, where bombs were tossed at the trucks by the gangs who felt he was encroaching on their territory. Among those involved was Llewelyn Murray Humphreys, an associate of Al Capone, who kept records and spoke to enough others so that the Kennedy name was known.

Likewise, men such as Meyer Lansky, whose New York-based gang was frequently at war with New England bootleggers, were found to be involved with hijackings of liquor. Sam Giancana also talked of this period, as have others. (Ironically, Giancana was pro-Kennedy and eventually helped with the 1960 presidential election, rigging the Illinois returns in favor of Joe's son.)

Joe did not see bootlegging as a primary source of income, but it was an excellent one and the organization with which he worked was extremely aggressive. Mobster Frank Costello claimed to have been a partner in the trade and may have handled the shipping arrangements. In addition, two of Rose's uncles, James and Edward Fitzgerald, were involved in one of the typical drugstore operations where liquor was dispensed by prescription in the front, and illegally for cash out the back door. The rear of the building, which was located on Rose Wharf, had a trap door release to send the liquor into the water if the store was raided, according to Goodwin's interview with James's nephew, Tom.

It is doubtful that Kennedy stayed active in bootlegging after the first five or six years of Prohibition, for he was involved with too many other ventures that offered both glamor and higher profit without the risk. He may have been a silent partner, receiving income from the business, or he may have stopped participating entirely.

Whatever the case, the bootleg activities were not perceived as appropriate for a man with presidential ambitions, which Joe Kennedy later developed for himself and then his sons. He did not worry about his documented reputation as an adulterer. He did not worry about the business ventures that bordered on the illegal, and that caused regulations to be passed to stop such abuses. But bootlegging became the first of the family's dirty little secrets to be carefully hidden. Most records of his activities have been sealed away or allegedly lost by mistake.

Joe Kennedy was a womanizer, a man unable to commit to his wife or anyone else, including his children. The closest family relationship he ever developed was with his second oldest daughter, Kathleen, the one child he could neither control nor bend to his will. Rose, his wife, was a conquest, a stepping stone for a man on the rise, a friend who willingly took him to bed in marriage as any good Catholic woman would do. She made few demands upon him, did not ask embarrassing questions about his business or his wealth. And after the first three or four years of marriage, she quite willingly let him lead a life apart from her.

The children were vehicles for his own ambitions. The boys would take control of the nation if he failed to do so during the period when he seriously considered running against Franklin Roosevelt for the presidency of the United States. The girls would do whatever he ordered to assure that the boys came to power. And the grandchildren, the third generation, would presumably extend the dynasty in the way he preordained.

Joe Kennedy always escorted his women more openly than most businessmen considered prudent. He seemed to savor his evenings with them in the same way some wealthy men took delight in Havana cigars and a fine cognac. They were a respite from the pressures of work and home, enjoyed as intensely as his mood and the moment allowed, then discarded. If ever one of the relationships passed for what he might have defined as love, it was his affair with Gloria Swanson.

Kennedy turned to Swanson with unbridled lust, the million-aire businessman and the most popular movie star of the era. She was uninhibited for the times, her idea of monogamy being to never take more than one lover during her frequent marriages, and smart enough to choose a man who could help her with her career. They had the right mix of passion and greed, each feeding off the best and the worst in the other, their relationship so intense that it almost shattered the Kennedy family and killed young Jack.

The idea to become more involved with Hollywood resulted from Kennedy's witnessing the control the motion picture com-panies and their distributors had over the film industry. The theaters were necessary for showing movies, but the motion picture had become one of the most popular pastimes in every country where it was available. As a result, whoever controlled the product could determine the price a theater owner had to pay. Many times distributors charged exorbitant exhibition fees, yet the theaters paid, for to not show a popular film meant losing business.

Kennedy decided that he wanted to make money from all facets of the film business, and to make more money than normal. That meant getting involved with a troubled company that was inexpensive, yet one that had potential for success. His chance came with Film Booking Office of America (FBO), a distribution company owned by Robertson Cole Pictures Cor-poration. FBO had long supplied films for Kennedy's chain of theaters.

The parent company had invested $7 million in FBO, but Kennedy felt that its rising debts and other problems were such that the owners would let it go for $1 million. He raised the money with four partners (though he always talked of the purchase as though it was his alone) and attempted to buy FBO. Although Robertson-Cole turned Kennedy down at first, they soon realized that no better offers were forthcoming. Less than a month after the first bid, the deal was closed on Kennedy's terms.

Hollywood at this time was newly urbanized, a farm area that was converted to the industry's needs. Actors working in New York studios could go to nightclubs, variety shows, theater, museums, and the like. In Hollywood there were no such diversions, nothing to spend the fabulous sums that the movie stars were making. The actors had good looks and were athletic (they performed their own stunts), but often had no prospects in any other field. They didn't know what to do other than to build large homes and spend their money and limited free time in the pursuit of sensual pleasure. Alcoholism, drug abuse, and promiscuous sex became the activities of choice for men and women who thought their success, and the money that came with it, would never end.

Joe Kennedy understood several things when he took the train west to Hollywood. First, he found that pandering to the greatest number of people had made FBO successful. The problems the parent company thought they had were not so serious as they believed. Instead, what created difficulties was the lack of day-to-day working capital.

Hollywood had no track record. Everyone was getting rich in the movies, or so it seemed. But this was a business too new to have a history during a period when speculation was destroying as many businesses as it was supporting. Banks provided short-term loans for movies only at usurious interest rates: 18 percent was common interest for the movie companies, three times the high end cost of money for other businesses.

Kennedy understood how to manipulate the stock market and arrange for credit. He simply created Cinema Credit Corporation, arranged to sell a large portion of the stock to one of his partners, Freddie Prince, then had Prince arrange a loan through another of Prince's companies that was well established in other businesses. Then it was a simple matter to obtain a one year line of credit from four banks, all the money coming at rates far lower than other studios had obtained. And for these efforts, Kennedy placed himself on the FBO payroll for $2,000 a week, separate from the profits he would share with his partners.

Kennedy treated FBO like any other business he had controlled. He cut costs, cut salaries, and allowed only himself to be hedonistically self-indulgent. He rented a mansion on Rodeo Drive, the luxury center of Beverly Hills at the time. There was a swimming pool and tennis courts—everything that was needed to delight his growing family. All that his California residence lacked was the family.

Joe and Rose repeatedly claimed in interviews that they made their children their best friends. They saw no need to rely on outsiders for companionship when there were so many Kennedys and they could be so happy together. Family, they claimed, not commitments to strangers, was the driving force of their marriage, of the way they raised their nine children.

In truth, Joe spent his children's childhood seeking wealth, power, and illicit sex. And unlike his youngest son, Ted, who has both wealth and greater long-term power as senior senator than even Jack attained, Joe used his power only to maintain or increase his wealth. The senator has a history of illicit sex at least as blatant as his father enjoyed, but he has used his power primarily for the public good, a situation he did not learn from his father's example.

The truth was quite different. Joe and Rose held the same biases as did the Protestants of Boston. They were racist and anti-Semitic, and believed that poorer Irish Catholics were inherently inferior. Only the Brahmins mattered, yet they were snubbed by the Brahmins, which ultimately led them to leave Boston and buy homes in New York, Hyannis, and Palm Beach.

The children were not their parents' best friends, though they were desperate to please their father whenever he was at home. However, the supposed focus on the children provided the parents with several advantages. First, it gave them an excuse to miss events to which they were not going to be invited because of bias. The implication was that they were home with their family by choice, not because they were unwanted elsewhere.

Second, it enabled Joe to make certain Rose was tied down on the East Coast while he was living the life of the wealthy, oversexed bachelor on the West Coast.

And third, as with all dysfunctional families in which there is emotional or physical abuse, the insular attitude was a way to hide Joe's dirty little secrets. So long as his wife and children thought that the family was more important than anyone on the outside, they would endure the hell the members caused, certain that anything else could only be worse. Ultimately this led to the majority of Joe's children becoming drug and alcohol abusers.

As for Rose, she distanced herself from her children in her own way. Before I came to work for her, she had maintained a small house in Hyannis that was separate from the main house she shared with the growing family. She spent extensive time alone there performing the religious rituals she had learned from the nuns. During this period she insisted that the children leave her alone and that they participate intensely in physical activities.

Joe also bragged about his desire to keep his children independent of him, to give them the funds so they could tell him off and go their separate ways. Toward this end, he claimed in interviews in the 1950s, trust funds were established for the children shortly after he first moved to Hollywood.

The truth was that Kennedy was taking gambles, and knew he might lose. He was speculating in land, speculating in business. The trust funds let him secure a source of money should he make a serious mistake.

There were three trusts in all. (Rose was the trustee when the funds were originally vested.) The first trust was established during the Hollywood years, with additional trusts created in 1939 and 1949. More than $180 million would eventually be set aside this way, with income from the trust coming to each child upon his or her twenty-first birthday. However, the trusts were not irrevocable instruments that could be used only by the children. In essence, they were protective shelters for Joe's money. If his speculations failed, he would have access to millions his creditors could not touch. And if he was even more successful, he had preserved family wealth safe from taxes and death duties.

The money was used at least once for purposes other than income for the children. Joe Gargan told me that when Sargent Shriver decided to run for the Democratic presidential nomination in 1976, part of his campaign funds came from money originally set aside for Rosemary's trust fund. It was only because the seeming altruism of a trust fund for his children looked better for Joe Kennedy's image that he failed to tell the truth.

In addition to succeeding in the movie business, Kennedy wanted to have inside information on actors' personal lives. He arranged with Arthur Houghton, an employee at the Hays Office,* to provide him with the latest Hollywood gossip and covered-up scandals, an interest he would pass on to his son, John.

Joe Kennedy decided to use Hollywood for more than money and gossip, however. He had failed to gain the respect of the Protestant Eastern establishment despite his great success as a businessman. Accident of birth had robbed him of the chance to be acknowledged by Boston's elite. He seemed to feel that it was time to buy special privilege, and Hollywood seemed the vehicle for achieving that end.

Once Joe knew the Hollywood moguls, he approached Harvard about arranging for course work for the serious study of

*The Hays Office was the group established by the motion picture industry to police itself. It operated under the direction of Will Hays for many years after its founding. It established fair business practices, dealt with scandals in the industry, and ultimately became a censor for the industry.

the film industry. A course in how the film industry operated would be a requirement for every second-year business student. And the introduction of the new course would be through a conference at which the heads of the major studios would lecture.

Wallace B. Donham, the dean of the Harvard Graduate School of Business Administration, recognized the importance of the film industry, and agreed that the study of American business was incomplete without a course on the movie industry. But Donham's influence on Harvard's administration, especially college president Lawrence Lowell, was not so great as Kennedy would have liked. The most vehement spokesman against the new program was the highly influential William Marston Seabury, whose great-great-grandfather was the first bishop of the Protestant Episcopal Church in America. The heads of the major movie studios were un-American in Seabury's eyes. Of those he knew about, there was one whose family had come from Germany, two from Hungary, and the fourth came from that most terrible of cities—New York.

Kennedy was again faced with the realization that even the most successful Irish Catholics would always be second-rate in the eyes of the old-line Protestant families. So he struck a deal. He contributed $30,000 to Harvard's Fogg Museum to establish a film library. In exchange, he was allowed to present a series of lectures by a dozen heads of the major studios.

When the series was completed, Kennedy was feted on both sides of the continent. The lecture series had put the industry into perspective, and the men who had spoken—Cecil B. De Mille, Jesse Lasky, Harry Warner, William Fox, Robert Cochrane, Marcus Loew, Adolph Zukor—were the ones who had nurtured the business that was changing the world. No matter what anyone thought of Kennedy, the result was worthy of praise.

In order to further enhance his reputation, Kennedy published a book that was a compilation of the lectures, titled *The Story of the Films*. Each industry leader was credited for his contribution, but Kennedy's name was on the cover, and the reviewers referred to him in their articles.

During the Hollywood years, Joe Kennedy essentially divorced himself from his family. The luxury trains on which he traveled from coast to coast took four to five days in each direction, time spent out of contact with his growing businesses. Whether or not he maintained a friendship with his wife, he had the money and the power to attract every beautiful woman who thought that having sex with the tall, skinny producer would be the way to a starring role. He seldom traveled unescorted, even taking women to many of his business dinner meetings. And he knew that, because of the way she was raised, he could always return to his wife's bed and enjoy her favors whenever he was at home.

Yet the women Joe was known to be dating were using their bodies, not their brains, seeking to benefit from a man's weakness, not meeting him head on as a strong equal. Until Gloria Swanson.

If Rose Kennedy had not been rigidly molded by the Catholic Church, and if she had pursued the lifestyle she enjoyed when acting as her father's representative during his time as mayor, she would likely have been the emotional twin of Gloria Swanson. Both women were bright, aggressive, eager for all the experiences of life, and hedonistic enough to enjoy the lifestyle seemingly unlimited access to money allowed. But Gloria had been raised without constraints, given limited formal education, and was sexually liberated in a manner that made her comfortable experiencing whatever the man in her life desired. Married or single, she made her choices and let the man make his. Convention was for others.

By the time Joe Kennedy met Swanson, she had become one of the powers in Hollywood. She was twenty-eight, having moved to California when she was sixteen to get more involved in movies. She had started out in bit parts, became a major player in Mack Sennett comedies, and then a star at Famous Players-Lasky earning $5,000 a week. She was married to French royalty (Henri de la Falaise, a bankrupt French nobleman), and legally able to take a title for herself. She had been divorced twice, delighted in frequent affairs, had two abortions, given birth to one child, adopted another, and been feted in some of the most glamorous cities in the world. The problems she had experienced had been of her own making. And after she joined United Artists in 1925 and became her own producer, her successes increasingly became her own, too.

In comparison to most people, Swanson was fabulously wealthy. She had turned down an offer of $22,000 a week— more than $1 million a year—from Famous Players-Lasky when she joined United Artists. Her New York estate had a full-time press agent, four secretaries, several servants who maintained her property both there and in California, and several business managers. About $10,000 a month went for personnel.

Clothing was the next largest expense for Gloria. Many of her pictures were society films where she was expected to dress in the most lavish of costumes. Since fans wanted movie stars to be seen in real life as they appeared in their films, Gloria had to own enough clothing to stock a luxury boutique. She spent $50,000 a year on gowns, and an additional $35,000 a year for fur coats to cover the gowns. For shoes, stockings, and perfume, she annually spent $5,000, $9,000, and $6,000, respectively.

Finance was Swanson's major weak point. She not only had no comprehensive business sense, she had no interest in dealing with details on the sets and the overall financial framework of each movie. She came face to face with her shortcomings when trying to film *Sadie Thompson,* a controversial story that threatened to run afoul of the Hays Office. She sank $200,000 into the film, convinced that no matter how much she spent the movie would be a success. However, she soon found herself in financial trouble due to personal overspending. That was when a friend introduced her to Kennedy. It was the end of November 1927, and the two met for a business lunch at the Savoy Plaza Hotel on Fifth Avenue in New York.

Much has been made of the meeting between the banker and the actress, somehow implying that each was instantly taken with the other. But if anything came from that first meeting, it was only the mutual realization that they both had an excellent grasp of motion pictures as business. Kennedy enjoyed the gossip of the industry, and his grasp of the intricacies of foreign sales, rights, accounting procedures, and all the other details of production that could ensure success exceeded Swanson's. Swanson was not just a pretty face; she knew production, distribution, and the roles of all the people involved in making a movie.

Kennedy returned to FBO's New York office, where he spent his business hours when he was not away from his family. There he checked on the sales of Swanson's most recent films. He wanted to provide a loan to her only if the potential of *Sadie Thompson* seemed great enough based on her track record. Once he was ready to make the deal with her, he invited her to dinner, hoping to learn more about her. He gave her a copy of the book he had edited from the Harvard talks, with her name embossed in gold on the covers.

(The dinner conversation gives additional insight into Kennedy's lifelong anger at the social conditions that had so long victimized him. Swanson later quoted him as saying of the Boston Protestants, "The Cabots and the Lodges won't be caught at the pictures or let their children go. And that's why their servants know more about what's going on in the world than they do. The working class gets smarter every day, thanks to radio and pictures. It's the snooty Back Bay bankers who are missing the boat.")

By December 1927, Kennedy and his staff, working from their rented home in Beverly Hills, had completely changed Swanson's finances. He analyzed her income tax deductions, the money she was paying for staff, the ways in which she made movies, and everything else that related to her business.

He realized that she was a woman in complete control of almost every aspect of her life. Of limited education, without adequate guidance, and with a series of crises women with twice her years might not have handled effectively, still she triumphed. She learned from life, from both mistakes and successes. She was also quite beautiful, and the way she had conducted her personal life prior to marrying Henri meant that she might see sex as Joe did—recreation frequently unrelated to love.

It is uncertain just when Kennedy decided to sleep with Swanson, though it is known that his closest associates helped him. Joe, his business staff, Gloria, and Henri were in Palm Beach in January 1928, working on her business affairs. The rest of the Kennedys were up north. Perhaps he carefully plotted that first day's sexual escapades. Perhaps he came to the conclusion that the timing couldn't be better. Whatever the case, it happened when Eddie Moore, Joe's closest assistant and the man for whom Joe's youngest son would be named, convinced Henri to go deep-sea fishing. The entire crew was supposedly going. But by the time they were ready to leave, Gloria convinced her husband that she was afraid of small boats and needed to do some shopping. Kennedy had important business calls to make.

Swanson did go shopping, then returned to her hotel. She was in a kimono, lying on the bed, talking to the hotel florist when Joe entered the room, having come into the suite as the maid was leaving. As Swanson later wrote in her autobiography:

> He wasn't listening. He just stood there, in his white flannels and his argyle sweater and his two-toned shoes, staring at me for a full minute or more, before he entered the room and closed the door behind him. He moved so quickly that his mouth was on mine before either of us could speak. With one hand he held the back of my head, with the other he stroked my body and pulled at my kimono. He kept insisting in a drawn-out moan, "No longer, no longer. Now." He was like a roped horse, rough, arduous, racing to be free. After a hasty climax

he lay beside me, stroking my hair. Apart from his guilty, passionate mutterings, he had still said nothing cogent.''

Swanson had no illusions about the relationship, nor any wish to end it. Kennedy was a staunch Catholic, married to a woman for whom the teachings of the Church were to be followed so rigidly it would not matter if her personal life was in tatters. Gloria was married to a kind man with little ambition but a desire to help his wife succeed. She had no interest in divorcing Henri, and knew that Joe would not leave Rose for her.

The relationship between the two lovers was brief, stormy, and well known. Even today, a stop at such Hollywood insider locations as Musso and Frank's Grill on Hollywood Boulevard uncovers photographs showing the couple as obviously intimate. However, each had the good fortune to be married at the time. No one felt pressured to break up an adulterous couple so long as they were reasonably discrete, not living together or having parties for the press, and could trot out their respective spouses when needed.

Because of this, the relationship took on a rather outrageous nature when Joe agreed to produce Gloria's first all-talking picture, *The Trespasser*. It would have its premiere in London, where Gloria and Henri, along with Joe and Rose, would attend the opening.

Before going to England, Gloria and her daughter came to Hyannis Port in August 1929 to visit with the Kennedys. Joe had bought what was originally called the Malcolm Cottage in Hyannis. This was the origin of the Kennedy compound there.*

---

*The home, located on a bluff, had two-and-a-half acres of land and beach. Although originally built as a summer home—Joe and Rose used it as such when they rented it earlier in their marriage—the Kennedys remodeled and enlarged it after buying it. Eventually, the main house had twenty rooms, nine-and-a-half bathrooms, and a private movie theater with a commercial movie projector. Next to the theater was the doll room, where Rose put the dolls she collected from all over the world. Special glass-enclosed shelves lined the walls to display and protect the dolls. There were numerous and varied antiques.

Gloria noticed that Joe was different at home than he had been in Hollywood. Instead of the wealthy playboy and business genius, Gloria saw a proud, seemingly loving father. He was always a fantasy figure for his children, the one person who both seemed to care for them and who was forever somewhere else. Rose, in her pain over the condition of her marriage, withdrew from the children and traveled as much as she could. (She made seventeen European shopping trips in the six years following the stock market crash.) The children seemed to ignore or fear her, but they treasured their frequently absent father. When he was home, they were determined to take advantage of him, to play with him, to show off for him, to win his approval one way or another. It was almost as though they felt responsible for his frequent absences, determined to do everything right so he wouldn't leave them again.

It is impossible to know what Rose saw during this period. The summer people were visiting Hyannis Port in large numbers, and Joe regularly introduced Swanson as his most important business associate. He referred to her as Rose's friend, though Rose did not know the movie star. As for the community, most people viewed movie stars as magical. They delighted in Gloria's presence, gossiping about her, observing her, becoming almost giddy with each new contact. Many of the children in the area had trouble believing that the girl playing with Pat Kennedy and going to school with her was really Gloria's daughter.

Rose continued to do what she always did, including going to mass at St. Francis Xavier Church each morning, then returning for breakfast with her older children. There was some time for Joe to be alone with his girlfriend, but not nearly enough. He decided to take her on a sailboat he had purchased in 1927, a vessel ironically named the *Rose Elizabeth*.

For example, the Kennedys had two plates that were used by George Washington, as well as a lock of his hair. Joe and Rose liked best that the grounds could be used for competitions among their children and other family members, whether sailboat racing, football, or baseball.

The *Rose Elizabeth* was large enough to have a hold in which a twelve-year-old boy could hide, a trick Jack decided to pull when his father and Gloria went sailing together. She was unable to swim, but Joe was good in the water and skilled with the boat. Years later Jack's friends from that era told of the incident, and he reportedly discussed it with close associates at the White House. In addition, the rather terse harbormaster's report following the incident contained some details. Jack sneaked up on deck, discovered his father and Gloria in an intimate embrace. Shocked by what he witnessed, he leaped over the side and began swimming away from land.

Joe, knowing that his second son was sickly and not strong enough to survive long in deep water, leaped into the water and saved his son's life. The incident seems to have been an emotional turning point for the future president. Many of his cavalier attitudes toward women as sexual objects, especially his relationship with actress Marilyn Monroe, seem to have stemmed from his shocked disillusionment with his father. In the future there would only be one serious relationship for Jack, and that would be with Inga Arvad, whom he met at the start of World War II, and whom his father eventually kept him from seeing.

On the ocean voyage to London, Joe's only effort to be discrete with Gloria was to spend the nights with Rose. He frequently ignored everyone except Gloria, and once threatened to punch a man whom Joe felt was staring at Gloria. Gloria was embarrassed by this attention and certain Rose would be irate. Instead Rose played the role of the naive wife, talking delightedly with Gloria, sharing stories of their respective children.

In London, however, the affair was obvious to Henri, who had arrived there from France. He refused to wear the blinders to his spouse's infidelity that Rose perpetually used. Yet with both Henri and Gloria owing substantial incomes to the work they were doing with Joe, neither would stop the affair. For Gloria, sex with Joe was pleasurable and the price she paid to have him take care of her finances. For Henri, his willingness to share his wife discretely was an aspect of himself he had never previously wanted to face. It was easier to go on pretending than to admit he could be bought by his wife's lover.

It was near the end of 1929, after the Great Depression had begun, when the next dramatic incident allegedly occurred between Joe and Gloria. This was reported by Swanson, although it has never been confirmed.

According to Swanson, Boston's Cardinal O'Connell came to New York to see her. He explained that he wanted to talk about her association with Joe, and while they both avoided specifics at first, Gloria soon recognized he meant the personal side of their relationship.

According to Swanson, Joe had no intention of divorcing Rose to marry her. First, it was not permitted by the Catholic Church. Second, there would be too many financial considerations at stake. There would have been family settlements to make that Joe was too cheap to consider. Joe was too greedy, too frightened of losing even a portion of his wealth to consider divorce. What he sought was the right to maintain a separate home with Gloria away from Rose.

O'Connell explained that Gloria had become an "occasion for sin" every time the two were together. Joe was supposedly one of the most prominent Catholic laymen in America, so his public appearances were closely scrutinized. (In reality, Joe distanced himself from the Church as much as possible, except when its leadership or its members could be used for his own ends. However, the potential for scandal was there.)

Gloria was irate. She informed the cardinal that what he was discussing was Joe's problem. If he was not at peace with his faith, then *he* would have to take some action. She told Cardinal O'Connell to talk with Kennedy, not her.

There are those who have tried to dispute the story, to say that O'Connell did not make the contact or that he did not make it when claimed. More likely the story is true and that the source of the information concerning Joe was Rose. Sending the cardinal may have been what she felt was a last chance to stop her husband's public mockery of his marriage vows. Not surprisingly, after the affair with Swanson was over, all of Joe's relationships were adequately discrete.

Joe's film production career was short-lived, primarily because of his ego. (It did add at least $5 million to his personal fortune.) He wanted to become a famous producer, and he wanted Gloria Swanson to be his leading lady. He commissioned a comedy for her, but the screenplay that resulted was terrible, and Kennedy was convinced by others to have it changed. Ultimately a quality comedy was developed utilizing the talents of such individuals as Sidney Howard, a Pulitzer Prize-winning playwright, who also came up with a new title for the movie— *What a Widow*—for which Joe gave him a new Cadillac.

What a Widow was a success with *Daily Variety,* but the more important New York critics were less enthusiastic. Even more embarrassing for Joe, whose name had not been on the highly successful *Trespasser,* the titles for *What a Widow* were animated at great cost, and the result was riveting. No one could miss the credit that read "Joseph P. Kennedy Presents," a credit Joe thought would assure that everyone knew the brilliant Swanson success was his doing. Unfortunately the public, like the critics, was not impressed.

Comedics such as *What a Widow* had lost their popular appeal by 1930 as more and more Americans were out of work. Based on the ticket sales, Americans wanted either the glamor of elaborate musicals or the drama, violence, and ultimate "good guy" triumph of gangster films. Comedies did not offer the type of pure escapism the public was seeking. And while Swanson's popularity had not slipped, her name alone was not enough to sell a movie. With the special credits, the last film of Joe's Hollywood career would always be seen as *his* flop.

Kennedy decided that it was time to get out. On December 6, 1930, the film industry and Gloria Swanson learned the truth about Joe. As the *Motion Picture News* for that day explained, Joe sold Pathe, which he headed, to RKO for $5 million. Joe personally made millions, but the other stockholders collectively lost millions, and were convinced that they had been victims of deceit, mismanagement, the illegal use of proxies, and other frauds.

There were other discoveries as well. The dressing room of the bungalow Kennedy had arranged for Gloria Swanson to have when she was on the lot had a listening device Kennedy planted in case Gloria cheated on him with someone other than her husband. (Joe considered himself monogamous because he could brag to Gloria that, for the previous year, Rose had not gotten pregnant.) In addition, the Cadillac given Howard had been billed to Gloria's personal accounts instead of to the cost of the film as agreed. (Joe's accountant kept the books until their parting.) The fur coat that Joe gave Gloria was charged to Gloria's personal account, as was the price of her bungalow. And she later learned from other movie executives that Joe had acted behind her back to prevent her involvement in films that could have brought her greater income and prestige. They would have required Gloria to work with other producers, and Kennedy would hear nothing of such arrangements. In effect, Kennedy had wooed and won his mistress with her own money.

For his part, Joe returned to Wall Street without saying good-bye to Gloria. He stayed with his family in Bronxville most nights and every weekend. He had sex with his wife once again (Teddy became the ninth Kennedy child), and she felt that both he and their seventeen-year marriage had been saved. In reality, the philandering was simply on holiday, though the children were happier than they had been for most of their lives. For the moment, their father was home.

Joe Kennedy was scared when he returned East. He made money buying stocks following the Wall Street crash, and in 1930 was worth at least $100 million by most conservative estimates. But Kennedy also had a sense of what the Great Depression could mean for the country. People were homeless. Drifters were riding empty railroad cars, going from town to town, seeking work. Families were starving or being split up as everyone tried to find work. There were radicals calling for drastic changes in politics and society. There was a chance of revolution. Certainly it was to Washington, not the business community, that the public would be looking for help. In the near future, if a man wanted ultimate power, as Joe Kennedy did, he had to look to government. Whoever was in the White House or held a meaningful position with the national government would have the power and respect that major business executives previously held. While he had not yet formulated thoughts of running for the presidency, he decided that he could at least buy government prestige.

Joe felt that he could give a few thousand dollars to Franklin Roosevelt's campaign treasury and the Democratic National Committee and have his choice of government positions. However, even after he gave $25,000 to Roosevelt and loaned $50,000 to the committee, his fantasy did not carry over into reality. Although he was given a position on the campaign finance committee, no one felt obligated to Kennedy because of his contributions. Joe had the cynical attitude that everyone had a price, even those at the top, and that he could buy the loyalty of anyone he chose. He underestimated Roosevelt.

Roosevelt had a skill rarely encountered in politics at the top levels, though ironically John Kennedy would come close. Without saying anything misleading, he could convince anyone that they were more important to him than they really were.

Years later, Angie Dickinson, Joey Bishop, and others would tell of conversations with John Kennedy where he would indicate he was truly interested in their work. He seemed to genuinely want to know, to put their interests over concerns of the nation. He made them feel important and they repaid him with intense loyalty on the campaign trail. It was a trait he had learned, in part, from watching his father's nemesis.

Many have accused John Kennedy of being shallow and almost transparent about his actions, even though he did love Hollywood gossip. Certainly his father recognized that Jack was using Roosevelt's technique, yet in the 1930s, Joe was taken in by Roosevelt's approach even though some of the closest campaign (and later administration) personnel deliberately showed their disdain for the businessman. However, he never realized that the staff was reflecting their boss's attitude.

Roosevelt's election delighted Kennedy, who planned to take advantage of it in several ways. He had developed a friendship with James Roosevelt, the president's son, which he intended to utilize for business. And he fully expected to be named secretary of the Treasury so he could control the nation's money supply.

But Roosevelt understood men like Kennedy. In politics, as in business, the more he achieved, the more he would want. Kennedy could become a political opponent if the president was not careful. Thus, Roosevelt first thought he would make Kennedy treasurer of the United States, a high-profile position without authority. His name would appear on the nation's currency, he would be feted and photographed, but he would be dead-ended without being a danger to anyone.

Kennedy was infuriated at the way he was shunted aside. With characteristic lack of tact, in February 1933 Kennedy invited Raymond Moley, one of Roosevelt's closest advisers, to spend a few days in Palm Beach. Moley later stated, "There I heard plenty of Kennedy's excoriation of Roosevelt, of his criticisms of the president-elect who, according to Kennedy, had no program—and what ideas he had were unworthy of note." Roosevelt continued to ignore Kennedy.

Angry over the rejection, Kennedy informed men close to the president that he might sue the Democratic Party for immediate repayment of the $50,000 loan. Then he turned to bribery, offering to establish a fund to support Moley in a better lifestyle than his government salary would allow. But Moley had too much integrity. Rather than hurt Kennedy, he said that his tastes were simple, the salary adequate under the circumstances.

Kennedy did manage to turn the Roosevelt connection to his advantage in one way. It was obvious to everyone that the end of Prohibition was near, and anyone who could gain the right to legally import liquor from Britain would make great profits. England was anxious to improve its relationship with the U.S.

government, and a business opportunity that would connect the president's family with one of its industries was an opportunity to be encouraged.

Kennedy had met and befriended the president's oldest son, James, during the campaign. In September 1933, the Kennedys and the Roosevelts took the boat to England, where Joe and James called upon the important distilleries in the London area. James's presence implied that if the companies did business with Kennedy, the White House would be pleased. As a result, Joe was given the chance to handle John Dewars Scotch, Haig and Haig, and Gordon's Gin. Although Prohibition was still law, Kennedy's company, Somerset Importers, could bring liquor into the country legally under Joe's medicinal license. Joe would be able to supply commercial buyers with an extensive quantity of real liquor the moment Prohibition ended.

Joe Kennedy was not the only person to gain the right to legally import liquor. King's Ransom Scotch and House of Lords Scotch signed with Alliance Distributors, a company owned by mob leader Frank Costello. Meyer Lansky became a liquor importer, as did Lucky Luciano. Ultimately there were alliances between these figures, sometimes loose, sometimes as solid as any business partnership. Kennedy became connected with Sam Giancana, among others, a connection that would be utilized in another setting. Giancana's organization allegedly handled the rigging of election results in parts of Illinois during the 1960 presidential election. And President Kennedy also shared Giancana's mistress, using her to pass messages when Kennedy needed help from organized crime.

When President Roosevelt finally got around to a post for Kennedy, it turned out to be what at first sight was the least sensible appointment—chairmanship of the newly created Securities and Exchange Commission (SEC). The SEC was to be the watchdog for the public to end the excesses and frauds on Wall Street. Roosevelt knew that Kennedy had been thoroughly disreputable. He had proven himself unethical at best, an uncaught violator of numerous laws at worst. Yet there was great wisdom in the appointment. First, there was no one with more knowledge of how to improperly manipulate the stock market than Joe Kennedy. Thus, he would be the perfect man to devise ways to prevent people such as himself from taking advantage of Wall Street. Second, Roosevelt knew the size of Kennedy's ego. The SEC appointment would bring him massive public attention. He would do everything in his power to prove his value so he would get public acclaim.

As SEC chairman, Kennedy performed as Roosevelt thought he would. Kennedy used his knowledge to help clean up Wall Street, to improve disclosures of stock offerings, and to publicize the inner workings of corporations. For the first time, small investors had the opportunity to understand the potential for success of the companies whose stocks were for sale. And speculators were denied many of the vehicles for making money they had previously enjoyed. Kennedy emerged a hero, unrepentant in his personal ways, yet performing what amounted to truly valid public service for the nation.

Two other important events took place during this time, one of which revealed the ever-widening gap with Rose, and the other being a major step toward creating the Kennedy myth. The first was the renting of Marwood, a 33-room house on 125 acres of land in Maryland near Washington, D.C. His companion there was Eddie Moore, the same man who had been with him in Beverly Hills (and for whom Joe's youngest son, Edward, was named). And though he claimed he chose the place because it would house Rose and the children for the year he planned to remain as SEC chairman, he never intended to have her present. The estate became the scene for lavish parties, whose guests and activities went unreported in the newspapers. Franklin Roosevelt could play there without bringing his wife, and journalists knew they were invited precisely because they could keep quiet. Silence was the price of access, and access was such a privilege that everyone played the game.

The second situation was a friendship with Arthur Krock, Washington bureau chief correspondent for the *New York*

Times, a position that made him one of the most prominent reporters in the United States. Perhaps because of his relatively poor roots, Krock was fascinated by the wealthy and the powerful. However, because he had become a *Times* columnist by 1932, writing "In the Nation," he actually was more influential than many of the men of whom he was in awe. Yet he delighted in special favors from the politicians, and his observations depended upon how he was treated.

Krock was a brilliant writer and a usually careful researcher who both won the Pulitzer Prize and was involved with the committee that issued the Pulitzer. However, he also could get carried away when he wanted to impress someone, as he wanted to impress both Kennedy and Roosevelt, who asked him to interview the new SEC chairman. As a result, the article that appeared on July 4, 1933, was filled with unchecked half-truths. Kennedy became a "famous ballplayer" at Harvard. He was credited with being Roosevelt's business and financial campaign manager during the election. And in the most outrageous nonsense of all, Krock claimed that Kennedy had "never been in a bear pool in his life or participated in any outside move to trim the limbs [Wall Street terms for the types of deals that, in truth, had added immensely to his wealth]. He has been a member of but two pools of any kind. His Wall Street operations have been with his own money, in the interest of his own holdings." Naturally, Joe loved it. If Krock was misled before the article was published, there were plenty of experts attempting to correct his statements. He received a number of letters pointing out Kennedy's dishonesty, his lack of business ethics, and the financial woes he created for others in Hollywood. Krock did not care, however. His friendship with Kennedy was more important.

Eventually Krock turned against the family, or at least was more open to the truth. But in the early years of their relationship, Kennedy provided insider information about the government for Krock, and Krock wrote glowing articles about Joe and the members of his family. He was feted at the Kennedy's Palm Beach estate and was frequently at the Marwood parties.

He also helped John Kennedy gain his first recognition as an "intellectual" by helping to gain him the Pulitzer Prize for his book *Profiles in Courage.*

Kennedy resigned from the SEC in the fall of 1935, the departure planned from the start and thus not a surprise to anyone. His tenure had been successful, and he had shown his critics that he could have integrity. He also claimed to have no political ambition, though he continued to advise Roosevelt from time to time, especially after taking a European vacation where he visited nations of concern to the United States.

After leaving the SEC, Kennedy wanted a more important post in the administration. In order to help assure Roosevelt's reelection in 1936, and to keep his own drive for government power alive, Joe "wrote" his second book, *I'm for Roosevelt.* He undoubtedly outlined the ideas he wanted to convey, but then he offered Arthur Krock a five-week contract at $1,000 per week to do the actual writing. Krock accepted the job but claimed he took no money.*

I'm for Roosevelt was released in August 1936. It pictured the president as being the savior of capitalism. It implied that big businessmen were given too much respect, that regulation of business in the manner Roosevelt had started was in everyone's best interest. The price of the book for Roosevelt? Another appointment for Kennedy, and one with more power, influence, and prestige.

After the reelection, Kennedy was offered a chance to return to government service. In spring 1937, he took the chairmanship

---

*This may or may not be true. If it is, there are probably two interconnected reasons. The first was that Krock was desperate to maintain the friendship with Kennedy. The second was that, being one of the top journalists in the country, Krock knew that Kennedy's effort to appear more scholarly would be instantly attacked if it became known how much Krock had been paid. Working without pay would imply that Krock made an occasional editorial suggestion for what was truly Joe Kennedy's book.

of the Maritime Commission, which had been established under the Merchant Marine Act implemented the previous year.

Kennedy's work was again impressive. He restructured the country's outdated merchant marine, handled claims against the government, altered improper contracts, and handled the selling, scrapping, or refurbishing of government-owned ships. In addition, he helped Roosevelt develop plans for the transportation of various military items to the Far East, where China and Japan were at war, using private vessels. In that way the government could allow the sale of weapons and other supplies to the Asian antagonists without being directly involved, financially or politically. Kennedy spent less than a year on the job, living once again at Marwood away from his family, but when he was done, the merchant marine was in a position to handle the extraordinary demands of the war years to come.

The year 1937 marked the high point of Kennedy's government career. Robert Bingham, ambassador to England, was terminally ill. Joe Kennedy wanted to take his place.

Becoming ambassador to England promised Kennedy everything he had dreamed about since he was first understood the disdain the Brahmins held for Irish Catholics. He had received a Harvard education without being accepted by the Protestant elite. He had become a self-made multimillionaire and not been accepted by them. He had become a movie mogul, a government leader, a man who was being written about in the major newspapers and magazines of the day. And still the family was not accepted. To be the first Irish Catholic ambassador to England would give him a chance to thumb his nose at the people he had hated all his adult life.

Thanks to Arthur Krock and other reporters who looked favorably upon him, Kennedy was receiving the type of press that was making him a national figure. He had wealth and knew how to influence others. It was obvious that he had political ambitions, and there was some hint that he might become a candidate for the presidency. Kennedy had the money and the reputation to challenge Roosevelt in 1940 if he so chose, and there was a chance that he could sway enough party leaders to be successful. Roosevelt saw him as a man who could undermine his efforts through criticism in the press or displace him on the party ticket in the future. Getting him out of town in a manner that fit Kennedy's desires was appealing to the president.

Roosevelt also had a sense of humor about the appointment. He knew that Kennedy would both shock and impress the British. There was no way that Kennedy was going to be so pompously formal as most diplomats, a fact that would upset staid London. At the same time, Kennedy wanted to impress the British and had the personal fortune needed to underwrite the cost of putting on the lavish banquets expected of the ambassador. As James Roosevelt said of his father's reaction to the discovery that Joe Kennedy wanted the position, "he laughed so hard he almost toppled from his wheelchair."

Roosevelt actually had second thoughts about the appointment. He sent his son James to see if Kennedy would accept the appointment of secretary of Commerce instead. According to Krock, who was present at the time and recorded the incident in his memoirs, Kennedy was outraged. The London job was the only appointment he would accept. One week later the appointment was approved, Krock breaking the news on December 9, 1937.

Roosevelt administration aide and long-time Roosevelt friend Henry Morgenthau wrote in his diary following the appointment that Roosevelt "considered Kennedy a very dangerous man and that he was going to send him to England as Ambassador with the distinct understanding that the appointment was only good for six months and that, furthermore, by giving him this appointment, any obligation that he had to Kennedy was paid for." Morgenthau also noted that Roosevelt had said to him: "I have made arrangements to have Joe Kennedy watched hourly—and the first time he opens his mouth and criticizes me, I will fire him."

* * *

Joe Kennedy arrived in London in 1938 with three concerns on his mind. The first was the official agenda for the U.S. government. Britain and Ireland were at odds, Roosevelt trying to act as mediator between them, using his ambassador, Kennedy, to relay messages to both sides as they attempted to work out their differences. In addition, Kennedy was to handle problems related to some Pacific islands in a trustee dispute, and he was to negotiate a trade agreement between the United States and Great Britain.

The new ambassador's second major concern was to upgrade his family's social standing. America may have rejected royalty for its own government, but Americans embraced the idea that kings and queens were special, somehow a step above mere mortals. To be in the presence of royalty was to achieve a singular honor, and the debutante daughters of Americans living in England were regularly presented to the ruling king or queen, as would Joe Kennedy's daughters.

In recent years, Rose had been an almost dowdy housewife whose occasional sprees, such as going shopping in Europe with Kathleen, were aberrations. Yet those sprees were like an ember of the fire that was within her when she was still the companion for Honey Fitz in the days before his fall.

With the change in Joe's status, Rose was suddenly turned into an international figure. She decided to eliminate her distinctive Boston accent, so voice lessons were provided through Michael Scanlon, the protocol expert at the American embassy. Then Scanlon's wife, Gladys, took Rose to Paris so that she, Rosemary, and Kathleen would have the proper gowns for meeting the queen. The Scanlons were close friends of the royal family, as well as with the notorious American expatriate Wallis Simpson, who would lead the playboy Duke of Windsor to denounce his throne. Thus they knew not only the flawlessly correct ways to meet royalty, but also the gossipy, scandalous, or amusing incidents that took place when the Windsors let down their crowns.

Next came curtsy lessons, which lasted several days. Rose was given a diamond-and-ruby tiara by Lady Bessborough for the occasion, and Joe was so delighted by the way she looked that he gave the impression that he would truly enjoy dating his own wife again.

The youngest of the Kennedy children were the delight of the British press. There were stories of little Teddy holding a camera upside down while taking a picture of the changing of the guard, and of Jean challenging her teacher's criticism of her math test by claiming that, in America, nine can be divided evenly by five.

But the warmth with which the British embraced the family was countered by Joe's third agenda. He wanted to make very clear that the United States was not going to get involved with war.

The upcoming war would bring great personal tragedy to Joe Kennedy, but to say that concern for the safety of his sons affected his attitudes is to apply hindsight to what was taking place. Joe still believed that war was bad for business. It could endanger his personal wealth, and anything that might effect his personal income or holdings was bad. There was no thought to public good or the needs of a world outside of his family. If he could have predictably gotten richer during a major conflict, his opposition would have drastically diminished.

Kennedy wanted to separate the United States from what was taking place in Europe. Toward this end he gave his first speech on March 18, a speech that was meant to present the American foreign policy toward Europe. He explained that Americans were placing their self-interest before the interest of other nations. They had not been attacked, did not expect to be attacked, and had no plans to attack anyone else. Should there be war, the United States had no intention of getting involved.

Kennedy was in a position to talk with representatives of the Third Reich, including Herbert von Dirksen, who gained the ambassador's sympathy. Von Dirksen helped Kennedy understand how effective Hitler had been in restoring Germany's shattered economy. As for the problems with the Jews, a reading of von Dirksen's personal papers and dispatches indicate that he believed Kennedy was in sympathy with the German leadership's desire to rid the nation of the "problem." He noted that Kennedy had mentioned accepting the exclusion of Jews from Boston golf and social clubs all his adult life. Denying Jews full access to society was not a major concern, though both men apparently wished the Jews would be quieter about what was happening to them.

Kennedy, working with Chamberlain and von Dirksen, wanted to give Germany a free hand to do whatever the leaders felt necessary in Poland, Central Europe, and the Balkans. All their economies would be strengthened in that manner. The fact that treaties were violated meant little. In Kennedy's view of history at the time, there would always be periods when a government or an approach to social order had outlived its usefulness. Change was a normal process, and there was no reason to risk the problems that would come from fighting the inevitable.

Kennedy was in England only a short time before he sailed back to America to watch his oldest son graduate from Harvard and to meet with Roosevelt. He arrived in New York on June 20, holding a brief press conference where he assured reporters he did not plan to run for president in 1940. Prior to that, no one seriously thought he would. His declaration of noncandidacy made him a possible candidate for the first time.

Roosevelt was irate with Kennedy, though not yet enough to fire him. Roosevelt's contacts in England made clear that Joe was speaking for himself, not the White House. He was reinforcing the interests of the isolationists in the United States, a group Roosevelt neither supported nor was ready to deny.

No decision was reached as to what to do with the ambassador. For the moment, Roosevelt decided to have him return, following a dressing down, because it was too soon to replace him without serious international repercussions. He also related to Secretary of the Interior Harold Ickes, a long-time friend who kept a detailed diary of his years with the administration, his belief that Kennedy would not last more than a couple of years. Roosevelt believed that Kennedy followed a definite pattern in the jobs he took on. He would throw himself into the work until a crisis arose, then bail out. Certainly that had been his pattern in Hollywood, and there was no reason to think the international arena would be different.

Despite the problems, Kennedy's candidacy for president was being hyped by friends in key positions. For example, Doris Fleeson and John O'Donnell, both friends and both working for the *New York Daily News,* then the largest circulation newspaper in America, wrote that Kennedy's being made ambassador was because he was "the Crown Prince of the Roosevelt regime—FDR's personal selection as his successor." The *Boston Post,* a supporter of a native son, said that "this country will either select a next President of the Kennedy type—or it will wish it had." Arthur Krock added his support, of course, though rumor had it that Kennedy was trying to use financial pressure on the *New York Times* to assure that Krock would be named managing editor. *Liberty* magazine did a serious analysis of the possible candidates in 1940 and found that Kennedy, though a long shot, seemed the likely winner. He had the personality, drive, and ability for the job.

Joe returned to England with little trust of or from Roosevelt and the career personnel in the State Department. The entourage Kennedy had taken with him when he first arrived included the only men and women he trusted. He felt that the State Department was incompetent and unprofessional, and that it kept his information from Roosevelt. He was certain that the personnel did not know what was really taking place in Europe, though the truth was they were more realistic about Hitler than Kennedy.

The trip back to England on the *Normandie* included sexual dalliances by Young Joe and Jack. Their father had stressed that it was important for men to have sex as often as possible, with as many different women as possible, and they eagerly obeyed their elder. According to Arthur Krock's memoirs, he was also on that trip, and he described one of the incidents he witnessed:

> The ship's company was gay, and there was a beautiful actress aboard to whom young Joe was very attentive. This annoyed his father, because he thought that the boy might perhaps be a little too impulsive and the girl be making a play for a youth of his prominence and wealth. Jack was also staying up late at night, with a girl I think his father didn't know about. So he imposed a curfew on the young men; they would have to be in their quarters in his suite by midnight or thereabouts.
>
> They made the first deadline. But the suite had a service door, distant from the bedrooms. So when thereafter I saw them as my fellow-conspirators, enjoying themselves in the ship's salons in the small hours of the night, I assumed they must have used this facility to elude the curfew.

The time in England would set the stage for many of the events in the lives of not only the Kennedys as they were, but the as-yet-to-be-born next generation. There were machinations of sex and power, with political intrigues on both sides of the Atlantic.

Joe Kennedy and Franklin Roosevelt were in a complex game of mutual manipulation, each without the other's full awareness. The American Embassy had secret listening devices planted by the British in areas where the ambassador conducted his work. Whenever Kennedy was involved with policy decisions that went counter to what Winston Churchill and other British leaders sympathetic to Roosevelt knew were the president's wishes, transcripts of the recordings were dispatched to Washington.

Roosevelt knew that he needed to keep a firm grip on the man who was supposed to be representing the White House. At the same time, he was hoping he could keep Kennedy's public support long enough to use him if a forthcoming political crisis evolved at the time of the 1940 election.

Other than Kennedy, the most likely challenge to Roosevelt's third term was going to come from then Vice President John Nance Garner. (Garner certainly wouldn't have challenged Roosevelt if the president's popularity remained high.) James Farley, who had been one of the advance men for Roosevelt's campaigns, agreed to be vice president if Garner ran. The shift did not reflect dissatisfaction with Roosevelt on Farley's part so much as the recognition that taking the vice president's position was the only way he personally would ever have national power.

If Garner ran, one of his reasons for using Farley was that he was an Irish Catholic. If Garner ran, Roosevelt planned to strengthen his own Irish Catholic support by asking Kennedy to be his vice president. Of course, Roosevelt's popularity did not slip, so the Irish Catholic issue did not have to be considered.

Kennedy never knew of Roosevelt's plans, and even if he had, he was foolish enough to trust his instincts in an area he knew nothing about—the American electorate. He was convinced that Americans were as strongly committed to isolationism as he was. What he did not understand was the depth of awareness concerning Hitler and the Nazi party. Many Americans were first or second generation Eastern Europeans. There were Jews who had fled the horrors of the Nazis and others whose families, still in Austria, Poland, Czechoslovakia, Germany, and elsewhere, were either alerting them to what was taking place or suddenly disappearing. Americans were increasingly willing to go to war for the sake of humanity regardless of the economic penalties. Joe Kennedy had never placed the lives of strangers ahead of acquiring wealth, so he could neither understand the change in sentiment nor the reasoning behind it.

Whatever plans Roosevelt had for Kennedy were ended after September 12, 1938. Roosevelt did not see Hitler limiting his territorial aspirations. He recognized that eventually the Americas would either be isolated from the world, perhaps waiting for the day when transportation advanced to a level where an aggressor felt comfortable crossing the oceans, or the last target of a war that would already have destroyed Europe. Neither scenario was comfortable. It was better to stop Hitler before he completed his conquests.

Roosevelt had to find a path among all sides. He wanted Chamberlain to know that the United States would support whatever decision he made concerning what to do about a move into Czechoslovakia. However, the prime minister was also to understand that the United States was not comfortable with any compromise that might be reached with Berlin. The implication was that Washington was not about to tell London to use its military to stop German expansion into Czechoslovakia. But if London felt the need to use force, Washington would back the British to whatever degree was necessary. It was a backdoor agreement to go to war that probably would not find serious opposition from among the vast majority of politicians. Roosevelt could be involved with stopping Hitler before matters got out of hand without taking a stand in such a way as to cost him reelection. The maneuver was brilliant, but it needed to be executed by Ambassador Kennedy.

Kennedy ignored the president's strategic chess game. He constantly stressed that there was nothing to be gained by war. The Czech people were not worth the spilling of American and British blood. The United States, Kennedy said, would maintain neutrality.

Prime Minister Chamberlain met with Adolf Hitler on September 15 in the Berchtesgarden. Acting based on his principals and the belief that he had the tacit support of the United States, among others, Chamberlain agreed that it was time for Germany to have the right to self-determination. The Sudetenland issue would be resolved peacefully, and Hitler would not invade the area as matters were negotiated.

Roosevelt, irate, summoned British Ambassador Sir Ronald Lindsay to the White House. The president explained that he was in a bad position. If he formally called for resistance, the Czech people would rise up in arms against an overwhelmingly superior German force known for its unrelenting brutality. He also could not stand by and let the British think that he wanted a sellout of the Czech people. He explained that American troops would be dispatched the moment Britain was invaded. However, if Britain was willing to push the issue with Germany, there was probably a way that troops could be dispatched to Europe without a declaration of war and without the White House obviously violating the Neutrality Act.

The final round of negotiations between Chamberlain and Hitler ended on September 30. The Czech president wanted Roosevelt to demand that Britain and France support his country by force if necessary, something Roosevelt refused to do. Roosevelt also refused to let Chamberlain make a radio broadcast to the American people, since that broadcast would stress support for appeasement. It was obvious that Chamberlain's course was being determined by his own intransigence and the support of Kennedy's statements.

As Kennedy would later explain to the guests of the annual Trafalgar Day dinner of the British Navy League, "It has long been a theory of mine that it is unproductive for both the democratic and dictator countries to widen the division now existing between them by emphasizing their differences, which are now self-apparent." He explained that there were very basic differences in the two types of power structures. "But there is simply no sense, common or otherwise, in letting these differences grow into unrelenting antagonisms. After all, we have to live together in the same world whether we like it or not."

It was the speech of a man who felt the reasoning of business should always take precedence over all other issues. The domination of one country over another, the changing of boundaries against the wishes of the governed, and the other problems known to be taking place with Hitler were not a concern. He feared for his sons in a war. But more than that, he feared for the state of his wealth.

Kennedy's speech seemed to others to be the new American foreign policy, wrecking Roosevelt's careful efforts to walk the fine line between appeasement and war. Kennedy favored the fascists, many alleged, and they wondered if what Kennedy had said was Roosevelt's true feelings. The press savaged Kennedy, making him aware of how much public opinion had changed in recent months. Writer Heywood Broun, a former classmate of Kennedy's, suggested that Kennedy be dropped in Boston Harbor to mingle with British tea. Arthur Krock tried to shield his friend from criticism, but even he realized the serious error Kennedy had made.

In the end, the Munich pact gave Germany the Sudetenland, providing it with the natural resources it needed to fully prepare for war. Kennedy, refusing to admit a mistake, later argued that the sacrifice of the Czechoslovakians gave France and Britain an extra year during which to build their militaries. But the extra year allowed Hitler's totalitarian regime to put all its efforts into building up its forces, which assured German domination in the early years of the war.

The pressures against Kennedy were now mounting. As Roosevelt had predicted, once public opinion turned against him, Joe's tendency was to get out. This time he used Arthur Krock to contact Princeton University to see if the school would give him an honorary degree in June 1939. If they were willing to do so, he would announce his retirement from the ambassadorship, return for his solicited honor, buy a partnership with a respected investment house, and return to making money. He was spending $250,000 a year of personal funds in England to cover the cost of entertaining, as well as the excesses of his wife and other family members. Since the world was not responding to his ideas the way he had hoped, and since the option of running for the presidency was slipping from his grasp as his press relations deteriorated, it seemed time to leave.

There was no honorary degree and no resignation. The world Joe Kennedy so foolishly sought completely fell apart around him on September 1, 1939, when Germany invaded Poland and Britain and France declared war. Kennedy was convinced that

Britain could not win, that the world as it had once existed was lost to everyone forever.

Diary notes and internal dispatches by the British leaders indicate that they not only were hostile to Kennedy, they felt his talk of trying to bring about peace with Hitler after Poland was meant to protect his wealth. His world view was so narrow to them that there was interest in forcing his recall.

As part of being on war footing, the British government arranged to tap the telephones used by key foreigners, including those of Kennedy and his staff. Once again greed had gotten the better of Kennedy's judgment. He was allegedly making investments based on his inside information concerning what was happening in world affairs. By knowing when announcements would be made that would affect the way investors looked at stock, he could position himself for a quick killing.

Investigations over the years failed to turn up records of transactions Kennedy made. However, a number of career diplomats from various countries who worked with Kennedy in England, such as Sweden's Ambassador Baron Erik Palmstierna, all made the same allegations. The allegations are presumed to be accurate, and because the British often passed on to the White House transcriptions of recordings they made of Kennedy, it is assumed Roosevelt was aware of the problem. Certainly the desire to make money using whatever information was at his disposal was routine for Kennedy. Unlike his image concerns when he headed the SEC, Joe's being ambassador was presumably not a reason for him to change his ways.

Jan Masaryk, the Czech leader in exile in London made a similar accusation. He claimed that Joe's investments in Czech securities were sold in such a way that Kennedy made almost $100,000 profit on his country's crisis. The ambassador always understood that there could be money made in the misfortune of others, just as he had done with his early real estate business that foreclosed on the poor.

Roosevelt recognized that his world view was diametrically opposed to Kennedy's. He began making direct contacts with men such as Winston Churchill and various close assistants of Chamberlain. There were times when Kennedy learned of Roosevelt's work only when messages had to be sent back to Washington via the embassy. The British naturally realized that the president had no faith in his ambassador, and Kennedy's influence quickly deteriorated. He returned to the United States at the end of 1939, staying for almost three months, much to the relief of the British.

Kennedy met with Roosevelt after greeting the reporters in a friendly manner and kissing Rose, who raced through the crowd to embrace him as he stepped from the plane. He acted as though all was well, that Britain was comfortable with America staying out of the war. He then endorsed Roosevelt for a third term, apparently a way of easing whatever wrath he expected to encounter when he reached the White House. However, on February 12, the *Boston Post* was headlining the story that Kennedy might run for president. Eventually all three Boston papers editorialized in his favor, and Roosevelt had no illusions that Kennedy was doing anything except trying to imply that he had a grassroots mandate to run.

Kennedy's return to England was not a happy one for the British. He sailed on February 23, 1940, hating the trip and feeling that there was no reason for him to go. The State Department personnel and the British government felt the same way. Increasingly Roosevelt was having to be his own representative with key heads of state, but as much as Kennedy was hated in England, Roosevelt was even more concerned with keeping him out of the country until after elections.

What drove Kennedy to ignore all criticism of him was his firm belief, frequently contradicted by facts, that any hostility toward him came because he was Irish Catholic. He retained the same siege mentality with which he had grown up. He had the wealth to create his own private world, whether that was through the manipulation of his family, the wherewithal to have housing that would give him as much privacy as a feudal king in a castle, or a wife so compliant because of her religiosity that he could chase other women with impunity. He did not let himself feel anything but anger toward outsiders, so he could use the fact of their attacks to justify his original attitude. And when they ignored him, he could call them bigoted.

Earlier there had been an incident that showed how oblivious Joe Kennedy had become to the world of the diplomat. It occurred in March 1939, and foreshadowed the callousness that added to the British displeasure with his return. Pope Pius XI had died, and on March 12, Eugenio Cardinal Pacelli had his coronation as Pope Pius XII. Since Kennedy was Catholic, an ambassador, and had had Cardinal Pacelli to his home two years earlier, he was sent to represent the United States in Rome.

Joe and Rose had a delightful time. They felt themselves seeing a friend who so wanted them there that they and five of their children had the best seats at the ceremony. Rose got to see the cardinal who had married her, and the entire event seemed to have been staged in their honor.

However, the church hierarchy saw things differently. Pope Paul VI (Cardinal Giovanni Battista Montini at the time of the coronation), was later interviewed about the incident as part of the oral history collection at the John F. Kennedy Library. Pope Paul VI stated:

It happened that the Ambassador of the United States to London, Mr. Kennedy, father of the dead President, was charged by his Government to represent the United States at the ceremony; and indeed he arrived punctually but bringing with him five children, who proceeded to occupy places that were reserved for the members of the official Missions, with the result that the arrangement of places was altered; and when there arrived the Italian Minister of Foreign Affairs, Count Ciano, the son-in-law of Mussolini, he found his seat in the Gallery of the official Missions was occupied and he began to protest, threatening to leave the Basilica and to desert the ceremony. The situation was immediately resolved; but there remained in our memory the procession of the children of Ambassador Kennedy.

Cardinal O'Connell, who had come from Boston, was upset with what was taking place, though he had no influence. The one humorous part of the entire trip was a comment by Rose concerning the seven-year-old Teddy who was given his first rosary by the pope. "I thought that with such a start he would become a priest or maybe a bishop," she was later quoted as saying, "but then one night he met a beautiful blonde and that was the end of that."

Eventually Kennedy's unwillingness to go outside the family would produce a legacy of tragic dimensions, preventing even the third generation from reaching their full potential without loss. But for the moment, the wall of anger, ego, and money protected Joe from reality. His girlfriends enabled him to use sex as an alternative to love. His millions enabled him to rent palatial residences for himself and Eddie Moore, letting him live the life of a rich playboy while his wife and nine children were somewhere else. His fawning apologists in the media, most notably Arthur Krock, enabled him to ignore the much more objective editorial information that revealed his failings. And his friendship with the weak, foolish Chamberlain let him consider himself a statesman instead of the man who may have been a key player in the loss of thousands of lives when Czechoslovakia was willingly abandoned to the Nazis.

It was Winston Churchill who would hasten Kennedy's decline in power. He was given command of the Admiralty by Chamberlain that September, and he was made a member of the War Cabinet. When Hitler sent his troops on a surprise, though long-anticipated Western offensive on May 10, 1940, Chamberlain was forced to step down in favor of Churchill.

On May 14, when the neutral Holland had its forces surrender to the Nazis, and Kennedy contacted Roosevelt with a telegram, he stated his usual pessimism:

> I just left Churchill at one o'clock. He is sending you a message tomorrow morning saying he considers with the [likely] entrance of Italy, the chances of the Allies winning is slight. He said the German push is showing great

power although the French are holding tonight, they are definitely worried. They are asking for more British troops at once, but Churchill is unwilling to send more from England at this time because he is convinced within a month England will be vigorously attacked. The reason for his message to you is that he needs help badly. I asked him what the United States could do to help that would not leave the United States holding the bag for a war in which the Allies expected to be beaten. It seems to me that if we had to fight to protect our lives we would do better fighting in our own backyard. I said you know our strength. What could we do if we wanted to help you all we can. You do not need money or credit now. The bulk of our Navy is in the Pacific and we have not enough airplanes for our own use and our Army is not up to requirements. So if this is going to be a quick war all over in a few months what would we do. He said it was his intention to ask for the loan of 30 or 40 of our old destroyers and also whatever airplanes we could spare right now.

He said regardless of what Germany does to England and France, England will never give up as long as he remains a power in public life even if England is burnt to the ground. Why, said he, the Government will move to Canada and take the fleet and fight on. I think this is something I should follow up. . . .

Certain that either Kennedy was wrong about what he had been saying, or that because of his personal bias his statements should not be trusted without a second opinion, Roosevelt planned a secret mission to England by his longtime friend, Colonel William J. Donovan.

Instead of echoing Kennedy's pessimism, Donovan noted that England had done everything possible to assure that Hitler could not be readily victorious. The men at arms were well trained and determined to fight. Bases and radar stations had been so dispersed throughout the nation that Hitler could not stage a massive strike that would make a major difference in the country's ability to resist. There was a good chance that Britain had the defense capabilities to keep the German air force from devastating the country, as well as being able to stage retaliatory strikes of its own. The only way an invasion of England was possible was through such a massive loss of men and equipment that Hitler would probably lose more than he gained.

The only thing Donovan did not do while in London was meet with Ambassador Kennedy. Naturally the ambassador was both angry and hurt when he discovered what had happened. He was even more irate when Roosevelt had a member of the U.S. Army General Staff make a trip as a follow-up to Donovan, again without consulting Kennedy.

Feeling more and more isolated—his family was back in Hyannis, his government was ignoring him—Kennedy finally demanded to be recalled in October 1940. The State Department finally agreed, and he arrived home on October 27. He had thoughts of endorsing Wendell Willkie for president, but after a meeting with Roosevelt, at which the charming president managed to deflect Kennedy's anger toward him, Joe made a radio speech endorsing the president, and saying that Roosevelt was the best man to keep the country out of war.

There was another reason for Kennedy to bow to Roosevelt's will—the future of the second generation of Kennedys. That year, Young Joe, 24 years old and interested in politics, had become a Massachusetts delegate to the Democratic National Convention. Young Joe's idol seemed to be his grandfather, John Fitzgerald, with whom he regularly had dinner after he was enrolled in Harvard Law School. Honey Fitz was living in the Bellevue Hotel in Boston, directly across from the state house, and it was he who suggested that Young Joe try for the convention.

The Massachusetts delegation was pledged to Roosevelt's opponent, Postmaster General James Farley, and they voted that way even though Roosevelt wanted his nomination to be unanimous. But to maintain Young Joe's viability in the

Democratic Party, Joe Sr. couldn't rebel against Roosevelt. Thus, even as the national political influence of Joe Sr. was coming to an end, the groundwork was being laid for the children to go even further than their father had.

4

THE SINS OF THE PARENTS VISITED UPON THE CHILDREN

They were always in competition with one another and the world, the best of friends, the greatest of enemies. They were molded into a life that bordered on the incestuous, then forced to fight amongst themselves for the attention of their perpetually absent father and their emotionally distant mother.

Their father claimed that they never competed with one another in their drive to win anything at any cost, no matter how trivial. He proved his point by showing how they were each enrolled in competitions appropriate for their ages. What went unsaid was that to not win in one's category was to gain their parents' wrath and their siblings' ridicule. "Daddy was always very competitive," Eunice Kennedy Shriver later commented. "The thing he always kept telling us was that coming in second was just no good. The important thing was to win—don't come in second or third—that doesn't count—but win, win, win."

Childhood was not a happy time for the Kennedy children. The money bought big houses and occasionally the chance to travel. But though the family could readily afford it, the children were given little opportunity to have their own identities. Bedrooms were used at random: a child might sleep one place one night, a different room a night later. There was no chance to hang photographs, display toys, or otherwise show personal expression. Only Joe and Rose's sleeping arrangements, as well as the location of the regularly filled nursery, were consistent.

What mattered was pleasing Daddy, being a winner, establishing dominance. When their father was home, the children had a demanding schedule to which they were expected to adhere without question. In addition to their physical rigors, they were to arrive at the dining table exactly five minutes before mealtime, or face their parents' wrath. There was no small talk, no laughter while eating. Each child had to make intelligent comments when asked about the events of the day, either in their own lives or in the world at large. Sometimes Joe would lecture them, often using a map or some other prop. Other times the meals would be more casual, but the tone would be set by the father. The children were not allowed to be young and carefree. They had to fit a role that their father would define when he was home and that Rose would perpetuate when he was away.

Rose was feared by the children, not loved or respected. Her temper was vicious, and the children later talked in front of me about the times their mother struck them with wooden coat hangers. Although Rose downplayed this punishment, implying that it was within normal discipline, that perception was challenged by incidents that occurred many years later.

One such incident happened when I was working for Rose, then in her eighties. Rose felt it was sensible at her age to begin distributing to her children the family acquisitions. One day, Rose said Eunice would be dropping by to go over the silver pieces in the attic. Rose was concentrating on getting things "in order," as though she were the captain of a ship that was sinking, and she was disposing of any items of value or disbursing them to the family members.

We went up the stairs to the attic and I opened my inventory book. The room where we were standing was one of the smaller rooms of the attic, with low exposed beams and one small window, which was our only source of light.

The door slammed on the first floor, and the shout of "Motha" from Eunice, and then her banging noisily up the stairs let us know she had arrived.

She came running into the room where we were standing, of course with no hello or salutation, just an obligatory brief grin. She was dressed in faded shorts of nondescript color and a dingy white T-shirt, her usual attire. Her hair, which had been permed but was presently uncombed, was pulled back on the side with a comb, and she was barefoot. Of course, she wore no makeup, not even lipstick, to soften that leathery, weathered skin. Her jewelry was a large sapphire ring surrounded with diamonds and a wedding ring, on the left hand.

She was out of breath and obviously wanted to get on with the job, but Rose was intent on unwrapping the two pieces of silver in question, and she was taking her time doing so.

Rose had told Eunice she wanted her to have an English silver sauce boat and two other pieces of silver, but since the sauce boat had been bought by Joe in England during World War II and was part of a collection, she wanted Eunice to pay $4,000 for it. Eunice, of course, balked at this and wanted to make sure of the authenticity before she committed herself to that amount.

There was another sauce boat of similar description, but a different pattern. The three of us, heads bent over the list, were intent on determining which piece fit the description of the expensive one, when Eunice started to disagree with her mother. Rose then stood upright and, eyes blazing, said "Eunice, be still!"

As Rose calmly went back to the list, Eunice immediately closed her mouth, turned, and walked over to the corner of that small room, and stood with her arms folded in front of her. It was as though Eunice had returned to early childhood, the punishment so ingrained from so many repetitions that now, when she was of an age to be a grandmother herself, it was automatic. This fear of her mother remained intense until long after Rose was helplessly debilitated by a stroke.*

By their father's example, the children were also raised to hold Rose in contempt. The boys learned that womanizing was all right—not only did Joe Sr. occasionally bring one of his girlfriends home, but he also made passes at the friends of his daughters. The girls came to look upon their mother as a fool, a martyr to a way of life they would not tolerate. However, they would be torn between the teachings of the Church and the belief that philandering, at least for males other than their husbands, was acceptable. And all the sisters married philanderers. And all the sisters at least tacitly encouraged Jack's bragging about the women he had had (including at least two different women a day while in the White House). Pat, while married to actor Peter Lawford, even allowed her home to be used as one of her brother's Hollywood trysting places.

All the Kennedy children were expected to develop unique lives of their own—provided they became exactly what their parents demanded of them. In theory, Joe was responsible for the education of the sons and Rose for the daughters, but that related mostly to which school each child attended. Neither parent was interested in nurturing any unique character traits among their sons and daughters. They only took pleasure when their children, acting on their directions, were "winners," and it did not matter at what.

For example, during summers in Hyannis, the children reported to the beach by 7:00 A.M. to meet with their physical

---

*There was revenge of a sort later, according to one Kennedy employee, although the story could not be confirmed. After Rose's first stroke, Eunice insisted that Rose be sat at the dinner table with the rest of the family. Rose would be propped in her chair like a slightly stiff rag doll, five minutes before the meal was served, the exact timing Rose had once demanded of her children. Her nurse stood at her side to keep her from falling out of her chair. Then, every few minutes during the meal, Eunice would tell the nurse, "Mother's hungry. Feed her." The nurse would spoon whatever soft food Rose could handle into her mouth. Sometimes it went down her throat, sometimes down her chin, but Eunice was determined that home life should be "normal."

fitness instructor. There were calisthenics before breakfast, then sailing, tennis, and swimming during the day. Joe kept abreast of all public competitions for children in the area, entering his kids in the appropriate age brackets. In theory they were not competing with one another, but each knew that if he or she didn't win, Joe would be angry. Winning meant attention from father; losing made you an outcast. If one child came in first and another didn't, the successful child would taunt the other just as unmercifully as if they had competed with each other.

The Kennedys liked titles. They established identity, brought respect, and made the bearer seem better than others, or so Joe and Rose believed. From the moment of his appointment as ambassador to England until long after his death, the family always called Joe Sr. "the Ambassador." Rose was known to the staff as "Madame." Jack ultimately became "the President"; Robert first "the Attorney General" and then "the Senator," the same title Teddy would later enjoy. The daughters never received titles, as they were secondary Kennedys who would provide support for the achievements of the males. And Joe Jr., the best and the brightest, was "Young Joe," a title intended to be worn until he entered politics.

Young Joe (and later Jack) was sent to an elite Protestant private school, Choate. Joe Sr. chose the school not for its excellent curriculum, but because it was a school the Brahmins would respect. Jews and Catholics were admitted, though in few enough numbers that Joe could see his son having achieved what he had not.

Young Joe respected the Catholic religion, though like his mother his interest was in ritual and social trappings. When he eventually joined the Navy during World War II, he was president of his cadet class's Holy Name Society. He attended church regularly, and once allegedly did penance by dropping to his knees, then climbing the steps of St. Peter's. Cynics who knew the youth assumed that he performed the act for the sheer challenge of doing it. This was certainly true for his skiing; he always tried to go down hills rated beyond his skill level, although he usually crashed. Very often, more advanced skiers who were accompanying Joe deliberately went to easier slopes because they feared he would be injured trying to compete with them.

But no matter what he accomplished, no matter how he outshone his brother Jack academically, athletically, and with girls, Young Joe desperately needed to be best in his father's eyes. His competition with Jack had an angry edge. There are numerous stories of battles between Young Joe and Jack. Some were the unavoidable pummelings of close brothers over some often exaggerated slight. Other fights mentioned by family and friends over the years were more serious. Author John Davis, for example, reported on a bicycle race around the block, each of the boys traveling in opposite directions to see who could get back to the start first. When they arrived simultaneously, rather than veer away they deliberately raced toward each other, trying to make the other brake. Neither could yield without losing, and the crash sent Jack to the hospital for twenty-eight stitches. The boys were battered and bloodied, but both could tell their father that they had won.

The often vicious rivalry between the brothers was caused by more than just the desire to please their father by winning. Young Joe was a natural athlete who was also under strict orders to teach John about proper behavior, games, school, and other activities. In fact, each child was expected to teach the next younger. And while sometimes Young Joe would directly discipline Teddy, Jean, or one of the younger children, usually Joe would tell Jack, who would tell Rosemary, who would tell Eunice and on down the line until the message got to the offender.

Young Joe was supposed to take his brother under his wing, to make him a man. Yet the sibling rivalry was too intense. When playing football, Joe liked to slam the ball into Jack's belly as hard as he could to hurt him. There was frequent bullying and little effort by either parent to interfere.

Perhaps it was Jack's illnesses that made him seem a threat to Young Joe. While Joe Sr. did not seek extra time with his second son, his periodic medical needs occupied a good chunk of the time that Joe spent with the family. Rose also had to get involved, if only because she was the parent most often home during hospitalizations or doctors' house calls.

Jack was not a natural athlete. Although the Kennedys would create the myth of a strapping lad brought to his knees in agony by a war injury, he was actually a weak, sickly, though driven child. His back was slightly deformed at birth, and medical knowledge was not yet advanced enough for corrective surgery to be risked. He was often in severe pain. In fact, while some of his later girlfriends discussed the "kinkiness" of sex with Jack, such as his lying in a bathtub with the girl on top, the variation was actually necessary to keep his pain from preventing his pleasure.

Because of his health, Jack spent much of his time either in bed or sitting quietly. He became the reader of the family, yet he was not an intellectual. He read for entertainment, not to challenge his mind. He was supposedly a history buff, yet his ideas parroted those of his father even after time had proven Joe Sr. to be wrong. He seemed to retain little information relative to what he read, and he had limited ability to analyze. His grades were so poor that his father had to use influence to get him into Harvard. His spelling was always atrocious. Yet despite his deficiencies, he was determined to keep pace with his siblings whenever possible, which resulted in the frequent hostility of Young Joe.

When the family moved to England when Joe Sr. became ambassador, Joe, Jack, and Kathleen became closer. They were given more freedom, a chance to travel together unchaperoned, a chance to be more adult. Only then did their natural personalities make for a pleasant blend—Joe bright, aggressive, determined; Kathleen (called "Kick") intelligent, outgoing, open to new experiences; Jack shy and eager to see things, yet not anxious to participate.

It was in September 1935 that Kathleen Kennedy was taken to Europe to spend at least a year at the Sacred Heart convent in France in order to mimic her mother's education. Jack was on his way to the University of London for a semester.

Joe and Rose took their children to Europe on the ship *Ile de France,* and Jack and Kathleen thought that they could regularly visit each other. What neither expected was that Jack would develop jaundice and become so ill he would have to return home, eventually spending time in Arizona in order to regain his health. Kick, suddenly alone in Europe, not only hated the structured life of the Sacred Heart Convent, she refused to continue her studies there. She would not be broken like her mother, and her parents agreed to transfer her to a far more liberal convent school in Neuilly, just outside of Paris.

Kathleen spent as much time traveling as possible. She skied in Switzerland, heard Mussolini speak in Rome, had an audience with the pope, attended art exhibitions in Paris, and generally enjoyed herself. Then, in April, her mother came to visit her, the two of them traveling to the Soviet Union for a visit hosted by William C. Bullitt, the U.S. ambassador to the Soviet Union.

The trip to the Soviet Union was an important time for both mother and daughter. Joe had always delighted in his daughter, though never becoming close to her in the manner of Rose and Honey Fitz prior to Rose's marriage. Rose had always seemed to be a somewhat emotionally distant person to her second oldest daughter. But in Europe, it was as though mother and daughter had become like wealthy school girls running away from repressive responsibilities. Rose seemed to see herself as she had been when young and filled with hope in the personality of her oldest daughter. Later the inability to tame her daughter in the manner she felt proper would cause her both pleasure and heartache. For the moment, though, the future did not exist. The women were not "sisters" in attitude or appearance as some writers have maintained. They were in a more important relationship than that. After years of isolating herself from her children, Rose and Kathleen had become friends.

Jack entered Harvard as a freshman the same year that Young Joe was a junior. However, unlike the time at Choate, neither brother felt the need to compete. As earlier, Young Joe was well established—holding a position on the student council, excelling in athletics, getting excellent grades.

Jack tried to follow his father's athletic desires, but all he did was hurt himself. An attempt at football, despite having only 149 pounds on his six-foot frame, led to a ruptured spinal disk that would add to his life-long back trouble. And though a strong swimmer, especially in the backstroke, he lacked the endurance needed for the team, making himself sick enough trying to achieve beyond his abilities that he had to go to the infirmary. However, he found that he made friends easily, and that he was able to enjoy a variety of social activities that made him more popular, though less respected, than his older brother.

The academic activities of the younger children were but a diversion to Joe Kennedy. All his thoughts eventually focused on his appointment as ambassador to England, and it was with great pride that he took his family to London, arriving early in March 1938. He was an Irish Catholic representing the United States before a country whose history was one of Irish Catholic repression. There was irony, anger, and a sense of triumph. It would prove to be a time that would reveal to the world the dark side of Joe Kennedy, a side that could not be hidden in the manner of his involvement with organized crime or the destruction of his oldest daughter, Rosemary.

The society that existed when Rosemary Kennedy was growing up was not equipped to understand a person like her, who existed outside the norm. People understood her father, who had spent more time socializing than studying while in school, then mastered the world of business through different jobs. And they understood her mother, a woman who had a lust for learning that was partially quashed by social convention and the convent schools she was forced to attend. But a child who was different from friends and siblings, who did not learn as they did, who seemed to lack the abilities of the others, who was out of step with both family and community, was not considered acceptable. There were only two labels possible for the child. She was either a "bad seed" or she was retarded. Rosemary Kennedy was neither, though she would pay the price for her father's desires and his lack of compassion, and the lack of knowledge about learning disorders.

Kennedy family members, friends, and historians like to tell stories of the childhoods of Joe Jr., Jack, and Kathleen, the most aggressive and charismatic of the children, or of the younger family members, such as Eunice, Bobby, Teddy, Jean, and Pat. But the family's first daughter is like the tragic heroine of a Victorian novel, a daughter destined for misfortune. She might just as well be "Poor Rosemary," a sad sigh escaping the lips of anyone who mentioned her.

Some have noted that Rosemary was shy, quiet, slow, fat, obviously troubled. Yet others have described her as the prettiest of the sisters, sweet, friendly, and delighted with attention. What was done to Rosemary had a greater effect on the family and the nation than has previously been examined. The deliberate destruction of her life, followed by a coverup that remains to this day, was certainly a major factor in the way the children responded to their father. And the person who may have been most affected was Senator Ted Kennedy, just nine years old when his sister "disappeared," and later the male who would have the greatest influence on the majority of the third generation of Kennedys.

Since 1961, allegedly the year Rose learned the full truth about her daughter, there have been at least seven different versions of what happened to Rosemary provided by the family and their spokespeople. Each "official" account varied slightly from the preceding one, and all of them rang slightly hollow. That the stories should be questioned was reinforced by three subtle clues in Rose's memoirs, *Times to Remember*.

First was Rose's comment about Rosemary: "When she was old enough to learn a little reading and writing, the letters and words were extremely difficult for her, and instead of writing from left to right on a page she wrote in the opposite direction." Such mirror writing we now know is caused by dyslexia, a common learning disability.

The memoir hinted that there was a limit to Rosemary's abilities, mentioning the numerous misspellings she made when she was old enough to have a better sense of the language. However, if Rosemary's writing is compared with Jack's, the average person would conclude that spelling was not a Kennedy strong point. Personal letters in the Kennedy Library and documents in the possession of those who once worked for the family show that Jack was a poor speller throughout his adult life.

Second, there had been stories over the years of Rosemary's temper tantrums and violent outbursts. These were necessary to imply that Rosemary fit into a category of brain-damaged individuals for whom surgery was sometimes used at that time. In *Times to Remember* Rose quoted Mary O'Connell Ryan, described as one of her closest friends, who mentioned that Rosemary seemed rather shy, but that those who knew the family recognized that younger sister Kathleen was so outgoing and vibrant that it was natural for Rosemary to be uncomfortable. Mary Ryan said, "So that's the way it was, nothing to indicate that Rosemary had any special problem, because I'm sure lots of little girls could feel inhibited by an especially beautiful baby sister. And on Rose's part, nothing, nothing at all. Nothing was ever said even to very close friends. No one outside that family—except I suppose some doctors—knew or suspected that Rosemary's condition was that unusual." She then said that the first she knew that Rosemary was retarded was when Joe Kennedy mentioned the "fact" during an interview he gave in 1960.

Third, Rose mentioned that Rosemary and Eunice traveled throughout Switzerland in 1937, when Rosemary was nineteen and Eunice sixteen. There was no chaperone, although a paid escort could have been readily arranged. Given the moral standards for Irish Catholic women, to which Rose strictly adhered, it is almost impossible to believe that a retarded young woman and her younger sister would have been allowed to travel to Switzerland unaccompanied by a responsible adult. And since, in the Kennedy family, the older children took care of the younger, Eunice would not have been made responsible for Rosemary. However, nineteen-year-old Rosemary, learning disabled rather than retarded, would have been allowed to take her younger sister.

In 1977, I made an interesting discovery—Rosemary's diaries covering the years immediately before World War II. The myth of Rosemary's retardation had long been accepted by everyone except for the nuns who cared for Rosemary in a special home in Wisconsin. *Times to Remember* had been published in 1974, and Rose wanted it to serve as the official family history. The Kennedy Library was being developed to handle the bulk of the family's historical records. But while too many knew the truth about Joe's philandering and bootlegging to cover them up completely, Rosemary could remain the family secret. Rose told me to throw the diaries out.

(Rose never liked to talk about Rosemary. When Rosemary was mentioned, a look of disgust would come over Rose's face as she thought about what had happened to her oldest daughter. Once, when Rose, Jean, and I were at the pool in Palm Beach, Jean mentioned to me that she had seen the movie *One Flew over the Cuckoo's Nest,* and that she had liked it very much. Rose asked about the movie, and Jean replied, "Oh, it's not a movie for you, Mother. It's about a man who has a lobotomy." When any of the family members would talk about Rosemary, especially about matters of her care in Wisconsin, Rose would simply close her ears to the conversation.)

I didn't throw the diaries away. I first offered them to the head of the Kennedy Library for inclusion as part of the family record. The information they contained, and the facts revealed about the normal, healthy young woman who had been lobotomized in an attempt to make her fit the family mold, would add depth to the family story. And while what happened to her would cast a cloud over her father, it added a dimension of understanding to the pain borne by the other children. Thus, it made sense to me that they should be in the archives, even if sealed from the public.

The library did not want the diaries, agreeing with Rose that the papers should be discarded. Next, I asked Pat Lawford, who said, "Do whatever Mother says."

Since I had formerly been employed by the FBI, I knew that an item in the trash may be taken by anyone and owned with clear title, just as if it were a gift or a purchase. So I took the diaries home from the trash.

Among the diaries were records from the London trip Rosemary took in the spring of 1938, when her father became ambassador to England. She talked of shopping and clothes, of movies seen, and of the diet she was trying based on tips from Gloria Swanson, the most famous actress who had been Joe Kennedy's mistress.

She detailed the activities of each day, from when she arose through afternoon tea and bed. She mentioned the courses she was taking from some nuns, and her athletic activities, which appear to have been successful, contrary to the image of an uncoordinated child her mother tried to convey. Games of tennis against schoolmates, casual swims with friends (not the competition she faced with her siblings), trips to Buckingham Palace, and the like were all part of the reminiscence.

If anything, the diaries are fascinating for their ordinariness. There is no real depth, no glowing details or insights about what she saw. Yet that superficiality makes her diary similar to those kept by the rest of the family. The diaries were a discipline, not a creative tool. For example, there might be, "Have a fitting at 10:15 Elizabeth Arden's. Appointment dress fitting again. Home for lunch. Royal tournament in the afternoon." Or, while traveling on board the ship en route to London, she detailed: "Up too late for breakfast. Had it on deck. Played pingpong with Ralph's sister, also with another man. Had lunch at 1:15. Walked with Peggy. Also went to horse races with her, and bet and won a dollar and a half. Went to the English Movie at five. Had dinner at 8:45. Went to the lounge with Miss Cahill and Eunice and retired early."

Unrelated to the British trip, Rosemary described active participation in family doings. On January 19, 1937, for example, she told of meeting President Roosevelt, his son James, and various diplomats at the White House. Later she talked with Betsy Roosevelt and attended the reception for Postmaster General Farley.

All through the pages are the notes of a girl entering womanhood, engaging in all the ordinary activities of one with a father as prominent as hers. Yet Rose tried to imply in her memoirs that her daughter was carefully controlled and had to be specially rehearsed for extraordinary events, the diaries only occasionally confirm such preparation. She was rehearsed before meeting the queen, but so was Rose and the other children present. By contrast, when meeting Roosevelt and his family, no such preparation is indicated. There was no "tight leash" to keep her from embarrassing herself or others, for there was no need for one. Rosemary was not retarded.

So what did take place? Rosemary Kennedy was dyslexic, a condition that affects as many as one in ten individuals to some degree. In the extreme, reading and writing become difficult, including the tendency to write letters and words backward. It is not retardation, nor does it reflect the eventual success the person will achieve in life.

Then why were the Kennedys troubled? Apparently the problems arose not from Rosemary, who did extremely well in her education despite her disability, but from the expectations of Joe and Rose.

Rosemary was not a winner. When she engaged in athletics, she did so for enjoyment, not to be the best. She hated competition with her sisters, frequently rebelling against Eunice's attempts to push her into activities such as swimming and boating. On her later visits to the family homes, I would watch in horror as Rosemary would yell almost hysterically as her sisters forcefully encouraged her to participate in whatever athletics they thought would be good for her.

Joe wanted a quick fix for his daughter, having no patience with the special schooling and additional time she needed.

During his affair with Gloria Swanson, Swanson overheard him speaking to an East Coast hospital official from his Beverly Hills home. He was talking about Rosemary, and she described his voice as going "up and down with impatience and annoyance" as he spoke. He was trying to bribe the official with a special ambulance if a cure could be guaranteed. It was such impatience to make her well that only caused greater problems for Rosemary.

Rosemary was also enjoying men. Rose's biggest fear was that her daughter might be seduced by any man she happened to meet, for she felt she could not count on Rosemary's adhering to strict Catholic teachings as she could with her other daughters.

In addition, Rosemary's dyslexia was frustrating for her. Her parents thought they were helping her by demanding that she do what the other children were doing. They seemed to feel that with the right encouragement, she would either succeed or feel better about herself. Yet the pressures were so intense that she was increasingly angry and rebellious. She would lash out in frustration, verbally and physically. She was not dangerous to herself or others, and the tantrums were a sign of immaturity and overwhelming stress rather than declining mental health.

Rosemary might have led a normal life had she been allowed to stay in England. There she was attending a school where the staff understood learning disorders. She had thrived in that environment, but Joe did not want Rosemary remaining during the war. He brought her home, and by 1941, he was determined to correct her problems.

Exactly what happened next is uncertain. There were reports of rages where Rosemary smashed whatever was within reach. And there was a report of Rosemary kicking her grandfather, John Fitzgerald, as the man sat on the porch in Hyannis during the summer of 1941. If the incident occurred, no one discussing it knew the details. Certainly the idea of a powerful young woman beating a frail old man is a horrible one. But what preceded it, the reasons for the loss of control, and other factors remain a mystery.*

It is uncertain when Joe decided to stop his daughter once and for all, or who knew about it. Whatever the case, without discussing it with his wife and without her approval, Joe arranged for Rosemary to have a prefrontal lobotomy at St. Elizabeth's Hospital in Washington, D.C., in the fall of 1941.

We now think of a lobotomy as a cruel form of destruction. However, more than half a century ago, it was considered by many doctors to be a state-of-the-art technique for controlling behavior. It was frequently used to help self-abusive psychiatric patients who otherwise would have to be physically restrained, and it was even found to improve the condition of some catatonic patients. However, there had been enough failures with the procedure that Boston-area hospitals had strict standards for which patients could undergo the treatment.

The more liberal attitude in Washington, D.C., was because the St. Elizabeth staff included Dr. Walter Freeman who, along with Dr. James Watts, were among the first physicians to try the technique. Freeman thought the procedure could be done

---

*Speculating further about what happened between Rosemary and her grandfather would be fruitless. But with a family as complex and insular as the Kennedys, each incident can be better understood when placed in the context of other things that occurred.

Joe Kennedy was desperate not to be Irish Catholic, and his father-in-law was a constant reminder of the old-style Irish machine politician. In 1946, Fitzgerald supposedly stopped by grandson Jack's campaign headquarters during Jack's first congressional race to see if he could help out. Joe Kane, the campaign manager (and Joe Sr.'s cousin), turned to the old politician and, with Jack's awareness and seeming approval, shouted, "Get that son of a bitch out of here!" For Fitzgerald, such a rejection was more vicious than anything Rosemary might have done to him in 1941. But Jack was the heir apparent after Young Joe's death in the war. Rosemary was just a woman, and not an emotionally strong one. Both instances were acts of violence, yet one was used to justify destroying Rosemary, and the other was business as usual in a politician's life.

in a manner that would prevent obvious scarring or disfigurement of the patient. Determined to find a method that would not be so disfiguring, he studied the anatomy of the skull and found that entry could be made through the upper portion of the eye socket. This was far enough away from the eye so there was no risk of blindness, and because the brain cannot experience pain, recovery was both rapid and without discomfort. The only problem was that his efforts were not exact. He used a gold-plated ice pick, and there was a dangerously wide variation in where he struck. Although he performed more than 4,000 procedures with his ice pick, the results were not always predictable.

What did Joe Kennedy expect would be the result of the procedure? No one knows. Based on the literature of the time, he most likely expected a passive child, a daughter who would be more like an obedient staff person than a vibrant, aggressive Kennedy. She would not be much help in fulfilling the plans he had for his sons, as the other girls would be, but neither would she cause him embarrassment. When Rose was out of town, Joe had Rosemary admitted into St. Elizabeth's for the procedure.

The procedure was a disaster. Rosemary went from an attractive young woman to a perpetual five-year-old child in a woman's body. Kennedy had orchestrated the destruction of his oldest daughter's mind.

The coverup was swift and brutal. Allegedly on the recommendation of Archbishop Richard Cushing, Rosemary was sent to St. Coletta's School in Jefferson, Wisconsin. She was not allowed to return home. It was as though Rosemary had to be thrown away after failing to come through the operation in the manner her father desired.

The other children were not allowed to ask what happened to their sister, though Kathleen, Joe's favorite daughter, apparently knew. Rose claimed that she did not learn the truth until 1961, but she did not try to see her now-retarded daughter for many years. Eunice was put in charge of overseeing Rosemary's care. Yet if Rosemary's interactions with Eunice during her occasional visits to the Kennedy home after Joe died were any indication, she viewed Eunice with fear.

Joe refused to ever see Rosemary again, and made sure that only lies were printed about her. For example, in 1958, when Jack had been unofficially running for the presidency for more than a year, Joseph Dinneen interviewed father and son for a book titled *The Kennedy Family.* Dinneen made every effort to be objective, but he had to use the information provided. He wrote:

> In large Catholic families, it is a commonplace that at least one child shall have a "vocation," a divine call to the priesthood, the Christian Brothers or a woman's religious order. All of the Kennedy children loved rough and tumble sports except Rosemary. She cringed and shuddered at violence of any kind; she was a spectator, but never a participant. Unlike her siblings, she shunned the limelight and was shy and retiring. It was inevitable, perhaps, that she should study at the Merrymount [sic] Convent in Tarrytown, New York, and devote her life to the sick and afflicted and particularly to backward and handicapped children.
> She is the least publicized of all the Kennedys. She prefers it that way and her wishes are respected. . . .

What has gone unpublished to this day is the way the surgery affected the other children. In a family where neither parent ever felt the need to provide more than shelter for their children—where the children had no room they could call their own, to put up mementos, pictures, or accumulated treasures; where the children were moved about from home to home and school to school—the removal of Rosemary would have rocked whatever security the children could have found. Teddy especially was moved about the world so often, he later mentioned in front of me, that it was no surprise he was having so much trouble as an adult. He had gone to fifteen different schools by the time he graduated high school.

The disappearance of Rosemary when he was only nine, when combined with the pressures his parents placed on him, was probably a major factor in forcing Teddy to sublimate all personal desires. Desperate for stability, for parental approval, and for love he probably seldom felt he experienced, he witnessed his oldest sister, a sweet, gentle girl as he remembered her, seemingly rebel against their father. She did not behave the way Joe wanted a Kennedy to behave, and one day she went away, never to come back. He was not allowed to ask what happened to her. He was not allowed to question where she was or what might be happening.

The message was clear: Disobey Joe and Rose and you will cease to exist. From that time forward, Teddy placed his own emotions on hold, never letting himself become too close to anyone, carrying anger, fear, and guilt trapped inside his troubled heart. It was the destruction of Rosemary, along with the reinforcing negative factors in his life, that ultimately led to the surviving male child becoming a drunk, a womanizer, and a periodically violent man.

When Joe Kennedy Sr. took his family to London in 1938 to take up the post of ambassador to England, he entered a world where he was wiretapped, spied on, circumvented, criticized, and ignored. However, his wife and children thrived in England. The youngest were in school, oblivious to the machinations of politics. The oldest four seemed to come into their own for the first time.

The British educational system to which Rosemary had access was far more adept in handling students with learning difficulties than were the American schools she had attended. They nurtured her in ways her parents, her siblings, and her American teachers had not.

Rosemary's school was run by Montessori teachers. Located in the countryside, she could live a life based on her needs and wants for the first time. Did she have difficulty studying in the early afternoon, becoming cranky and frustrated? The staff taught her to take a nap, then arranged her schedule so she could do so. Not only did her ability to learn improve, she began helping with the young children who attended the facility, reading to them and assisting their teachers. No one thought of her as retarded, and her skills increased greatly. She could finally work and learn at her own pace, not the pace of a Kennedy. She did not have to win at something each day, did not have to compete. She blossomed into an independent person—happy and successful. In fact, her joy at this school was so complete that her depression, anger, and violent outbursts after she came back to the United States in 1941 can probably be traced to her having been forced to leave the first home where anyone cared about her.

Kathleen also fell in love with England, and to both Joe and Rose's frustration and delight, the people who were London's equivalent of the Brahmins also fell in love with her. Kathleen, often with Joe or Jack, spent weekends at the home of the Duke of Marlborough, Lady Astor's country place, or some other home owned by the British ruling class.

It seems that no one was certain how intelligent Kathleen was, though she was probably the equal of Joe Jr. School was not important to her in the manner it had been for her mother when Rose still hoped to go to Wellesley. Kathleen did think she might go to college in England, if only to keep herself from being bored. However, in England, education for a woman seemed to be disproportionate to her station in life. Working-class girls were most likely to attend college, preparing themselves for the world of work and professions. The aristocracy thought they would never have to experience this life, and so the wealthier and more high-born a young woman, the less it was considered proper to get an education. And Rose definitely wanted Kathleen to be the equivalent of the wealthy, even if it meant reducing her opportunities in life.

Rose decided to have Kathleen make her debut in England, not the United States. Like Joe, she still held lingering anger over how Boston society had treated her. As the ambassador's daughter, Kathleen was treated in London in the manner which

Rose once coveted. Equally important for Rose was the fact that coming out in England involved protocol that helped her own image. Kathleen was invited to all the important debutante parties. Once the invitation was given, the invitee's mother had to approve. This meant that the mother of the girl who was coming out had to pay a social call on Rose. It had taken yet another full generation, but at last the Brahmins were coming on their knees to beg the Kennedys to grace their homes. Or so it undoubtedly seemed to Rose.

Kathleen held no lingering anger, no need to get back at anyone. She was sensitive, sensual, outgoing, lively, and crazy about boys, though her intense Catholic upbringing kept her out of trouble. She made friends easily, and was interested in all things British. It was as though she saw herself as having been permanently transported to a strange country where she wanted to be assimilated as thoroughly and rapidly as possible.

Kathleen and Rosemary dominated the society functions in 1938. They came out together and made the round of balls together. Both danced all evening at the affairs and spent time with the various boys. Rose later tried to impress people with how generous Kathleen was to help her older sister, but there is no indication that the boys, the other debutantes, or their parents ever suspected there was something wrong with Rosemary.

(Eunice had her coming out party in 1939. She had begun dating, but young men took little interest in her. She was considered awkward, unable to wear her clothing well, and rather shy at social events. She was not comfortable in the world in which Kathleen moved with such ease. In fact, even Rosemary handled her year of debutante parties with more grace, beauty, and happiness.)

It was July 18, 1938, when Kathleen began a course that her mother became convinced led to her death as a punishment from God. At a party given by the king and queen at Buckingham Palace, she met Billy Cavendish (William Cavendish, the Marquess of Hartington, eventual heir to the title of Duke of Devonshire, and considered a proper suitor for Princess

Elizabeth), a tall, lean youth who was as quiet as she was out-going, and with whom she talked for two hours. A week later she visited his family home.

Billy's parents delighted in Kathleen. They seemed to enjoy the novelty of the friendship between an Irish Catholic, who had been raised to dislike all Protestants, and their son, whose father was as hostile to the Catholic Church as old Joe was to the Brahmins of Boston. Any sort of intimacy between the couple would have been attacked, but Kathleen, though smitten enough to begin a scrapbook containing every article she could find related to Billy, was considered nothing more than a friend.

Kathleen had a very different reaction to the impending war than did her father. She and her British friends discussed what was happening without illusions. Hitler was on the march, they were threatened, and they had to stand together to stop him. They were all surprised about the doom and gloom the relatively isolated, probably quite safe Americans were expressing. The boys she knew understood as best as their parents could tell them what hardships were coming, and while they did not wish to fight, if that was what it took for the survival of England, they were not afraid to do their part.

Of all the Kennedys, it was probably Kathleen who best understood what would happen in the war. She, Joe Jr., and Hugh Fraser, a mutual British friend, went to Spain in July 1939, four months after the end of the Spanish Civil War. When they returned, Young Joe talked of the remarkable spirit of the Spanish people, who had undergone such terrible suffering. He was thrilled that Franco was triumphant so that the people could at last get on with their lives in a positive way. His enthusiasm for Franco, a violently oppressive dictator, fit nicely with his father's attitudes toward dictators.

Kathleen, on the other hand, was sensitive to the realities of what had taken place. The bodies were buried by the time she arrived, and the bloodstains had darkened to little more than dull mosaics on the walls of buildings, on the floors, and in the streets. But she knew that the government had been wrong, that the dictatorship of Franco was not a blessing, that peace had come through vicious suppression and was better only by contrast to the war that had gone before.

As war approached, Kathleen's debutante friends began deciding what they should do. Generally factory work and the military service seemed the most attractive because the factory uniforms were flattering to young figures and the military had the best hats. Alternatives including working for the Red Cross. As fall approached, the young men enlisted in the military and some of Kathleen's female friends looked seriously into jobs building bombers. She wanted to do her part, but was devastated to learn that her father was sending the family back to the United States in September. Only Rosemary would remain because she was doing so well at her school in the country, farther away from potential German bombing.

Back in the United States, Young Joe began his first year of law school, Jack was finishing at Harvard, and Kathleen enrolled in the finishing school Finch, a quasi-junior college catering to the wealthy but less-than-academically-inclined daughters of the rich. She had wanted to attend Sarah Lawrence, a highly respected experimental women's college, but had been rejected. The three siblings frequently made weekend trips to Manhattan, listening to the jazz and big band music at the Plaza Hotel, the Stork Club, Roseland, and the Paramount.

Young Joe did not do well at Harvard Law School. Whatever academic ability he had shown as an undergraduate did not transfer to his study of law. There was a chance he would flunk out of school, so Joe Sr. arranged for private tutoring each night. With his usual flamboyance, Joe hired Superior Court Judge John H. Burns for the job.

Young Joe was an angry youth. He wanted to be the center of attention, telling of his exploits in Spain. He would sometimes leave a room in a huff if he received less attention than he desired. Mostly Young Joe tried to be with Jack or Kathleen. However, when his more gregarious siblings asked a friend along, turning the trio into a foursome, Young Joe became either sullen or ridiculed the friend.

Kathleen dated frequently, though not seriously. The press frequently intimated that she might be engaged to Winthrop Rockefeller, but she tended to play the field. She frequently would go to parties or dances with one boy, then leave with another one, a breach of etiquette Jack occasionally lectured against. However, Kathleen knew that he was trying to have as many different girls as possible, and if his letters to friends are to be believed, enjoying them sexually as well. She used to laugh at his pompous double standard behavior, and carried on as she chose.

Prior to his return to the United States, Joe Sr. had given Jack the opportunity to travel throughout Europe on his behalf. He visited Bucharest, Prague, Moscow, and other cities, sending back letters to his father concerning the politics and economic problems he encountered. As his father was the ambassador, the State Department had to make arrangements for such visits, offering him whatever assistance he needed.

The European travels of Jack—and of Young Joe before him—were treated with derision by the Foreign Service. Their college-level insights were useless. In addition, Jack's atrocious handwriting made his letters an embarrassment. As George Kennan wrote in *Memoirs, 1925-1950:* "His son [Jack] had no official status and was, in our eyes, obviously an upstart and ignoramus."

Harvard tended to agree with Kennan's evaluation during Jack's first two years. His grades were only average, and in his sophomore year he was considered to be undisciplined and without much original thought. However, Jack's grades improved during his junior year, after Young Joe moved on to law school. In his senior year they were even better, his political science grades so strong that he could graduate with honors if he wrote a strong undergraduate thesis. Jack decided to write about the Munich pact.

The quality of the 150-page presentation was such that the Harvard readers felt he should graduate magna cum laude.

However, they also noted that the writing was poor and the analysis of the reasons that Chamberlain made the pact with Hitler was quite faulty. This despite the fact that his father paid for a personal secretary to assist Jack.

Joe Sr., convinced that his son could gain fame from the thesis, decided to have it published. Young Joe had commented to his father that "it seemed to represent a lot of work but did not prove anything." However, Joe Sr. passed off the reaction to sibling rivalry. Besides, the ideas reflected his own, and that seemed to be enough proof of its value.

As usual, Joe Sr. contacted a number of people to produce an image-building book for his son. Arthur Krock reworked the thesis so that it made more sense, the grammar was correct, and the book was in publishable form. Then he arranged for Henry Luce (publisher of *Life, Time,* and *Fortune*) to write a forward. Then Krock used his and Luce's reputations to get an agent to sell it.

The book, *Why England Slept,* came out at the end of July 1940. The thesis had been submitted for credit at Harvard on March 15, 1940, and assuming the reshaping was accomplished after that time, the project was rushed into print far faster than normal. Luce wrote, "I cannot recall a single man of my college generation who could have written such an adult book on such a vitally important subject during his senior year at college." Then Luce put Jack's picture on the cover of *Time,* adding a lengthy laudatory review. (For years afterward, the Kennedys and the Luce publications had close working relationships that were always favorable and rarely objective.)

The total number of copies of the book actually sold to the public is unknown. Joe Sr. wrote to Jack with the comment, "You would be surprised how a book that really makes the grade with high-class people stands you in good stead for years to come." And to help his second oldest boy have such high standing, Joe bought between 30,000 and 40,000 copies, storing them in Hyannis Port, placing the book on the hardcover best-seller lists in September. Through 1941, the book had sold a total of 80,000 copies.

The success of *Why England Slept* increased the tension between Jack and Young Joe. Not that Joe Sr. wanted his oldest son to be without glory in his own right. He had tried to get Young Joe to develop his experiences in Spain at the end of the Civil War into a book well before Jack wrote his senior thesis. Young Joe dutifully tried, but even with his father's influence and money, the task was impossible. Interest in Spain was eclipsed by the German actions. In addition, Young Joe didn't know anything. He had not experienced the fighting, nor had he interviewed the leaders or the people who endured. The project was quietly abandoned, and Young Joe had nothing else he could parlay into fame.

Young Joe must also have sensed favoritism toward Jack on the part of his father, though such favoritism did not exist. Young Joe was the focus of his father's life and ambitions. Whatever the father did not achieve, he expected to experience vicariously through his namesake's achievements. But Young Joe did not understand this, and the pain he felt after the release of *Why England Slept* would be magnified by subsequent events during wartime. The probable suicide of Young Joe, long hidden as a hero's death, stemmed from the blow to his self-esteem that began with the depression he felt following the carefully orchestrated and heavily underwritten "spontaneous" success of his younger brother.

In the fall of 1940, Jack Kennedy, extremely ill with ulcers and other problems, headed west to California while his father was finishing his time as ambassador. He wanted no pressure, yet he knew he would become bored if he only pursued sunbathing and chasing girls, his two primary pastimes while regaining his health. For that reason he decided to audit classes at Stanford Business School while pursuing females with the assistance of actor Robert Stack, whom he met in California.

Stack and close friend Alfredo de la Vega had convinced their mothers to help them pay for a small apartment on Whitley Terrace in Hollywood. They told their parents that they needed the space as a retreat where they could study and think. In truth, they mostly used it as a place to entertain and be entertained by girls.

The bedroom was so small that there was only room for a full-size bed, and Stack said the ceiling was too low for an adult to stand upright. The ceiling was plastered with small copies of flags from every nation. "I devised a game that required the lady of the evening to memorize the flags on the ceiling in a given time or pay the penalty. Since she was already in a horizontal position, paying the penalty was usually no problem," Stack commented in his autobiography *Straight Shooting.*

> The Flag Room became as well known locally as the Pump Room in Chicago. De la Vega brought a nice-looking fellow to the studio one day, and introduced him as "Ambassador Kennedy's son John." I am happy to say that Jack Kennedy found occasion to further his geo-political studies and gain future constituents at our little pad on Whitley Terrace. (When campaigning for the presidency and talking about his experience in international relations, he never publicly discussed the Flag Room. Yet Alfredo and I always believed ourselves responsible in some small way for Jack Kennedy's early interest in remembering which flag represented which country.)

The Kennedy myth machine made more of the respite in California than was there. Author James MacGregor Burns later told of Kennedy attending six months of business school at Stanford, though Kennedy left after half that time. And Rose had him spending a semester in which he studied "economics, finance, and business administration." There was nothing wrong with what Jack had done, but recovering from illness and acting like an adolescent youth did not make so interesting a story.

While Jack was recovering, the nation was getting ready for a war that everyone knew was coming. Young Joe entered the navy. He had joined the Naval Aviation Cadet program during his last semester at Harvard, and then became a seaman second class in the U.S. Naval Reserve in June 1941. He was stationed at Squantum Naval Air Facility near Boston.

In August, Jack also entered the Navy, though he was singularly unqualified for the military. He had a bad back and numerous other problems that should have made him 4-F. It is not known if he wanted to serve, if he entered in order to compete with Young Joe, or if his father insisted that a military career was important for future ambitions. Whatever the case, Joe called on Capt. Alan Kirk, then director of the Office of Naval Intelligence, whom he had met in England, to be certain that Jack passed his physical. When the doctors finished faking their reports on the state of Jack's health, he became an ensign in the Naval Reserve.

Once committed to the service, Jack seemed to see himself as a heroic figure, strapped in a corset, having to sleep on a board, suffering from asthma and an ulcer, yet somehow going heroically into battle. The fantasy was fine, but the reality was that he was assigned to a desk job at the Office of Naval Intelligence in Washington, D.C. Most likely, had it not been for an arrangement between his father and FBI Director J. Edgar Hoover, he would have fought the war behind that desk. Instead, he would end up with sea duty, nearly kill all the men under his command, and generally make a fool of himself while his father created the myth of heroic service. There was a woman involved, of course. There was always a woman, though this one was different, certainly more important than any relationship Jack had had before and perhaps after.

The situation began with Arthur Krock, a friend of Frank Waldrop, who was part-owner of the *Washington Times-Herald* as well as its editor in chief. Krock, although politically conservative and trying to maintain perhaps a better image than he deserved in his private life, liked pretty women. Whether he was physically involved with many of them or just handled his lust vicariously, he enjoyed helping women interested in journalism with their careers. And while he had no influence on the *Times* in this regard, his friendship with Waldrop enabled him to assist both the women he liked and the daughters of friends.

Krock obtained jobs for what he considered his protege, Inga Arvad, for Kathleen Kennedy, and in 1951, for Jacqueline Bouvier. But it was with Arvad that Jack was first concerned.

Inga Arvad was the older woman in Jack Kennedy's life. Twenty-eight to his twenty-four, she was a tall, blond, professional journalist who had been born in Copenhagen, educated in Brussels, London, and Paris, and then married to and divorced from an Egyptian diplomat before her twentieth birthday.

Arvad was an aggressive woman, filled with both a passion for life and a curiosity about the world. She won a beauty contest in France, which she apparently entered for the fun of it. Her interest was not in herself but in others, and she took a job as Berlin correspondent for a Danish newspaper, her beauty immediately catching the attention of the German High Command.

She was the perfect person to be in Germany in 1936, the year of the Munich Olympics. She had the appearance of the Nazis' Aryan ideal, and she arrived at a time when Hitler was attempting to gain the world's sympathy and support. The Nazis were denying Germans freedom of the press, but they were still friendly toward outside journalists. As a result, she was able to interview Joseph Goebbels, Hermann Goering, and even Hitler himself, who made her his personal guest at the Olympic Games.

Arvad used the friendliness of the German high command to gain information for stories, but quickly fled when the Nazis approached her about returning to Paris to work as a spy. Knowing that her effectiveness as a correspondent was in danger, she temporarily left news work, using her appearance to gain a small role in a low budget movie being filmed in Denmark. It was there that she met her second husband, Paul Fejos, a director.

Eventually there was an apparent affair with the wealthy Swedish industrialist Axel Wenner-Gren while her husband was recording an archaeological dig, and finally Inga, married but separated, reached New York where she enrolled in the graduate program of the Columbia University School of Journalism. There she met Krock, who was a consulting professor.

Inga proved to be an excellent writer at the *Times-Herald.* She was assigned a column that profiled Washington's politically and socially prominent. She and Kathleen Kennedy, who also worked for the paper, found enough similarity in temperament that they became friends. Through Kathleen, Inga met Jack Kennedy.

The importance of Inga Arvad in Jack Kennedy's life cannot be overstated. Much has been made of his sexual exploits, including the fact that he liked taking his girlfriends to the White House where he risked being caught by Jackie. There is no question that he was no more committed to monogamy than his father had been. He would later confide in his brother-in-law, Peter Lawford, the husband of his younger sister, Pat, that he liked to have a woman three different ways before he was through with her. He was callous, crude, and oblivious to the feelings of the women he knew. Except with Inga.

It is extremely difficult to find direct proof of Jack Kennedy's relationships with women in his personal materials. Peter Lawford retained some items, and many friends talk quite freely. But the family had made certain that the record was purged of almost all that might show him in a negative manner. Yet in the archives were letters Inga had written to Jack, love letters, personal stories of their time together.

Jack saved Inga's letters through the war. He saved them when he was in Congress. He saved them when he married Jackie, when he entered the White House, when he had his children. Inga obviously meant more to him than any other woman he had known, and he visited her with some frequency long after they had broken up.

The letters from Arvad are loving, sensitive, the writing of someone who cared deeply for the man. She wrote of wanting to have Kennedy's baby. There was an intimacy to her words: ''You once said—as a matter of fact last Sunday 'To you I need not pretend you know me too well.' I do, not because I have put you on a pidestal [sic]—you don't belong there, nobody does—but because I know where you are weak, and that is what I like.''

From a letter dated January 27, 1942:

Distrust is a very funny thing, isn't it? I knew when Kick got a letter from you today why you haven't written to me. There was a peculiar feeling at the realization that the person I love most in the world is afraid of me. Not of me directly but of the actions I might take some day. I know who prompted you to believe or rather disbelieve in me, but still I dislike it. However I am not going to try and make you change—it would be without result anyway—because big Joe has a stronger hand than I.

Probably the above is a thing which will put a wrinckle [sic] of bitterness to my mouth, but why worry, why actually care? That is the trouble dear, I care too much. The realization was brought to me tonight, when I came home. Since you left Washington I have been restless, wondering what I want to do next, but having a distinct dislike of going out with anybody. When I do I am bored and want to get home to my solitary abode. The same tonight. I went to a coctail-party [sic] at vonKeller, and as soon as I left, I went over to Dorchester House. It looked pretty much the same—a new Gainsborough has arrived but is still unpacked, so I didn't see it. Betty is more or less the boss, and Kik [sic] is already a little sad about the whole arrangement, I wonder how long it is going to last. Please dont [sic] say anything about it, as it actually is none of my business. I stayed around for a little while, but left pretty soon, because I wanted to be alone—Garbo-stuff.

Home alone, I sat down and started to think, however I stopped promptly as the problems are unsolvable to me. . . .

Untill [sic] then all that is good, decent, honest and loving
in me belongs to you Jack. Love from Me.

When Kennedy was ailing and living out of town, she wrote
of having to work over the weekend, saying, "My impulse is
to throw everything overboard and get away. Not because I
want you to make love to me and say charming things. Only
because I wish more than anything to be with you when you
are sick."

It is not known exactly who decided to wiretap Inga Arvad's
apartments and office telephone, but the surveillance was extensive. There were wiretaps on Inga's telephones, as well as
hidden microphones. Her mail was intercepted, carefully opened,
read, copied where appropriate, then returned. She was followed
to see with whom she had any contact, and her apartment was
periodically entered while she was at work so that everything
could be examined.

The official story is that the investigation began because of
Inga's known "connections" in Nazi Germany. A second story,
unprovable yet credible given Joe Kennedy's friendship with
FBI Director J. Edgar Hoover, was that the older Kennedy
was concerned with the seriousness of his son's relationship.
Women were to be used for sex, then discarded. Not only was
Jack heavily involved with Inga, she was totally unsuitable for
him as a spouse. She was married, not Catholic, and not someone who could help the political career Joe was planning for
him.*

---

*Most books say that Jack Kennedy had no interest in being president until
after his brother's death, when his father pressured him to enter politics. While
there is no question that Jack expected Joe to go to the White House and was
pushed to take over, letters from Inga to Jack indicate that they had talked
about his becoming president. Apparently he was planning to follow Joe into
office in much the manner of the Massachusetts Senate seat that was supposed
to be passed from Jack to Bob to Ted.

It is believed that Joe Sr. was routinely shown transcripts of the surveillance tapes. Joe mentioned some of the activities he knew about to his embarrassed son, though Jack continued the relationship. However, Inga knew the intensity could not continue, that there would be no future together. In a letter dated March 11 (presumably 1942), she wrote:

> A human breast to me has always been a little like a cage, where a bird sits behind. Some birds sing cheerfully, some mourn, others are envious and nasty. Mine always sang. It did especially for a few months this winter. In fact it sang so loudly that I refused to listen to that other little sensible creature called reason. It took me the F.B.I., the U.S. Navy, nasty gossip, envey [sic], hatred and big Joe, before the bird stopped.

Hoover eventually used the Arvad files as part of his blackmail of John Kennedy in order to retain his director's position with the FBI. He combined them with the files on other sexual dalliances, including a reported half-million dollar pay-off that went to one of his girlfriends after Jack had married Jackie. Then those files were used to force Bobby Kennedy to retain him in power after Bobby became U.S. attorney general, Hoover's official boss.

Jack never fully broke off with Inga, keeping in touch during and immediately after the war. However, from March of 1942, when his father pulled strings to get him assigned to active duty in the Pacific with a PT-boat squadron, until 1947, when Inga married retired cowboy star Tim McCoy, their relationship lost its ardor.

Inga Arvad died of cancer in 1973, having refused large sums of money to tell the story of her relationship with Kennedy. She had loved him too much to cheapen it. Instead, after working with McCoy's traveling rodeo and wagon show, she joined her husband in running a horse farm in Nogales, Arizona, along the northern border of Mexico. Together they raised two sons, apparently living happily together. Jack Kennedy, who was

murdered ten years earlier, retained her love letters the entire
time.

If Kennedy was committed to Arvad, he still had trouble
with sex. Attitudes toward women among Joe, Jack, and Ted
Kennedy, and to a lesser degree with Bob, seem to have been
molded around the idea that a woman was to be controlled,
dominated, dismissed, and forgotten. The longest-term relationships Kennedy would have in his later years—affairs with
Judith Exner and Marilyn Monroe, for example—seemed to
exist as a way of showing off. Exner reported that Kennedy
was constantly questioning her about Frank Sinatra and organized crime figure Sam Giancana, other man with whom she
was involved. It was as though his mind was on them, on being
more macho than they were.

Likewise it was impossible to tell whether Jack Kennedy
was interested in Marilyn Monroe or in showing his father that
he, too, could have the most famous actress of the time as his
toy. None of the Kennedy men would ever be close to women.
Sometimes they were distant. At other times they were abusive.
Yet to the public, the fact that Jack Kennedy would have children born in the White House, that Bobby and Ethel Kennedy
would have eleven offspring and that old Joe had nine, all
seemed to imply commitment. The public equated the size of
a family with the attitude toward that family. Having children
meant a loving home. No one wanted to think that the Kennedy
men were using their wives as sex objects, and that the pregnancies had nothing to do with love.

There have been many explanations put forward not only
for the reasons John Kennedy went from a seemingly serious
relationship to an endless series of meaningless dominations
that could not have offered much greater pleasure than mastur-
bation. The first had to do with his handicap. John Kennedy,
though seemingly a vigorous member of the generation ''born
in this century, tempered by war,'' and bringing a fresh perspective to the nation, as he would be touted in his various political
campaigns, was perhaps our most seriously ill president when
he entered office. More than Lincoln, suspected of having Mar-

fan's syndrome and, possibly, a venereal disease, more than Eisenhower whose heart attacks in office raised questions of emergency powers, more than Wilson and Franklin Roosevelt who became increasingly incapacitated in office, Kennedy was not vigorous. He was a sick man with problems with his adrenal glands, periodically crippling back pain, asthma, allergies, stomach ulcers, and other disorders. He also was addicted to amphetamines through the ministrations of Dr. Max Jacobson, who came to be known as "Dr. Feelgood" because of the so-called vitamin shots he was providing a number of major political, business, and entertainment figures. Jacobson mixed amphetamines, steroids, animal cells, and, presumably, some vitamins. He eventually lost his license because he both misled his patients and concocted combinations of chemicals that had no known therapeutic value. Thus Jack Kennedy never had the vigor created by the family myth machine.

There were published rumors that John Kennedy had a roving eye when he ran for president. A few reporters knew the truth about his womanizing, including the callous extent of it, but they chose not to reveal it. Instead, the public's image was that of a youthful, handsome, powerful married man who delighted in winking at ladies, kissing them, and touching them in a friendly manner that was neither brotherly nor sexually threatening.

The truth was that the Kennedy men had learned to hold women in disdain. They feared their mother more than respected her, and even her power was diminished when old Joe flaunted his latest mistress by bringing Gloria Swanson on board the ship the families took to England. Sex was a method of control. Women were trapped, dominated, then discarded, as though the sex act erased their individuality, their uniqueness, their personhood.

Sex so frequent as to be either meaningless or a pathological pursuit was constant proof to Jack that he was still a whole man. He would fail in wartime, have to wear a brace during the family touch football games that caused him intense pain, and be unable to drink alcohol at a time when drinking was a sign of manhood. All he had was the frequent conquest of women, and he acted like a prehistoric hunter who was able to bring back more prey than other men of his tribe.

Typical of the adolescent callousness would be a story actor Peter Lawford told about the first time he, Jack, Ted, and some of Jack's friends from Harvard gathered in the White House. All of them were womanizers, including Lawford, who was married to Kennedy's sister, Pat, at the time.

The men set aside Lincoln's bedroom as their target point for having sex with a woman, any woman, so long as she wasn't their wife. Each would try to get a woman to the White House. Each would try to get her to the Lincoln bedroom. And the first one to score would collect a pot of cash to which each contributed.

Peter Lawford was the first to have a chance at the money when he left his wife in their California home, then flew cross country to the White House. Along the way he was served by a beautiful flight attendant. She was off duty after the plane landed, so Peter, who was enjoying her company, invited her to the White House for lunch.

The woman was dazzled. They were met by a limousine, and when the White House guards saw who was inside, they immediately let Peter pass. Finally they arrived at the entrance and met the president, who told Peter that his bags would be placed in his "usual place," the Lincoln bedroom. The couple was encouraged to go there and relax until lunch.

Peter knew the woman had no intention of just jumping into bed with him, so he began making his moves slowly. Though he was not rebuffed at first, even when they kissed, the woman stopped him before he could become more amorous. She told him she liked him, that he was fun to be with, that he was good looking. However, she couldn't have sex with Peter because she was deeply in love and had to remain faithful to her lover— another woman. She wanted no hard feelings. She really did like him, and the excitement of going to the White House and having lunch with the president of the United States. . . . She just couldn't resist accepting the invitation.

After getting over his shock, Peter convinced her to act loving around him when they went to lunch. Figuring it was a small price to pay for a meal she could talk about with her girlfriend, the flight attendant agreed.

When Peter and his date went to the dining room, Kennedy took one look at them, then pulled Peter aside. "You son of a bitch," Peter later said that he commented. "I knew you'd be the one to win."

When war eventually intruded on everyone's good times, Jack became captain of a PT boat.

The PTs were not sturdy craft. Made of plywood, they were propelled by three engines and carried 3,000 gallons of gasoline. That amount of fuel made the boats inherently unstable and extremely explosive. Even a rifle bullet could readily penetrate the hull, setting off a cataclysm if enough oxygen was present.

The armaments seem impressive at first glance, but not under closer scrutiny. The torpedoes the PTs were supplied with were too often defective, bouncing off the hulls of their targets or exploding before reaching them. The PTs were supposed to attack in packs, so that the sheer volume of fire might damage larger Japanese boats. However, it was never learned if the strategy was truly effective, since the undertrained PT commanders seldom coordinated their attacks in the manner desired.

The vessels' equipment was also bad. The engines were not protected from water, and the radios had been taken from airplanes and converted in a manner for which they were not designed. When the sets worked, frequency drift was a common problem, interrupting conversations.

Jack Kennedy's body was in at least as bad shape as the typical PT just before he received his training at Northwestern University's Midshipmen's School. His back condition had flared up, making corrective surgery probable, though he was first prescribed a series of strengthening exercises to make him well enough to handle the surgery. After ninety days of stringently supervised exercising, his back was considered strong enough so that he could avoid surgery. However, avoiding surgery, normally the last resort at that time, and enjoying an improved back condition were two different things.

Again myth held that Kennedy was vigorous when he went to the PT training school. In truth, he was in such bad shape that he had no business being on the water on a small craft. The repeated shock of waves against the hull practically guaranteed new back problems, which ultimately did occur. However, Joe Sr. wanted Jack away from Inga, and so pushed Jack's training.

There was another consideration for Jack. Young Joe had graduated from flight training with his wings and his commission as an ensign in the Naval Reserve. Jack felt he had to stay even with him in the endless, pointless competition for their father's approval.

The commanders of the PTs often thought of themselves as an elite group. Most objective observers said that they were an elite group of fools. They were chosen from among those rich kids who had grown up on their families' cabin cruisers, sailboats, and other vessels similar in size to the eighty-foot PTs. The similarities in the craft enabled them to be trained more quickly than would otherwise have been possible. They had far less oceangoing and military experience than those who commanded larger vessels. They were frequently unable to work together, each trying to be a hero, as though war was just another yacht race.

Jack graduated from training school on December 2, 1942. Since it was obvious to his superiors that his back would make him unfit for sea duty, he was asked to stay and teach. However, when the training vessel was sent to Jacksonville, Florida, Jack, through Joe Sr., arranged to go to the Solomon Islands in the South Pacific, an active war zone. Jack would certainly see combat, something of which Joe had to have been aware.

Why would Joe Kennedy, who had been so opposed to the war, pull strings to send his own children into the path of enemy fire? One possibility was that Joe Sr. was still trying to prove his value to Roosevelt. As much as he disagreed with the president, as much as he had fought him, he wanted to be viewed as serving the government in time of crisis. If he couldn't keep America out of the war, he could at least show that he was a loyal American by sending his draft-age sons to face the enemy.

Whatever the reason, for the first time the Kennedy brothers experienced a role reversal. Young Joe hated what seemed to be taking place. Jack was going off to war while Young Joe was relegated to reconnaissance flights in gull-winged PBY-4 planes out of Puerto Rico. Instead of Joe leading the way, showing Jack how to be a man, Jack now seemed to be getting ahead.

The PTs probably would have seen little combat if it had not been for "the Tokyo Express." When Jack arrived in the Solomons, there was a passage through the islands the Americans had not been able to seal off, and the Japanese were using it to supply their troops in the area. Japanese destroyers and cruisers would nightly escort the vulnerable supply barges through the channel. Since they were light, maneuverable, and capable of hiding before they struck, the PTs were brought in to help stop the Express. But their record against the Japanese was abominable. Many had broken down prior to battle, and others had been outgunned and outmaneuvered.

In May 1943, the Navy decided to use the PTs during the invasion of New Georgia. Kennedy was in charge of *PT 109* during a refueling, and decided to have some fun by racing the others. He did not realize how bad the equipment was until he was almost to the dock and slammed his three engines into reverse. All three engines broke down. The resulting crash knocked everyone on deck into the water. This was a warning of things to come for the young lieutenant.

It was in July 1943 that *PT 109* joined with other PTs to try to close the Tokyo Express. The PTs, traveling in packs of fifteen to twenty, would be used to locate and attack supply barges at night, while alerting heavier vessels as to the whereabouts of the Japanese. Unfortunately, the PTs left a phosphorescent wake as they sliced through the water that was readily visible from the air. Japanese planes spotted the wakes, and then dropped flares to alert nearby ships, which would fire on the thin-hulled PTs.

On August 1, 1943, Jack Kennedy demonstrated the problem with the undertrained PT commanders. Fifteen PTs, including Kennedy's, located four Japanese destroyers carrying cargo and troops in the Blackett Strait. Suddenly the Japanese vessels turned on their searchlights and began shooting. The PTs could either move into the fray, hoping to outmaneuver the larger Japanese boats, or they could take evasive action, and then reform and attack the destroyers from different angles. Fourteen of the fifteen PTs coordinated for an attack from a different angle. The undertrained Kennedy ordered *PT 109* to take evasive action and flee. No one was hurt by his action, and no one called Kennedy a coward. Yet general consensus held that Kennedy was not ready for command. He lacked the experience to make effective decisions under fire.

PT 109 regrouped with two other PTs after the battle. The Japanese destroyers reached their destination, quickly unloaded, and started their return some time after 2:00 A.M.

For some reason, Kennedy did not have his men on full alert. Four were resting, two of them asleep. The radio man was talking with Jack at a time when radio communication was critical. All three engines, fresh ones after the dock crash, were in good shape, but Kennedy left only one in gear despite being part of an impending attack. Squadron policy called for all engines to be ready in such a case.

Suddenly the Japanese destroyer *Amagiri* appeared in the distance. The other PT crews spotted it immediately. The vessel was approaching Kennedy's starboard bow, its wake obvious, and there was plenty of time to get out of the way. When *PT 109* remained dead in the water, attempts were made to radio her, but no one was listening. There was nothing the other PTs could do but watch in horror as the boat was sliced in two by the *Amagiri*.

Later Kennedy would claim that he was alert, that he had

turned his boat for full attack at the last moment, implying that he was bravely going into battle. Experienced PT commanders said that such a maneuver was counter to proper training and assured a crash.

The fuel-laden PT erupted in flames, two men dying immediately. Later Kennedy claimed that the deaths were caused because the other PTs did not immediately begin rescue operations, but the truth was that such efforts were impossible at that moment, and the deaths were the result of his incompetence. Rescue efforts could have been made as soon as the crew abandoned ship had Kennedy fired his flare gun, but again he made a bad decision. He feared that the flare would bring the Japanese. Of course, so would the dawn.

The fire burned itself out in twenty minutes, at which time the men helped each other grab the still floating bow. Jack personally helped save crewmen Charles Harris and Patrick McMahon, for which he received honors. Two other officers acted in a similar manner and were also honored. There should have been a life raft for the men, and there had been one originally. However, Kennedy decided he needed more firepower, so he had replaced the raft with a 37mm gun. The mounting plank for that weapon became a float for the men, who used it to reach an atoll approximately three-and-a-half miles away.

It was during the four-hour movement through the water to the atoll that Kennedy truly performed heroically. McMahon had been so badly burned that he could neither swim nor hold on to the plank. Kennedy gripped McMahon's life jacket in his teeth and began swimming, towing McMahon to the island.

Once safely on the atoll, Kennedy reverted to his earlier incompetence. The crew had been spotted earlier by Lt. Arthur Evans, an Australian positioned on the nearby Kolombangara volcano. Spotting and rescue efforts were under way, friendly natives in the area alerted, and all the men had to do was to remain visible to be seen and rescued at once. Instead, Kennedy ordered the men to hide anytime they heard a plane. While he could not be aware that Evans had spotted him, standard procedure required making certain they could be seen by search crews. The risk of being attacked by the Japanese was less than the risk of not being rescued when they hid as improperly ordered.

Next Kennedy again defied logic and training by deciding to go for help in unfamiliar waters. At 8:00 P.M., a time when PTs might be in the area, he decided to swim through the area known as Ferguson Passage. He had only had a half hour's rest and would carry only a lantern and pistol with which to signal the boats. He exhausted himself, nearly drowned, and returned to the atoll, ordering crewman Barney Ross to make the same swim the next night. Ross halfheartedly agreed, though returned before he was in as bad a shape as his lieutenant.

The third day the men began moving to another island from which Kennedy and Ross would together explore surrounding islands. They found enough food and water to keep them going, then were eventually discovered by natives while Kennedy and Ross were away.

It took a week before everyone was reunited, the crew known to be safe, and reporters had the story. Truth was distorted at once. The *New York Times* headlined the fact that Joe Kennedy's son saved ten crewmen in the Pacific. According to those first press reports, Kennedy had spotted the destroyer traveling at a speed of at least forty knots. The crew was summoned to general quarters, and they quickly prepared for torpedo attack. They were too close, though, and the *Amagiri* rammed them. The implication was that there was no way any commander could have avoided such a tragedy, and at least Kennedy went down trying to fight.

Kennedy was first recommended for the Silver Star, an honor it was quickly discovered he did not deserve. He had failed in battle, should not have been hit, and did not lead the rescue. It was finally decided to give him the lifesaving medal, and even that seems to have been done under pressure through Joe Kennedy's friend, Undersecretary of the Navy Forrestal.

The truth did not matter to Joe Kennedy, who needed war heroes for sons, and he was not about to let Jack's incompetence hurt the family name. Contacts were made with everyone who could be of value. Friendships were used, and when those weren't strong enough, it is believed that Joe Kennedy's money was placed in the appropriate hands.

The first publicity came from Pulitzer Prize-winning writer John Hersey, who was a friend of Jack's. His article about Jack's heroism under fire appeared in the *New Yorker,* and then was condensed in *Reader's Digest.* The crash was unavoidable in that version, the destroyer barely visible when Kennedy saw it, reacting instantly, flawlessly, but against a ship moving too fast to be outmaneuvered by the time it was visible.

The truth was effectively suppressed until long after Kennedy's death. Even during his 1960 presidential campaign, Jack used the story to prove his leadership abilities, his courage, and his coolness in a crisis. Fortunately no crisis that struck during his time in the White House ever brought out the same poor judgment he had shown that night in the Pacific.

Joe Kennedy used his son's survival for his own purposes. The Boston newspapers had an artist recreate the seven days the survivors spent before their rescue, naturally playing up the heroism of the local boy. Both newspapers and political gatherings toasted Ambassador Kennedy, the "father of the hero." The issues of Joe Kennedy as pro-Nazi, Joe Kennedy the anti-Semite, Joe Kennedy the counselor of appeasement, were all forgotten.

Tragically, Young Joe was also forgotten.

Young Joe had never avoided courageous duty. He learned to fly, learned to handle observation craft, and did his job professionally. He was far more competent than his brother, yet even if anyone had admitted that Jack's failings, not his skills, were what had given him short-term hero's status, Joe's pain would not have been lessened. Jack had been the first to win at the game of war. Young Joe, once his father's favorite, had been bested. He had to retake the lead.

The humiliation Young Joe felt was even worse because he

was at home on leave when his father was being feted for Jack's alleged heroism. According to Joe Timilty, a friend of Joe Sr.'s, he shared a room with Young Joe during that visit. After a dinner celebrating Jack's success, he heard Young Joe weeping in frustration.

The answer for Joe came with the Aphrodite Project. Germany had developed rocket technology. The V-1 rockets, called "buzz bombs," were causing some havoc and more fear in England. The Allied command determined to destroy the launch sites of these weapons.

The supposed launch sites in occupied France were identified, and allied bombing missions were immediately dispatched to destroy them. They were unsuccessful. The Allies lost 154 planes and 774 crewmen, and still the V-1s came. So the Allies planned to destroy the V-1s with their own missile. The answer seemed to be to counter the missile with an Allied missile.

Unlike the V-1s, the American "missiles" were jury-rigged affairs. First a plane was modified so it could be flown by remote control from a mother ship. A television camera was placed in the plane's nose to provide more accurate guidance to the target. The plane was loaded with high explosives, and a pilot would fly it close to the target before bailing out and letting the remote controller take over. The pilot would supposedly be on the ground and well away from the attack site before the explosion occurred.

Preparation took place in a remote section of England. While one plane—a PBY 4—was modified for the attack, Young Joe and others practiced taking off, moving into position, and then switching on the remote control device when they were given the code words "Spade Flush."

There were two different target areas planned for the earliest Aphrodite missions. One was to be handled by the Army Air Force, the second by the Navy's air wing, to which Young Joe belonged. A week before Young Joe was scheduled to go, word came that the Army strike had failed miserably. It had come nowhere near the target.

The official story of what happened next, as told by the

Kennedys, made Joe another war hero. He had taken flight training because it was the most dangerous branch of the service, something that pleased Joe Sr. He had volunteered for an extremely important mission, knowing that he might not return. Someone had to take out the V-1 launch sites. Young Joe had no wife and no children, and he was a man who would prefer to take the risks than to endanger a fellow pilot.

However, almost from the start there were comments among others in the program that Joe had a death wish, that he did not want to return, that he didn't care what happened. He had been depressed since the colorful story of *PT 109* was reported.

The story that seems to be the most accurate is the least pleasant. It was determined after interviewing people who knew Joe, extensive research in the Kennedy Library, and studying the books that have been written and the quotes of people who were there. It appears that Young Joe deliberately committed what amounts to suicide, acting in a reckless manner he knew would probably get him killed. And if suicide was not his goal, he was comfortable with death, knowing that returning alive from such a mission would probably pale as an act of heroism when compared with what Jack had achieved.

On August 11, the night before takeoff, electronics officer Earl Olsen explained to Young Joe about problems with the circuits on the plane. The electronics had to be working perfectly or the switch to remote control could result in premature detonation, killing anyone on the plane. Olsen needed just one more day to make things right and asked Young Joe to delay his flight.

The discussion was apparently quite specific, and there seemingly was no doubt in Joe's mind that going ahead as planned would kill him. He divided his possessions among his friends and wrote out what amounted to a will. He made every preparation for death he could think of, his only regret being that he could not call his girlfriend, Pat Wilson, to say good-bye.

There was no strategic reason for the flight to be made when Young Joe made it. Another day or two would not have hindered Allied operations or caused terrible destruction. The weather was holding nicely. To go up when Joe did was unnecessary. Olsen could have finished the necessary work.

The top officers of Aphrodite were uncertain about what to do and left the decision to the pilots. Waiting a day was not avoidance of duty. All the men were volunteers. All were experienced pilots, well trained for the mission. If they chose to override Olsen's judgment, no one would stop them. Only Young Joe made that choice. He took off at 6:00 P.M. and was blown to pieces in the air.

Two priests arrived at the Hyannis house on Sunday, August 13, 1944. They told Rose that Young Joe was missing, then asked to see Joe Sr., who was taking a nap. Only with the father would they tell of the death twenty-eight minutes into the mission, just after Young Joe had thrown the switch on the electronics he had not given Olsen time to fix.

No one can say how another person handles shock and grief. No one can say what someone feels and why. Yet the way in which the Kennedy family reportedly handled the news seemed to be a metaphor for their lives.

Joe Sr. gathered onto the back porch those children who were at home, including Jack, who was on leave, still somewhat crippled and recovering from malaria. He broke the news to them, told them to carry on, and retired to his room to grieve. Rose, as usual, was left alone, barred from her husband's intimacy at a time when others would have shared.*

And the children did what their father wanted. There was a sailboat race that day in which they were entered. They were to compete regardless of the loss of Young Joe. No one could think of a Kennedy dropping out of a competition, no matter

*Doris Kearns Goodwin, a highly respected biographer who was extremely close to the Kennedys, tells a slightly different version in *The Fitzgeralds and the Kennedys: An American Saga*. "When the priests left, Joe held on to Rose for a moment and then went into the living room to break the news to the others. 'Children,' he said, 'your brother Joe has been lost. He died flying a volunteer mission.' Then, with tears in his eyes and his voice cracking, he said, 'I want you all to be particularly good to your mother.' And with that he retreated into his bedroom and locked the door."

how meaningless, especially under the circumstances. However, not even the Kennedys were so callous as to note the results of that race.

There was one exception, the one person who understood war and failure, life and death, and what Joe's loss would mean. That was Jack, instantly the heir apparent to his father's desires and demands. Not allowed to share his grief with his parents, and unable to "be a Kennedy" with his siblings because of his injuries, he went to the beach and began walking, a solitary figure lost in thought, overwhelmed with pain, recognizing that he was facing a very different future than he previously imagined.

Perhaps more important was the impact on Ted. Twelve years old and intensely alone, the boy was essentially abandoned as a result of the death of his older brother, a man who had been more of a father to him than Joe Sr.

It is easy to dismiss Ted, even though he has become one of the most powerful people in the U.S. Senate. He is a periodic alcoholic, a womanizer, a man whose willingness to drive while under the influence of intoxicants took a woman's life, a man who liked to take girlfriends on camping trips with his sons and nephews while still married to Joan. If ever someone was self-destructively acting out in a way that would assure public condemnation, it has been Ted Kennedy. Even the name by which he is known—"Teddy"—implies a small boy at play. It is not the name of a senior statesman.

Under the best of circumstances small children have great difficulty understanding and accepting dramatic changes in their lives. Children frequently blame themselves when their parents divorce, for example. They think that if they had acted differently, everything between their parents would have been fine.

Ted knew nothing but rejection, albeit inadvertent, throughout his childhood. He experienced the world, yet never had his own bedroom. He was sent to so many different schools that he never had time to make friends before he was transferred, sometimes more than once in the same school year. He was always the loner, always the stranger, always the fat kid who became the joker, the tease, the life of the party in order to be accepted. His father was seldom home and his mother ridiculed him, again unintentionally. Over the years she wrote letters to her children, especially during wartime when they were so scattered. She did not write to each child individually. Instead she wrote family letters describing the activities of each child that she thought might interest the others.

Reading the letters from Rose to her children in the Kennedy Library is like taking a course in child psychology where the inadvertent but often searing pain of language is explored. Rose wrote of Ted's attempts to learn to dance and how clumsy he was. She wrote about his being short and fat—always about being fat—and about her pleasure when he finally found a little girl who was seemingly as clumsy, unattractive, and short as he was so he would have a dance partner. There was never anything Ted could do right. His triumphs came from making less of a fool of himself than usual. He was the family joke, the perpetual holder of second place in a family where everyone was either a winner or a loser.

Ted had been close to two siblings growing up. The first was Rosemary, who adored small children and was always kind to Ted. But she disobeyed her father and was sent away when Ted was nine. Even speaking her name was forbidden, as though having once loved his sister was suddenly somehow shameful.

The second was Young Joe. If there was a gentle side to Young Joe, it was revealed in his relationship with Ted. There was no competition between the two, no anger. Friends, family, and biographers cite numerous instances of the brothers' closeness, of Ted racing to greet Young Joe, of being lifted into his older brother's strong arms. If there was any nurturing within the family, Young Joe gave it to Ted. And just as Ted was entering puberty, a time of intense emotions, of self-doubt, of fear of the unknown, Young Joe was gone.

Ted Kennedy has never discussed that time, and his adult behavior has been so outrageous that most biographers have not bothered to look back that far. But there are appropriate questions that would provide essential insight into this now-powerful senator.

Did Ted know that his father pulled strings to get his oldest sons into the war? If he knew, with Rosemary "disappeared" and one brother dead, did he fantasize that his father was so powerful that he dared not lead a life in conflict with the man? Years later, when helping Jack with his race for the presidency, Ted fell in love with the American Southwest. He talked seriously of moving there, of setting up a law practice, and thus leaving New England and the family behind.

Joe would hear of no such decision, of course. Ted had to take the "Kennedy seat" in the Senate. His future was in Massachusetts. He could visit the Southwest, but he would live and work where Old Joe said he would. And Ted did not rebel, even though the rest of the family would not have cared—unless Old Joe did.

Or did Ted come to the conclusion that he was worthless, someone who had to be told what to do and how to do it because he could not make such decisions himself? The alcoholism and inability to commit to a relationship certainly are typical of people filled with self-hate. For many years, Ted would stop drinking and lose weight during the first months of the new year, a discipline that seemed to help him feel in control of a life that was like a roller coaster. Yet such personal challenges are common among some alcoholics and drug addicts, a way of reminding themselves that they can quit any time—though they choose to spend the rest of the time engaged in self-destructive behavior.

Whatever the real Ted, the loss of Joe, coming so soon after the loss of Rosemary, had to profoundly affect the youth. Yet neither his parents nor his remaining siblings reached out to comfort him, to help him through the crisis. Expressions of love, compassion, nurturing, and caring were not part of the Kennedy makeup. Only aggressiveness, winning, playing through the pain, and triumphing over others mattered in the family.

* * *

There was yet one more Kennedy life that would end in the years surrounding the war, and another that would be tinged with fatalism. The death was Kathleen's, the candle who burned the brightest while having the courage to follow her heart. The fatalism was Jack's.

Kathleen had returned to England to help with the war effort, as beloved by the people who knew her as her father was hated. There the romance with Billy Hartington blossomed.

Rose Kennedy was horrified by the thought of Kathleen marrying an Episcopalian. Even worse, Kathleen remained a devout Catholic, her only lapse, in her mind, being the desire to marry the man she loved. She would not change her devotion to the Church for that reason, and she did not want the Church to abandon her. And Joe was sympathetic. Only a hypocrite could have led the kind of life he had and not quietly approved of his daughter's actions, although he didn't tell Rose.

Joe asked Francis Cardinal Spellman if there was some way the Vatican would approve a church marriage for Kathleen and Billy, but that was impossible. In the end, the couple had a ten-minute civil ceremony in England on May 6, 1944. With luck there would come a time when the couple could marry in the Catholic Church. Until then, they would make the best of the situation.

Jack probably approved his sister's choice. Young Joe certainly did, for he was at the ceremony as unofficial family representative.

Kathleen and Billy had a little more than a month together. They spent the time as so many wartime couples did before the husband was sent back to the front. They explored a sexual relationship, they talked, they went out together, and each day moved too fast.

Billy was part of the Normandy invasion that began on June 6, 1944. Kick, now Lady Hartington, was visiting in Hyannis Port when she received the news of Billy's death on September 10. She returned immediately to England, to what she now considered her home. Rose privately claimed that God had handled the improper mixed marriage in His own way. And Billy's sister found that Kathleen apparently shared some of the same feelings. She was later quoted as saying of Kathleen following the death: "I never met anyone so desperately unhappy in my life. I had to sleep in her room night after night. Her mother had tried to convince her that she had committed a sin in this marriage, so that in addition to losing a husband, she worried about losing her soul."

Kathleen returned briefly to the United States in 1946 when Jack ran for Congress, but it was a hard time for her. She had become the family embarrassment. She couldn't be seen with Rose. She couldn't be seen with Jack. She had adopted Britain as her home and had married a Protestant in a civil ceremony. She could not take the sacraments of the Catholic Church. In many ways Rosemary's situation was less troublesome than Kathleen's, and so she returned to England, deeply hurt and even more alone.

Family exclusion could not be corrected, but loneliness could. There was the delightful Peter Milton, Lord Fitzwilliam, whom Kathleen began to see. Unfortunately, he was also the very married Peter Milton. Now Kathleen was acting like Gloria Swanson—a single woman helping a married man commit adultery. The difference between Milton and Joe Kennedy, though, was that Milton sought and won a divorce.

By 1948, Kathleen made it known to her family that she intended to marry Milton. Rose was scandalized. If Hell had been but an option with Billy Hartington, it seemed a certainty if Kathleen married a divorced Protestant. But Kathleen knew where the power in the family was. Joe was visiting Paris, and Kathleen decided to stop there with her lover on the way back from a holiday in Cannes. They were flying in a private plane and could handle the trip in any way they desired.

When they were readying to leave Cannes, the weather changed. They had a lunch date with Joe in Paris, and both were too anxious to get there to worry about the rain. They told the pilot to try to outrace the storm, but the winds caught the plane, smashing it into the side of a mountain. All three were killed.

Rose, again witnessing the hand of God, knew her daughter was in purgatory and refused to attend the funeral. Kathleen had played with fire and was consumed in it. There would be no grieving, except, perhaps, for the wrongheaded decision. Only Jack and Joe Sr. were extremely shaken, both shattered by the loss of all but one of the oldest children.

In 1947, Jack discovered that he had Addison's disease, a failure of the adrenal gland that was frequently fatal prior to the 1939 development of a chemical that affected the cortical hormones. Addison's causes jaundiced appearance, extreme exhaustion, and reduction of the immune system. The sufferer is susceptible to illness and infections, frequently losing appetite and experiencing severe weight loss. Cortical hormones, taken in conjunction with oral doses of cortisone, could help the person live a normal life. Without the medication, Jack would have died. With it, along with the other drugs he was taking, there was a good chance he would be dead by middle age.*

*The truth about the Addison's disease was discovered slowly over the years, the coverup involving Kennedy's personal physician, among others. One of the earliest reports, without Kennedy's name being used, was published in the November 1955 issue of *Archive of Surgery*. The article, titled "Example of a Patient with Adrenal Insufficiency Due to Addison's Disease Requiring Elective Surgery," told of Kennedy's surgery in a New York hospital on October 21, 1954: "A man 37 years of age had Addison's disease for seven years. He had been managed fairly successfully for several years on a program of desoxycorticosterone acetate pellets of 150mg. implanted every three months and cortisone in doses of 25 mg. daily orally. Owing to a back injury, he had a great deal of pain which interfered with his daily routine. Orthopedic consultation suggested that he might be helped by a lumbosacral fusion together with a sacroiliac fusion. Because of the severe degree of trauma involved in these operations and because of the patient's adrenocortical insufficiency due to Addison's disease, it was deemed dangerous to proceed with these operations. However, since this young man would become incapacitated without surgical intervention, it was decided, reluctantly, to perform the operations by doing

Kennedy arranged for quantities of the drugs he needed to be available in safe deposit boxes throughout the United States in those cities to which he knew he would be traveling with some frequency. With them he could stay reasonably vigorous and healthy-looking. However, if anyone asked about his health problems, he stressed that they were related to his time in the Pacific. It was better to be crippled by war than by a body that had not been healthy from birth. The Addison's became another of the little family secrets.

the two different procedures at different times if necessary and by having a team versed in endocrinology and surgical physiology help in the management of this patient before, during, and after the operation.'' The report didn't mention that Kennedy was close to death after the surgery, and that last rites were administered several times. It was one of the few times that an Addison's patient had withstood the trauma of major surgery.

The Kennedy office, denying the Addison's, said he had a bout of malaria, less ominous and more heroic since he supposedly got it in the South Pacific. However, this was years after he had been in the South Pacific. (The same excuse was used six years later when he had treatment at George Washington University Hospital in Washington, D.C.)

Another denial occurred on June 14, 1959, following a *Des Monies Register* newspaper report that he had Addison's. Dr. Janet Travell, who treated Kennedy for back and leg pains, issued a memorandum on July 21, 1959, that was thoroughly incorrect:

"In 1943, when the PT boat which he commanded was blown up, he was subjected to extraordinarily severe stress in a terrific ordeal of swimming to rescue his men. This, together perhaps with subsequent malaria, resulted in a depletion of adrenal function from which he is now rehabilitated.

"Concerning the question of Addison's disease, which has been raised. This disease was described by Thomas Addison in 1855 and is characterized by a bluish discoloration of the mucous membranes of the mouth and permanent deep pigmentation or tanning of the skin. Pigmentation appears early and it is the most striking physical sign of the disease. Senator Kennedy has never had any abnormal pigmentation of the skin or mucous membranes; it would be readily visible."

Travell had a degree in pharmacology, not endocrinology. Cortisone, which Kennedy was taking, would clear up any discoloration.

5

THE MAKING AND UNMAKING OF CAMELOT

They were different after the war years. More insular. Young Joe was dead, and Rosemary might as well have been. They had been the oldest, the ones responsible for everyone else.

Kathleen lived for just four years after the war, but she had effectively broken with the family when she moved back to England. Eunice had become her mother's special child, taking on the Kennedy women's mantle of power that she seemed to wear with both smug satisfaction and the dangerous wrath of unfocused frustration. Jack, who had a very brief, thoroughly meaningless stint as a reporter/correspondent for the Hearst newspapers, agreed to enter politics. Bob came of age. Ted moved solidly into his teens. Pat and Jean followed their mother's lead by looking to convent school educations.

Joe noticed the change in his children. He mentioned that he doubted his children would marry. They were too close to each other.

There was nothing incestuous about the family. Amoral in their relationships, perhaps, but they had taken their lead from their father in that regard. He just saw that they had so much fun with each other, so little tolerance for outsiders, that he doubted anyone would be acceptable as a mate for any of the children still at home.

In 1946, Jack took up the mantle left by the death of Joe Jr. and entered politics. As friends from that time have noted, it was perhaps not his first choice. It was true that he had talked with Inga Arvad about politics and the White House. And it was also true that after Young Joe's death he knew he would be carrying on his father's plans. But all of that was theoretical, not real yet. The war ended. He came home. And when he and his friends sat around the VFW meeting place, drinking beer, playing cards, and talking, Jack Kennedy thought about travel, maybe trying to be a journalist. But he did not need to think about such things. Joe Kennedy did that for him.

In April 1945, Joe used friends to arrange for Jack's appointment as co-chairman of a committee making an economic survey of Massachusetts. It was the same technique John Fitzgerald had used many years earlier. The committee would gain extensive publicity no matter what its findings. Then, in November 1945, the congressional seat from Boston's Eleventh District came open when the popular James M. Curley was elected mayor. With this opening, Joe saw that his son could take his first political office.

In February 1946, Kennedy began working the streets, perhaps the most difficult aspect of campaigning for him during those early years in politics. Jack was not like Honey Fitz. He was uncomfortable walking into saloons and pool halls to introduce himself, to shake hands, to work the room. There was a joke that Jack was the only pol in Boston who refused to go to a wake unless he knew the deceased. Because of this, the idea of Coffee with the Kennedys was developed. The gatherings were more relaxing and less formal.

It was Coffee with the Kennedys. Have a few friends in to meet a handsome young bachelor, back from the war, wanting to go to Congress to make sure no one has to die again. Or if he couldn't drop by the house for coffee because . . . well, you know how these young people are. Always running here and there. So many people to meet. So many things to do. Busy all the time, but the boy has stamina, vigor, enthusiasm. And you can meet him another time because, right now, his mother, Rose, is here. Or his sister Eunice. Or his sister Pat. Or his sister Jean. Or his brother Bob. Or his brother Ted.

Joe orchestrated his son's campaign and the other family members' involvement. Rose spoke, held receptions and teas. Eunice worked from the Boston office and also in Cambridge. All the others were involved, including fourteen-year-old Ted, who ran errands, and twenty-year-old Bob, just out of the Navy, to try to influence the East Cambridge wards.

Bob, who would soon become known as one of America's most hated ultra-right radicals when he worked with Senator Joe McCarthy, was actually of tremendous help during the campaign. East Cambridge was mostly laboring Italians, and Bob spent much of his time talking with people and eating spaghetti. But he understood how the community evaluated whether or not someone cared for them. When he saw a group of children playing softball in a park across from the office he was using, he closed the office, walked to the park, and joined in the game. He gained more votes for his brother from that action than resulted from the campaign promises of any of the candidates.

Handouts were numerous, including 100,000 reprints of the *Reader's Digest* condensation of John Hersey's *New Yorker* article on *PT 109*. The war hero image was more important than substance.

The elder Kennedy also bought votes, though in an extremely subtle way. Anyone giving a tea would receive $100 to help with the expense of cleaning their home. In addition, several large families were given $50 each to help at the polls, even if they chose not to show up.

Favors were called in as well. The *Boston American,* a paper owned by William Randolph Hearst, refused to acknowledge the existence of Mike Neville, one of Jack's opponents. In the two months prior to the election, Neville's name was not mentioned and political advertising was not accepted from him. Later it was learned that this was in response to a request by Joe, who had earlier helped Hearst with his finances.

The final touch was to add an image of accessible royalty to that of Bob's "regular guy." The Kennedys held court.

The Democrats had developed a voting list, and a group of women volunteers decided to personally write to every name on it, inviting the people to a formal reception and tea at the Hotel Commander in Cambridge. It was a fancy dress version of Coffee with the Kennedys, with every woman and her escort expected to be formally attired. Some of those invited were wealthy. Others would have needed to skip an occasional meal to be able to afford an appropriate outfit to attend.

Approximately fifteen hundred people showed up, the women dressed in the finest gowns they owned, could buy, rent, borrow, or make, the men in formal wear. The receiving line snaked through the hotel lobby, outside, and down the street. The people attending met not only the candidate, but also the former ambassador to England in full formal white tie and tails. In a sense, those in attendance were paying homage to royalty and having royalty pay homage to them. It was a heady experience, and it helped clinch the election to Congress.

Years later, when Jack Kennedy was in the White House, formality was routine for many well-photographed White House gatherings. But the royalty seemed accessible, and the Kennedys were beloved for it, the family becoming part myth and part myth makers. And the technique began as an experiment in the congressional campaign.

Jack did not appear to take his time in Congress particularly seriously. He lacked the opinions of his father, had no agenda, and seemed to weigh every vote based on how his district would be interested. He maintained an office and a three-room apartment in his district, but made his primary residence the luxurious Georgetown section of Washington. There, in a three-story row house, he lived with Eunice, who held a job with the Justice Department, and his friend and secretary, Billy Sutton.

Jack was lucky in the rather conservative Eightieth Congress. His committee appointments would have delighted his grandfather Fitzgerald because they allowed him to make headlines without having to get involved with substantive issues that could backfire later. He was on the subcommittee of the House Veterans' Affairs Committee, the District of Columbia Committee, and the House Committee on Education and Labor. The latter enabled him to be in the midst of issues dealing with organized labor and a growing awareness of national illiteracy. Veterans were also clamoring for help as they restored their lives, and their numbers were so great that their gatherings regularly made the press.

The actual work seems to have been handled by his Washington secretary, Mary Davis. Beyond not caring about the daily activities, Kennedy did not care about his appearance. He was more than casual, his attire closer to that of a high school student rebelling against his parents than a freshman congressman. He was frequently mistaken for one of the pages, and his only interest in life seemed to be fantasizing about being a football hero.

There were a few other freshmen in Congress who became friends with Kennedy. They had greater ambition and spent more time working, but they would frequently come to small parties Jack held at Georgetown. Among these guests were Richard Nixon and Senator Joe McCarthy. Girls were also familiar visitors, especially airline hostesses and secretaries. He wanted no commitments, no women who would make more demands on him than those he could handle sexually.

Kennedy was also becoming increasingly shy around girls, an ironic situation given the family history. By the time he was in the Senate, I was working on Capitol Hill. Jack was known as somewhat of a joke among the attractive single women like myself. They would frequently go to a bar named Mike Palms, where many government workers, including Kennedy, hung out after work. It was a place to relax, a place to talk about shared concerns, and a place to pick up dates in a safe environment.

Jack Kennedy did not have the nerve to join with the others. He would send an aide to the young woman he was interested in to make his approach and ask her if she would be interested in going out with the senator. Almost every time, the woman refused. She had no illusions about the senator, and his methods were both juvenile and insulting. As a result, most of his women in later years were either provided by friends and family members, or approached him because of who he was and the glamor associated with his name. (This same situation would recur with John Kennedy Jr., most notably with singer/actress Madonna, who claimed to have deliberately seduced John Jr. because she wanted to be like Marilyn Monroe.)

Jack began to take control of the myths about his life. Where the *PT 109* incident had previously been an embarrassment for him, he began talking about it as though the fantasy actually happened. He selected staff people who would not embarrass him with the truth, who were so honored to be a part of his entourage that they would do anything necessary for him. He used his friends for entertainment and to run his errands. Their skills and interests meant nothing; his pleasure was his overriding concern.

No one complained very loudly, of course. Just to be in the Kennedy inner circle was an honor in itself. Thus, Joe Gargan, a Kennedy cousin (in other words, a related outsider), gave up a law career to do whatever was needed for the Kennedys, including protecting Ted when Mary Jo Kopechne was killed at Chappaquiddick.

Kennedy served three terms in Congress before making a move for the Senate. This included a trip to Europe in early 1951, arranged by Joe. Joe knew that his son had little knowledge of foreign affairs and even less interest. This "fact-finding mission" lasted five weeks, although it was not part of his congressional duties. Joe paid for the trip, so there could be no charges of misuse of public funds. He also arranged for Jack to meet with willing heads of state, and had his PR people publicize Jack's action, including his testimony before the Senate Foreign Relations Committee upon his return. The report he gave to that committee showed no great insight into the problems of Europe, and the testimony was allowed more as a courtesy than because anyone thought the young congressman could provide substantive information. However, he gained the public image of statesman.

That first overseas trip garnered such favorable press that Joe underwrote an October vacation/business trip for Jack, Bob, and Pat. This time they visited Israel, India, and Vietnam. This trip was too strenuous for Jack, and he was rushed to a military hospital in Okinawa with a 106° temperature. His adrenal glands were failing him because of the Addison's, and his personal physician called over to suggest the use of adrenal hormones and penicillin. The treatment saved his life, but it was obvious he would never have the natural stamina for the rigors of the presidency. Only the later use of amphetamines would keep him alert and active in the White House.

Kennedy's opposition in the 1952 Senate race was the perfect test of Jack's power and the changes in the state. He was Henry Cabot Lodge Jr., a Harvard-educated Brahmin whose family once stood for everything Joe hated. He had entered the Senate in 1936 when he was 34. He had also been a true war hero, resigning his Senate seat in 1944 to serve in the army, where he won the Bronze Star, among other honors. Then, in 1946, his liberalism on domestic matters, the military service his constituents knew he could have avoided, and his record of competence in the Senate, led him to a third-term victory in which he crushed his Democratic opponent.

In theory, Lodge should have beaten Kennedy. He was a serious politician, concerned about his state and the nation. He cared about people from all economic backgrounds, and had the legislative record to prove it. By contrast, Kennedy was a lightweight politician who had accomplished little during his six years in office.

Unfortunately, Lodge made two mistakes. The first was that he looked at the relative records of himself and his opponent and determined that no one would bother to vote for Kennedy. The second was that he did not recognize Joe's drive to make his oldest surviving son president, a drive that would not allow for a loss.

Joe met with Massachusetts Governor Paul Dever, who was trying to decide whether to take on Lodge or to run for a third term as governor. After the meeting, Dever declared that he would seek the governor's office once again. As part of the agreement, his campaign expenses were mixed with Kennedy's, giving Dever greater financial backing. He had been bought.

No one knows how much money Joe Kennedy spent to make his son senator. Officially, the family spent about $70,000, a figure quoted by a number of writers who researched the campaign. However, such accounting does not include numerous private committees, all funded by Joe, that were under no requirements to report the source of their money. Experts analyzing the cost of billboards, media, giveaways, and television, a rarity in 1952, place the expense in the range of $500,000-$1 million. In addition, Joe Kennedy used another $500,000 to "bribe" John Fox, the editor of the *Boston Post,* to endorse his son.*

Joe also used the campaign to bring Bob into politics. The next-oldest son was just 26 years old, politically naive, with no experience in much of anything. He graduated from the University of Virginia Law School, married Ethel Skakel, whose background also included great wealth, and worked for the Department of Justice for a few months. Although quite different from his older brothers, Bob was then his father's eyes, ears, and mouth. Whatever Bob said was considered a directive from the father. Unfortunately for those involved with the campaign, Bob was also viewed as unpleasantly self-

---

*The Fox money was a much-needed loan to the head of the strongly conservative newspaper. Fox had approached other candidates for loans, offering to endorse them as part of the repayment. In an interview several years later, Jack Kennedy admitted to journalist Fletcher Knebel that the *Post*'s endorsement had been bought.

important, pugnacious, and capable of carrying a grudge to such an extreme that he alienated people who might otherwise have helped him.

Bob was the ambitious Kennedy among the surviving brothers, and he married a woman aggressive enough to have been born a Kennedy. Ethel Skakel was the sixth child of another self-made family. Though mere multimillionaires, the family fortune that enabled them to live in a Greenwich, Connecticut, mansion came from the Great Lakes Carbon Corporation. The couple met and married while in school, almost immediately having the first of their eleven children, Kathleen. (The godfather was Senator Joe McCarthy.)

The Skakel background was somewhat like that of the Kennedys, and Ethel was the one spouse who would be able to hold her own amid the often vicious, demeaning family into which she married. Ethel was taunted by her older brothers when she had dates. They used to take air rifles, then hide on the grounds while Ethel's dates approached the house. They would fire stinging BBs at the young men who had no idea why or from where they were being assaulted.

Bob was an odd young man, intensely moral in the manner of the young, dividing all life into good or bad. His greatest weakness was that he could not see the human qualities in others—the good that existed in the worst of men, and the bad that existed in the best of them. He was easily led by superficial realities during those years, a fact that made him the most dangerous and dedicated of the brothers.

Bob also identified more with Rose than with Joe. He wanted a large family, equating the presence of children, dogs, a loving wife, and the sound of laughter with happiness. At the same time, he was driven like his father to spend long hours at work, though in his case it would be as a lawyer, U.S. attorney general, and senator from New York rather than as a businessmen. His children, undoubtedly loved, lacked discipline and guidance, a fact that made them hated by Joe and Rose's household staff when they came to visit. Thus, while there was talk of ideals, Bob's children would eventually lead the most troubled lives, not only involving themselves with drugs and alcohol, but also having marital difficulties, a scandal in which Bob's oldest son paralyzed a young woman, and a son, David, who was abandoned during times of critical need, resulting in what might be called a family-assisted suicide.

Bob and Ethel imitated his parents with dinner lectures and catechism training. Family friends told of Bob quizzing his children at dinner about people in the news. And others talked of asking the children about the catechism when they drove to church, then questioning them about the sermon when they drove home.

But, as with Joe Sr., such rigors only occurred when Bob was present, and his career in government allowed him less and less time with his family. Discipline was so lax that unless all the children had to be somewhere at the same time, they arose when they felt like it and ate when they felt like it. The house cook in McLean, Virginia, was expected to serve as short-order provider. If the children arose at eleven different times, then eleven different breakfasts were cooked. Naturally this carried over into lunch as well. a fact that made the retaining of staff a difficult task. Secretaries also quit, blaming the undisciplined children, frequently calling Ethel ''Mommy Dearest.''

What mattered to the Kennedys was that Ethel could handle any family member's taunts, challenges, or attacks. There were those who looked upon her as the sister of Eunice, Jean, and Pat, not the sister-in-law. And her love of Bob was intense, the couple fiercely devoted to each other.

Ethel was as devoted to helping the Kennedy brothers achieve their father's political ambitions as were the Kennedy sisters. She would travel, give speeches, make coffee, and do anything that was necessary to achieve victory. However, she made her greatest impression by chance during Jack's first Senate campaign. On September 23, a very pregnant Ethel made a speech at Fall River, Massachusetts, and then went into labor, giving birth to the couple's first son, Joseph Patrick II. Archbishop Richard Cushing, soon to become cardinal, presided at the baptism, a well-publicized event that seemed to imply the

Catholic Church's approval of Jack as senator. Of course, there was no such endorsement, but the image remained.

Two brilliant moves by the Kennedys were orchestrated by Bob with his father's guidance. The first was the development of a staff of 286 committee secretaries throughout the state. These were officially part of the Democratic Party system within Massachusetts, but they were really Kennedy organizers and spies. They worked with Larry O'Brien (later National Democratic Party chairman) and Kenny O'Donnell to organize 30,000 workers and 21,000 regular volunteers. But the secretaries were considered a shadow organization whose first allegiance was to Jack Kennedy, and by extension, to all the Kennedys.

The Kennedys' state organization was unlike anything that had ever been seen before. Every community with more than 600 people had a professional Kennedy organization. Although it took only 2,500 signatures to be on the ballot, the Kennedys worked until the last minute for filing, getting 252,325 names. This was a race between an Irish Catholic and a Boston Brahmin, and Joe was willing to bankroll whatever was necessary to win. Jack was going to achieve in the state what Joe had been unable to do, and Bob was coordinating it all.

The second essential move was finding and registering 100,000 new voters in the state, most of them sympathetic to the Democrats.

Jack Kennedy, single, handsome, and rich was seen as having great appeal to women. This sex appeal was utilized by having handwritten invitations prepared by the statewide organizations. These went to women inviting them to a "Reception in honor of Mrs. Joseph P. Kennedy and her son, Congressman John F. Kennedy." There were thirty-three such events in addition to the traditional Coffee with the Kennedys. Jack would always be present at these, along with one or more family members, frequently including his mother. Dave Powers (later head of the Kennedy Library) would unobtrusively stand with a counter, taking down the numbers. Approximately 70,000 women passed through the receiving lines of these events, according to his totals.

The importance of the receptions and the voter registration cannot be underestimated. When the election results were in, Jack's margin of victory was 70,737 votes.

Bob was the next to enter politics—again in a high-profile, non-elective position. In 1953 he joined Senator Joe McCarthy's Subcommittee on Investigations. Joe Kennedy wanted his son named chief counsel, figuring that the exposure would be good for him. Instead, that position went to Roy Cohn, a young, arrogant, flamboyant attorney. However, Joe Kennedy's control and influence in the selection process were obvious all the way through. Cohn discussed the incident in his autobiography:

> Bobby Kennedy, who had to settle for assistant counsel, never forgave me for landing the top job; he thought it was coming to him by birthright. In fact, birth was all he had going for him—and it was almost all he needed. Despite the fact that he never tried a case or conducted a hearing, that he had absolutely no experience in dealing with subversives, Joseph P. Kennedy pressured McCarthy relentlessly, and nobody could put on the heat like Papa Joe. He'd been a friend and confidant and big-scale contributor to McCarthy and now he was presenting all his markers for Bobby.

Bob Kennedy's focus was international trade in violation of sanctions against Communist countries, especially mainland China. American goods could not be legally sent to any such areas. However, American trading partners, including the wealthy Greek businessman Aristotle Onassis, were violating the intent of the law. They would buy American goods and ship them to another country that was a legitimate trading partner. Then the goods would be loaded on to a foreign vessel going to their final destination. Bob's investigations resulted in little that was substantive because there was really nothing America could do about the situation.

Bob left the committee in July 1953, but returned in January 1954, just as McCarthy was taking on the U.S. Army. The result was disastrous for McCarthy, as he was exposed as a fraud and was eventually censured by the Senate.* Bob's bad timing left him being remembered for his role in the disreputable action that finally destroyed McCarthy, and it was not until his years as attorney general that he was incorrectly anointed as a liberal by his supporters. And once the label of liberalism is provided a politician, it is harder to lose than the virginity of the sole survivor of an island shipwreck. And by the time the label was truly deserved, Bob had very little time to live.

It was 1953 when Jack Kennedy was told to marry. His father had positioned him for a presidential run that would have been unlikely for a handsome bachelor. A man in his thirties (Jack was thirty-six) could be seen as having "escaped" marriage. A man in his forties, even if just as handsome and seemingly desirable, would raise questions among the voters as to whether or not he was a homosexual. In fact, because his bed-hopping

---

*When McCarthy was falling, Jack Kennedy was in the New York Hospital for Special Surgery for the back surgery that he almost died from. He was recovering, although not yet able to return to a normal work schedule, on December 2, 1954, when the Senate voted to censure McCarthy. In the oral history made by Kennedy's friend Charles Spalding for the Kennedy Library, Spalding told how Kennedy joked about what he would do when asked about McCarthy. " 'You know, when I get downstairs I know exactly what's going to happen.' He said, 'Those reporters are going to lean over my stretcher. There's going to be about ninety-five faces bent over me with great concern, and everyone of those guys is going to say, "Now, Senator, what about McCarthy?" ' And he said, 'Do you know what I'm going to do? I'm going to reach back for my back and I'm just going to yell, "Oow," and then I'm going to pull the sheet over my head and hope we can get out of there.' "

Actually, that would have been more courageous than what he did. He did nothing, and no one would ever be able to prove that he was actually a supporter of Joe McCarthy.

indicated such disdain for women, rumor had already begun in Washington that the senator liked men. The fact that the rumors had already started, as unfounded as they appear to have been, means that Joe Kennedy's political instincts were correct. A bachelor Jack Kennedy would always be a U.S. senator. Married, the White House was within the family's grasp.

It is easy to glorify or denigrate Jacqueline Kennedy Onassis. Many of her biographers, either writing exclusively about her or focusing on the couple, have wanted to avoid certain facts about her. Sometimes it is because they hate their subject, as one biographer claimed he did when he wrote about her (ironically the writer was a womanizer, had been in trouble with law enforcement, and was abusive to his own wife on whom he cheated repeatedly). At other times, there is intense compassion for a widow who was filmed experiencing her husband's assassination. Documentaries from the era contain the haunting images of Jacqueline Kennedy climbing onto the back of the open limousine, in shock, grabbing at her husband's brains, trying to restore the skull shattered by his killer's bullet.

But an objective look at Jacqueline Bouvier, the woman who married Jack Kennedy, reveals someone who was unattractive, flashy in dress as a way of keeping strangers from looking deeper than the superficial; extremely bright, articulate; and like most Kennedy spouses, a child abuse victim. In fact, it seems that almost all of the Kennedy children married men or women who had been emotionally and/or physically abused when growing up. Their self-hate would later become evident in drug abuse, alcoholism, emotional sadism, and similar examples of self-loathing. They were traits that would leave indelible marks on the third generation as well, the reason that just surviving being a Kennedy grandchild would be a sign of unusual success.

Jacqueline's father was Black Jack Bouvier, a wealthy stockbroker who would eventually spend all his money on failed schemes and pleasures of the flesh. He gave his daughters monthly allowances, established charge accounts for them, bought them horses to ride, and paid for their education. After Jacqueline's mother, Janet Lee, divorced him for his womanizing, he never remarried, so when he saw his daughters, he always made the events special, taking them to expensive restaurants or buying them whatever they desired. Love, to Jacqueline and her sister, Lee, meant money, gifts, and periodic special attention mixed with long, lonely absences. The sisters were raised to have values and ideas about love typical of kept women.

Thus Jacqueline's attraction to an older (Kennedy was thirteen years her senior), wealthy man whose approach to courtship kept her as off-balance as she had been as a child, would be unusually intense. Kennedy was not deliberately trying to seduce her in the way he treated her, though that was the result. He either spent money lavishly on her, and then become sexually aggressive, or he would essentially ignore her, missing dates and forgetting to call when he promised. She could not count on the senator any more than she could count on Black Jack, but when Kennedy did show, he was seemingly interested in no one else.

There was always more and less to Jacqueline Bouvier than people gave credit, a paradox that would haunt her all of her life. She was not pretty as a young adult. The looks in the family went to her sister, Lee. Age and maturity gave Jacqueline her beauty, an unpleasant situation when you're still young and feel yourself in competition with others.

But Jacqueline had skills her sister did not. Both tried their hand at writing, yet it was Jacqueline whose work appeared in *Vogue* without the support of a powerful, doting father. And it was Jacqueline who obtained a job with the *Washington Times Herald,* where she handled a "Man on the Street" column.

One of Jacqueline's male friends was stockbroker John Husted, who was successful by the standards of average citizens. He was earning $17,000 a year when he knew her, a sum several times the income of the typical American family of four. But they could not have an estate, their own horses, or any of the other privileges with which Jacqueline's mother, Janet Bouvier Auchincloss, had been raised. Her father, James Lee, had hated Black Jack Bouvier so much that he had granddaughters Jacqueline and Lee sign agreements that they would make no claims against his estate, and then disinherited them. Having seen the way her own father cut off her children, Janet felt that a woman's station in life depended upon whom she married. Husted was not appropriate in her opinion.

When Husted proposed and Jacqueline said "yes," she was driving a used car, barely getting by on her $42.50 weekly income from the *Washington Times-Herald.* Her mother held a large party at the Auchincloss home in Virginia, a mansion where Jacqueline had grown into young womanhood after her mother's remarriage. It was a further reminder of what she was accustomed to experiencing, yet would never predictably have with Husted.

The engagement lasted four months, during which the couple was usually separated, Husted working in New York while she had her job in Washington. Finally she called off the engagement, either because of maternal pressure or because she was seduced by John Kennedy, in many ways a young version of Black Jack.

Many friends interviewed by biographers of Jacqueline Bouvier say that ultimately she was motivated by money. Jack Kennedy certainly represented financial security, as well as power and access to some of the most important people in the United States. However, she was little prepared for the pressures she would experience as the wife of a U.S. senator, and even less for the stress of marrying a Kennedy.

The engagement announcement, the courtship, and even the wedding seemed to foreshadow the real relationship that would follow. *Life* magazine had been planning to run an article on Senator Kennedy titled "The Senate's Gay Young Bachelor." It was a puff piece orchestrated by Joe, but it was also good copy. Jack Kennedy was handsome, rich, single, and perceived to be a war hero. He was single at a time when the women who read the magazine were considered to have marriage and family as their primary interests. Every mother of an eligible daughter would read the story and fantasize that Jack Kennedy might become her son-in-law. Single women could fantasize marrying the senator. Rather than risk killing the story or making a change that would shatter part of the illusion, Jack delayed announcing his engagement until after it appeared. Then, during a time when most engaged couples are together as frequently as possible, Jack took a European vacation with his friend Torby MacDonald, sending Jackie only a simple "Wish you were here" postcard.

Ultimately the wedding was a show, from the five-tiered cake to a blessing sent by the pope and the presence of the most important leaders of the church, including Archbishop Cushing of Boston. Joe brought in two truckloads of quality champagne, arranged for the wedding to be a front-page story of the Sunday *New York Times,* and made certain that the 3,000 spectators who gathered outside the church were noted by the press.

The one person who was truly happy was Joe Kennedy. His son was marrying someone he believed to be a French Catholic, a woman of culture and breeding who could enhance the Kennedy image. It didn't matter that Jack didn't love the woman, nor did it matter that his daughters hated her, ridiculing her voice, her shyness, her love of the arts, and even her name. Jacqueline was pronounced "Jack-leen," and Ethel, the honorary sister, joked about how it supposedly rhymed with "queen." However, Jacqueline would prove to be the one Kennedy outsider who maintained control. She was able to mock the family behind their backs, to stand up to them when appropriate, and to ignore them the rest of the time. She treated Jack's siblings like an indulgent parent watching a group of small children play meaningless games while taunting and challenging one another to engage in activities even they felt were foolish.

If there was any strain with Joe, it was Jacqueline's lack of interest in politics. The manipulation of power was not important to her, yet it was all-consuming to the family. She often ignored such talk, whether at home or at parties, and was considered a potential liability by the Kennedy sisters. Jack's wife seemed to be a snob, someone who spoke foreign languages fluently, loved the arts, and did not see the winning of an office worth the phoniness of being everyone's friend long enough to win a vote.

During the convalescence, Kennedy prepared the second of his books, *Profiles in Courage.* The story of this book is subject to controversy. Like all Kennedy books, *Profiles* was ghostwritten, this time primarily by historian and author Theodore Sorenson. However, several factors make this book different. Unlike *Why England Slept,* this book has more reason to be considered Kennedy's own in the manner of many "ghosted" volumes.

Theodore "Ted" Sorensen was officially a legislative assistant for Kennedy, but he was actually a great deal more. The 24-year-old man was an attorney who worked for the Federal Security Agency and the Senate subcommittee studying the railroad retirement system. He was a pacifist, strongly interested in civil rights, and active in the Democratic Party. He did not seem to be the type of man who would be comfortable with someone who refused to attack Joe McCarthy, However, he was also relatively closed in. He might write an impassioned article about civil rights, but he would be extremely uncomfortable going on the streets to be actively involved with others.

Sorensen became Kennedy's "ghost," writing for publications ranging from the *New York Times Magazine* to *Atlantic Monthly.* It was because of his efforts that Jack Kennedy began to be seen as an expert on international relations. The only problem the senator had was that he had difficulty reading Sorensen's speeches. His delivery style was weak, something he developed more effectively over the years, just as Sorensen learned to phrase ideas in a manner Kennedy could deliver well.

The idea for *Profiles in Courage* was Jack Kennedy's, though he turned immediately to Sorensen for help. He wanted to prepare an article on the courageous stands taken by American politicians acting in the public good. He was fascinated by the strength of individuals acting against all odds, perhaps seeking comfort during his own battle with pain so intense that Dr. Janet Travell had begun giving him Novocaine treatments on a weekly basis.

Kennedy had little idea who he might profile, though with Sorensen's assistance, he began contacting experts—professors, historians, journalists, and others. Gradually it was clear that it would be best to expand the article into book form. Soon so much was being found that Sorensen spent most of 1955 involved with the project, working with historian Jules Davids. The latter's help was requested by Jacqueline, who was trying to better understand her husband's passion by taking a course in American history from Davids. The professor was exploring some of the issues that brought individual legislators into conflict with one another, their political party, and their constituents, the very issues Kennedy was exploring.

There are numerous notes relative to *Profiles in Courage* in the Kennedy Library, and their presence is supposed to prove that he wrote the book. In fact, they do not. What they show is that he was involved with the process of writing, selecting the men to be profiled from among those suggested to him, overseeing the work done by others. He conceptualized the project, coordinated the professionals, and made suggestions along the way. Davids and Sorensen were the primary writers. Among those who offered suggestions for inclusion were Ted Sorensen, Walter Johnson, University of Minnesota's John Bystrom, James MacGregor Burns, Arthur Schlesinger Jr., Arthur Krock, Arthur Holcombe, James Landis, Allan Nevins, and Davids. Evan Thomas of Harper and Brothers publishers handled the editing of the project, and publisher Cass Canfield (ironically the father of Lee Bouvier's husband) suggested the format. The primary structuring, the focus of the concept, and other details of the final book seem to have been developed from lengthy critiques by Nevis, Davids, and Schlesinger.

The tapes that Kennedy made, again in the Kennedy Library as "proof" of his authorship, are, for the most part, oral notes. Most of them are simply quotes from other sources, Kennedy apparently having taken a biography, then read from it into the recorder so he would have the information later. The most work he did appears to have been on John Quincy Adams.

Sorensen worked full time on the project, and along with Davids, had access to a study room in the Library of Congress, as well as the help of William Tansill of the Legislative Research Office. Hundreds of items were located by Tansill, photocopied, and forwarded to Sorensen, not Kennedy. Eventually Sorensen provided Kennedy with chapters on Adams, Thomas Hart Benson, and Edmund Ross, while Davids handled Lucius Q.C. Lamar, Sam Houston, and George Norris. Landis contributed the material on Robert Taft, initially opposed by Kennedy as too recent a figure and a Republican, as well as helping with the material on Daniel Webster. Both Davids and Sorensen developed complete material for the section in the book titled "The Meaning of Courage." However, Kennedy combined those into a cohesive approach with which he was comfortable. Again, he was an editor, not a researcher or original writer.

Kennedy was most heavily involved with the book in March 1955 when he was in Palm Beach, flat on his back, recovering from surgery. By May he was able to swim regularly, and that seemed to be his only other activity of importance to him.

Sorensen later explained how he and Kennedy worked on the book when he was interviewed by Ralph G. Martin and Ed Plaut for their 1960 book *Front Runner, Dark Horse*. He said: "The way Jack worked was to take all the material, mine and his, pencil it, dictate the fresh copy in his own words, pencil it again, dictate it again—he never used a typewriter."

Sorensen seems to have written complete drafts, which Kennedy would revise as he desired. Then, before sailing to Europe in August, Kennedy alerted Evan Thomas that the completed manuscript would be sent by Sorensen after the latter received the suggestions and comments of Allan Nevins. Again this implies the physical writing by others. However, as Thomas proudly stated when Joe Kennedy thought the final draft lacked polish, the book reads as though Jack Kennedy wrote it. Or more accurately, it read as Kennedy sounded in public, and

Sorensen had been one of the primary molders of that image through his speech writing.

Expenditures for the book by Kennedy were limited compared with what his father had spent for *Why England Slept.* A total of $4,503.75, according to Herbert S. Parmet, who made the most thorough study of the creation of the book for his own volume, *Jack: The Struggles of John F. Kennedy.* The money included advertising, the fee paid to Professor Davids, and similar expenses. Sorensen's pay was not included in that figure.

The book was a financial success before it was published. Kraft Theater bought television rights so they could produce the stories of the individuals profiled. *The Reader's Digest* decided to serialize the book, and excerpts were sold for use in *The New York Times Magazine, Collier's, Harper's,* and *The Boston Globe. Life* magazine did a photo story on Kennedy, and foreign language editions were sold.

Kennedy used most of his royalties, and they were considerable as the book sold approximately 125,000 hardcover copies total in 1956 and 1957, to pay for advertising. Not only did this sell more books, it kept the Kennedy name before the nation. In addition, he spoke about the book on television, appeared on Edward R. Murrow's immensely popular show *Person to Person,* and became the darling of the media. Here was a politician who was young, handsome, a war hero, and with a great future ahead of him who was also an intellectual and historian.

One of the greatest prizes an author can receive is the Pulitzer Prize, and in 1957 the judges for the prize for the best biography were Julian Boyd and Bernard Mayo. They selected four books as being deserving, then recommended that the committee making the final choice (always different from the judges) select Alpheus Mason's *Harlan Fiske Stone: Pillar of the Law.* Because the selection committee does not have to accept the recommendation of the judges, three other books were offered as being worthy. While the selection committee is allowed to choose anything it wants, traditionally it relies upon the knowledge of the judges who have reviewed numerous books in the field within the year of the selection. The other three choices were *Old Bullion Benton, James Madison: The President, 1809-1812,* and *John Quincy Adams and the Union.* The Kennedy book *Profiles in Courage,* though well written, was considered too lightweight a book to be considered when compared with the four choices.

The selection committee, known as the Pulitzer Advisory Board, included Arthur Krock, who lobbied on behalf of Joseph Kennedy. Members yielded to pressure and gave the Pulitzer to *Profiles in Courage.* It would be nice to say that the selection was somehow justified in the minds of the advisory board. The ideal situation would be for the members to have read all of the books and felt that for reasons of scholarship, popular appeal, and impact on the nation, somehow they should ignore the judges and make their own selection. But the only criteria was that Arthur Krock was successful in lobbying on behalf of a friend, and either the advisory board didn't care, was too weak to argue, or was bought in some manner.

Such harsh criticism may seem a bias against the book. However, the advisory board consisted of 12 men, all professionals, all respected in their various fields. According to J.D. Ferguson, the president of the *Milwaukee Journal* and a member of the advisory board, what moved the group was the statement that his twelve-year-old grandson had read the book and been deeply influenced by it. When Ferguson shared that information with the others, they immediately decided to give the prize to Jack Kennedy.

Although undeserving of the Pulitzer relative to that year's competition, at least in the eyes of the judges, what is of greater concern was the way in which Jack Kennedy handled the matter. Instead of giving credit to the team that produced the volume, Kennedy took sole credit for the writing. And the family would perpetuate the myth in later years by having an annual award created to honor people of courage who exemplify the type of individual immortalized by Jack Kennedy in his collective biography.

* * *

With the episode of the second ghostwritten book, Jack Kennedy made clear that he would be willing to live a lie for the rest of his life. A study of an early *Who's Who* entry has Kennedy claiming "Student of London Sch. Economics 1935-1936" when he actually dropped out without taking any classes. He saved a man's life after causing his PT boat to be destroyed, yet he took credit for saving the lives of three men. He also accepted the idea that he was a "hero" after he disobeyed orders, acted improperly, and created a crisis where none needed to exist the night his PT boat was sunk. *Why England Slept* was not an original work, nor was *Profiles in Courage,* though at least with the latter he could claim a greater degree of involvement. The man was not an intellectual, a writer, or motivated to help others. He was moving toward the greatest power the nation had to offer, and everything he did had to be recreated with that in mind. There were even *PT 109* tie clips used as giveaways, not just by Jack but also by his brother, Bob, when the latter entered politics. The lies, repeated often enough, sounded like truth; the hollow base for the images to come was given the look of substance.

There were other marriages during this period, less important at the time because they did not involve the two primary heir apparents. The most interesting was that of Pat Kennedy, who fell in love with actor Peter Lawford.

Peter Lawford fit nicely into the Kennedy family, not because he was accepted but because he didn't care. Lawford, like the others, had been raised in an abusive environment. His father, Brig. Gen. Sydney Lawford, was one of the great British heroes of World War I. He not only was a leader in battle, he frequently risked his own life to be certain the wounded under his command were evacuated before they could be captured by the enemy.

Sydney Lawford was a wealthy man, inheriting from ancestors who made their money in banking and business during the late eighteenth and early nineteenth centuries. A handsome man, his first wife died of cancer in 1900 after seven years of marriage. His second wife was Murial Williams Watt who, as would become typical for his courtships, was still married when he first began dating her.

After the war, with the general knighted so he could use the title Sir Sydney, the couple went to India where his deputy assistant was Major Ernest Aylen. The major was married to the former May Bunny, whose previous husband had been Harry Cooper, and May was determined to be a titled aristocrat. When it appeared that the major could not supply such a life for her, she seduced the very willing Sir Sydney, getting pregnant by him.

There are conflicting stories about Peter's birth. The truth was that May's first husband committed suicide, and that her second husband ultimately had the marriage annulled. Ernest Aylen eventually retired from the military as a lieutenant colonel, then committed suicide on October 12, 1947, after discovering that he had throat cancer. Muriel Lawford also sued Sir Sydney for divorce, both couples formally splitting within a year of May's giving birth to Peter in September 1923.

Peter later told a more dramatic story about his birth. He hated his mother, a vicious woman who ignored his education and his needs. He was raised throughout the world, barely literate yet a highly intelligent man, fluent in both English and French. His mother raised him as a girl for the first nine years of his life, and the photographs taken of him during this period look like an adorable female child of the flapper era.

When Peter was nine, his nanny taught him oral sex. Then she had a friend join her, and together they regularly used the boy.

May frequently ran from life, drinking heavily at times. She was quite clear about not wanting Peter and later claimed to have stopped having sex with the general after he was 62 and she was 44.

Peter was trained to have impeccable manners, to be polite,

and to be more involved with the adult world than with children his own age. He was always interested in acting and dancing, hating the idea of the military that had been his father's life.

Peter had his first professional acting role in the movie *Poor Old Bill,* which was released in 1931. Then, six years later, in the spring of 1937, while visiting France, Peter's career was almost ended when he accidentally put his arm through a window. He broke the glass, then jerked his hand back, cutting himself severely. Muscles and tendons were severed, and an artery was slashed. There was a chance he would die, though while his father was terrified for his health and anxious to get him to a hospital, his mother complained, "Couldn't you have done this another day, Peter? You knew I was dining out tonight."

The arm was saved, though Peter never again had real use of the arm or hand. He usually kept the hand in his pocket; when dancing on stage, he frequently looped his fingers into his belt, then used his left arm in a manner that made the gesture seem a natural part of the choreography.

After Peter's recovery, the family relocated to the United States, settling into an apartment in Los Angeles. But there were more financial reverses during this period, mostly because Sir Sydney was a sucker for bad investments. Among other schemes, he put money into a project to build houses from materials made from sugar beets. Eventually they moved to New York and then to Palm Beach, taking advantage of the kindness of relatives and socially prominent individuals who delighted in having a titled British couple in their midst.

Eventually, the Lawfords lost their curiosity value and had to move to West Palm Beach, the "wrong side of the tracks" in status-conscious Florida. Their new home was small and shabby, with leaking plumbing. May became despondent, then fueled her depression with excessive drinking. Peter had to take a job in a gas station, and later parked cars in a lot owned by Joe Kennedy. (Joe saw Peter playing poker with two black employees, and was outraged. He did not believe that a white boy should be involved with "niggers.")

It was the war that made Peter Lawford a star. Every able-bodied actor was going to be involved in some manner with the war effort after Pearl Harbor. This caused a desperate need for males over six feet tall who were ineligible for service. Peter, the right height, handsome, talented, with some experience, and with a useless arm, fit perfectly. He made his way to Hollywood and became part of the world of MGM.

Hollywood was where Peter Lawford came into his own with women. Handsome, muscular, an athletic surfboarder, he was also filled with self-loathing. He was unwanted by his mother, generally ignored by his much older father, molested by one of his caretakers, barely able to read and memorize scripts. Sex became a game, a reassurance, and an escape from the unpleasant realities of his life. He separated sex and love, frequently using sex as a part of friendships enjoyed both before and during his marriages.

No matter how destructive Peter became in his life, and his eventual intense use of drugs and alcohol would nearly destroy both his wives and his son, he maintained certain standards for his women. He wanted them intelligent, with a good sense of humor, knowledgeable about the world around them, and willing to have fun, whatever that meant at the moment. Looks were of secondary importance, as was a woman's wealth. Although Lady Lawford was concerned that Peter marry for money because life could bring financial setbacks otherwise, the wealth of a woman was not one of his criteria.

Peter first met Pat Kennedy in 1949 when both were attending a party in London. He had met Jack Kennedy five years earlier in Hollywood, though he had not been overly impressed with either the brother, the sister, or the family. They were just part of America's rich, no different than others he had known while in Florida.

For Pat Kennedy, Peter was a long-desired fantasy. She was an avid movie fan, had seen Peter's films, and was star struck. She also fit his ideal, being intelligent, tall, slender, not particularly attractive, but outgoing and friendly. She had attended convent schools, much to Peter's disgust, and then graduated from the private Rosemont College, a women's liberal arts school in Pennsylvania. Though Peter loved her, he later sarcastically remarked that waiting for her to say her prayers before they got into bed for sex was like trying to make love to the pope.

In 1952, both Pat and Peter attended the Republican National Convention. Pat claimed she was there as an "enemy observer." Peter, who had no interest in politics, was visiting Republican Henry Ford and went with him to see the show. While there, Pat kept making nasty remarks against the people giving speeches, while Peter would taunt her by taking the other side. He actually did not care but enjoyed baiting her, their arguments becoming heated, though only she was serious.

Pat and Peter had dinner together, Peter increasingly drawn to her. Intelligence and wit were aphrodisiacs for him, but they both went their separate ways after the convention.

There was another chance encounter, this one in Manhattan in November 1953. Pat was working in the television industry, and happened to be going grocery shopping when Peter passed her on the street. They had dinner together, then flew to Palm Beach where they were both spending the Christmas holidays, she at her family home, and he at the home of Henry Ford.

Joe Kennedy, recognizing that his daughter was in love with the British actor, had J. Edgar Hoover check on Peter's worthiness. Hoover's report indicated that Lawford frequently used prostitutes, a fact that delighted Joe. And when Peter, an Episcopalian, agreed to take instructions in the Catholic faith and to raise his children as Catholics, Rose felt he would be a good son-in-law. In fact, reading Peter's letters to his mother-in-law, it became obvious that Rose was probably closer to Peter than any of her other in-laws, especially Jacqueline.

When eventually reported to the press, the Kennedy/Lawford engagement made headlines throughout the country. Peter had a new, successful movie showing—"It Should Happen to You"—and where Peter was not well known, Joe Kennedy and Senator Jack Kennedy had great name recognition. May

Lawford was also interviewed, though she was quick to make clear that she was convinced the Kennedys were beneath Peter.

Pat and Peter married on April 24, 1954, at St. Thomas More's Church in Manhattan. The ten-minute ceremony attracted thousands of spectators outside the church because of the rich and famous guests present for the ceremony. But the marriage was an odd one from the start. The couple essentially led two separate lives for much of the time. He would travel on location and she would travel for pleasure. They maintained separate bedrooms because they felt they were too set in their ways to be comfortable sleeping together (though they did have sex). Peter paid for the mortgage on their home and part of the staff they maintained. Pat paid for their travel, food, utilities, part of the staff, and their parties. Peter was never allowed to know how much she was worth, though his ego was such that he began working more intensely in order to be better known than his wife.

Pat became pregnant four months after the wedding, and two months after that the couple rented a two-bedroom beach house in Malibu. (Ironically, it was a house that Joe Kennedy had used during his affair with Gloria Swanson.) Their first child, Christopher Kennedy Lawford, was born on March 29, 1955. Rose was visiting at the time, and she took charge of the child. When she left and Peter realized how demanding the baby was, he was extremely upset. To calm matters, Pat rented an apartment close by for Christopher and his nanny. They essentially divorced themselves from their son unless his presence was convenient.

Peter was having outside sexual relations almost from the start. He apparently was faithful at first, then became frustrated by Pat who had been a virgin at marriage and who seemed to view sex almost as a sacrament, not just a pleasurable experience. More important, as is common with adults who were sexually molested when young, Peter found "normal sex"— the missionary position—not particularly satisfying. What other couples might enjoy as a periodic variation became the norm for Peter. He longed for every variety, eventually using multiple partners and mechanical devices.

Pat suspected what was happening, and she began to hate Peter—not for the womanizing itself, but for the weakness of his character. She had married a handsome man whom she fantasized as being strong, always in control of life. That was the type of character he played in the movies, and she was naive enough to believe that was the way he really was.

The truth was that Peter was an extremely weak man. He was cowardly, and sought to avoid confrontation. He had no interest in the "killer" touch football games of the Kennedy family. He came to hate the younger brothers, though ultimately he loved Jack as the brother he never had. And the only in-law with whom he could relate was Jacqueline, the other outsider in the family. They became close friends, which further estranged him from his wife, who delighted in mocking her sister-in-law.

Jack and Peter quickly went "hunting" together, seeking women for casual sex. Peter was able to provide Jack with actresses in a way the young Robert Stack could not. And as Peter came to understand his brother-in-law's shyness, he was delighted to bring him together with whomever Jack desired.

Kennedy's first meeting with Marilyn Monroe occurred during the summer of 1954 when Peter arranged an invitation to a party at the home of agent Charles Feldman. Monroe, then married to Joe DiMaggio, was a guest, and Jack was fascinated by her. Nothing happened that evening, but both were strongly aware of one another, and Kennedy had the nerve to call her the next day. DiMaggio was home, though, and hung up on the young senator. Nothing happened between Kennedy and Monroe until after her divorce, and even then the relationship was slow in starting, confined mostly to meetings in New York when both happened to be there.

In order to understand the third generation of Kennedys, it is essential to look back at the high point of the family—the Kennedy presidency. Ask someone who came to adulthood during the early 1960s and you will hear of the time of myth and magic known as Camelot. You will hear of the White House as the culture capital of the world. You will hear talk of selfless giving, of strength in the face of international challenge, of civil rights advanced more than at any time since the Civil War, of love and glamor.

But ask specifically what happened, and the person usually will not know. There will be references to Reverend Martin Luther King Jr., to civil rights legislation, to relative peace in Vietnam, to leadership for all manner of causes. Yet when something concrete is mentioned, a closer look at the time usually reveals that it was the work of someone else—Lyndon Johnson, Hubert Humphrey, Dr. King, and so on.

John Kennedy never wanted to be involved with the Vietnam conflict, true believers will tell you. Dwight Eisenhower was the cause of that problem, having taken the war over from the French. And then came the terrible Lyndon Johnson, who also somehow created the horrible violence. Yet the truth was that Eisenhower committed 800 men to Vietnam. Kennedy, delighting in international intrigue, committed 25,000 men. And if Kennedy had lived, instead of damning Johnson with their chants, the peace demonstrators might have been marching outside the White House shouting, "Hey, hey, JFK, how many kids have you killed today!"

Kennedy, remembered as the great leader of the civil rights movement, did not consider it important to place blacks in positions of importance, nor would his brother Bob when he took control of the Justice Department. When running for the presidency, he promised to end housing segregation with the stroke of a pen. Eighteen months into his administration, progress was so slow that civil rights groups had their members mail thousands of pens to the White House.

As for the arts, popular myth has it that all culture stopped for the eight years of the Eisenhower administration. Ike liked Fred Waring and the Pennsylvanians. When the Kennedys moved into the White House, they had Pablo Casals and Leonard Bernstein in for gracious evenings of formal dress and classical music.

Yet under the Eisenhowers the arts flourished as much as they did under the Kennedys. Playwright Arthur Miller became internationally famous for such plays as *Death of a Salesman*. Leonard Bernstein composed some of his greatest work before the Kennedys came to the White House, his fame being the reason he was invited there. Frank Sinatra, who brought countless bobby soxers to vicarious orgasm after World War II, was, at first, the Kennedy equivalent of Fred Waring.

The Kennedys feted brother-in-law Peter Lawford, who was acting in light comedies and mysteries on television, work that was fun to watch but of limited import. Yet before Kennedy came to office, Rod Serling was writing brilliant dramas— *Requiem for a Heavyweight, Patterns,* etc.—for Kraft Theater. He was a brilliant playwright working in the medium of television, a pioneer in the arts.

Golf is remembered as the game of the Eisenhowers, yet Jack Kennedy enjoyed the game but refused to allow photographs of him playing. The image of Eisenhower leisurely strolling down a fairway was replaced by the violence of Kennedy cutthroat touch football.

It seems that everything that has shaped the third generation, including the transitional Kennedy, Ted, occurred because of the desperate attempt to create a White House that never was. And the often deadly desperation of the family, in what might be called the post-assassination years of the third generation, came from the perceived need to maintain the myths, to forever hide the truth.

Jack Kennedy was a "lightweight" in 1958, the year the national Democratic Party leaders recognized that he was the favorite for the 1960 presidential nomination. At least such was the opinion of the Democratic leaders within Kennedy's home state of Massachusetts. His voting record indicated frequent absences from the Senate, just as in the House of Representatives. He had no interest in social reforms, the economy, or international concerns. If anyone asked what John Kennedy stood for as a legislator, none of the men who knew him from his home state could have answered the question. Writers who tried to define Kennedy from the issues he had supported while in the House and Senate found that there was no set pattern. He was careful not to offend any large groups by supporting or opposing controversial programs.

Eleanor Roosevelt, a major figure in the Democratic Party, did not like Kennedy. She felt that Jack was trying to buy the nomination, for well before the convention Joe was using his money to have paid representatives in every state. Perhaps if Kennedy seemed independent of his father, Eleanor would have been more willing to take him seriously as a candidate worthy of support. She would have been more comfortable if he had shown the concerns for issues that Hubert Humphrey, another possible candidate, had revealed in recent years. In addition, she told an interviewer for *Look* magazine that she did not like Jack's unwillingness to speak out against Senator Joe McCarthy.

Kennedy was an intellectual lightweight as well, and under close scrutiny could not compare to the brilliant Adlai Stevenson, still a potential opponent. However, Ted Sorensen developed a brilliant strategy for countering this concern. In December 1958, Kennedy arranged for a meeting of what was called his "Academic Advisory Committee." This group, chosen by Sorensen, consisted of some of the most respected intellectuals, professors, and authors (John Kenneth Galbraith, Arthur Schlesinger Jr., Seymour Harris, and others) in the nation. The group was asked during the two years leading up to the election to prepare papers on public policy. The image was that not only had some of the best minds in the nation lined up behind Kennedy, but that they would also help him gain critical insight into the important issues facing the country.

Again the truth belied the image. The group's efforts proved meaningless and ineffective. They allegedly developed little that might seriously be used, and Kennedy ignored the majority of the suggestions that were practical. However, the association with the group made Kennedy seem both in their league and willing to use the best and brightest of America, and the image brought many former supporters of Stevenson into the Kennedy camp.

The future was fully plotted in 1959. Bob Kennedy was establishing his literary credentials with *The Enemy Within* (written with John Seigenthaler), which would set the tone for the future Kennedy administration's attacks against organized crime. And at the same time, the family, working under Joe's direction, was planning for Jack's taking the presidency in the 1960 election.

The importance of organized crime in what would become the Kennedy White House cannot be overstated. It was a factor in the relationship of FBI Director J. Edgar Hoover and the Kennedy brothers. It was a factor in the assassination. It was a factor in foreign policy. And it was a factor in determining Joe Kennedy's ongoing influence and credibility with former associates on both sides of the law

The full story behind the Kennedy brothers' war against the mob will never be known. Many of the organized criminals who had known Joe Kennedy during the Prohibition era liked him and hated his sons, a reaction ironically similar to J. Edgar Hoover's feelings. Other members of organized crime came to work with the brothers, such as Sam Giancana, whom the Kennedys used when they wanted to attack Fidel Castro, and with whom Jack Kennedy shared a mistress.

Organized crime activities gave the Kennedy brothers high profile coming into the 1960 campaign, but behind-the-scenes efforts were being made to utilize organized crime figures to support Jack's race. The reports have been slow in coming over the years, some supplied by Judith Exner in both her book *My Story* (written with Ovid Demaris) and her extensive interview with Kitty Kelley for the February 29, 1988, issue of *People* magazine. Others came from organized crime figures and their families, including Sam and Chuck Giancana's book *Double Cross,* statements by the son of Albert Anastasia, the book *Mafia Princess: Growing Up in Sam Giancana's Family,* written by Antoinette Giancana and Thomas Renner, as well as other sources.

What is known about this time is that, on February 7, 1960, Frank Sinatra introduced Judith Campbell (later Judith Campbell Exner) to Jack Kennedy. They were at the Sands Hotel, and Campbell was known among entertainment figures as a "starfucker." She was enamored with the glamorous men in show business, politics, and the underworld, and would do almost anything to be in their presence. She was a beautiful woman, bright, and sexually available to men in the right circle. In addition to Sinatra and Kennedy, these men included organized crime figure Sam Giancana.

While it is common for Hollywood stars to be connected with political candidates today, the relationship was not so common in the late 1950s. The idea that the most popular stars of the day would endorse a candidate, would sometimes travel with him, would lend the power of their fame to his efforts to achieve office, was new. Kennedy was the first candidate to use Hollywood on a grand scale, and his children, nieces, and nephews would perpetuate this relationship on a personal level. John Kennedy Jr. has frequently dated actresses and entertainers ranging from Daryl Hannah to Madonna. Maria Shriver married actor Arnold Schwarzenegger in addition to becoming a television personality in her own right. Christopher Lawford abandoned plans for a career as a lawyer to become an actor. And most Kennedy-sponsored events include actors and other entertainers as hosts or window dressing.

Giancana arranged for Kennedy to have every sensuous experience he could have in Las Vegas. Kennedy was given a suite of rooms, free gambling, free food, and beautiful women. Sinatra agreed to produce a campaign song for Kennedy. The introduction to Campbell seemed another part of the experience. The fact that she was the same type of beauty that Jacqueline had become also intrigued Kennedy. He did not realize that he was being drawn into a world that was setting him up for everything his new found criminal "friends" could gain.

The first mob arrangement was helping assure Kennedy primary victories prior to the 1960 Democratic National Convention. Meetings between Sam Giancana and Joe and Jack Kennedy led to an agreement mentioned in *Double Cross:* "I told Skinny [Skinny D'Amato, manager of the Cal-Neva Lodge, in which Sinatra was an investor] to tell Joe that I'll take care of West Virginia on one condition—that after Jack's President, Joe Adonis is allowed back in the country. The guys out east want Adonis back. Jack and his old man couldn't say yes fast enough . . . didn't have any problem at all bringin' a deported gangster back into the country. So we've got a deal for West Virginia."

In the national campaign, it was arranged for the Teamsters Union to back Kennedy, though not publicly. Again Giancana was quoted as saying, "I've already got it worked out with Jimmy to skim a couple million out of the union for Jack's national campaign, based on Kennedy's agreement that Bobby will leave Hoffa and the Teamsters alone."

During the national election pitting Kennedy against Richard Nixon, coordinators of the Kennedy Illinois activities included Sinatra (according to the Giancanas) and Richard Daley, the powerful Chicago mayor long involved with Giancana. The voter turnout was excellent, with large numbers of patriotic citizens making frequent use of the ballot boxes. They cast their ballots at polling place after polling place.

Hard-edged machine politics was also used in Chicago. As in the campaigns that John Fitzgerald ran in turn-of-the-century Boston, Giancana placed thugs outside polling places in the wards he controlled to alert the people going inside that they were to vote for Jack Kennedy. Anyone who challenged the system was beaten as a warning to friends. Finally, the election count was rigged to add even more Kennedy votes. These efforts turned out to be essential, as Kennedy defeated Nixon in Illinois by only 9,000 votes.

Besides this kind of help, the entire Kennedy family was put into action during the campaign. All the sisters traveled and made appearances. Jack's family seemed to be an extension of himself, an advantage he had over Nixon. If Jack himself could not make an appearance, many people thought they were having the same experience when they met with Pat or Ethel, Eunice or Jean, Bob or Rose.

Jacqueline also actively involved herself, though without traveling because she was seventh months pregnant with John Jr. Whatever support she gave was critical in case the press remembered Jack's callous actions toward her in 1956 following the Democratic convention. Jacqueline was having difficulty carrying a baby to term. She had miscarried their first year of marriage, and in 1956 she was eight months pregnant when Jack decided to take a vacation in France at his father's villa. He traveled with his friend George Smathers, Democratic senator from Florida, and several women, leaving Jacqueline at home.

This second pregnancy also ended tragically, Jacqueline undergoing an emergency cesarean section. The baby was still-born and Jacqueline was in such serious condition that a priest had to be called. Jack was notified in France that his child was dead and his wife was in critical condition, but he did not seem to care. His attitude was that everything was over, his wife was being attended to, so why not enjoy himself? Even the tolerant Smathers was appalled. Cheating on a wife was one thing; abandoning her when she was in danger of dying and emotionally overwrought was quite another. He insisted they return, which they did three days after they were alerted. The press was given the story that Kennedy had been unreachable at sea, and only a few newspapers chastised him for his absence at such a critical time in his wife's pregnancy. There was no hint of the emotional estrangement, though alert reporters might have made the connection if Jacqueline was not involved in the run for the presidency.

The answer was for Jacqueline to make radio and television appearances, record messages in four of the languages in which she was fluent, and to write a newspaper column. She also adopted in public the attitude that would be most in line with 1950s thinking when describing her role in the family. She said that her primary duty was to create a smoothly running household and to create an environment for her husband that would enable him to be as effective as possible in service to the country. She also portrayed herself as a full-time mother, working alone to raise their daughter, Caroline. She did not mention that Maud Shaw, the live-in nurse, handled the child-rearing. Nor did she mention the intense efforts of Mary Gallagher, her secretary, implying that she handled her mail herself.

As usual, if there was a Kennedy family disappointment during the elections, it was Ted. He was assigned thirteen states, mostly in the West and Southwest. But at twenty-eight, he had little understanding of what to do or how to do it. The Southwest was an area where any Kennedy would have had trouble. Arizona, for example, was as insular a state as the Kennedys were a family. It was the last mainland territory, its statehood little more than three decades old. It was dominated politically by a handful of families—primarily the Babbitts, Goldwaters, DeConcinis, Rosenzweigs, and Funks. Population was limited, and the vast majority of the land was either protected wilderness or Indian reservations. The political deals were based on friendships gained in high schools and on softball teams sponsored by the businesses of the early families. The alliances crossed party lines, but the people were more in tune with Nixon than with Kennedy. When Ted campaigned the way he would in New England, passing out *PT 109* tie clips, singing "Sweet Adeline" to Anglos and "Jalisco" to Hispanics, shaking hands, and talking in his Boston accent, few cared. The people were not impressed with him or the Kennedys, and ten Southwestern states in Ted's trust went solidly for Nixon.

The election returns showed Kennedy with 49.7 percent of the popular vote, Nixon with 49.6 percent. Neither candidate could convince even half the people that he was the better man. But that did not matter to the Kennedys. Once again one of their own had won, and this time it was the biggest prize of all—the country.

* * *

The post-election period was one of personal turmoil. As was becoming routine, Jack left his very pregnant wife in order to be in Palm Beach right after Thanksgiving. Jacqueline was going to deliver their second child, John Jr., by cesarean section and wanted her husband present. He chose not to be, then discovered his wife needed an emergency delivery within hours of his leaving. She was rushed to the hospital with a priest, and though she would be fine, his new son was not well and it was thought that he might die within hours or days. This time, as president-elect, Jack had the sense to return immediately to Washington.

When the crisis was over, the Eisenhowers gave Jacqueline a tour of the White House, and the president gave Jack more intense briefings on the international situation, the nation, and the ways in which the government operated. It was a time when the outgoing couple and the incoming new first family found they truly disliked each other. Jacqueline hated the furnishings of the White House as well as the way sections had fallen into disrepair. Eisenhower held all three Kennedy brothers in disdain, saw Jack Kennedy as having a relatively meaningless Senate record, and felt that the victory was the result of Joe Kennedy's money. Eisenhower wondered if Kennedy could comprehend the balance of payments problems, the bureaucracy, Cuba, and similar areas. Likewise, Kennedy wondered if the outgoing president had such comprehension, finding him shallow. Later Kennedy would comment to Peter Lawford that his greatest shock upon taking office was discovering that the country was in as bad a shape as he had been saying.

There were also days of trying to fill key cabinet posts and other high-level jobs—1,200 in all. Blacks were never seriously considered, though the name of William Dawson, a respected congressman, was mentioned to the press so they would think that blacks had a chance. Those who were sought were white, mixed by region and religion, brilliant in their fields, and totally loyal to the Kennedys.

Jack Kennedy's White House staff set the tone for the men and women who would work for Bob and Ted, and for Joe II when the third generation started in politics. In every instance, the first criterion was loyalty. The closer someone came to the seat of power, the more they were exposed to the weakness of the person in that position. Kennedy had no vision for the world. He had no vision for America. The Secret Service agents derisively talked of his early period as being a 10 A.M.-to-2 P.M. presidency, the rest of the time devoted to pursuits of the flesh. And while the statement was an exaggeration, he was not dedicated to guiding or shaping the nation. Thus, the top men often were individuals without passion or ideology who could get work done effectively and with the least fuss. They were not typical bureaucrats, and they cared nothing for the chain of command. Bob Kennedy, in his role as attorney general, might call an FBI agent working in the field for a report rather than contacting J. Edgar Hoover or a high-ranking supervisor, as would better fit with established protocol.

Among the intellectuals chosen for involvement in the inner circle, Kennedy preferred those who would work with blinders, recording the glories and the heroism, not the flaws of the leader. The brilliant Arthur Schlesinger Jr. became what might be called court historian, ultimately producing books on both Jack and Bob that ignore all flaws of character. That the limitations of some of what was written can be shown just by a visit to the files of the Kennedy Library is unimportant. His books were so rich in detail, so eminently readable, that it would seem impossible that anything could be omitted. Yet others with similar skill but a certain amount of distance, such as author John H. Davis, a cousin of Jacqueline, were kept at arm's length. Such men were dangerous in that they could not be controlled, would balk at blinders, had no sense of editing for the president's desires and sensibilities.

The inauguration took place on January 20, 1961, at 12:51 P.M. Ironically the aggressive attitude of the speech that day was in sharp contrast with the attitude of the one American who understood war, politics, and business better than anyone in power at the time. Dwight Eisenhower, the general who had led the Allied forces to victory in the European theater during World War II, before becoming president of the United States, was wary of the power of the "military-industrial complex." He was concerned that the economy and the nation would be controlled by the wants of the ever-growing armed forces and the billion-dollar businesses that supplied the equipment needed by the military. He saw the need for a change to an economy based on peacetime concerns.

Kennedy, on the other hand, seemed to welcome the possibility of having to use force at the same time that he called for an international reduction of arms. "Let the word go forth from this time and place, to friend and foe alike, that the torch has been passed to a new generation of Americans—born in this century, tempered by war, disciplined by a hard and bitter peace, proud of our ancient heritage—and unwilling to witness or permit the slow undoing of those human rights to which this nation has always been committed, and to which we are committed today at home and around the world," Kennedy stated.

"Let every nation know, whether it wishes us well or ill, that we shall pay any price, bear any burden, meet any hardship, support any friend, oppose any foe, to assure the survival and the success of liberty."

As he came to the end of that inaugural address he added, "Now the trumpet summons us again—not as a call to bear arms, though arms we need—not as a call to battle, though embattled we are—but as a call to bear the burden of a long twilight struggle, year in and year out, 'rejoicing in hope, patient in tribulation'—a struggle against the common enemies of man: tyranny, poverty, disease, and war itself.

"In the long history of the world, only a few generations have been granted the role of defending freedom in its hour of maximum danger. I do not shrink from this responsibility—I welcome it. I do not believe that any of us would exchange places with any other people or any other generation. The energy, the faith, the devotion which we bring to this endeavor will light our country and all who serve it—and the glow from that fire can truly light the world.

"And so, my fellow Americans: ask not what your country can do for you—ask what you can do for your country."

In context, the most quoted of statements was actually a call to sacrifice in war as well as peace. It was more pugnacious than reflecting a future of caring and sharing among the people of all nations. And it is this fact that has helped create the odd legacy of the Kennedy years.

Before briefly looking at a handful of the key issues in Kennedy's brief term as president, issues that would have impact into the third generation, it is important to try to understand the Kennedy era legacy.

John Kennedy was killed before he completed his first term in office. Nothing in the Kennedy legacy is more important to remember than that fact. He became a mythic figure who was granted a future of reverential respect he possibly otherwise never would have experienced.

Name a social or international problem of the decade that followed and you are likely to hear, "Had Kennedy lived, he would have done . . ." Civil rights? International affairs? Poverty? The economy? Whatever the concern, there is frequently the belief that somehow, with Kennedy, life would have been different.

The war in Vietnam was the result of Lyndon Johnson, according to many Americans, even though John Kennedy escalated American involvement more than thirtyfold after he took office. The most sweeping civil rights legislation in history was created and pushed through Congress by Lyndon Johnson. Kennedy, by contrast, was inundated with pens after failing to keep his election promise to end discrimination in federally supported housing with the stroke of a pen. Kennedy was supposedly for peace, yet he created the greatest number of covert operations against governments he did not like, including encouraging assassination attempts against foreign leaders.

Kennedy was the man who represented the values of traditional families—large, loving, boisterous, and monogamous. Yet he was an adulterer who engaged in sex with the devotion of an aerobics addict.

The glory that now adorns the Kennedy era is a world filtered through sycophants, totally dedicated aides, and writers who were so proud to be touched by closeness with the White House that they overlook or deliberately ignore anything that is negative. Yet the opposite is also true. Kennedy was neither amoral nor evil incarnate during his administration. His often serious mistakes must be viewed in context with what was happening in the nation at the time.

The administration of President John Kennedy represented the image of hope that had not existed since the Great Depression. Bob Kennedy did not want to have Dr. Martin Luther King Jr. and other civil rights leaders embarrassing his brother through the massive March on Washington and similar events. White House and Justice Department support came only after it became clear that anger over past abuses and the desire to change were so strong that they could not be denied. Demand for reform, the willingness to die for such fundamental rights as the chance to vote, and efforts to create equality of opportunity in education, business, and where people could live developed because many Americans viewed the Kennedys as providing the moral and spiritual leadership for such change. In truth, the Kennedy brothers were followers, the legacy of a domineering, manipulative father who allowed his children the freedom to do and be whatever he wanted. The formerly disenfranchised and underrepresented Americans who stood together to demand what others considered basic freedoms were the leaders of that era.

Many Americans found courage within themselves because of the support they perceived they were experiencing from the Oval Office. In truth, leadership was like a train running backwards, the endless line of cars dragging forward the engine they thought was powering their movement.

Would Kennedy have changed if he had lived? Would he

have supplied the social leadership seen in the actions of Lyndon Johnson? No one knows. If Jack Kennedy's brother, Bob, is any indicator, the first sign of personal change came only after he witnessed the aftermath of riots in the Bedford Stuyvesant section of New York City. But fantasy hindsight is not important.

The legacy of Jack Kennedy's term was the sense of strong spiritual, moral, and personal leadership in the White House. Anything was possible. Wrongs could be righted. The common person uplifted. Morality would triumph. The individual would regain self-respect. The arts would flourish. The nation was becoming a center for all that was good, pure, decent, and uplifting, a beacon light of history illuminating the best and the brightest.

Not that the reality matched the legacy. Lyndon Johnson took office with civil rights promises unfulfilled, with families and the nation almost as divided over the Vietnam War as it had been with the Civil War. The first amendment freedoms of those who criticized the administration, especially critics from the entertainment field, were being challenged through subtle reduction of the opportunities for men like Mort Sahl to be able to work. And issues of due process in the courts were abandoned in the pursuit of major career criminals, no one recognizing that the loss of rights for one segment of society eventually could affect the rights for all segments of society.

Yet the memory remains a call to change. The memory remains an image of the best and the brightest. The memory has encouraged politicians of both political parties to try to link themselves to the image (never the all too human reality) of Jack Kennedy.

The truth of this time is not yet known. Jack Kennedy liked to tape-record his White House conversations. It was something that Franklin Roosevelt had done, and the equipment had long been in place. The reasons for the actions were unclear when it came to Kennedy. Were they to be a memory device when he wrote his memoirs? Were they to be used for blackmail if someone present lied about actions taken or not taken, planned or ignored? Did he, like J. Edgar Hoover, view information as power and tried to gather as much as possible, even if there was no use for it in the foreseeable future? It is now known that the Kennedy brothers occasionally kept files on their enemies, including Hoover, to neutralize blackmail efforts.

No one knows, and many of the men present, as well as the apologists who tried to create a more innocent Kennedy presidency, were shocked to learn that 325 tapes exist from this period. They are all in the Kennedy Library, but the vast majority are not available to the public.*

Yet the aftermath of the Bay of Pigs fiasco was the greatest clue to the attitude of the Kennedy White House. An immediate study into the expansion of guerrilla warfare in other countries was ordered. How could such actions be improved, expanded, and more effectively utilized in the future? At no time was the moral issue of whether or not such covert actions against sovereign governments should be continued ever debated. Covert action had an excitement to it that was addicting to Jack

*The Kennedy Library, just outside Boston, serves many functions. As with most presidential libraries, it provides largely partisan resources for research. To use the facilities of the Kennedy Library and not material in the Franklin Roosevelt Library is to get an incomplete picture of Joe Kennedy's activities, for example. But it also is surprisingly filled with documents, tape transcripts, and other material that reveals what might be called the darker side of Camelot. Pro-Kennedy writers often point to the fact of its existence, on file in a library where researchers are permitted, as proof that the Kennedys are not trying to hide facts about the era. However, the truth is that the existence of the materials does not mean that they can be used. They have not been destroyed, it is true, but they are often sealed until a date in the future when the second generation, at least, can be presumed to be dead and thus safe from embarrassment. Other papers and tapes require special permission to review. The special permission has, so far as is currently known, never been provided to anyone who is not a strong partisan.

Kennedy, America's most disabled president when he took office. The fact that it was in violation of numerous international treaties was not important. Like his fictional hero James Bond, he just had to make certain he was not caught.

It was easy to justify the Bay of Pigs by arguing that Kennedy supported self-determination and Cuba was a dictatorship, yet that belied two facts. The first was that, at the time of the Bay of Pigs, Castro maintained strong support within Cuba despite his strong arm tactics. He was still less corrupt and more concerned with the welfare of the nation than Batista, and there was no person available offering superior leadership potential. He may have been a bad lot, but he was better than the previous "bad lot," and the nation was still in a rather rocky honeymoon stage with their leader.

The second was that decisions as whether or not to take covert actions were based on whether or not the leader of a country was positively involved with the United States. There were "good" dictators and "bad" dictators by this double standard, never openly expressed, yet obvious in the actions taken. If we had a strong trading partner, a favorable arrangement for a military base, friends in a strategic location, or some other benefit, there was no criticism of an equally totalitarian ruler. Castro made the mistake of not honoring Joseph Kennedy following the revolution that removed both Meyer Lansky and Batista, and he also looked to Russia for financial aid when the United States cut him off. Those actions made him a "bad" dictator.

In addition to failing to review the moral aspects of such covert operations, Kennedy failed to understand what went wrong. He blamed the Central Intelligence Agency instead of looking to the fact that Bissell and others involved with the project had ignored the agency's own internal analysis *before* Kennedy authorized it. The director had tried to make clear that intelligence reports indicated that the only strong hostility to Castro was within the exile community in Miami. The people living in Cuba supported Castro. There would be no popular uprising because the leader was popular.

Robert Kennedy was encouraged to move to the CIA, letting others run the Justice Department, but that idea, conceived by Jack, met with too great a hostile response from more level heads. Instead, Bob Kennedy, working with Gen. Maxwell Taylor, became part of the counterinsurgency organization called Special Group CI (Counter Insurgency). Playing off Jack's love of manly action regardless of the law or the realities of international politics, CI created guerrilla warfare groups such as the Special Forces. Vietnam would be the training ground for such new approaches to action.

CI also helped train Latin American leaders in preventing revolution within. This assured close relations with "good" dictators who later were found to use torture and other oppressive measures to assure their control. Counterinsurgency experts became the most important players in the way Kennedy perceived the new military, and they were shown to best advantage in Vietnam.

The only action apparently approved by Jack Kennedy but to which Bob was hostile was what was called Operation Mongoose. This was the renewed effort to murder Castro. Bob Kennedy was apparently comfortable with the plot's existence, but became angry when he learned, in May 1962, that Giancana and Rosselli were still an integral part of the plot. He remained serious about prosecuting the Mafia, despite his father's past, his brother's help during the election, and the general family attitude that they were too helpful to destroy. Bob did not want government action that would prevent his special Justice Department units from destroying organized crime in the United States.

Lyndon Johnson, who stopped many of the excesses of secret operations after he took office, including ending Operation Mongoose, was convinced that Castro organized the assassination of Jack Kennedy. Johnson, in interviews with the press, including ABC Television news veteran Howard K. Smith, stressed his outrage over what he called "a damn Murder Incorporated in the Caribbean" sponsored by the Kennedy brothers. He was convinced that the murder was a retaliation by Castro.

Unlike the dozens of assassination books on the market and continually going to press, this book is not concerned with who killed Jack Kennedy. The only concern is how it affected the Kennedy image and the impact on the third generation. However, when the authors were researching this book, as well as other books each had written, including on Peter Lawford and the Teamsters/Mafia connection, several stories emerged. Johnson blamed Fidel Castro, and there appears to have been a contract against Kennedy in retaliation for the Kennedy effort to murder Castro.

Likewise, there was a Mafia contract against Jack Kennedy for his turning against the men who had helped him over the years. He had long made himself vulnerable to the mob, yet he tried to both utilize and simultaneously destroy major organized criminals. The Mafia has long maintained that a man must be all honest or all dishonest. Someone who walks the line in between, being honest or dishonest as it suits his purpose, is a man who will be deemed undeserving of respect.

A third contract was allegedly placed by lower level members of the Teamsters Union seeking to avenge Bob Kennedy's endless attempts to destroy Jimmy Hoffa. The death of Kennedy was to be a gift to Hoffa, who allegedly became irate when he learned such an assassination was contemplated. At the same time, men close to Hoffa felt that he was also planning his own murder, or at least talking about it seriously enough that it was thought that had Kennedy not been killed in Dallas, Hoffa might have paid for an attempt at a later time.

And Peter Lawford's notes indicate that the Kennedy family thought the murder was orchestrated by two extremely wealthy Dallas businessmen who felt a personal grudge against the president's attitude towards their work. This belief was bolstered by information placing everyone originally considered in some way involved with the murder of Kennedy or its aftermath—Lee Harvey Oswald, Jack Ruby, David Ferrie, and others—in the building from which the businessmen worked. And they were there within two weeks of the assassination.

John H. Davis presents yet one more case, and his is probably the most accurate. Davis did not just focus on the discrepancies of the Warren Report, an extremely incomplete document from a committee denied access to critical FBI records and other information available in 1963 and 1964. Instead of working to disprove or challenge anyone, he looked at the people who had been involved with the Kennedys over two decades to see who would care to murder the president. He interviewed men such as New Orleans organized crime leader Carlos Marcello, had access to the second major congressional investigation into the assassination that was conducted in 1978, and was able to truly explore all mob connections. He discovered that the assassination almost certainly was coordinated by Marcello, possibly working with current or former CIA men—though those men were not necessarily working under CIA orders. Men who have worked with Marcello confirm what Davis discovered, and though they were not privy to plans to kill the president, they felt that since all the other facts were accurate, the conclusion is logical. For the full story, see Davis's book *Mafia Kingfish*.

Unfortunately a full investigation was never ordered by Bob Kennedy into any of these possibilities, or any others. The Warren Commission acted, of course, but the Kennedy Justice Department did not. Dirty little secrets had to be protected, and it was better to let the investigation focus on one of the participants, the man with the rifle, then to look to others who might have been involved.

Such an attitude was not challenged by J. Edgar Hoover, who was not yet ready to admit that organized crime existed in America. Hoover was only comfortable with the idea of a Communist conspiracy, and since Oswald had been a Marine Corps defector living in Russia for a while, it was easy to justify the limited investigation. It was never mentioned at the time that Hoover deliberately suppressed the evidence of organized crime activities. Knowledge of Marcello and the others existed, but it was not made available to investigators.

* * *

The only problem during this period that did not become a family concern was Jack Kennedy's drug use. He had always been intrigued by the recreational drugs in which Peter Lawford indulged. Before he was in the White House, the two men occasionally enjoyed one or another chemical together. After Kennedy was president, though, Peter fought his brother-in-law's experimentation. For example, one of the more popular drugs at the time was butyl nitrate. It gave a flush and a high, and Kennedy wanted to try some. Lawford, refusing to allow such a thing, instead gave the drug to two women who were Kennedy hangers-on. They had been adoring fans whom Kennedy took into his entourage, giving them meaningless secretarial chores. One worked for Evenly Lincoln, the other for Pierre Salinger. Both, though college graduates and probably qualified for meaningful work, served primarily for presidential amusement. The Secret Service nicknamed them "Fiddle (21 years old)" and "Faddle (23 years old)," and Kennedy was fascinated by watching them on the floor, reacting to the drug.

There were women who talked about sharing drugs with Kennedy, especially marijuana, while he was in the White House. One talked about their joking that he would be high when he had to launch missiles against Russia. However, Lawford, more experienced than Kennedy, tried to induce some controls when he was present.

The most serious drug problem was with the shots that Dr. Max Jacobson ("Dr. Feelgood" according to both the press and some of his clients) had been giving Jack Kennedy since the fall of 1960. The primarily amphetamine combination of drugs acted as a pain-killing stimulant, artificial "high," and stay awake drug. When Clem David Heymann interviewed Ruth Mosse, the nurse who worked for Jacobson, for his book *A Woman Named Jackie,* he quoted the nurse as saying:

"Max was totally off the wall. When he gave an injection he would just spill the contents of his medical bag on the table and rummage around amid a jumble of unmarked bottles and nameless chemicals until he found what he was looking for. . . . Max was out of his mind. He would see 30 patients or more a day. He worked 24 hours a day, sometimes for days on end. He was a butcher. Blood was splattered all over his whites. That's why when they came to pick him up for Jackie, we would make him change. And because he was injecting himself with the stuff, his speech often became slurred. It was difficult to understand him at times. My father, who was a psychiatrist, made me quit the job because he feared that Max might begin to inject me.''

By 1961, both Jack and Jacqueline were addicted to the amphetamine portion of the drugs, which also contained steroids. However, all Kennedy cared was that he could function in ways that were not previously possible. He used Jacobson's service during the missile crisis, during the period of the Bay of Pigs, and when he went to talk with Nikita Khrushchev in Moscow. What impact the drugs may have had on his thought process is unknown. What mattered to Kennedy was that, despite the Addison's, the pain from his back, and the jet lag caused by the time difference between Washington and Moscow, he was able to function nonstop. He gave the press and the Soviets the appearance of youthful vigor. In reality, his health was being dangerously jeopardized.

It was on December 19, 1961, before Jack had faced a full year of crises and responsibilities, before Ted had joined the Senate, before Bob had faced the full weight of civil rights issues as attorney general, that the unthinkable came to pass. Joe Kennedy, seventy-three years of age, seemingly healthy, and vigorous enough to be playing an active game of golf in Palm Beach, had a stroke. He was with his niece, Ann Gargan, who had long been devoted to him. The nieces and nephews had received much of Joe's largess with few of the expectations that drove his children. He had paid for their college educations, for example, an unusual act of generosity that was generally ignored by the public.

Ann put Joe to bed, then immediately alerted Rose. In the Kennedys, the power of the first generation was so great that it was to whichever one was present that everyone turned in an emergency. Joe or Rose would be called before a doctor because seemingly their knowledge was greater. Perhaps more to the point, their wrath would be terrifying if a decision was made with which they disagreed. In this case, Rose felt Joe just needed rest. Four hours later, when the seriousness of Joe's condition was apparent to everyone, an ambulance was called to take him to the hospital. Rose, who by then hated her husband and no longer cared whether he lived or died, played a game of golf, then went swimming before bothering to stop by the hospital.

Joe's right side was fully paralyzed, he could not speak, and he required life support equipment to such a degree that the family had to decide whether or not to keep him alive. A priest delivered last rites, but Bob insisted that his father be allowed to fight for his life with the support equipment.

Joe would never really recover. The elder Kennedy developed pneumonia, blockage, and had to have a tracheotomy, yet he rallied. Some portion of his brain was lost forever, and his motor skills were severely affected.

Joe Kennedy came home in a wheelchair. His face was distorted, and he had no control over the right side of his mouth as he ate, drool dribbling down his chin. He could make sounds that were variations of *yes* and *no,* and he regularly attempted to write instructions for his staff with his left hand.

In the weeks that followed Joe seemed to have a mind that was still strong, and a body that was out of control. Family members read to him and talked about things that made him laugh, always in appropriate places, showing them that he understood what they were saying. Jack, who had to use a cane much of the time due to his back problems, knew to hide the cane from his father, not to spare him the sight of an ailing son but to avoid his wrath for showing weakness. Joe attacked anyone in sight with whom he disagreed, using verbal and as much physical violence as his limited movements allowed.

Rose wanted nothing to do with her husband. She bought the black mourning dress she would need when he died, then made Ann Gargan Joe's primary caretaker, including giving her responsibility for the nurses. She threw Joe away in the same manner she had thrown away Rosemary so many years before. The idea of Joe dying was not just accepted, it was almost eagerly anticipated. The man who had been a philandering embarrassment had become a nuisance. When he lingered enough years to see both Jack and Bob killed by assassins' bullets and Ted disgraced at Chappaquiddick, Rose frequently commented that she wished Bob had lived and Joe had died.

The stroke also resulted in estrangement between Joe and his grandchildren. They were too young to understand what had happened to their grandfather. He was a distorted figure, looking like something from a horror movie rather than the vibrant old man they saw at family gatherings. Joe seemed desperately to want their closeness, and the fear that they obviously felt in his presence caused him deep anguish.

The second generation of Kennedys was suddenly without their leader. He was alive, yet his pleasure or displeasure no longer mattered very much. He could no longer be consulted on matters of money, politics, world affairs, or anything else. The stroke created a situation that might be likened to what would happen in a zoo where animals, raised their entire lives in close confinement, suddenly were uncaged. Freedom of choice would be exciting, intriguing, and terrifying. They were not equipped for such a life.

On November 22, 1963, while on a political trip to Dallas, Texas, President John Fitzgerald Kennedy was assassinated at the age of forty-six. Cynics have called the death the most brilliant political moves the family could have made. By not having to face reelection, by not having to defend his administration's record, by not being called accountable for the civil rights failings, the more than thirtyfold increase in troops in Vietnam, and the other actions Americans later unfairly attacked Lyndon Johnson for creating, John Kennedy became a mythic hero. Bigger than life, more heroic than any politician before or since, compassionate for all, he was an American superhero who could bleed and die, but whose noble stands represented the best and brightest of the new generation.

The images of Kennedy's funeral added to the impact. There was Jacqueline, tall, strong, dressed in black, refusing to weep in public yet obviously enduring almost unbearable grief. There was John Kennedy Jr.—"John-John" to the American public—a small boy in his best coat, saluting the passing casket bearing his father's corpse. There was Bob Kennedy, strong, sure, at his sister-in-law's side, determined to carry on regardless of the forces of evil.

Robert Kennedy, the attorney general of the United States, dared not open an investigation into his brother's murder because of the dirty little family secrets that would be revealed. No matter who was behind the assassination, the Kennedy relations with the Mafia, vote fraud, legal violations in order to attack the Teamsters, and so many other problems would come out. If J. Edgar Hoover had been pressured enough, there was a chance he would even release some or all of his private files that would add jealous husbands to the list of people who might want Jack Kennedy dead.

It was better to limit what was known, to control the damage, to pay the unexpected price of winning, even at the cost of revenge. And Bob Kennedy was a man who wanted revenge almost as much as he wanted to be president.

Robert Kennedy went on to become senator from New York, a stepping stone to the presidency, which he sought in 1968. He was the heir apparent, his appeal to the young who saw him as their leader. Yet whether or not he had been changed remained to be proven by his actions, not by fantasizing in hindsight.

During interviews in Boston, several men who knew and supported Bob Kennedy's run indicated that New York City's

Bedford-Stuyvesant riots in 1967 changed his understanding of black America. The riots, among several that occurred in New York's black neighborhoods in the mid- to late-1960s, might have revealed frustration to him, but whether or not they suddenly gave Kennedy an understanding of the problems of low-income American minorities is not known. However, his friends say that he stopped being someone who had all the answers, and became someone who asked a lot of questions.

The nation was never to learn how this change might have affected it. Once again, on June 5, 1968, as Bob's son David watched live television coverage from one of the Los Angeles Ambassador Hotel rooms, a Kennedy was murdered.*

*Members of organized crime families, when interviewed about the matter, often claim that Bob Kennedy was killed by the Mafia as, they claim, Jack was. This cannot be discounted since the Mafia may have used a fanatical political partisan to achieve their desires. However, the Kennedy assassinations have probably become Mafia myths, or stories told to impress people with the power of the Mafia. A story repeated by men connected with mob figures in the Bonnano, Genovese, and Gambino families tells of the Mafia having Jack and Bob Kennedy assassinated because of what they did to Jimmy Hoffa. Then, the story goes, a representative went to see Ted Kennedy. He was told that, because he was too young to have been involved with his brothers' fight against Hoffa, he would be left alone so long as he stayed a senator. However, because he was still a brother, his punishment was to be an emotional one. He knew, as they did, that he had a good chance to become president if he ran for the office. However, his penalty was to be the knowledge that if he ran and won, he would be murdered like Bob and Jack. Thus, he could only stay alive by not running. For an ambitious man, this would be painful knowledge to be carried all his life.

6

DAVID KENNEDY: THE THIRD GENERATION'S FIRST TRAGEDY

The only exception to the family's habit of rallying around one of their own had been with David, the third son of Robert Kennedy. David was a weak link in the constricting Kennedy family chain—the unwanted Kennedy, the throwaway child, the addict who overdosed on drugs partially supplied, it is believed by some of the Kennedy household staff, by one of his cousins in a misguided attempt to help him.

It took Robert Kennedy twenty-six hours to die after he was struck down by an assassin's bullets. It took his son, David, sixteen years to die after that event. The first tragedy was perhaps unavoidable, being due to the actions of a man bent on destroying what he thought was an enemy of the Arab people. The other tragedy might not have occurred had the Kennedy family been able to nurture one another.

The full relationship between Bob Kennedy and his family is one that can only be guessed at. He seemed closer to his wife than any of the other second-generation Kennedy men were to theirs, yet he cheated on Ethel with some frequency. It is certain that he had an affair with Marilyn Monroe, had sex with her the day she committed suicide, and may have contemplated leaving Ethel for Marilyn after he entered the White House. (The Kennedy brothers had long been taught to think ahead. Jack had yet to complete his first term, and would definitely have run for a second term. Thus, Bob could not have run until 1968 at the earliest.) There would be stories in later years of Bob's involvement with other women when he was attorney general. The stories ranged from an alleged affair with Marilyn Monroe during the time Jack was tiring of the actress to involvement with singer Claudine Longet when she was still married to singer Andy Williams. The latter stories were reinforced by the fact that Williams, following his divorce, became the frequent companion of Ethel after she was widowed. But whatever his lapses, Bob was the Kennedy brother who liked being married, liked having a family, and genuinely enjoyed his wife. His cheating, fairly well documented by the late private investigator Fred Otash, was so seldom that, by Kennedy standards, he probably should be considered monogamous.

Both Bob and Ethel were extremely aggressive, and Bob was probably the most ambitious of the surviving brothers. Many who had to work with him strongly disliked his personality. They found him to be pugnacious, unpleasant, and willing to carry a grudge long after a more reasonable individual would have forgotten about whatever minor disagreement had occurred. It was this singlemindedness that would cause him to take any action needed to fight his enemies, including some actions later proven illegal. It was also this attitude that alienated people who might otherwise have helped him at a later time.

Bob identified with his parents in their areas of concern. He wanted a large family, equating the presence of children, dogs, a loving wife, and the sound of laughter with happiness. Perhaps he wanted Rose's approval by duplicating the type of family in which he had been raised. At the same time, he was driven like his father to spend long hours at work.

Harrison Rainie and John Quinn, in their book *Growing Up*

A young John, Jr. explores his father's office, 1962. *(UPI Bettmann)*

President Kennedy claps as Caroline and John dance around the Oval Office (1962). *(UPI Bettmann)*

John F. Kennedy, Jr. stands by his mother, Mrs. Jacqueline Kennedy, and his sister, Caroline, and salutes as the casket carrying his father passes before him (1963). *(UPI Bettmann)*

Caroline and John, Jr. wait with their mother for the commencement of the funeral procession to the Capitol (1963). *(UPI Bettmann)*

Maria, Timothy, and Robert Shriver III stand smiling around their father Robert S. Shriver, Jr. *(Globe Photos)*

Jacqueline Kennedy Onassis and John, Jr. race through Central Park (1970). *(UPI Bettmann)*

The daughters of Patricia Kennedy and Peter Lawford: Robin, Victoria, and Sydney Lawford relax in Hyannisport in 1983.   *(Brian Quigley)*

JFK, Jr. (3rd from right) at a Boston political gathering (1986) with some of his cousins: (from the left) Amanda Smith; Douglas Kennedy; Emily and Bob Kennedy, Jr.; Chris Kennedy; Ted Kennedy, Jr.; John; Kara Kennedy; Patrick Kennedy.   *(Brian Quigley)*

Chris, Victoria, and Robin Lawford with Kerry, Doug, Max, and Christopher Kennedy congregate in Boston for a political gathering. *(Brian Quigley)*

Caroline Kennedy sits next to her cousins Ted Kennedy, Jr. and his younger brother Patrick.   *(Brian Quigley)*

The oldest and youngest sons of Bobby and Ethel Kennedy—Joe and Douglas Kennedy in Hyannisport in the late 1980's. *(Brian Quigley)*

David Kennedy and Christopher Lawford in New York, 1979. *(Brian Quigley)*

Chris Kennedy, Joe Kennedy, and David Kennedy at their brother Max's graduation from prep school in 1983. *(Brian Quigley)*

Bobby Kennedy, Jr. and his brother David playing tennis in Hyannisport a year before David's death in 1984. *(Brian Quigley)*

Before journeying to India, JFK, Jr. arrives at NYC disco for his going-away party (1983). *(Brian Quigley)*

During a visit to Kenya, twenty-year-old Bobby Kennedy learns the correct way to hold a spear from a Masai warrior. *(Globe Photos)*

Ed Schlossberg, Caroline Kennedy, Jackie, JFK, Jr. and Senator Ted Kennedy attend Caroline's graduation from Columbia Law School in 1988. *(Brian Quigley)*

JFK, Jr. in Central Park. *(Brian Quigley)*

JFK, Jr.   (Brian Quigley)

Caroline Kennedy and Ed Schlossberg
with her cousin Willie Smith waiting
for a plane to Martha's Vineyard,
1985.   (Brian Quigley)

Kennedy cousins: actor Chris Lawford, lawyer Caroline Kennedy, and environmental lawyer Bobby Kennedy, Jr. *(Brian Quigley)*

The oldest Kennedy grandchildren, Joe Kennedy and his sister Kathleen Kennedy both ran for Congress. (1986). *(Brian Quigley)*

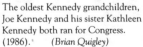

William Kennedy Smith after the alleged rape of Patty Bowman. *(Globe Photos)*

(From the left) Anthony and Mark Shriver, John, Jr., and Bobby Shriver dressed for Timmy Shriver's Washington, D.C. wedding in 1986. *(Brian Quigley)*

Victoria Lawford at her wedding with husband Robert Pender in Southampton, NY, 1987. *(Brian Quigley)*

John, Jr. and Caroline
(Brian Quigley)

(Left to right) Sheila and Joe Kennedy before their divorce; Ethel Kennedy and brother-in-law Steve Smith; political columnist Art Buchwald; Courtney Kennedy Ruhe and ex-husband Jeff; Michael Kennedy (1986). *(Brian Quigley)*

Joan Kennedy and her daughter Kara at an antinuclear concert in New York, 1983. *(Brian Quigley)*

Rose Kennedy celebrates her 92nd birthday surrounded by her children and grandchildren. (Left to right) Sydney Lawford, Kathleen Kennedy Townsend, Rose Kennedy, Eunice Kennedy Shriver, Rory Kennedy, David Townsend (Kathleen's husband), unidentified woman, Ted Kennedy (1982). *(Brian Quigley)*

Ted, Joe, and Bobby Kennedy, Jr. in Boston, 1980.   *(Brian Quigley)*

The last photo taken of actor Peter Lawford and his son Christopher, also an actor (1983).   *(Brian Quigley)*

Courtney, Caroline, Rose, and Ted
Kennedy in Hyannisport.
(Brian Quigley)

Rose Kennedy 1982
(Brian Quigley)

Robert and Ethel Kennedy pose with their children in the mid-sixties. *(Globe Photos)*

Ron Galella captures a moment shared by Jackie and her daughter Caroline, 1969.   *(Ron Galella)*

The omnipresent photographer Ron Galella catches Caroline and John, Jr. at Athens Airport, Greece, 1970. *(Ron Galella)*

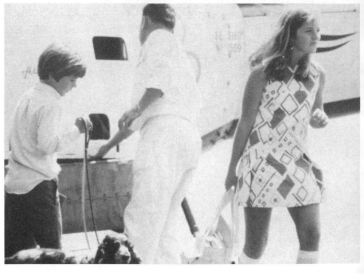

Willie Smith with his adopted sisters
Amanda and Kym in Southampton,
Long Island, 1987.   (Brian Quigley)

The young Christopher Kennedy here
in the 1970's. He is now vice president
of marketing for the Kennedy owned
Merchandise Mart Properties Inc.
(Ron Galella)

Doug Kennedy in 1983 is now a freelance writer in New York City. *(Ron Galella)*

Michael Kennedy, Bobby Kennedy and a friend leaving a family wedding in style.   *(Steve Heaslip)*

Patrick Kennedy arriving for Kerry Kennedy's wedding. *(Globe Photos)*

Max Kennedy with a friend at Chasen's Restaurant in California, 1989. *(Ron Galella)*

Kathleen Kennedy and David Townsend—"Just Married".
(*Ron Galella*)

Maria Shriver and Arnold Schwarzenegger's wedding day.
(*Steve Heaslip*)

Caroline Kennedy in her Scaasi bridal gown. *(Steve Heaslip)*

Ted's daughter Kara at her wedding to Michael Allen. *(Steve Heaslip)*

Sargent Shriver and son Mark.
(Brian Quigley)

Tim Shriver and his mother Eunice at
a family wedding in 1991.
(Brian Quigley)

Anthony, Eunice, Sarge, Maria, and
Bobby Shriver in New York.
(Brian Quigley)

Bobby Shriver at the Holyfield vs.
Bowe boxing match in 1992.
(Globe Photos)

Ted Kennedy, Jr. with wife Kiki Gershman; Ted's sister Kara Kennedy with her husband Michael Allen.

Rory Kennedy (the youngest child of Robert and Ethel Kennedy, born six months after her father's assassination) with her brother Michael in Boston, 1993. *(Brian Quigley)*

Joe Kennedy and fiance Beth Kelly in Hyannisport, July, 1993.
(Brian Quigley)

(Left) Steve Smith, Jr. and his cousins Chris, Kerry and Max.
(Brian Quigley)

Robert Kennedy, Jr. and his family at the opening of Arnold Schwarzenegger's restaurant Planet Hollywood in 1991. *(Ron Galella)*

In happier times: Ted Kennedy, Willie Smith, Ted Kennedy, Jr. and Joan Kennedy—long before Ted and Joan's divorce and Willie's trial. *(Brian Quigley)*

Maria and Arnold at a gala with fellow
actor Chevy Chase (1990). *(Globe Photos)*

William Smith. *(Globe Photos)*

Caroline and husband Ed at cousin Max Kennedy's wedding in Philadelphia, 1991. *(Brian Quigley)*

Arnold and Maria with 2½ year old daughter Katherine. Linda Potter Shriver and son Timmy in front. Newport, RI, 1992.

JFK, Jr. and Jackie Onassis at the JFK
Library in Boston, 1991. *(Brian Quigley)*

Bobby Kennedy, Jr. and his brother
Joe at their sister Kerry's wedding in
Washington, DC. *(Brian Quigley)*

JFK, Jr. and Darryl Hannah at President Clinton's Inauguration, January 20, 1993.   *(Brian Quigley)*

Survivors of cancer, alcoholism, and drug abuse, Ted Kennedy, Jr., his brother Patrick, and their cousin Bobby, Jr. in happier times on the Hyannis Port pier. (*Credit: Kevin Wisniewski/ Silver Image*)

Dr. Willie Smith (with unidentified girl) enjoying happier times boating after his acquittal on charges of rape. (*Credit: Kevin Wisniewski/Silver Image*)

John F. Kennedy, Jr. with the one consistent relationship he enjoyed prior to his marriage—his German Shepherd, Sam. Photo taken in Hyannis Port. (Credit: Kevin Wisniewski/Silver Image)

John Kennedy, Jr., campaigning for his Uncle Ted's reelection campaign for Senate, shows the charisma that made family members hope he would go into politics. (Credit: Kevin Wisniewski/Silver Image)

President Bill Clinton said Jack Kennedy was his idol. In 1993, he went boating with Ted Kennedy, Jack's widow, Jacqueline, her lover, Maurice Tempelsman, Hillary Rodham Clinton, their daughter Chelsea, Ed, and Caroline Kennedy Schlossberg. (*Credit: Kevin Wisniewski/Silver Image*)

The almost marriage that never was—John Kennedy, Jr. and actress Darryl Hannah. (*Credit: Kevin Wisniewski/Silver Image*)

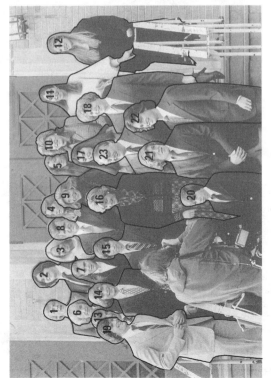

When the Kennedys gather, it is never certain who will be in politics and who in rehab. 1. Steve Smith; 2. Willie Smith (acquitted of rape); no contest to bar fight; 3. Joan Kennedy, former alcoholic who divorced Ted; 4. Sydney Lawford; 5. Robin Lawford; 6. Ethel Kennedy; 7. Amanda Smith; 8. Ted Kennedy; 9. Eunice Kennedy; 10. Pat Lawford; 11. Victoria Lawford; 12. Kara Kennedy; 13. Michael Kennedy—dead from playing football and videotaping while downhill skiing; 14. Anthony Shriver; 15. Max Kennedy; 16. Jean Smith; 17. Maria Shriver; 18. Ted Kennedy, Jr.; 19. Timothy Shriver; 20. Douglas Kennedy; 21. Mark Shriver; 22. Bobby Shriver.

(Credit: *The Boston Globe*)

Bobby, Jr. and his Uncle Ted after an appearance in the court house following his arrest with cousin Bobby Shriver for possession and use of marijuana. He would not get control of his drug habit until after he nearly died from free basing on an aircraft.
(Credit: The Boston Globe)

Paid staff provided much of the nurturing for many of the third generation. "Mamselle" was the beloved nanny for the Lawford children, including Robin. Later she was Rose Kennedy's cook. When she retired, Pat Kennedy Lawford refused her a pension which was later provided, secretly, from Rose Kennedy's funds.

Barbara Gibson, co-author of the book, who for ten years was
personal assistant to Rose Kennedy. She was one of the most intimate
outsiders to witness the third generation come of age.

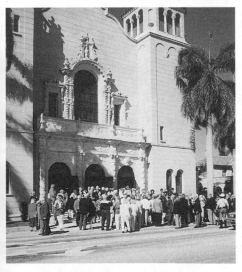

When Rose Kennedy had
her funeral at St. Edward's
church in Palm Beach
(1994) a mob of mourners
stood outside, weeping for
the matriarch of what once
seemed American royalty.

Home Of Senator Robert F. Kennedy

The home of Senator Robert Kennedy and the eleven children whose lives would combine triumph and tragedy.

Home Of President John F. Kennedy

The home of President John F. Kennedy where the myth of Camelot was nurtured.

Home Of The Late Ambassador Joseph P. Kennedy

The home of the late Ambassador Joseph P. Kennedy, for many years the regular gathering place of all the children and grandchildren. (All are at the "Kennedy Compound" in Hyannis Port, Cape Cod, Massachusetts)

Kennedy, quote Ethel on Bobby's character: "For him, the world is divided into black and white hats. The white hats are for us and the black hats are against us. Bobby can only distinguish good men and bad, good things and bad. Good things, in his eyes, are virility, courage, movement, and anger. He has no patience with the weak and the hesitant."

Bob's career was always high profile, whatever his office. The only time he was out of the news for very long was when he was handling one of his brother's election campaigns, and even then he got press because he was a Kennedy.

It was the home life of Bob and Ethel that mattered most to the children, though. They were raised on a six-acre estate in McLean, Virginia. They had two swimming pools, a trampoline, and a father who was intensely involved with them, playing with them and refereeing their games. He also took them with some regularity to the White House for dinner, though only the oldest among the children have memories of that.

In 1988, Kathleen Kennedy Townsend, Bob and Ethel's oldest daughter, was interviewed by Lester David for the article "My Father, Robert Kennedy" in *McCall's* magazine. She discussed the close relationship of Bob with his children:

> When he came home from work, all of us would rush to the door and wrestle him down to the ground. We'd drag Mother over, too, and we'd tickle-tumble him and each other, rolling on the floor, laughing and shouting, until he cried "enough."
> Next morning, when he left, he never got away without another round of tickle-tumbling, which he endured happily. I guess that's why he always looked so rumpled when he got to the Department of Justice or his Senate office!
> You don't forget those little moments of happiness. That's why the five Townsends tickle-tumble every evening before dinner and every morning before we start the working day. It may rumple David and me, but we glow inside.

There were also some carryovers from the way Joe and Rose raised their nine children. The youngest children ate separately from the older children and their parents. At the larger table, though, Bob questioned the school-age children closely about history. They were expected to get the right answer every time, or earn their father's disapproval.

Ethel was not really a part of such activities, other than as a listener, but she was also not particularly interested in the daily aspects of rearing a family. It seems harsh to make a negative comment about one of the prettiest and most dynamic of the Kennedy women, yet despite her eleven children, she was not capable of nurturing others. She had a large estate on which to raise the children, and the money to hire a staff to help her. But the children were ultimately left to raise themselves. She never seemed interested in their day-to-day development, never gave them the discipline that growing children need, never gave them rules to obey. The children were closer to their father than their mother because, though he was the more physically distant of the two, he was at least emotionally close to them when he was at home.

Ethel had a volatile temper, and it did not help that she was in the habit of retiring at night with wine and sleeping pills, something that troubled me every time she visited her mother-in-law. She was publicly honored for the quantity of her offspring and not the way she raised them. She was unpredictable, and the boys, especially Joe and David, seemed to take the brunt of her anger in their early years.

Bob passed on to his children the characteristic Kennedy trait—win at everything. As Kathleen related in the *McCall's* interview:

We had to be first in sailing and skiing races. We had to beat our opponents in tennis and get more runs than the other team in softball. And if we didn't he'd get mad. Very, very mad! It was made clear that we weren't to take these sports halfheartedly.
And to make sure we were in condition for athletics,

Father had the Green Berets set up an obstacle course on the grounds. Peals of laughter. Can you believe it! Green Berets! We climbed ropes, jumped, ran, swung, and we toughened up all right.

Because of Bob's absences and Ethel's laxness, their children lacked discipline and guidance. Unless all of the family had to be somewhere at the same time, they arose when they felt like it and ate when they felt like it. The cook in McLean was expected to serve as a short-order cook: if the children arose at eleven different times, then eleven different breakfasts were to be provided. With such chaos, it was hard for Ethel to keep cooks. Secretaries also quit, blaming the undisciplined children, and the fact that Ethel had the tendency to berate the staff viciously for minor infractions, and to otherwise treat them shabbily.

One of Ethel's secretaries, who worked in Ethel's Washington office, told me this story: One summer, Ethel told her that she needed her at Hyannis Port, and that she could stay in the house in the compound where the Secret Service agents used to stay. Then, part way through the summer, Ethel told the secretary that she would have to leave the house, because Ethel was holding a party and needed the space for her guests. However, there was nowhere else for the secretary to stay, so Ethel told her to go back to Washington for the weekend, as the chauffeur was driving Ethel's car back there. When she was back in Washington, the secretary got a call from Ethel's personal secretary, telling her that Ethel no longer needed her in Hyannis Port. All the secretary's clothes were at the Cape, however, and Ethel promised to send them on to Washington. A week later, the secretary received her clothes in the mail, knotted and clumped, and wrapped in a plastic bag.

Ethel was both cheap and dishonest. There are numerous stories of her buying an expensive dress, wearing it to a party, then returning it to the store for a refund because it supposedly did not fit correctly. Rose and Eunice also did this frequently. Once, Ethel's daughter Mary Kerry visited Rose in Palm Beach, and brought a huge pile of such clothing that her mother wanted returned. It fell to me to bring the clothes back to the stores. Some luxury stores in Palm Beach eventually refused to sell to her, although in most instances the glamor associated with the Kennedy name caused them to go along with the well-known charade so they could brag that a Kennedy shopped there.

Ethel would also go to designer showings and order a style she liked in several different colors. When the garments were delivered, an assistant would inform her that she couldn't afford them. Rather than making arrangements to pay for the custom clothing over time, she would return them and refuse to pay the bill. A person of lesser fame would have been sued by the designer for payment for these custom orders.

Instead of hiring professional help for the house, she hired college students during the summer so she could pay them less. After watching her angry outbursts at her children, the students began calling her "Mommy Dearest," after the title of Christina Crawford's shocking book about her mother, Joan. She also frequently lost her temper with the young adults, slapping one of the college students during an out-of-control rage.

A secretary from the Park Agency told me that Ethel's Skakel family inheritance was tied up, and that she had to live solely on Bobby's trust fund for her. This sum, paid annually, was probably in six figures, but it was never enough to meet Ethel's wants. She was frequently in debt because of her extravagant lifestyle and entertainments, and was unable to pay for the maintenance of her home. The front porch was rotten, and a repairman told me he could see the sky through the holes in the attic roof. Her family comfort and safety were not so important as her personal possessions. Jacqueline Onassis personally paid for a new roof after Joe Gargan had tried to get other family members to restore the house because it had historical value. But though they could afford it, sibling rivalry did not permit their helping a Kennedy-by-marriage who could not manage her money.

Early in 1968, Bob was trying to decide whether or not to challenge for the Democratic nomination for president. Despite the enthusiasm Bob had for the presidency when Jack was alive, Jack's assassination, Bob's work as senator, and other factors made him at first reluctant to attempt the campaign. Ted's staff felt that the next Kennedy president should be their man. Many others in the family felt that either Kennedy should wait until a proper national organization was in place that could assure victory. This would delay a run until 1972. Other Democrats felt that there were better candidates, whether Lyndon Johnson, who did not take himself out of the race until March 31, Hubert Humphrey, or Eugene McCarthy. The one person who had absolutely no doubts about making the run was Ethel. She thought that Bob would know when he was ready, and that when he decided to run, he would win.

Although popular support for Bob's candidacy was building when he was killed, winning the nomination and taking the general election was not a sure thing. Had he done so, it would have been without the cohesive support of a totally dedicated family, a major factor in Jack's victories and the political survival of Ted following each of his major scandals.

As the 1968 California primary approached, Bob campaigned hard throughout the state. He had gotten a late start in the race, and he needed to win California to have any chance at the nomination.

On primary day, the family was at the Malibu home of director John Frankenheimer. During a break, the family went swimming in the ocean where David, then thirteen years old, got caught in a rip-tide and was dragged away from land. Bob, a strong swimmer, went after his son, saving the boy's life. It was almost a repetition of the act Joe Sr. performed when he rescued young Jack in the waters off Hyannis after Jack saw his father making love to Gloria Swanson.

The situation was later described by Theodore White, the political writer and family friend who was present. White wrote in *The Making of the President 1968*:

A huge roller [wave] came in from the sea, and the bobbing head of one of two children went under. Bobby dived. For a moment one could not see them in the surf until he came up with David, whom he had pulled from the undertow. A large red bruise now marked his forehead where he had bumped either sand or the boy; he chided the boy gently for going beyond his depth, but the boy was safe.

The event brought the two closer together—it was a bond between the two. David had overreached himself, a trait the Kennedys admire as symbolic of pushing past personal limits. And Bob had shown how much he cared for the boy. This last act of closeness between father and son was a life-saving one that would hang over David after his father's death.

To await the primary returns, the Kennedys had taken the Royal Suite of the Ambassador Hotel in Los Angeles. The suite had a large room in one section and isolated bedrooms in another. A party could take place in the large room while others slept undisturbed in the bedrooms.

Five of the Kennedy children were with their parents—David, Courtney, Michael, Mary Kerry, and Max. David, who would turn thirteen in a few days, was staying up later than the others. He wandered about the large room where the party was taking place, though most of the guests ignored him. They were long-time Kennedy family friends, such as ex-Los Angles Rams lineman Roosevelt Grier, Olympic champion Rafer Johnson, and former astronaut John Glenn. Six television sets were spread throughout the suite, each tuned to coverage of the primary.

David was still with the adults when it was announced that Bob had won South Dakota, the other primary held that day. The state meant little in terms of popular or electoral votes, but the fact that Bob won gave everyone hope for California. It was eleven o'clock when David was sent to his bedroom. He was given permission to watch television provided he kept the sound low. David found a channel that was showing live coverage of the primary—the returns, the campaign workers, the parties, and the speeches. He watched from bed, dozing on and off.

Later that night, the TV commentators declared Bob the winner in California, and Bob went downstairs to make his victory speech. The results were showing that he had a comfortable lead in the state, effectively ending Eugene McCarthy's bid for the nomination. Only Hubert Humphrey remained an obstacle to Bob's nomination, and Bob was comfortable in a two-way race. Bob was also buoyed by the knowledge that what he had achieved had been earned on his own. He was no longer in Jack's shadow. His father, who was not happy with his decision to campaign, had been proven wrong.

Elated, Bob made his victory statement, then went through the hotel kitchen to the press conference. Exactly what happened next is debated by assassination theorists. All that is certain is that an Arab youth named Sirhan Sirhan shot Kennedy with a .22-caliber handgun. He was angry with Kennedy's politics, and according to psychiatrist/attorney Ron Markman, who examined him later, felt that shooting the candidate was proper. He came from an area of the world where assassination of office-seekers was fairly common.

David was startled by a shout coming from the television. He heard gunshots and screams, saw Rosie Grier subdue Sirhan, saw his father lying mortally wounded on the floor. A reporter said that his father had been shot and was being rushed to the hospital. David saw the live coverage, witnessed what would prove to be the slaying of his father. Earlier, his father had seen him dying and saved his life. Now David saw his father dying and could do nothing.

What happened next is uncertain. Some writers tell of Michael, sharing David's room, awakening and asking what had happened. Other stories tell of David being alone with the knowledge. Whatever the case, he was the only child to witness the murder.

It seems that the first person to think of the children, especially David, was Theodore White. In an article about the death he later wrote for *Life* magazine, White explained that he cradled David, talking with him, letting him cry, ordering hot chocolate for him as a way of helping him through the trial. Reports by Kennedy family supporters indicate that White came almost immediately. Other sources indicate that it was a matter of two or three hours. Whatever the case, White acted on his own. None of the adult family members thought of David or the other children.*

After Bob was declared dead, his body was flown back to New York to lie in state in St. Patrick's Cathedral. Richard Cardinal Cushing said the mass, and then the family and 1,000 mourners boarded a special train for the trip to Arlington National Cemetery. Ethel invited David's friend from Hyannis, Phil Kirby, to keep David company on the trip. But rather than this being a thoughtful addition to a time of closeness with her son, the reality was that Phil's presence allowed the adults to ignore the traumatized David.

*The April 26, 1984, *New York Post* credited John Glenn with breaking the news of Bob Kennedy's death to the Kennedy children in the hotel. The article seems to indicate he broke the news of Bob's death, not the shooting. This is probably correct. However, another source contradicts White's account of who helped David at this time. In another article in the April 26, 1984, *New York Post,* Larry Nathanson quoted Harrison Rainie and John Quinn's book *Growing Up Kennedy:*

Around dawn, David's mother, Ethel, asked friends Nicole Salinger, wife of Pierre, the White House press spokesman for John Kennedy, and John Glenn to check on the children at the bungalow.

A frantic search turned up David at the hotel. When they opened the door they could hear the television newscast. David was sitting on the bed.

"David," Nicole called. The child continued his glazed stare at the screen. Glenn gently lifted him from the bed and told the silently grieving boy:

"Son, we'll take you out of here now. You'll be all right."

As the train made its way slowly to Washington, bystanders pushed close to the tracks to get a closer look at Robert's casket, which was placed at window level in the funeral car. South of Elizabeth, New Jersey, a group of people jumped down on the tracks to see the casket, but a northbound train came roaring through, killing two and injuring six others. One of the dead was cut in two by the engine, and David stared out the window at the blood, the gore, and the horrified witnesses. A Secret Service agent reached out to him, pulling him completely back into the car, and getting him to sit down. The act was a compassionate one. As happened so much with David, it was also the act not of a family member, but of a stranger.

David, a shy boy with a lisp, was overshadowed by others in the family and overwhelmed by life. He was the fourth child, born in 1955, and as he grew older, his father seemed emotionally closer to him than to the other boys.

Bob had borne his own problems when growing up. Also the fourth child, he had been small and slight, unable to compete with the older children. Joe Jr. and Kathleen were close. And by the start of World War II, Jack had become close with the two oldest siblings. But no one seemed to care about Bob. Joe Jr., the hero of the children, made Teddy his favorite. And Jack, in generally poor health, received extra attention from his parents. Kathleen was stubbornly independent, and Rosemary, by 1941, was institutionalized. Bob was, in a way, the family outsider. Thus, the special attention he gave his son David seemed to be related to his own position as the runt of the second-generation litter. Yet this attention may have antagonized Ethel.

David desperately needed a sober friend or loving adult during the troubled time, but there was none available to him. He had recurring nightmares about his father's death, and Ethel could not cope with her son's anguish. Instead, she teamed David with his cousin Christopher Lawford, who was less affected by the murder yet extremely disturbed in his own right, and sent the two to a ski and tennis camp in Austria.

Peter Lawford was an uncaring father, an alcoholic, and a drug addict. He had been his brother-in-law Jack's procurer of starlets, a go-between with Frank Sinatra, the Kennedys, and the mob. He hated most of the Kennedys, yet would do whatever they asked, even after he was long divorced from Pat and remarried again and again and again. His idea of being a good father was to give Christopher cocaine for his twenty-first birthday. Four years later, when Chris was twenty-five, he was arrested for possession of heroin, attempting to illegally obtain the painkiller Darvon, and other drug-related problems. At one point, after Peter was living with Patricia Seaton, the woman who would be his fourth wife, Chris was so high that he climbed out onto a balcony to try to fly.

To allow two thirteen-year-old boys, both emotionally disturbed from overwhelming trauma, to travel in Europe showed a lack of judgment on their mothers' parts, as well as the extent to which they had stopped caring. Austria was too far away for the boys to get into trouble that would affect their mothers. And if David seemed to be happy with Chris, then why worry about anything else?

The boys' destination was Meyerhoff, the camp run by former tennis star Bill Talbert. While the grounds were patrolled for safety, as at all ski resorts, the boys were not given any special attention or chaperoning appropriate to their special needs. They soon discovered that their famous name and Bob's recent death created the perfect environment for learning about sex. There was a dormitory where a number of older girls were staying, and it was a simple matter for the boys to sneak over at night. Some of the compliant girls wanted to "fuck greatness," others wanted to soothe the boys' tragic lives through sex. Most likely, none of it made much sense to the boys, but they let themselves enjoy the experience.

The boys, who had entered puberty with the exuberance they previously were ordered to show in constant competition, stopped caring about the future. They were confused by what had happened, by the devastation of the family even though they were constantly trying to do the "right thing" by their family standards. It was as though both the Kennedy ethos and God had failed them. Christopher Lawford was later quoted by authors Peter Collier and David Horowitz (*The Kennedys: An American Drama*) as saying, "David and I sort of decided together that there really wasn't any reason to try to be good any more, so we might as well try to be bad."

When the boys returned from their summer abroad, nothing was right at home. Ethel, who paid her staff poorly to begin with, was making increasingly unfair demands on them, and consequently was having trouble keeping any help. And the children, undisciplined and with all sorts of unresolved feelings, were seemingly running out of control. Rose eventually warned me and the other staff not to leave money or valuables where her grandchildren could get to them, because they would steal whatever was lying about. The maid at Rose's house informed me that she wanted to know when the Lawford children would be arriving for their annual summer stay in Hyannis Port so she could leave beforehand. She said she hated the Lawford children, especially Victoria, for their stealing and the obnoxious way they treated her. Among other complaints, the maid said that Christopher had broken the window to the president's bedroom so he could sneak his girlfriend inside to spend the night. He didn't use the front door because he was afraid Rose would hear. Rose was aware of this situation and always allowed the maid the time off.

Ethel also began giving huge parties, as though gala events would help her forget what had happened or protect her from her emotions. Every weekend she would invite famous people to the compound, filling the main house, the two-room apartment in which the Secret Service stayed, and even the Doll House, a tiny building with two beds that had been built by Joe Sr. for his young daughters. I came to work one morning and found David Hartman, former host of *Good Morning, America*, coming out of the Doll House, his tall frame just unfolding from the night in the cramped quarters. Since Ethel had eleven bedrooms in the main house, the overflow was an indication of how many people she tried to cram into her life to help her emotional state.

David, after returning from Austria, still needed to talk about his father's death. He sought out family friends, but either they turned away from him or his mother made it clear that she would not tolerate talk about the murder. She was determined to handle grief in her own way, even if that meant acting in a manner destructive to her children. She either did not care about the kids, or she simply did not meet their needs.

Bobby Jr. discovered recreational drugs as his way of coping. He obtained and sold LSD, though how frequently he used it is unknown. At one point, he brought out some mescaline, which he had used, and dared his brother David to try it. A Kennedy competed no more fiercely than when going against another member of the family, so David accepted the dare. His foray into the world of drugs had begun, and his first pusher, like his last, was a member of his own family.

By fall 1970, David transferred to Middlesex to be with his cousin Chris. They had been set adrift with no experience in dealing with life's ups and downs, let alone traumas like death and separation. They were unable to provide emotional support to each other, yet somehow being together seemed safer than being apart. Each was a seeming outcast. Each at least understood the other's pain. And each liked to use drugs.

Ethel next sent David to the Blackfoot Reservation in Montana in spring 1971, ostensibly to make him more sensitive to the needs of less-fortunate people. Instead, he discovered marijuana on a section of the land, harvested it, and smoked it.

Ethel continued to send David anywhere but home, to anyone other than those he needed to know loved him. He went to boarding school. He worked as a laborer at Caribou Ranch just outside Boulder, Colorado. He became involved with Pam Kelley, the sister of Kim Kelley, with whom his brother Bobby had been intimate.

Sorrowfully, Pam became yet another victim of the Kennedys. David adored Pam, finding solace in the most intense relationship he had experienced. Each was having trouble at home, according to comments she later made to reporters, and they found great comfort with each other. They were friends, they were in the early stages of being lovers, and they had found safety and hope in their relationship.

It was August 1973. David and Pam were camping out in the Doll House on the Hyannis estate. Joe had been meeting with his mother and his Uncle Ted to discuss his own behavior, since Joe was the heir apparent to the political dynasty. Joe was staying in Nantucket for the summer.

By the time Joe was done talking with his mother and uncle, he was on an emotional high. He had enrolled in the University of Massachusetts starting that fall. He was going to get his degree. He was going to go into politics. He was going to be what his father wanted him to be, whatever that meant. (Because Bob died before his children were of an age when they could have substantive talks about adulthood, no one ever knew what Bob wanted for his children except as it was filtered through others. The legacy was often obscure or even contradictory, but no one seemed to care. Again, image, not substance, was always what mattered.)

On Sunday, August 13, Joe, David, and Pam were swimming off Nantucket Island. They had spent the night there, having held a cookout that lasted well past sunset. Joe borrowed a friend's sport vehicle to take them back to where they could sail to the mainland.

As Joe drove recklessly through the woods, Pam and David were standing up in the back, holding on to the roll bar. Joe would drive in circles, going on, off, and over the highway. Suddenly, a station wagon came down the road. Reacting late, Joe swerved sharply to avoid a collision, and the Jeep struck a ditch, broke an axle, and flipped. Both Pam and David were thrown from the car. David's vertebrae were shattered, his body placed in traction. Pam's injuries were worse. She would never walk again.

In the hospital, although Pam's senses were dulled for a time by painkillers, she was visited by Ethel, Rose, and Ted. When she was able to maneuver herself, the Kennedys brought movies to her, set up a projector, and had some of the staff in the room watching. Pam would later say that during some of the films she eased herself into her wheelchair and sneaked out to smoke a cigarette, with no one missing her. The Kennedys, however, never expressed sorrow or remorse over the incident, and when Pam was out of the hospital and an insurance settlement was made, the Kennedys seemingly dropped her from their lives.

The Kennedys did not tell David the extent and permanence of her injuries. Instead, it was one of Pam's friends who broke the news to him. He was horrified that none of his family cared enough about him to let him know.

David did not know how to handle the traumas that occur in the best of relations in real life, and he certainly did not know how to love a disabled Pam. He wanted her to be well, he wanted her to be able to heal, and he wanted her compassion for his own pain. In some ways he seemed to be in competition with her, as though his needs were being upstaged by someone else and he resented that she was suffering more than he was. He would sometimes yell at her because she wasn't more concerned with his pain.

David became a hard-core addict as a result of the hospital stay, but not for the reasons apologists would like to believe. Many people involved with the family want to talk about David getting hooked on painkillers as a result of his injuries. The implication is that his addictions were to prescription drugs, and that somehow this made a difference.

In truth, David wanted the escape the drugs—any drugs— offered. He wanted to stop feeling the emotional pain that had become so much a part of his life. He had neither the knowledge of how to cope with life on his own, information his siblings, aunts and uncle also lacked, nor the loving support of a nurturing adult.

David had become that worst of all possible Kennedy types— the family embarrassment without redeeming power position. Ted Kennedy could be an embarrassment, of course, but Ted was the senator. He had power, he had influence, he deserved damage control. David was a kid who had never proven himself, and who lacked the charisma of his brothers, his aunts, and his uncle. If David had any value, it was to make the other family members feel healthy by comparison. But reaching out to David would have forced introspection on the part of at least some of the rest of them, and introspection was an act the Kennedys always feared.

David continued to bear the pain of his father's death. The family kept him at arm's length, and when Sargent Shriver attempted to win the Democratic nomination for president in 1976, David was not allowed into the glare of publicity. There was no support for him. Even worse, in 1976, David developed the heart ailment bacterial endocarditis, directly related to his drug use, and required a stay of six weeks in Massachusetts General Hospital. Only after that did he get psychiatric help, and then he was given more pills. From 1977 through 1979, David fell so low that he had to seek help. He went to a Cambridge, Massachusetts, psychiatrist who indirectly became another of his pushers. Whether he believed David needed to maintain his addiction while working out his emotional problems, or whether he was simply not competent to handle a cross-addict, he allegedly provided David with fifty prescriptions over eighteen months, primarily for Percodan, though David also took Dilaudid, which was one of Peter Lawford's favorite drugs, assuring David of another source for pills, and quaaludes. (One of David's doctors ultimately lost his license for careless prescriptions.) None of the drugs served any purpose relative to David's physical health. And the drugs kept his mind clouded enough so that he could not effectively review his life.

During this time, David enrolled in Harvard, where his brother Bobby had been remembered for his daring, his skill, and his intellect. David was an alcoholic by then, fellow students commenting about his never being without a container of Colt 45 and a cigarette. Unlike his brother and cousin, David wore his addiction like a Halloween costume of death. His skin was a sickly pale tone, as though his body was slightly poisoned at all times. He was thin to the point of malnourishment. When he was with his family, he kept himself apart, having the maid bring him food, reading, resting, and always filled with self-pity. He was constantly at odds with his mother, whose attitude toward him seemed to be one of hate. He was desperate for attention and approval, yet he was too much of an outcast to get it from the family. He became involved with journalist Hunter Thompson, a writer for *Rolling Stone* magazine, among other publications. Thompson often talked of using drugs and alcohol, and his counter-culture life-style reinforced the worst in David at a time when neither his mental nor physical health could tolerate further abuse.

The Kennedys began seeking places to treat David. Ted, Steve Smith, Joe, Robert Coles, and others persuaded him to attend one facility where Chris had gone. The rehab center had not helped Chris, which should have been a warning, and David's three weeks there were wasted. He hated the place, and his one family contact, his sister Kathleen, was torn between wanting to help him and wanting to please the family, who felt he should not be trusted. She was in her mid-twenties, relatively newly married, with one daughter.

Kathleen had no business being the liaison with David in a weak variation of Eunice's caretaking role for Rosemary. She was too young and it was unfair. There was no reason for her to be placed in this role, usually taken by the parent or other responsible older adult. At the same time, she would ultimately prove one of the best and brightest members of her family, a person who would do the good works and meet the public needs that so many others only handled when they were high profile, offered quick gratification, and served other ends. Unfortunately, because Ethel refused to have anything more to do with her son, Kathleen was made trustee.

But Kathleen was still quite young when David was in trouble, and the others seemed more concerned with keeping David out of the way as Ted considered a 1980 run for the presidency. Eventually David was sent to Sussex, England, to be treated by Dr. Margaret Patterson and her "neuro-electric therapy." David had to wear a Walkman-like headset to affect that part of the brain that was involved with drug dependence, a situation that was difficult to take seriously. To add to the oddity of the therapeutic experience, he boarded with Pentecostal evangelical Christians who spoke in tongues. Two months into the treatment, David came home.

The return could have brought happiness if it had not been for the drugs. He became involved with actress Rachel Ward, whom he met at the Xenon disco in New York City, and the two were serious about each other. She wanted to get an apartment with him, though he had the sense to avoid the issue. He was taking a minimum of forty Percodans a day, along with heroin, in addition to whatever other drugs he could get.

David's lifestyle with Ward was not conducive to healing. They were frequently at Xenon, a location that appealed to a fast crowd seeking sensual pleasure of all types and having the money to pay for anything they wanted. He was being photographed at the club because of his name and the women he accompanied. There was even a photograph of him dancing with his leg in a cast following an injury during a 1979 touch football game.

Such publicity further upset the family. They did not want to see anything published that could hurt Ted's chances with his next run for the presidency. The last campaign appearance for David was when the family had gathered in Boston during Ted's run for reelection to the Senate. Mrs. Kennedy had given a speech, and David sat on the stage. Christopher Lawford was assigned the task of tucking David's shirt into his pants and generally keeping his cousin presentable. Fortunately all eyes were on the matriarch and her son, the senator. Had they truly studied the family, David's appearance would have alerted them to his troubled life.

* * *

David's dangerous life was rapidly catching up with him. On September 6, 1979, he went with a friend to the Shelton Plaza Hotel in Harlem. He was driving his BMW, and he left his friend to watch the car while he went to meet his dealer.

The hotel clerk showed no recognition of a Kennedy being present as she sat inside her bulletproof cage, a faded picture of President Jack Kennedy hanging on the wall behind her. David was just another white addict coming for drugs. But he was well known to the dealers as "White James," the result of his having been introduced to the hotel's illicit businessmen as "James." This was a common name, but only among the black junkies. That was why they called him "White James." It gave him a uniqueness. He would be remembered.

If there was a difference this time, it was that David decided to argue about the price he was being charged. When David refused to go above the price he thought was right, the dealer mugged him, taking his money. The friend fled, calling the police, then fleeing in a cab.

David Kennedy identified himself to the disbelieving police officers. He was terrified that the press would hear about it. All he wanted to do was go home to Hyannis, and one of the officers offered to drive him to LaGuardia Airport for the flight to Boston, but before he could, the detectives arrived and took charge.

The story that came from the 28th Precinct house was meant to help the Kennedy family. David was supposedly out driving in late afternoon. When he came near the hotel, he was signaled by two men. They were trying to get him to come over, and apparently being a friendly or curious sort, David complied, parking his car and joining them. There was a brief conversation, then the men went into the lobby with David. They dragged him to an empty staircase, beat him up, and left him after stealing $30 of the $200 he was carrying.

At this time, someone became aware of the struggle. It was that person who called 911 to say that a white youth was being mugged in the lobby of the Shelton. At least that was one of the stories.

The psychiatrist's prescriptions for the Percodan were found in the car. The illegal volume was enough to prove that the doctor was acting both in violation of the law and in violation of medical ethics. Proceedings were started to strip him of his license, and David was taken to Massachusetts General Hospital, where he was placed on methadone to get him off heroin.

In the world of narcotics treatment, there are good and bad addictive drugs. Those that endanger life, health, and relationships are bad. Those that are addictive but allow an otherwise normal lifestyle are good. According to experts in the field of addiction, methadone may be a valid alternative for heroin if the addict refuses all other approaches. But the ending of all addictive drug use should be the only goal of therapy, and when it is not, the patient has not been fully helped. For the Kennedys, though, methadone represented a quick fix, something the second generation always preferred. It was just like Ted's annual test of discipline when he neither drank nor overate for from six to eight weeks each year as a discipline to prove he could exercise self-control. The fact that he drank to a degree that seemed to indicate alcoholism (alcoholics can be periodic, going long periods of time between drunks, yet having just as many problems as the person who is always drinking), and ate himself into obesity the rest of the year was ignored. The quick fix meant he was all right. No one wanted to look beyond that with Ted or David.

Steve Smith avoided the issue when the press learned of the incident. He just stated that David was suffering from ''an ailment similar to drug addiction'' (*Boston Herald*, September 13, 1979).

David also suffered a new bout of endocarditis, and during his stay in the hospital, he reluctantly agreed to give the family a six-month guardianship over him. The family wanted lifetime control, which would enable them to put him away in a manner similar to the institutionalization of Rosemary. The difference was that Joe had destroyed Rosemary. David was destroying himself.

David was sent to a drug rehabilitation program in Sacramento run by a therapist named Don Juhl. Visitors were allowed, though no family member bothered to come to see him. There were too many other things to do, important things. Ted Kennedy wanted to run for president, and with David out of the way, the family could concentrate on what truly mattered—primaries.

Only David seemed to have a direction, and that was trying to kill himself more slowly than his skills as an addict allowed. He returned to Harvard on probation, began seeing a psychiatrist, and failed to make any sustained progress in his fight against drugs. Instead, he became the first of the Kennedys to seriously look at the life they had led. He came to understand the emotional abuse from the family's pursuit of fantasy and glory. He decided that politics were "crap" and that America needed "a rest from the Kennedys." He even challenged his siblings to face their own drug abuse. His attitude was moving in the right direction, but he lacked the inner strength to act on his own.

The warning signs were everywhere. Periodically he would go to Rose Kennedy's New York apartment at 59th Street and Central Park South, overdose, and thrash about and make noise until someone heard and alerted the doorman to check on him. Several times the building staff had to call the police to break in because Rose had four or five locks on the door to protect her from whoever she feared might break into the high-security suite. David apparently had used all the locks so he would not be disturbed.

When I stayed in the apartment while working for Rose, evidence of David's past visits were everywhere. All the floor lamps had their cords cut off so he could use them as tourniquets on his arm in order to make his veins bulge for drug injections.

The Kennedys soon insisted upon further isolating David. His trust fund access was reduced to $1,500 per month, more than enough to get by, though only as a normal person. He was living with New York photographer Paula Sculley, whom he seemed to love, yet ironically feared marrying Paula because his family seemed to approve of her being in his life. He also began spending time with Nancy Narleski, his former girlfriend who hated the Kennedys for their destructiveness with David.

The murder of Robert Kennedy was also in the news again during this period. Dr. Thomas Noguchi, long the coroner for the county of Los Angeles, wrote his memoirs. In them he noted that Karl Uecker, the assistant maitre d' who had accompanied Kennedy through the kitchen area and was standing by the senator when the shooting broke out, noted that Sirhan never was close enough for a point blank shot. There was every indication that there were at least two gunmen, and that Sirhan, who hated Kennedy and would have gone along with any assassination attempt, may have been as much a diversion as one of the killers. Noguchi also showed how the distance the bullets traveled, based on autopsy evidence, made the idea of a single gunman difficult to believe. The first shot was within three inches of Kennedy's head, with other shots coming from much further back. The movement necessary for Sirhan to have accomplished all that on his own would have been difficult to make and highly unlikely.

News shows discussed the new book, and television stations frequently rebroadcast the film taken when Bob Kennedy was murdered. If David paid much attention to the media, there was a good chance that he was emotionally thrown back to the night of the death. There was no escaping the nightmare, and no one in the family or among family friends was willing to reach out and help him with the ordeal. No one wanted to be bothered.

Finally it was Easter weekend 1984, and the family was gathering in Palm Beach where Rose Kennedy was seriously ill. What happened next has been reported in pieces over the years and is perhaps one of the ultimate Kennedy tragedies. Even Caroline Kennedy was dragged into the scandal, with some household staff members citing her as possibly an unwitting contributor to her cousin's death.

David arrived in Palm Beach on Thursday, April 19, taking a room at the Brazilian Court hotel, a rather sedate luxury facility typical of the subdued elegance of the area. The family claimed that there were too many people staying at the house for there to be room for David. The truth was that there were never too many people at the house—David was told he was not welcome. His ninety-three-year-old grandmother, confined to her room, had no such rules for the home she dominated. Ethel might have gotten involved, but she was not present and was not interested in the son who arrived from St. Mary's Rehabilitation Center in St. Paul, Minnesota. She did not know if he had done well in the program or simply abandoned it. She also gave no indication of caring to those who were around her at the time.

Although some news reports say that David began visiting his grandmother each day, he actually visited her only once, according to both the maid and affidavits filed with the court. During that single visit, he faced the shock of her extreme ill health and the scorn of other family members. He left the room crying, tears streaming down his face, horrified by her ill health and the apparent loss that might take place at any moment. He had not realized that she was as seriously ill as she was. Months earlier, the last time he saw her, she was still the powerful matriarch, loved, feared, or hated by the family, but always in charge. The stroke she had suffered left her little more than a shell, and the nursing staff would later wonder if they had done her a kindness in resuscitating her. When David arrived, the family was certain that Rose would die at any moment. Instead, her mind essentially stopped functioning, but her heart and lungs, strong from more than ninety years of activity, continued functioning without life support. For David, the shock of the unexpected devastation of Rose's mind and body, added to his already depressed emotional state, triggered a desire to flee in any way possible.

Not everyone hated David, of course. Some of the cousins

cared deeply for him, though they did not know how to help him or what to do on his behalf. Sometimes they would help him obtain drugs or even share drugs with him. Sometimes they would talk. But they had no experience themselves in how to heal, and their parents tended to throw away the broken members of the family.

Drinking began early for David. He took double vodkas because, in theory, they left no evidence except in the bloodstream, and the alcohol content was enough to give him a solid kick.

How much David drank is unknown. When he was unwilling to try to cope with the family hatred, he was reported to order three double vodkas at a time. All that is certain is that he tended to be the first to enter the hotel bar, and he would drink late at night, in the hotel and in the area bars.

The Brazilian Court staff was accustomed to the eccentricities of the rich, and were not shocked by the physical degeneration of someone with a famous name. David was unusual only because of his age, and while he was so gaunt, frequently unshaven, and sickly looking that few recognized him, word quickly spread that his American Express card bore Ethel Kennedy's name.

The police investigation into what happened to David soon turned up that he was also taking Demerol, an extremely dangerous drug if used improperly. Demerol has long been a popular prescription painkiller, an effective drug when used under carefully controlled circumstances. The problem with Demerol comes with either an overdose or its use in combination with narcotics, alcohol, or other depressants.

So long as the person who has taken too much Demerol stays awake, he or she will be fine. There will be a conscious act of inhaling and exhaling to sustain life. But let that person fall asleep, and the Demerol so suppresses body action that he or she may die. They neither remember to breathe nor are conscious enough to fully rouse themselves before they begin to suffocate. Death from a Demerol overdose is almost always death by suffocation.

Rose Kennedy was legitimately being given Demerol as she lay in her bed. An order for the drug had been placed with a nearby pharmacy shortly before David and some of his cousins arrived. When it arrived, the nursing staff discovered that they had far more than needed, but it was likely that Rose might be given small doses over a prolonged period of time, eventually using up the extra Demerol. And since the nurses carefully controlled the amount injected, Rose could not be hurt by having the extra available in the bedroom.

All the older grandchildren were familiar with drugs, either from personal use or having cousins and friends involved with them. David may have been the addict most closely associated with flirting with death that drugs could bring, but Bobby had overdosed on a plane in 1983, and Christopher Lawford was two or three years from stopping his heavy use. Chris's sisters had a father notorious for abusing himself, and even Caroline Kennedy was regularly around drugs, though neither of Jacqueline's children became seriously involved.

Among the drugs that killed David was Demerol stolen from his grandmother's room. This is certain, and the family has allowed the story of David's stealing the Demerol to be reported as much as possible. Ultimately the family fought having documents concerning the case released to the public. They did not want any of the facts brought out for fear they would reveal the dirty little secrets of the third generation. What they did not count upon was the animosity toward the family that had developed in the years just before and since that incident. Staff members have been willing to talk provided they were granted anonymity. Some documents have legitimately become public record, and some have been deliberately leaked by those who hated the truth that was being hidden.

According to individuals who were present, it is believed that David did *not* take the Demerol from his grandmother. There were two reasons for this. The first was the people present claimed to have watched him closely. Although the arrangement of Rose's room and sickbed were such that she could be afforded privacy when someone visited, a visitor could also be watched surreptitiously. David was not given a chance to be truly alone because the staff was aware of his addictions, of the medication available in the room, and the risk of theft. They were alert to his presence the one time he came by for a visit, or so they claim.

According to the staff, the Demerol seemed to be missing after a visit by Caroline Kennedy and Sydney Lawford. No one has said for certain that the Demerol was present just prior to their appearance in the room, and that it was missing just after they left. However, the staff opinion is that one of the two girls was involved in taking it, not David.

The idea of either Caroline or Sydney, or both cousins acting together, taking the drug is not a condemnation of them. Had David not overdosed, it never would have mattered. And most Americans, including the Kennedys, are not truly aware of the dangers in prescription drugs. They are not aware of the addictive factors. They are not aware of the chemical interactions that can turn two or three seemingly harmless products into a lethal mix in the blood stream.

Excessive use of both prescription and illegal recreational drugs was a common practice among the Kennedys, their wealth enabling them to purchase anything they desired. These two evils—money and drugs—combined to fuel the fantasy of the third-generation Kennedys' presumed destiny to achieve ultimate power and respectability with minimal effort via public service.

But this problem did not begin with the second or third generation. I discovered that Rose Kennedy took sleeping pills as part of her daily regimen, no different than attending mass, taking walks, and going for swims. They were prescribed for her by her doctors, who were perhaps negligent or naive. Sleeping pills are meant for short-term use. Studies on sleep indicate that they do not result in proper rest and should not be used for long periods of time. However, her doctors were only slightly cautious.

One doctor, either in Massachusetts or New York (possibly both), gave Rose prescriptions that would enable her to take sleeping pills no more than once every two days, a control of sorts but still a dangerous amount. The second doctor, in Florida, made the same arrangements. Together, Rose always had enough drugs for every day of the year.

Eventually Rose gave me the impression that the Florida physician discovered the game she was playing. Unwilling to be a party to addictive and self-destructive behavior, he refused to continue treating her. She then obtained the pills from friends who were returning from Europe. For example, I witnessed one occasion when author Irwin Shaw, residing in Switzerland, sent a gift of sleeping pills to Rose via his good friend Pat Lawford.

Another time, when we were at the Cape, Sarge Shriver returned from Europe with a bottle of Rose's favorite drug. He sent the sleeping pills through his son, Anthony. Sarge called me in advance, explaining that he was sending a container of sixteen pills and asking that they be counted in Anthony's presence. He wanted to be certain that his son did not use the drug he was giving to his mother-in-law.

Ironically, the Shrivers did not mind their son engaging in sex at an age when most parents would be irate. The family was in Palm Beach when the then sixteen-year old actress Tatum O'Neal came to visit Anthony. O'Neal had become successful, both acting alone and in the film *Paper Moon* in which she appeared with her father, Ryan O'Neal. The bedroom that Anthony shared with Tatum was so close to that of the Shrivers, he apparently knew they would not mind the youthful sex. Only drugs were a concern.

Ironically, photographers for a German news magazine had rented a boat and were anchored off the coast, telephoto lenses at the ready. They had been hired to photograph Tatum O'Neal and had followed her to Palm Beach. However, instead of recording the actress, to their amazement they captured a very fat, very naked Ted running down the beach.

The photograph was run internationally, including in *Time* magazine. Nellie, the cook, confided to me that, as a result of the picture, American nudists emotionally embraced the senator. He received numerous invitations from various nudist colonies and clubs, asking him to visit their locations.

Mrs. Kennedy was so heavily addicted that she got into a routine that prevented her functioning effectively. She would go to bed at 11 P.M., decide she could not sleep, and take a sleeping pill. Then she would lay down for an hour, and when the pill had barely started to work, she would grab a second one, certain the first had failed her. Since only one was necessary, it was difficult or impossible for her to rouse herself in the morning.

There was one incident that occurred when Rose had to arise at what, for her, was an early hour. She overdosed as usual, and at 8:30 the next morning I received a frantic call from Jeanette, the maid. Rose could not be roused, and Jeanette and the gardener, who was the only ones present to help her, were desperate.

Rushing over, Barbara found Rose being balanced on the side of the bed, struggling unsuccessfully to put on her pantyhose. Rose's mind was so befuddled that she thought she was in New York, not Massachusetts, and that the urgency was because the taxi had arrived to take her to mass.

Later that morning, after coffee and something to eat, I walked her back and forth on the front porch. I tried to impress upon Rose the disaster if she died from an overdose of sleeping pills. When Rose did not respond, I reminded her that it was spring, the anniversary of Jack's birth was coming, and people would think she deliberately committed suicide. Rose agreed that such a situation would be bad, but she did not stop. Similarly frightening incidents occurred in Palm Beach.

Worried about the addiction, I took it upon myself to contact Ted Kennedy to alert him to the problem, but Ted was afraid to confront his mother directly. Instead he arranged for a cocktail party in Palm Beach, then had Rose's New York physician, who regularly visited Palm Beach's Everglades Club, join them at the party. The doctor was to subtly examine Rose to see if he felt there was a problem. Unfortunately, nothing changed and Rose continued with her pills. Ted just told me that Rose looked fine to him and did not want to hear anything that might require him to get involved.

Only Jean Smith had some concern. When I continued to express my worries, Jean told me that, when Rose wasn't looking, I should steal the pills and flush them down the toilet. This I did, but Rose confronted me after the fact. When I told her that Jean had told me to do it, she became irate. "I won't be treated like a child," she shouted, and then ordered me to get hold of Jean so that she could talk with her. However, Jean, expecting such a call, had her maid tell me that she was out of town.

Later I talked about the abuse with Ethel Kennedy's secretary. Ethel's secretary said that, although the two Kennedy women were some forty years apart, their regimens were quite similar. "She takes a sleeping pill every night before retiring," the secretary said of Ethel. The difference was that Ethel used the potentially lethal combination of the pill and Pouilly-Fuisse wine of what she considered a good year, frequently the 1964 vintage. Like her mother-in-law she had to drug herself to sleep, though Ethel did it with what seemed to be an attempt at class and sophistication. In fact, if the stock ran low, staff members, friends, and anyone else who might be able to find that favored vintage had to scour liquor stores in an ever-widening area until her needs could be satisfied.

Once, when Ethel was going on a skiing trip, she called Ted's secretary in his Boston office to demand that she run down a case of the wine and bring it to her at Logan Airport. The task was assigned to Frank Crimmins, who was also present at Chappaquiddick. When he successfully located and bought the vintage and got to the airport on time, he discovered that she had arranged for two others to do the same thing. She so feared being without her nightcap, she refused to trust the effort to just one person. Frank, outraged, picked up a telephone and mercilessly cursed Ted's secretary.

Peter Lawford claimed that some of his earliest addictions

occurred with his wife, Pat Kennedy Lawford. He claimed that their late-night poker games with friends caused havoc with his sleep and work schedule in Hollywood. Through her suggestion he began taking sleeping pills at night and stimulants in the morning. It was an era when drugs were routinely available from doctors in the movie colony, and the world of addiction was not understood. They thought they were doing nothing wrong, never realizing that they would not easily be able to stop.

The Demerol was undoubtedly given to David to ease his emotional pain. It was not viewed as particularly dangerous, even if it was a controlled substance. And in a sense, it was not dangerous. The problem was that David was a cross-addict, a user of more than one addictive substance.

Among the drugs to which David was exposed that Easter weekend was cocaine, which he allegedly purchased from two bellhops. He was also drinking a lot of vodka.

David's drug use was leaving him exhausted. Some time early Tuesday morning, when David finally crashed in his room, he hung a "Do Not Disturb" sign on the door, took the telephone off the hook, and went to bed. Family members trying to reach him became worried as the lunch hour approached, and finally they asked the staff to check on him. Bell Captain Doug Moschiano knocked on the door, then, getting no answer, he used a passkey to enter. David was in bed asleep, the telephone off the hook. There was no crisis.

Carol Wright, a reporter for the *Palm Beach Daily News,* discovered that on Monday night, David met Marion Neimann, a forty-one-year-old German woman at the popular Chuck and Harold's Restaurant on Royal Poinciana Way. He invited her to dinner, and they ate at the Rain Dancer Restaurant in West Palm Beach where they would have greater privacy. She estimated that he drank as many as seven vodkas at dinner, then invited her back to his room at the hotel.

It was 10:30 at night, and the time was spent talking. David allegedly left the room briefly, returning with cocaine he claimed he purchased from the bellman. Then he snorted it, using a $20 bill, and as the cocaine countered some of the depressant of the alcohol, Neimann was quoted as saying, in her broken English, that David talked about his life. "I cannot forget when I see my father," she said he related. "On this television and this time I can, I never find peace inside. I've been full of pain. . . . And I say you need help David and he said, yes, I am crying for help."

Neimann left between 11 and 11:30 p.m., after which David visited Harriet Couch, a member of the New York Opera Company, who was also staying at the hotel. They had met on Easter Sunday when both of them, along with Douglas Kennedy, were at the pool. The Monday night meeting was chance, though, because she happened to be at the Kenya Club in Palm Beach, and David dropped by for more drinking. He was also carrying more cocaine, though whether he bought additional or had some left over from what he used when he was in the hotel is not known. Whatever the case, he became increasingly incoherent, asking Couch to take him back to his room. It was early morning, and that was when he removed the telephone from its hook.

Eventually David roused himself, taking a cab to visit his grandmother. It was during that visit that the Demerol supposedly disappeared. Off the record, some staff members say otherwise. The truth does not matter only because David was not suicidal, and neither Caroline Kennedy nor Sydney Lawford wished their cousin further harm. In fact, their involvement with him was a loving act. They were among the few family members who would reach out to him, who would visit him, who seemed to truly care, though in a manner that was seemingly naive. Certainly, if they were the ones who gave him the Demerol, they did it because, in their own minds, it would help.

Caroline and Sydney were the only family members comfortable with David that Tuesday. Douglas had flown back home the day before, leaving David alone at the hotel. And while

David was allowed to visit his grandmother, it was obvious each time that it was only because she was his grandmother and she was ill that he was permitted into the family home.

The death was discovered as a result of a call a hotel desk clerk thought was made by Ethel Kennedy. David had not been on a scheduled flight back to Boston, and the woman who called was worried when she could not get an answer in his room. However, Joe Gargan later told me that he suspected it was David's girlfriend who made the call, not Ethel. Whatever the case, initial reports indicated that Betty Barnett, a hotel desk clerk, and Douglas Moschiano went to the room, again using a pass key to enter when there was no response to the knock. They found David lying face down on the floor between the two beds, his head twisted against the night table. There was no sign of violence in the room, nothing obviously out of the ordinary. Open suitcases were present, as though he had either been packing his bags or unpacking them. It was as though he fell asleep on the bed and fell off.

The police reports released to the press conflicted with comments made by insiders. Palm Beach Police Chief Joseph Terlizzese made the statement prior to the autopsy that, "We have no evidence at this time of any drug use." He then added, "There was no drug paraphernalia in the room."

The latter statement was accurate in terms of special holders, needles, and syringes. But drug taking by injection, or the smoking of drugs through special pipes, are not the only ways someone ingests drugs. Palm Beach South paramedic Lt. Ronald Perron saw a half-filled bottle of amber-colored prescription pills on the bed next to David Kennedy's corpse. He was the first official on the scene, having been summoned by hotel owner Dennis Heffernan.

Palm Beach chief medical investigator Rick Black's first comments were in line with Perron's findings, though the autopsy had not been performed. "We are leaning toward natural or accidental death," he told reporters. "An accidental overdose is still a possibility."

But there were other drugs in the room. A total of 1.3 grams of cocaine were found by the police investigating the accidental death, and traces of more drugs were found in the toilet. Someone had entered the room and tried to dispose of drugs by flushing them. No one ever thought David wanted to rid himself of any excess.

According to hotel concierge Douglas Moschiano, Caroline Kennedy and a second woman, believed to be Sydney Lawford, were at the hotel the morning that David's body was found. It was later speculated that they entered the room and disposed of the drugs. (Caroline denied personally entering the room, according to a sworn statement released January 14, 1985, by Palm Beach County State Attorney David Bludworth.) The drug residue in the toilet confirms that someone hid the drugs, though whether or not it was Caroline, Sydney, or another family member is unknown.

The paramedics worked to try to resuscitate David. Life support equipment was utilized, and defibrillation equipment was used to try to jump start his heart. It was all to no avail. The body, which was eventually identified by both Caroline and Sydney, was removed on a stretcher.

Eventually the two men accused of selling David Kennedy cocaine were placed on trial, but their participation meant little. David's death came because he used a deadly mix of drugs by choice, stopped breathing because he failed to understand that you cannot take a large quantity of Demerol and then go to sleep, and suffocated. The Demerol was stolen from Rose Kennedy, probably by his cousins who had no intention of doing him harm. Family members also were likely to have participated in the destruction of some of the evidence of David's drug use, an action that was stupid but had nothing to do with his death. And when it was over, the prosecutor kept the situation quiet, not releasing information to the press. The family asked that records be sealed, which some were, and teams of lawyers were called in to protect everyone involved. It was just another coverup, though this time the tragedy was one where the truth would have made the family more sympathetic than the appearance of having something to hide. By clamping a lid on David's death, the family guaranteed that outsiders would think that more foul play had occurred. It also guaranteed that the family wouldn't have to take a close look at its myths and legends and see what they were doing to the third generation.

7

TED KENNEDY: THE MAN BETWEEN GENERATIONS

The one Kennedy who was freed the most when Joe Sr. was incapacitated by his stroke was probably Ted. He had graduated from the University of Virginia Law School, the same one attended by Bob. His record was undistinguished, and class-mates interviewed generally considered him both self-centered and a terrible touch football player, perhaps the ultimate insult for a Kennedy.

It was 1958 when Ted married the former Joan Bennett, a beautiful, quiet woman who loved music and had always shunned the pressure-filled, active life of the Kennedy women. Ted married her on the rebound, having been serious about another woman, quite similar in appearance, who had spurned his advances. She claimed that she loved Ted but would not marry his family.

Although Ted had not yet established himself in any career, the fact that he was a Kennedy and that his father would guide his life meant that he was "important." Cardinal Spellman presided at the wedding, and the bride and groom were carefully wired for sound for the movies made of the event. No one was certain when such film might be important in the career of what would likely be the third Kennedy president.

Joe, having decided that Jack would be elected president in 1960, wanted to be certain Jack's Massachusetts Senate seat went to Ted in 1962. This was perhaps his greatest political manipulation, since the Senate seat was not a beginner's post. Few men even ran for the position without a solid background in government service of one form or another. For example, prior to Ted's running for the office at 30, the minimum age, one of the youngest people to have joined the Senate was Georgia Senator Richard Russell, who took the post at age 36. Unlike Kennedy, who was barely out of law school, Russell had been a county attorney, member of the State House of Representatives, Speaker of the Georgia House, and governor.

When Jack won the presidency and resigned from the Senate, the Massachusetts governor was expected to appoint a successor to finish the term. The governor, who was ending his career, was Foster Furcolo, who hated Jack Kennedy.

The feud dated back to 1954 when Furcolo ran for the Senate seat held by Republican Levrett Saltonstall. He thought that Jack Kennedy would support his effort because of party loyalty. However, Kennedy had analyzed the election and realized that Saltonstall would likely not be defeated. Kennedy knew that when he ran again, he would want Saltonstall on his side. He felt that by refusing to endorse Furcolo, Saltonstall would repay him by staying out of the future race. It was a tactic that worked, though Furcolo felt that it went against party norms.

The Kennedys were in a bind. The decision had been reached to make Bob a part of the new administration, and even if it hadn't, Bob did not want the two-year Senate appointment. This left the Senate seat to Ted, who was too young under the Constitution to take it, or to a surrogate who would step down when Ted was ready to make his move. The family decided to seek the surrogate, either from the outgoing Furcolo or the governor-elect, John Volpe.

Furcolo buckled to the pressure, naming Benjamin Smith II as interim senator. Smith, a classmate of Jack's, was a friend and loyalist with no ambition. He was content to be a place marker in the family's as yet unwritten history book.

Within weeks of Smith's taking the Senate seat, assisted by a staff selected by the Kennedys, Ted made a fact-finding tour of Africa with three senators. He had earlier spent a year traveling in both North Africa and Europe prior to entering the University of Virginia Law School. Later, in 1961 and early 1962, he visited Europe and South America. None of the trips were meant to reveal anything, and the press in Israel and elsewhere chastised him for creating publicity for himself.

In order to have the image of a young man working seriously for the people, Ted took a job as assistant district attorney, working under District Attorney Garrett Byrne. His pay was $1 a year, and he earned every cent of it, though not much more. His caseload was so minimal that it was valid to claim, as his opponent in the 1962 primary, Edward McCormack, later stated, that Ted had never held a job in his life. However, his true intentions were revealed in November 1961, when Ted sent introductory postcards to every Democrat in Massachusetts who had been a delegate to any of the three previous Massachusetts Democratic conventions.

In the 1962 primary, McCormack, the Massachusetts attorney general, began as the far superior candidate. McCormack was first in his class at Boston University Law School. He became financially successful, then entered politics, first joining the Boston City Council, and then successfully running for attorney general in 1958. Two years later, he was reelected with a 400,000-vote margin. Because he was such a formidable opponent, McCormack was approached by the Kennedy family and asked to step aside. The implication was that there would be rewards in the future, and the implications were probably true. However, the attorney general refused to accept the bribe.

Ted was running both with and against his family. He liked the campaign process, something quite different from his oldest brother. He delighted in being a ham, and just as Jack distanced himself from the brothers' maternal grandfather, Ted used the old style of politics, including singing renditions of ''Sweet

Adeline.'' He seemed genuinely to like people, a big friendly kid mothers wanted to baby and boys thought might be fun to take cruising for girls or drinking beer. Ted was the brother people thoroughly enjoyed.

The campaign was orchestrated by the most powerful non-Kennedy in the family, Jean's husband, Stephen Smith. Smith was the type of man Bob physically wanted to be in those years, though the two did not think alike. But Smith, like Bob, was relatively small, seemingly weak, yet a superb athlete and so tough that, unlike Bob, he never had to prove himself. He was also a pragmatist about life, marriage, business, and politics, making him the perfect individual to eventually be given control of the Park Agency in New York City from which the Kennedy businesses were coordinated and family funds dispersed.

Jean, a graduate of Manhattanville College, had worked for a while in the public relations division of the Merchandise Mart, then returned to New York to work for the Christophers. This Catholic organization, founded by Father James Keller, had as its mission at the time the fight against both corruption in society and communism.

Stephen, like his future bride, was the grandson of an Irish Catholic immigrant, though that man, William Cleary, made his fortune in fields requiring physical labor. He worked the Erie Canal until he had enough money to buy a boat. He had seen the amount of construction that was taking place along the Hudson River, and knew that massive amounts of rock and sand had to be transported there. Special barges were necessary for the hauling, along with tugboats to guide the vessels. There was room for extensive competition, the transportation need barely touched, and so he gradually built a fleet of such vessels. The profits were enormous, and the family grew wealthy.

A second grandfather had chosen politics in the manner of Honey Fitz, serving three terms in Congress. Thus, Stephen was a businessman who understood politics. And Ted, though inexperienced, was a good man to have when the competition became tougher than usual. The pols—the older Irish politicians raised with the campaign styles of men like Honey Fitz—hated the way the Kennedys ran for office. Instead of working with the established machines, they ran alone, relying on no one, buying whomever they needed instead of coming to the power brokers for favors. To counter their hostility, Ted quietly went to them and made it clear that with his brother as president, it was Ted's word that could determine numerous patronage jobs. He matter-of-factly told them to back him or suffer the consequences.

Smith added some unique contributions. There would be 1,700 delegates to the state Democratic convention that would name the candidate for the fall election. Smith arranged for each delegate to be investigated so that their interests and activities could be determined. Then a Kennedy supporter who was also involved in such activities would contact the delegate to talk about their shared interest and Ted Kennedy.

Ted also personally talked with as many delegates as possible, reaching an estimated 1,300 of them before the convention opened on June 8. He also worked with the state senators and representatives who controlled delegate votes, using indirect influence in the same manner as some of the ward bosses. In addition, the family and staff utilized the same state-of-the-art electronics gear for communication that had been used for the national convention. Television spots were purchased, and the family made certain they effectively outspent not only McCormack but the Republicans and Independents seeking the Senate seat.

By primary day, Ted had become the stronger of the two candidates. He was relaxed, friendly, obviously enjoying not only the campaign but the people he was with. It was almost as though he took their adulation to be the acceptance he had never realized in his own family after Young Joe died and Rosemary was sent to Wisconsin. The people of Massachusetts became his family, and the rapport he sustained in campaigning would have made him a formidable challenger no matter what his name. As a Kennedy, he took the primary by more than two-to-one: 559,303 to 247,403. He then ran against George Cabot Lodge, the son of Henry Cabot Lodge Jr., who had been Nixon's running mate in the 1960 presidential election. This time the victory was by a narrower margin, though Ted took a decisive 57 percent of the votes.

The reaction to the victory was often hostile outside the state of Massachusetts. Ted Kennedy was unqualified by any standard. Being the brother of the president, while giving him influence in the executive branch, meant nothing when it came to working in Congress. If anything, his win was demeaning to the Senate.

There was also the suspicion that somehow Jack had rigged the election. But perhaps the most humorous comment about why Ted was in the Senate was given by one of his sisters, quoted in an article written by Stewart Alsop for the October 27, 1962, issue of the *Saturday Evening Post*. She said, "Teddy had to do *something.*"

Ironically, Ted Kennedy, the most maligned of the brothers, the least honored, the most ridiculed, was also the one who truly did his job for the nation. He was not and is not particularly bright compared with some of his colleagues, though his wealth, his past proximity to the president, the belief that he might eventually go to the White House one day, and the power he would ultimately accrue as a senior Senator have all resulted in his being able to obtain and retain perhaps the finest staff of any senator in the nation. His seeming wisdom is the result of their collective wisdom. His success with the day-to-day business of the Senate is the result of their often brilliant work. Despite his womanizing, his professional work has been sensitive to all minorities as well as to women's issues. He has been as supportive of the advancement of women in most of his efforts within the Senate as he has been demeaning of them in his private life.

Yet through the years, Ted would also be the most obviously self-destructive of the second generation, and his destructiveness would have a negative impact on the third generation. Sex for him could be casual to the point of demeaning the woman, or almost brutal although consensual. While still married to Joan, he would take his sons and nephews on trips where, before heading for their destination, he would pick up his girlfriend of the moment. And his drinking, too heavy at best, alcoholic at worst, would lead to behavior that resulted in headlines and death.

Just as he had been demeaned in his family, the best of Ted Kennedy was frequently held in disdain by those who could not separate the personal from the public man. Yet he was as close to a statesman as the family produced among the second-generation males, and certainly far more of one than his father. He kept a low profile as freshman senator and was deferential to those senior to him. He avoided trying to make dramatic speeches or otherwise call attention to himself, including waiting seventeen months before speaking on the floor for the first time. He made no request for special committees, doing the grunt work expected of all freshmen senators. And he looked upon the Senate as a career rather than a stepping stone, a fact that earned him the respect and friendship of Lyndon Johnson, who hated the Kennedy brothers.

Unlike Jack and Bob's success, it is probable that Ted's success came, in large measure, from the *lack* of his father's influence. Once Ted proved that he was not using the Senate for higher office, though no one, including himself, doubted that there would come a day when he likely would run for the presidency, he turned away from his father's biases. He worked diligently to assure the passage of the 1964 Civil Rights Act, something both his brothers had avoided despite their reputations for caring. No matter how separate his life may have been from urban America, at least as a legislator, he exercised concern, compassion, and interest in America's underclass, the people who were disenfranchised from the mainstream regardless of race, color, or creed.

Despite his fine legislative record, in 1969, Ted Kennedy's actions would result in the death of Mary Jo Kopechne at Chappaquiddick. This would mark the beginning of the low point to which several in the third generation would be taken. Just as Coffee with the Kennedys began the family's ascendancy to glory, so would Mary Jo Kopechne's death begin its descent.

This time there probably was no sex before the crisis, though some believe an illicit rendezvous was possible that night, more because of Ted's reputation with others than because of anything else. There was a good chance that Ted Kennedy was being faithful to his girlfriend of the moment, though his wife Joan was pregnant with what would have been their fourth child.

The events leading up to the incident at Chappaquiddick were rather innocent. A group of young women had worked long hours for Bob Kennedy during his 1968 campaign. Their efforts had been intense, their loyalty unstinting, and their horror and grief at his assassination almost as great as the family's. As a result, the group, nicknamed the "Boiler Room Girls" because of the pressures under which they had worked, periodically got together to talk, have a few drinks, and reminisce. The gatherings were the result of the thoughtfulness of Kennedy cousin Joe Gargan. He was perhaps the closest non-Kennedy allowed inside the family.

Joe's mother was Rose's sister, and she died in 1936 when Gargan was six years old, his sister Mary Jo was four, and his sister Ann just a year old. His father raised the three primarily in Lowell, Massachusetts, until his death ten years later. Even when the elder Gargan was alive, Joe and his sisters spent extensive time with the Kennedys. Joe and Rose ultimately paid for their nephew and nieces' education, Joe being sent to Notre Dame University and Georgetown University Law School. The Kennedys also provided the two sisters with their coming out parties when they were ready to be introduced to society. Joe spent all his summers with the Kennedys, becoming close friends with Ted. Once in college, Rose paid for him to travel to Florida for winter vacations.

After he graduated from law school, Gargan held several

posts. He took charge of the Kennedy family properties, arranging for maintenance and other needs as necessary. He traveled to Europe with Ted, with whom he was more like a sibling than a cousin. He worked in the Massachusetts state attorney's office for a while, and then he went into private practice. However, every time a Kennedy ran for office, he would take a leave of absence to help with the campaign. For example, he was in the hotel kitchen with Bob the night he was shot.

Tragically, the Kennedys ultimately did not return his loyalty. After Chappaquiddick he was dismissed from the family circle to a great degree. Ted refused to let him work on his campaigns again because the family feared his presence would result in reporters asking questions about the death of Kopechne. The idea was nonsense, but the family felt safer throwing Gargan away.

There was also a love/hate relationship between Rose Kennedy and the Gargans. When Joe Kennedy had his stroke, Ann Gargan selflessly devoted herself to taking care of him, ignoring all opportunities for career and personal relationships. (She married only after Joe's death.) Yet Rose commented to me that none of the Gargans ever made anything of themselves. They were damned for being Kennedy loyalists instead of building their own lives, yet they were expected to be Kennedy loyalists at all times. There was no way they could gain full approval from their aunt and uncle.

Gargan was completely trusted by Joe Sr., though his position was more as a family retainer than as a son. Joe gave him the keys to his car, had him make reservations. Gargan and Ted might sail in a race together, yet while Ted celebrated the win, Gargan would remain behind to put away the sail.

How this affected Gargan is not known. He became a heavy drinker for a while, though whether that was a reaction to the life he led or the direct result of it is not known. He was in the midst of heavy drinkers, including Ted, and his desire for acceptance may have led him to overindulge without realizing the consequences.

Gargan had worked in both the Jack and Bob Kennedy campaigns, was close to the staff, and was known not only for his relationship with the Kennedy family but also for his kindnesses to the underlings. The Kennedys were notoriously thoughtless about anyone they perceived as inferior, including Joe. Yet he was thoughtful where they were not, and because he was a friend of Ted's, the presumption was made that Joe's kindnesses were Kennedy kindnesses.

It was Gargan who arranged for the Boiler Room Girls to gather on Chappaquiddick Island. He also arranged for Ted to be present, though no one else of importance in the family was there. Instead, a friend of Gargan's, former Georgetown Prep classmate Paul Markham, was there (Kennedy patronage helped Markham become U.S. attorney for Massachusetts), along with chauffeurs John Crimmins and Ray LaRosa (the latter only an occasional driver), advance man Charles Tretter (who was a lawyer, too), and Gargan.

Kennedy was staying in a room at the Shiretown Inn at Edgartown on Martha's Vineyard, where a regatta he was racing in was being held. The other men stayed in a house that had been rented on Chappaquiddick Island.

Ted, like his late brother John, suffered from a bad back. However, in the senator's case, it genuinely was from an earlier injury. On June 19, 1964, the small plane that he, Senator and Mrs. Birch Bayh, and aide Edward Moss were riding in crashed in a fog near Springfield, Massachusetts. The fog was so dense that the plane was landing with instruments and the pilot flew too close to the tops of trees. The branches ripped the underbelly of the aircraft.

The pilot was killed instantly, and Moss died soon after. Only the Bayhs escaped relatively unharmed. Ted had a punctured lung, three crushed vertebrae, and two cracked ribs. He spent six months recovering, but his back bothered him thereafter when he was not careful about his activities.

The injuries were so serious, Gargan later told me, that it had been necessary to attach Ted to a special bed that suspended him in a manner that prevented further deterioration. Without it he would have died. However, the nurses were unable to turn

Ted over onto the bed because of his weight. So Joe rounded up a dozen close friends, and together they linked their hands under the senator, creating a human webbing to give him support. This way, they flipped the senator to a proper position from which he was able to safely heal. It was in that awkward position that Ted began seriously painting, a hobby he had pursued in the past. He became quite skilled. Some of the paintings hang in various people's offices, and he sent one to Rosemary, which the nuns hung in her cottage.

The gathering of Kennedy mourners was difficult for Ted in many ways. Ted was never allowed to have a personal life that did not, in some way, include the dead. Only his work with the Senate was inviolate. Everything else he did, with the possible exception of casual sex (even then, some of the women undoubtedly wanted to go to bed with Jack's brother or Bob's brother, using Ted as much as he used them), somehow involved tragedies that should have been long over.

As an ambitious political animal, Ted had to continue to court those supporters of his brothers who might help him when he ran for president. Some were strategists, others speech writers, organizers, experts on special interest groups, and the like. Some were Jack Kennedy partisans and had to be handled in one manner. Others were Bob Kennedy partisans who had different memories, different dreams, and different expectations.

Ted had to listen to endless reminiscing about triumphs, problems, and the world that might have been had his brothers not been killed. In some instances he was not allowed to lay his own grief to rest, the healing scabs torn off again and again. In other instances it was like reading his mother's letters to his siblings when he was growing up. Ted was fat and awkward, and would never be as good as his brothers. He was special by birth and by association only, his own accomplishments not important. (Ironically, the achievements of his older brothers would pale by comparison with what Ted would achieve in the Senate.)

Eventually Ted would be seen as a man at peace with grief,

who was somehow a tower of strength in the midst of loss. But he could not be himself; he had to be a ''Kennedy''—the surviving son who would carry out his father's ambitions.

Even worse, Kennedy had to be a part of the families of the men and women who had helped his brothers, who might help him. He had to attend family rites of passage for people he barely knew and probably did not care about. He went to the weddings, funerals, birthday parties, and other events of strangers because such actions would ultimately help him. Yet unlike the gatherings of his constituents that he willingly attended, delighting in eating, drinking, and pressing the flesh like any old-fashioned Massachusetts politician, these strangers did not care about Ted. To them he was simply the only man left to support from a family that had produced two greater men.

Events such as the gathering on Chappaquiddick were emotionally destructive, creating pressures Ted did not know how to handle. Always before there had been someone in the family, bigger, older, more famous to tell him what to do; to cover for him; to take the attention. Always before he had been allowed to participate where he chose, to hide when he wanted to. He always had someone else defining the parameters of his existence.

As senator and sole surviving brother, he could no longer exist as he previously had. Publicly, he was not allowed to be a unique person, a man growing into prominence in his own right. Privately, he seemed to fear looking in the mirror. Sex may have been recreation, validation, or escape. Drink combined pleasure with escape, and may have lowered inhibitions in ways that were simultaneously liberating and inappropriate.

Whatever the underlying pressures, Ted was filled with self-hate, self-doubt, rage, frustration, and loneliness when he went to yet another party in remembrance of one of his slain brothers.

Since Ted was a womanizer, there have been allegations that he left the party to have sex with Mary Jo Kopechne, one of the six women who were present. Other stories say that he was drunk and bored, that Kopechne's presence was meaningless, and that he did not intend to have sex with her.

The truth is not known. The Boiler Room Girls who were present were too loyal, either to Bob's memory or to the last surviving male Kennedy, to ever turn against Ted. Even if the truth would ultimately help Ted more than what passed for an investigation, they would not have revealed it. To assure one's self that special place among outsiders, it was better to commit perjury, to "forget," or to otherwise avoid critical details than to break the Kennedy code of silence. Old Joe, incapacitated by his stroke, would have been thrilled by the reaction of the Boiler Room Girls.

What is known is that sometime that night, probably after 11:00, Ted and Mary Jo left in Ted's black 1967 Oldsmobile Delta 88 to take the ferry across the 150-yard channel linking Edgartown with Chappaquiddick. The last ferry made the four-minute crossing at midnight, plenty of time if the couple did what the witnesses claimed. The only problem was that the witnesses were inconsistent. Esther Newberg provided two interviews on behalf of the Boiler Room Girls, and both times she claimed to be unsure of the time because her watch was not working properly. However, when she appeared before the grand jury investigating the case, her watch had recovered and she remembered that the senator left at 11:15. The time, noted by looking at her watch, was confirmed by the others.

The three attorneys present at the party invoked the attorney/client privilege and did not testify, though whether or not such a relationship existed was not challenged. In fact, much was never challenged at the time. The Kennedys had endured enough pain in the previous half dozen years. They didn't need more grief over an obvious accident. And for those who thought Ted was not above the law, there were Kennedy minions who made certain that all the facts would never be known.*

---

*Joe Gargan ultimately was the weak link. He decided to straighten up his life, to stop drinking, to find an identity separate from the Kennedys. During this period he became one of over two hundred witnesses and participants in aspects of the death and investigation to be interviewed by Leo Damore. Damore's book *Senatorial Privilege* became the definitive study of an event

The official story was that Ted Kennedy, known to be a poor driver under the best of circumstances, tired, influenced to some degree by alcohol, and confused by the darkness, missed a turn and went from a paved road to the dirt lane called Dike Road a quarter mile from the cottage. Although the lane was deserted, Ted claimed he could not turn around. Traveling at between 20 and 22 miles per hour, by the senator's estimate, the car hit the wooden Dike Bridge, hurtled 35 feet through the air, flipped over, and landed on its roof.

Here is Ted's statement to the police concerning the accident:

On July 18, 1969, at approximately 11:15 P.M. in Chappaquiddick, Martha's Vineyard, Massachusetts, I was driving my car on Main Street on my way to get the ferry back to Edgartown. I was unfamiliar with the road and turned right onto Dike Road, instead of bearing hard left on Main Street. After proceeding for approximately one-half mile on Dike Road I descended a hill and came upon a narrow bridge. The car went off the side of the bridge. There was one passenger with me, one Miss Mary [here the police chief paused, indicated that Kennedy was not sure of the spelling of the dead girl's last name, and offered a rough phonetic approximation], a former secretary of my brother Sen. Robert Kennedy. The car turned over and sank into the water and landed with the roof resting on the bottom. I attempted to open the door and the window of the car but have no recollection of how I got out of the car. I came to the surface and then repeatedly dove down to the car in an attempt to see if the passenger was still in the car. I was unsuccessful in the attempt. I was exhausted and in a state of shock. I recall walking back to where my friends were eating. There was a car parked in front of the cottage and I climbed into the back seat. I then asked for someone to bring me back to

that would have forced a less influential man than Ted Kennedy into a criminal trial for negligent manslaughter, among other charges.

Edgartown. I remember walking around for a period of time and then going back to my hotel room. When I fully realized what had happened this morning, I immediately contacted the police.

Also in the report relating to the case was the statement by Chief Arena concerning the investigation. It included detailed drawings and notes from the scene, and said, in part:

Chief Arena first received word of the accident at approx. 8:20 A.M. when a call from a Mrs. Sylvia Malm was made to the Edgartown Police Station concerning a report received by her at her home from 2 boys who had been fishing on the Dike Road Bridge that they had spotted a car in the water upside down. The invest. officer arrived at the scene and upon observing the car for the first time found it almost completely submerged, part of the left rear tire was above water—the invest. officer entered the water and swam to the car but because of the strong tide each time he went under he was unable to determine whether or not anyone was in the car. Assistance was then requested from the Edgartown Fire Dept. scuba squad and one John Farrar came to the scene and was able to enter the car and with the assistance of the invest. officer remove the body from the car. The victim was a young lady, dressed in white blouse, black slacks, and sandals; she was dead when removed. Dr. Donald Mills, MD, of Edgartown, an associate Medical Examiner was notified and came to the scene and pronounced the victim (Miss Mary Jo Kopechne, 28, of 2912 Olive St., Washington, D.C.) dead of accidental drowning. Her body had been found in the rear of the car. Her body was ordered removed to the Martha's Vineyard Funeral Home.

Farrar found the situation even worse than the original report. The car was turned completely around from the way it had been traveling when it went off the bridge, the result, in Farrar's opinion, of excessive speed that was certainly greater than the estimate the senator gave. But even more horrifying was that the corpse's position showed Mary Jo had found an air bubble trapped where she could breathe. Eventually the air was replaced by carbon dioxide. When she died, it was from suffocation, not drowning.

Dr. Donald Mills, the associate medical examiner, made only a superficial check of the corpse. There were some minor hints of drowning. Water came from the mouth and nose with pressure on the body. However, without an autopsy, it could not be ascertained whether the water came from her stomach or from her lungs.

There was never an autopsy. Although the funeral home delayed embalming for a while on the assumption that a full determination of death would be needed, no examination was ever ordered.

How Mary Jo Kopechne died will remain a mystery. The death was certainly an accident—even Kennedy's most bitter enemies do not seriously consider him guilty of first-degree murder. However, what happened after the car went into the water may have cost her life, and certainly reflects on both the power of the Kennedy name and the cowardice and inability to take personal responsibility on the part of Ted, something soon to be emulated by the members of the third generation.

Ted was going faster than he should have, and much too fast for a road he had not expected to be traveling. He was under the influence of alcohol, possibly drunk, and certainly unable to think clearly.

Somehow Ted escaped from the Oldsmobile and returned to the surface. Whether he tried diving repeatedly, as he claimed, or simply went immediately back to the cottage is not known. On his way to the cottage, he passed at least two lighted locations where help was available, but he did not stop.

As for Mary Jo, it is not known how long she lived after the crash. Since the area was known to have scuba divers on call around the clock, had Kennedy or his friends simply called for help, it is possible Mary Jo would have lived. In hindsight it can be seen that such an action would have soothed the public's reaction to the horrors of the tragedy. Kennedy's hopes for the presidency might not have been ruined. There would have been sympathy for Kennedy instead of derision.

Instead, Kennedy met quietly with Gargan and Markham, apparently convincing them that he was going for help. Supposedly they drove him back to the ferry dock, where he swam across the channel. Others have suspected he used a small boat. Whatever the case, none of them made any effort to call for help. Even worse, at 2:55 A.M. Kennedy claimed that he was awakened by a noisy party at the hotel and made certain that the innkeeper on duty saw him. Again there was no mention of Mary Jo.

Kennedy was awake at 7:30, talking happily with the winner of the regatta. Still there was no indication that anything was wrong. In fact, throughout that weekend, except for the brief period during which the accident was reported, all those who encountered Ted talked of his laughing and joking. He seemed a happy man, relaxed, without serious worries.

It was 8:00 A.M. when Markham and Gargan met with Kennedy, discovering that he had not reported the accident. A half hour later Ted obtained New York and Boston newspapers from the inn's desk, then borrowed a dime for the telephone. It was time to get all the help possible. By 9 A.M., back on Chappaquiddick, Kennedy was using the telephone when the ferry came to fetch the victim's body. It was only after all of this that he finally faced the police and admitted what had happened. It was also at this time when the others in the house on Chappaquiddick learned that their friend was dead.

The research done by Leo Damore, for his book *Senatorial Privilege,* and others over the years, points to two considerations that seem to have come to Kennedy. The first was whether or not to ask Joe Gargan to claim he, not the Senator, was driving. Certainly Gargan would have taken the fall for his cousin if asked.

And the other consideration was whether or not to claim that Mary Jo had been alone, driving the car when it went off the bridge. Except for witnesses, that might have been a possibility. Certainly the way the body was found indicated only that she was trying to stay alive, not where she might have been seated when the car went over the side.

The greatest horror of the tragedy was a third consideration, the one that seemingly did not bother Ted. Was Mary Jo still alive? Could she have been saved? To worry about his own reputation, his own future, and not the condition of the woman who was trapped in the car was morally reprehensible. Dead or alive, the most damning aspect of Chappaquiddick, the most evident manner in which a Kennedy will sell his soul in order to pursue power or to salvage a career was that Mary Jo Kopechne was a distant afterthought, not the primary concern.

Joe Gargan told me that he and Paul Markham went down to where the car was in the water even as Ted was returning to the Shiretown Inn after the accident. Gargan dove into the water and managed to find an open or broken window providing enough space for him to wedge his way inside. He felt around, found Mary Jo's body, and could tell by the unnatural feel that he was too late.

At first Gargan thought he might be able to remove her corpse from the car, probably taking the body through the window. Then he realized that he could not hold his breath long enough with each dive to be effective, and his twistings and turnings were threatening to leave him trapped in the wreckage. He went back to the surface, and since he and Markham were certain that Kennedy would be alerting the authorities, they went back to the cabin. There they could get dry and prepare everyone for the emotional ordeal ahead when the police had removed the corpse and needed to speak with them. However, no one came.

Ultimately all manner of important men reached out to help the senator, both directly and indirectly. Stephen Smith was contacted on a European vacation, and it was he who began to coordinate whatever coverup seemed possible. Ted Sorensen arrived, along with Robert McNamara and Richard Goodwin. Dun Gifford removed the body, William vanden Heuvel went to see the Kopechnes, and Burke Marshall, once the most powerful assistant to Bob Kennedy in the Justice Department, was prepared to move in whatever manners were necessary to handle the legal problems. District Attorney Edmund Dinis was a Kennedy loyalist who could be counted upon to go slowly, and without being asked, delayed a request for an inquest until twelve days after the death. By then there was almost no chance of autopsy.

Additional help came from Bernie Flynn, the Dukes County district attorney's investigator, and a man who believed in Kennedy. He was convinced from the start that Kennedy had not been driving that night, that the senator was covering up for someone else. (The fact that Ted had never been altruistic apparently did not contribute to his decision.) Working with Stephen Smith, Flynn delivered information on what witnesses would testify about at the inquest. It would take six months for the inquest to be held, with Kennedy, the surviving Boiler Room Girls—Rosemary Keough, sisters Mary Ellen and Nance Lyons, Esther Newberg, and Susan Tannenbaum—and twenty-one other witnesses testifying. Ted's negligence was found to be the probable cause of Mary Jo's death, and he was guilty of leaving the scene of an accident. He received two months in jail—suspended—and was given a year's probation.

In the performance of his career, Ted then spoke before the nation. He told a version of what happened, invoking the name of his brother John to link himself closely with the myth of Camelot. He explained that there was no relationship between he and Mary Jo, and that he was not drunk. He had made a mistake, and he felt that perhaps he should resign from the Senate after seven years in office.

The reaction was what he and his staff had hoped. Hundreds of telephone messages, along with telegrams from throughout the nation, came into the Boston office from people telling of their support. Kennedy had his mandate to continue, and no one ever wondered why, if the party was both innocent and such a touching memorial, the participants were six married men without their wives, and six single women.

Eventually Mary Jo was buried, and efforts to have the corpse exhumed for an autopsy were successfully fought. The Kopechnes were given a $50,000 insurance settlement, another $90,923 from the senator, and may have received more money from Ted. (Rumors of regular checks being sent to the Kopechnes have surfaced in recent years, though they cannot be substantiated, nor is their existence important. The parents' grief has been endless, and they remain wondering exactly what happened that night).

By 1980, when Ted made his bid for the presidency, Chappaquiddick had become the subject of a number of studies that resulted in several theories that further destroyed the senator's credibility. Whether or not any of them were accurate was not so important as the fact that they were possible. They constantly reminded the public that the senator not only was responsible for a woman's death, he also avoided taking responsibility for that death for as long as possible.

Joan Kennedy, for her part, had had enough pain. She could no longer ignore her husband's immaturity, his philandering, his inexcusable actions toward others. She lost the child she was carrying (the couple never again attempted to have a child) and increasingly turned to alcohol. She stayed involved with the Kennedy family, though never actively, and played the role of the dutiful wife. But her husband had gone too far. The marriage was over in every way except legally. There would be nothing left except pain, humiliation, and the keeping of the dirty little secrets until she was overwhelmed, sought help for her alcoholism, and left her husband.

However, the fact that Kennedy saved his job in the Senate through his handling of Chappaquiddick would make the incident a model for the third generation. A Kennedy had enough friends to get away with anything, even someone else's death. And the damage control that was practiced to stonewall the public about Chappaquiddick was refined even further several years later when Ted's experience provided the protection needed by nephew William Kennedy Smith, whose rough, casual sex resulted in the greatest family scandal of the third generation to come to light.

And so life was set for the third generation of Kennedys. The burden they faced would have been difficult in a family whose members lovingly nurtured one another. With the Kennedys, the grandchildren of Joseph, who died in 1969, and Rose, the price for bearing the results of the sins of the grandparents would be frequent degeneration into drugs, alcohol, violence, and death.

8

WILLIAM KENNEDY SMITH AND PALM BEACH

Almost nobody heard of William Kennedy Smith when he was growing up. He is tall, with the slightly bemused, round-faced look of the perpetual fraternity good old boy. He seems the type of kid who is shy when sober, self-centered after drinking too much beer, potentially boorish in sex, and the youth most likely to dress up as the mascot of the local football team and make a fool of himself at the big game. I seldom noticed Willie when the Smith family gathered around Rose during my time as Rose's personal secretary. He was frequently sitting alone, staring off into space, his face a mask of indifference. It was impossible to tell if he was a youth of deep thoughts, seething anger, or just rather vacant mind despite having enough intelligence to successfully complete Georgetown University Medical School.

At his most gregarious, Willie could easily have been the type of used car salesman you know is lying to you about the vehicle you think is the car of your dreams. You know that somewhere deep in the engine, the brakes, or some other critical spot, there is a flaw that will cause you intense grief, yet you don't care. You let yourself be charmed into buying a lemon, and you even half-believe he didn't know about the rust, the missing spark plugs, the almost dead battery, the holes in critical hoses, and the rolled-back odometer.

But Willie was seldom that gregarious. Like his late father, Stephen Smith Sr., he avoided publicity. Stephen Smith was a skilled businessman who controlled the family fortune, paid the bills, and handled family problems, especially after the death of Joe Sr. He was also a campaign strategist who was the man to be called whether you were planning a run for high office or in trouble because Mary Jo Kopechne was dead in your car. He was a fixer, and perhaps because of this, there were rumors about a dark side to the man.

Peter Lawford claimed that Jean Kennedy Smith, Stephen's wife and link to the Kennedy fortune, could not handle his abusiveness and his womanizing. She eventually took a lover whom she decided to marry. However, after leaving her husband a note telling him what was taking place and flying to Europe, she discovered that her lover was taking advantage of her. According to Lawford, the man had told her he would marry her when she was free to do so, knowing full well that, as a devout Catholic, she would never be free. He could enjoy her company, assure himself of her devotion, and never have to make an actual commitment. He dumped her, and the shattered Jean returned home to face her husband. From then on they led two lives, he more openly involved with other women, frequently staying away from the family home. She allegedly began drinking, a not uncommon problem for the Kennedy second generation.

Willie Smith never wanted to be known as a Kennedy. The Lawford and Shriver children frequently made clear that they were Kennedys, but not Willie. He did not use his middle name, and refused to go to the same schools as the others. Born on September 4, 1960, he was three years younger than his brother Stephen Jr. However, where Stephen Jr. went to Harvard and eventually became a lawyer like so many others in the family, Willie deliberately chose Duke. Thus, for him to be the heir to Chappaquiddick, far more than the grandchildren of Joe and Rose who continue to bear the Kennedy name, was unexpected.

But if Willie was an unlikely candidate for Teddy-style notoriety, Palm Beach, Florida, where the kids spent a great deal of time, was not.

Palm Beach residents buy books, read books, may even collect books. They have little other entertainment except television, videos, alcohol, and sex. Yet even with the latter, they are a discrete group, one's awareness of an orgy coming in the retelling, not in witnessing the event. Thus Roxanne Pulitzer could scandalize the community by telling what happened behind closed doors, yet still remain an insider because she had the class to keep the events private while they were taking place.

Ethical standards for the Palm Beach Police Department are different than those for departments in other wealthy communities. Traditionally police keep a deferential distance from the people they serve. They try to avoid the appearance of impropriety, of possibly compromising the integrity of the departments for which they work. While some officers will accept free meals, especially at all-night restaurants where the proprietors feel the sight of armed officers in uniform eating in the early hours of the morning may discourage rowdies and hold-ups, most will not. Certainly they do not work for people whose actions may require a criminal investigation at some time in the future. And when a mistake is made, outside investigators from the Sheriff's Department, the state police, or, where appropriate, the FBI, are called in to help.

Civil rights are respected as official policy by most police departments, though there may be strong personal bias among the men and women who work for them. In Palm Beach, the civil rights of whites, especially wealthy whites, are respected. Several long-time police officers and men now retired from the force, though still working for the Kennedys and other wealthy families, talked freely about not allowing "niggers" in Palm Beach after dark. They laughed about escorting blacks, regardless of why they were in Palm Beach or how much money they had, across the bridge to the nonexclusive community of West Palm Beach once nighttime fell. Blacks are allowed to work in Palm Beach provided they dress correctly, know their place, are respectful, and stay out of sight at the end of the day. The racism is not so obvious as it was in the old South, when "colored" had their own eating establishments, drinking fountains, and entrances. But a contemporary presidential candidate making his primary residence in Palm Beach would be laughed out of the election as a racist elitist.

For many years, including the time I was working for Rose, anyone who worked in Palm Beach but did not live there had to carry a passport. The term is not technically accurate, of course, for Palm Beach is not a sovereign nation. It only thought of itself that way, and that was why every legal citizen of the United States who commuted in and out of Palm Beach to work each day was given a special photo identification card with a number registered with the police department. Not having such a card could get you "deported" across the bridge. The arrangement was unconstitutional and against the civil rights the Kennedys wanted the nation to think they supported, but it was the law of the rich, white isolationists who thought they could buy their own private world. Matters changed only when cartoonist Garry Trudeau, the creator of the comic strip *Doonesbury*, embarrassed local officials by satirizing the passports.

Ironically, as pure as Palm Beach leaders often like to present themselves, the community was built on scandal. The resort was first developed in the 1890s by Henry Flagler, a partner with John D. Rockefeller in the Standard Oil Company. He built a railroad down the Florida coast so he could commute to his ideal for a vacation home, then built a resort at the end of the line to justify the expense.

Married three times, Flagler's second wife went crazy. When it became obvious she would have to go into an asylum, he discovered that a man could not divorce a woman who had been declared mentally incompetent. Using his influence with the state legislature, he had the law changed specifically so he could get a divorce. Then, in 1901, he married Mary Lily

Kenan, who had previously been dating the relatively poor Robert Worth Bingham. The marriage to Mary Kenan was apparently a happy one for Flagler, though he cheated on her somewhere along the way, contracting syphilis, which had not revealed itself by the time he died in 1913.

Kenan immediately resumed her relationship with Bingham, who quickly married her. The Kenan and Flagler families were concerned that Bingham was just a gold-digger and asked that he not be made her heir. He declared undying love for Mary, not her money, and readily agreed to the arrangement. Then, when she was high on romance, he convinced her to change her will to make him the beneficiary of a small portion of her wealth—$5 million. She was dead five weeks later.

It is almost certain that Kenan died of the syphilis she had contracted from her late husband. Certainly that is the conclusion reached by contemporary researchers and medical historians. But Palm Beach residents prefer a nastier turn of mind. They spread the word of a murder, and Bingham was either feted or damned based on that conclusion.

More recent scandals have involved sex and money, the pursuit of which pass for entertainment in Palm Beach. For example, there was the 1982 divorce of sixty-one-year-old Peter Pulitzer and forty-year-old Roxanne Pulitzer. He was the heir to the newspaper family whose name is synonymous with the most respected prize in journalism. She was a former cheerleader and secretary.

Exactly what happened between them has been the subject of speculation and at least one book, Roxanne's *The Prize Pulitzer*. It was not the truth but the allegations during the trial that delighted local residents. He said she had extramarital sex with at least four men, though that seemed like a quiet evening's entertainment to some of the trendy bar crowd. Roxanne counterpunched by saying that he slept with his own daughter, Liza Pulitzer Leidy. No way, said Leidy. Roxanne was just saying such lies because she, Liza Leidy, had turned down Roxanne's sexual overtures.

Finally, Peter topped them all by saying that Roxanne had

an affair with Jacquie Kimberly, the wife of his good friend James Kimberly, heir to the fortune made from Kleenex brand tissue and other products. And how did he know? Simple—he had been in bed with them.

Tragically for the Kimberlys, the Pulitzer trial forced the couple to divorce in 1986. They had been together since 1967, when she was seventeen years old and he was sixty. Even worse by Palm Beach standards, James started living on his inheritance rather than the interest from it. He soon was forced to downgrade his lifestyle, moving to the decadent wilds of West Palm Beach and a "lean-to" of a house costing only $225,000.

The Palm Beach police officers are also employed by the local homeowners for private security matters. The officers, working off duty, are beholden to the wealthy locals for what are often substantial sums of money. This does not mean that they will not honestly do their duty, including arresting someone who has both committed a crime and previously employed one of the officers. However, such work can lead to corruption, is considered unethical by many police departments, and creates a potentially unhealthy environment. This was proven during a two-year period when the police were not allowed to work for the residents, the jobs going to members of the Florida state police. However, when the state police evaluated what was taking place, they decided that the risk of corruption was too great and ordered their men to stop. The jobs returned to the Palm Beach Police Department, and the Kennedy family was among the employers.

This is not to say that all Palm Beach homeowners are either racist or elitist. Palm Beach is a beautiful community, whether your home is on the water or in the less-pricey area back across the highway. (Homes there may still fetch six-figure prices.) It is a community where crime is frequently "victimless," such as the sale of illegal drugs purchased with one's allowance or inheritance. There are no homeless people on the sidewalks, no industries to pollute or even to remind the residents that, at some point in their past, their ancestors worked hard for the lifestyle they can now afford.

Many Palm Beach residents are compassionate, but it is a community where compassion can be exercised from a distance. You can write a check to build a soup kitchen in Miami. You can underwrite a hospital research facility where a cure for AIDS might be found. You can give of everything but yourself, or you can use the community for rest and recreation, periodically making excursions to give hands-on help to the impoverished in New York, Detroit, Cleveland, Philadelphia, or wherever you came from. The people of Palm Beach are often extraordinarily generous with their money, with their political contacts, with lending their names when their names are respected.

But ultimately Palm Beach is the good life for wealthy, white Americans. You go there to enjoy your money, not show it off. You go there to never have to fear the unexpected because the streets are run in whatever manner you and your friends pay to have them maintained. There are few surprises in Palm Beach, even with the much hated Kennedys who remained outside the social order that dominated. And even when there is a surprise, even when Dr. William Kennedy Smith engages in rough sex on the grounds of his family home, even he has the good taste to use the West Palm Beach Court House.

West Palm Beach is everything Palm Beach is not. There are blacks and Hispanics. People are sometimes hungry in West Palm Beach. People are sometimes homeless. There are movie theaters and places where the arts are more readily encouraged. It is a microcosm of much of what the people of Palm Beach have managed to avoid experiencing.

It was Good Friday, March 29, 1991, when a few Kennedys and friends gathered at the Palm Beach house, which would be passed on to the children and grandchildren of Joe and Rose Kennedy once Rose Kennedy died. The patriarch was dead, and their mother was so frail from a severe stroke suffered a few years earlier that she showed fewer signs of life than a newborn infant. She was spending her days in Hyannis, under constant care, her body seeming to grow smaller almost with each passing day, her capacity for speech gone. Those who hated her joked about her being maintained in Saran Wrap or having been freeze dried, then partially animated by the Disney studios. Those who cared for her cursed the decision to use heroic measures to keep her alive after her last stroke. Rose Kennedy was too strong of body to die, yet those who knew her, those who had loved the woman that was, knew she would not want to continue through life a vegetable, her mind and body forever separated by the infirmities of great age.

There were two bedrooms with exits to the outside on the south end of the Palm Beach house. To the left was a veranda that was on the ocean (southeast) corner. And next to that was the lake bedroom, which had a door leading out to the swimming pool. The next bedroom to the right, on the southwest corner, was called the president's bedroom.* That bedroom, so named because Jack frequently used it before the election, also had an exit going out to the pool.

Two of the bedrooms had doors that gave access to a stairway leading to the tennis courts and a series of dressing rooms, but the president's bedroom was most desired. It was bigger, lighter, and on the far corner, adjacent to the tennis courts and the bullpen—a location equipped with a telephone for any work that had to be done while sunning in the nude.

Both lower bedrooms had their own private baths. This enhanced their appeal because the room Rose used as her own

---

*Jack Kennedy never stayed at the Palm Beach family home after becoming president. There was no way to make it properly secure, nor could the communication equipment needed by the Secret Service be effectively installed. Instead, when he visited Palm Beach, he stayed down the road with Charles Wrightsman and his wife. Wrightsman had made his money in the oil business, becoming so wealthy that he was able to donate a suite in the Metropolitan Museum of Art. Kennedy would stay there with his security personnel, then walk up the beach to the Kennedy house.

did not allow the family matriarch to see Ted and the members of the third generation sneak their lovers of the moment inside. They could enjoy themselves without her disapproval. (Long privy to the most intimate of the goings-on, I became accustomed to all the members of the second generation—Eunice, Pat, Ted, Jean—conspiratorially pleading, "Don't tell Mother.")

There was another reason for selecting the sunny president's bedroom. As I learned when I worked in the Mediterranean-style home, the house was not the finest work of the famed Miami architect Addison Mizner. The house is extremely large, apparently the only requirement of Rodman Wanamaker, who commissioned its construction in the early years of the century. The trip to Florida was long, and the home was used mostly during the period when Palm Beach weather was most enjoyable. However, it was never designed for the use the Kennedys gave it, and Rose was too cheap to put any money into the place while she lived there.

Who owns the house is sometimes questioned. Some people say the family owns it. Others say that it is owned by the Joseph P. Kennedy Jr. Foundation, which was established in 1946. The truth is that a strip of land between the home's parking lot and the road is owned by the foundation. The house and other grounds belonged to Rose for as long as she lived.

The confusion stems in part from the way the foundation was established, which requires that the house, if owned by the foundation, cannot be used as a vacation home, the way the family members use it. As a result, the family has not transferred it to the foundation. However, when the police arrived after the first allegations of rape that Easter, they were denied entrance because permission allegedly had to come from foundation personnel.

The media presumed that either the statement was a ruse to delay an investigation, or the family was violating tax laws in the manner in which they are using their home. But there is a third consideration. When no one in authority was present and the staff had to give a stranger, including a police official, information concerning how to get permission to come on the grounds, they would tell the person to call either the Park Agency in Manhattan or the foundation offices. There was always someone available who could either speak for the family or quickly locate such an official. What could have been done that Easter but wasn't was for the police to get a search warrant to seek evidence of the alleged crime. Although legal, that might have been impolite, and in Palm Beach, law enforcement is almost always polite to the people who pay their bills. After all, Patty Bowman, even if a victim, had come from across the bridge. She did not deserve the same respect as the Kennedys.

Jack Kennedy never slept in the president's bedroom after his election, but it became the ideal family trysting place. I laughed when Maria Shriver, whose libido was as healthy as any of the other family members, appeared on the *Arsenio Hall Show,* and talked about her marriage to Arnold Schwarzenegger. She was working in television network news and apparently felt the need to maintain the image of the demure newlywed. She essentially claimed that she had never had the relationships of her famous uncles because of her strict Catholic upbringing and her intense work schedule, implying that she was an innocent virgin when she married Arnold. However, I remembered coming into the dining room and encountering Maria sitting at the table with her male friend from the night before. The maid was serving them breakfast, and later told me that Maria's actions were not unusual, especially when she knew there was no risk of her grandmother catching her. As the maid later joked about Maria's affairs during those nights in the president's bedroom, "She'll never die wonderin'."

Although the walls seemed to leak critical heat and cold, the size of the house, the layout, and the external construction were such that noise did not carry. It was likely that a woman screaming for help would not be heard from the beach. Even if heard, the sounds would not necessarily be unusual enough to attract attention.

* * *

Patrons have little loyalty to the nightclubs in Palm Beach, though each club has its own personality. Some are rowdy, others sedate. In some you can dance on the tables. In others, the idea is to drink, talk, and pick up sex partners. Au Bar, for example, the "in" place on the night Willie Smith became an unintended celebrity, was known by young men and young women as a location where you could pick up someone to get laid. The management did not encourage it, but the younger patrons who filled the location during the late night hours understood that anyone alone was fair game.

Au Bar was also a place where a cheeseburger sold for $12, and where celebrities often entertained. That Good Friday, for example, Ivana Trump stopped by Au Bar with a group of twenty people. Her presence, coming as it did when she and her husband were getting constant publicity because of his financial problems, his affairs, and their divorce proceedings, would have caused a great stir of excitement in most locations. At Au Bar, she was just another famous face contending with all the other famous faces for a place to sit or a spot on the dance floor.

For a time, Palm Beach night life had catered to the slightly more sedate residents and visitors. During that period, the swingers went "over the bridge" to West Palm Beach. There the variety of entertainment was greater, but you could not be as certain about the people you might meet. Many of them had attended public schools, and might be "only" in lower management positions, having yet to inherit either businesses or money. Many were young urban professionals with good incomes, but still having to save their money all week for their night on the town. They weren't the same type as those found in Palm Beach, and you never could be certain where or how they lived if you decided to let yourself be picked up. But if you had someone you were seeing, rendering moot all questions of new relationships and one night stands, then going over the bridge was an adequate alternative.

Au Bar changed that. Even West Palm Beach residents were willing to risk the disdain of their neighbors by coming over the bridge from the wrong direction in order to enjoy its night life. They traveled at hours when the rich and powerful were no longer dominating the club. They understood their place in the complex social hierarchy of the area. But Au Bar was the social center of the moment, and everyone wanted to be there, if only to say they had been present on the noisy, overcrowded dance floor where conversations were held by lip reading and guess.

Ted Kennedy, his son Patrick, and his nephew Willie Smith liked Au Bar. The bar made the double Chivas Scotch and soda that was the senator's favorite drink, although the late-night crowd at Au Bar tended to order champagne. Many of the girls hanging out at the club after midnight were from outside Palm Beach, and they were looking to pick up rich young men. Since it was difficult to pick out the wealthy guys by dress alone, a determining factor was the price of the drinks he would buy.

No one is certain how the Kennedy family arrived at Au Bar. The senator's story told of how he, his sister Jean, his son Patrick, Willie Smith, and William Barry and his son Patrick were at the Palm Beach house. (Barry was a retired FBI agent who had worked for Bob as a bodyguard, and who had been present the day he was assassinated.) They had dined together, then gone on to the patio to sip drinks and enjoy the ocean.

The talk apparently was maudlin, with reminiscences of Stephen Smith, who had recently died of cancer, as well as of Bob. It was yet another time when Ted was unimportant, someone who had value only because he had lived in the midst of his brothers. If anything made the night different from others Ted had endured, including Chappaquiddick, it was the fact that Jean, at 64, had become close to Ted. They were the "babies" of the second generation, good friends who seemed to understand each other's pain, each other's fears, each other's strengths and weaknesses.

According to Ted's statement, all of them went to bed around 11:30 that night, but he was unable to sleep. This was a period when he was drinking far too much, using alcohol to dull the night demons he was too insecure to try to exorcise through therapy. Alcohol would calm him, and going to Au Bar would quickly get his mind off the past. He may or may not have been interested in having sex, though he had long been sharing the dates of his sons and nephews. Often, the staff would see Ted and one of the younger Kennedys dancing with girls in the kitchen or some other part of the house. Ted would come on to the dates with some regularity, taking them off to another room for sex when they agreed.

Other depositions taken before the Willie Smith trial tell a slightly different story. Supposedly both Willie and Patrick had gone to a club called Lulu's with two sisters, the daughters of a friend of Jean. If the depositions given by both the sisters and several other witnesses are true, the two men were at Lulu's until at least 1 A.M. Then they dropped off the girls and eventually met up with Ted, either at home or at Au Bar.

Previous to that, at 10:45 P.M., Ted and Patrick stopped briefly at Ann'z, a relatively tame establishment, to have a quiet beer. They easily could have returned home and gone to bed, or Patrick could have joined his cousin prior to all three males meeting up at Au Bar. As so frequently happens with Kennedy family coverups, there were so many official stories and so many people anxious to have been witnesses to events involving them, that the truth has to be pulled from a grab bag of responses.

Whether Ted awakened his nephews from their beds, as he claimed, or they all went out before Patrick and Willie had considered going to bed, is not important. What matters was that they arrived, went to the bar, and stood drinking. Patrick and his father remained at the bar for forty-five minutes before they were able to get a table. Willie had no interest in male companionship, picked up a girl and went to the dance floor.

Ted and Patrick were quickly joined by two girls, one of whom was to prove to be an opportunist trying to capitalize on her moment of rather odd fame. This was Michele Cassone, and with her was Anne Mercer. (The Mercer deposition said that Ted and Patrick joined her, not the other way around.) Apparently there was an argument where Ted felt that Anne was being rude to his son, and eventually the senator, his son, and Michele Cassone went back to the house. Willie had to be driven back by the girl he was with, Patty Bowman.

There are two pictures of Patty Bowman that emerge when investigating her background. The first is that of a wild, wealthy young woman who would do anything for a good time. She was raised in Akron, Ohio, a city known as the rubber capital of the world. Her mother, after a divorce, worked as a secretary in the area, later marrying Michael O'Neil, the son of William O'Neil, the founder of General Tire Company. In addition to O'Neil's millions, Patty's mother added to her new husband's fortune by becoming a successful real estate investor. When Patty attended Hamilton Holt College in Orlando, Florida, her family was quite wealthy.

Patty worked several lower-paying jobs in the Palm Beach area, including with a law firm, the *Palm Beach Post*, and Disney World. She was known for reckless driving, including having her license suspended eight times in nine years, and she was considered a wild party girl. But when she fell in love with a wealthy West Palm Beach businessman, having his child, then discovering that he was unwilling to get married, her life seemed to change. By the time she encountered Willie Smith, she had moved to Jupiter, Florida, with her small child, living in a comfortable pink home provided by her stepfather.

Patty Bowman's life in Jupiter was a radical departure from the apartment in which she had been living in Palm Beach. The home was in the heart of a suburban, family-oriented community. In order for Patty to reach Au Bar, she had to arrange for a sitter, then drive a considerable distance from home. She obviously wanted to enjoy herself that evening, but she no longer would allow her personal life to be such that it would affect her relationship with her daughter.

What happened next? According to the police report filed by Detective Christine Rigolo:

> After 12:00 A.M., midnight, on 033091 [March 30, 1991] the victim met suspect, William Kennedy Smith at the Au Bar, 336 Royal Poinciana Way, Palm Beach, Palm

Beach County, Florida. At the Au Bar, the victim and Smith talked and danced together. Smith introduced the victim to his uncle, Senator Edward Kennedy and also to his cousin, Patrick Kennedy. Near closing time Smith stated that his uncle and his cousin had left. Smith stated that he did not have a way home, so he asked the victim for a ride to the Kennedy Estate, at 1095 North Ocean Blvd., Palm Beach, Florida. The victim agreed to give Smith a ride to the estate.

Upon arriving at the Kennedy estate the victim stated that she kissed Smith good-night and Smith asked if the victim would like to see the estate and also take a walk down to the beach. The victim agreed.*

Was Bowman "asking for trouble" by agreeing to go with Smith? When talking with people in Palm Beach, it becomes rapidly apparent that the Kennedys are an object of intense

---

*What was not stated in the police report, but what would become an issue in the trial, was the fact that Patty Bowman's pantyhose were removed and left in the car before she went on the beach. Bowman claimed that she could not remember taking them off, a statement the jury felt might not be true. The assumption was that she had taken them off in anticipation of having sex with Smith, an argument that cannot be refuted, though for which there is no corroboration.

Another possibility was that Bowman removed her pantyhose to keep them from getting ripped when going barefoot on the beach. Rocks, stones, sand, and other objects would almost certainly cause a tear. Stockings and pantyhose are so notorious for getting runs, it is likely that any woman planning to walk the beach might do what she did. The fact that the action may have been less modest than others would approve could reflect the woman's general attitude toward life, and it could just indicate that her inhibitions were lowered by alcohol.

A third possibility was raised by a staff person who was on the grounds shortly after the alleged rape and who knew both Smith and his uncle quite well. "I think she said 'yes,' then changed her mind. You don't change your mind with the Senator or with Will when they've been drinking. They'll just do it to you, and I think that's what happened with Patty Bowman. Will wouldn't take 'no' for an answer."

fascination. Most residents dislike them. They are not considered part of "proper" society, and they have few local friends. Yet the idea of being invited onto the grounds, to be able to see more of the house than is visible from the street, is exciting. An invitation, even at an early hour of the morning, is not to be turned down.

The victim stated that she and Smith entered a door leading into the kitchen area. The kitchen area is divided into three parts. For the purpose of this affidavit, the rooms will be designated as the "mud room," the "kitchen," and the last room is the "pantry," which also has a doorway that leads into the dining room. The victim stated that Senator Edward Kennedy and Patrick Kennedy were standing in the doorway that leads from the "pantry" into the dining room. She said that they turned and walked into the dining room when she and Smith entered the room.

The victim said that she and Smith talked for a short time in the pantry and then walked through the dining room and out a doorway on the east side of the house. She said that they walked to a stairway that led to the beach. The victim states that they again observed Senator Kennedy and Patrick on the property, but that no words were exchanged, and she assumed that the Senator and Patrick were walking back to the house.

The victim stated that she and Smith talked for a while on the beach and exchanged some kisses, but the victim states that she felt that there were no sexual overtures. The victim said that Smith asked her to swim but she declined. The victim stated that at no time did she remove her clothing or enter the water.

The victim said that Smith told her that he was going in for a swim and took off his shirt. The victim said that when Smith began unfastening his pants she became uncomfortable and turned away. She said that she called out to him and said that it was late and she was going to leave. The victim advised that she walked up to the stairway and climbed the stairs. She states that her left foot was on the top of the stairway and that her right foot was leaving the last stair when her lower right leg was grabbed. (On 033091 at the time the victim was making the report, there was some visible bruising to her lower right leg, just above the ankle.) The victim stated that she did not know Smith's intentions at that time. However, because of an old injury to her neck she feels that she is fragile and fears reinjuring a preexisting back injury. (It should be noted that when the victim was approximately 15 years old she was involved in a serious automobile accident. Medical records of the victim confirm that she suffered a severe neck and back injury. As a result of that injury the victim underwent surgery during which a bone graft was taken from her hip and used to fuse three vertebrae in the victim's neck.)

The victim stated that she broke free from Smith's grasp on her lower leg and began running south across the Estate lawn, toward the pool area. The victim stated that as she was running she was tackled from behind. She said that she was forced onto her back with Smith on top of her and that Smith held her down with his body weight and chest. She said that Smith pinned down her left arm out to her side and her right arm was pinned between them. The victim said that she tried to get up but that Smith slammed her back to the ground with his chest. The victim is approximately 5′ 6″, 130 lbs., and Smith is approximately 6′, 180 lbs. The victim said that Smith pulled her dress up and pushed aside her panties [rest of sentence blacked out before release to press]. She said that she [censored before release] attempted to push him [censored] but that he [censored] was trying to push her hand away and told her to, "stop it bitch." The victim stated that she screamed and told him, "NO" and to stop several times. The victim said that she remembers hearing herself screaming and wondering why no one in the house would come out and help her, especially since she knew that Senator Kennedy was in the house. The victim stated that she believes that Smith [censored].

The victim said that she got away from Smith and ran into the house. The victim stated that the reason she went back into the house was because she was unfamiliar with the layout of the property and had been brought out to the back yard through the house. (It should be noted that there is a north wall that runs the entire length of the estate, from the seawall, on the east, to North Ocean Blvd., on the west. Although there is a walkway from the back yard to the exit through the wall, the victim was unaware that it existed.) Once inside the house the victim stated that she was hysterical and extremely fearful that Smith was going to find her. She said that she saw an area in the kitchen between an ice chest and a cabinet and decided to hide there. That location was later determined to be in the southeast corner of the "pantry." She said that she tried to calm herself and noticed a red light on a telephone, which was located on a shelf adjacent to her. The victim said that she called a friend, Anne Mercer, who had been with her at Au Bar that night. She said that she told Mercer that she had been raped and that she needed her to come get her at the Kennedy estate. (It should be noted that Anne Mercer was at her home in West Palm Beach, Florida, with her boyrfriend, Chuck Desiderio at the time of the phone call.) Witnesses Mercer and Desiderio have stated that the phone call that they received from the victim, advising that she had been raped, was between 4:00 A.M. and 4:30 A.M. After the phone call they said that they drove immediately to the Kennedy estate.

The victim said that she heard Smith calling out her name [Censored. At the time the document was released, the victim had not been identified publicly.] and that she was afraid he was going to find her. She said that she started moving through the "pantry" and began entering the "kitchen," on her way to leave the house, when she felt her arm being grabbed. The victim stated that Smith grabbed her arm and she began screaming, and said "Michael, you've raped me." (It should be noted that the victim stated that she was extremely upset at that time and does not know why she called him Michael.) She said that Smith then grabbed her harder and said, "why are you calling me Michael? My name is William." The victim said that Smith's demeanor was "ferocious." She said, "I didn't know what he was going to do to me then. I was petrified that he was going to start hitting me, or that he was going to rape me again, or that he was going to kill me." She said that Smith pulled her into a room that had a stairway along the left wall and windows along the right wall. She said that Smith let her go and sat in an easy chair, crossed his legs and appeared very composed and sure of himself. The victim said that she then said, "you raped me," and that Smith replied that he did not rape her, and that no one would believe her anyway. The victim said that she believed Smith, that "no one would believe her."

The report continued, telling of Anne Mercer arriving to take her home. She explained that before leaving the house with her friend, she took a photograph in an inexpensive plastic frame, a yellow legal pad with some telephone numbers on it, and an urn. The latter was taken by Desiderio, who accompanied her through the property and back to the car. The items were turned over to the police department on Saturday, March 30, as proof that she had been where she claimed to have been.

The victim stated that she did not report the crime immediately because she feared that no one would believe her. She felt that due to the prominence of the suspect and his relationship in the Kennedy family, that the Town of Palm Beach Police Department would not believe her and would take no action on her complaint. She also stated that she was hysterical after the assault and did not know what to do.

Bowman talked with a Rape Crisis Line counselor at 9 A.M. Saturday morning. At the counselor's urging, a report was filed, the information taken at 2:00 P.M. by the Palm Beach Police Department. Three hours earlier she had attempted to register her complaint with the Sheriff's Office, but it was not that department's jurisdiction.

Before providing the other details of that weekend, it is important to keep several facts in mind. First, Patty Bowman called Willie by the name of Michael, something that troubled both of them. The name was also her stepfather's name, a fact that Kennedy supporters are quick to point out, seemingly trying to imply that perhaps there had been some trauma with her stepfather and that she transferred thoughts about him to Willie.

Such a story is intriguing, of course, with all manner of pseudo-incestuous ramifications. However, her body was bruised when she went to the hospital, and her injuries were severe enough so that there appeared to be a fracture of the seventh rib. (There wasn't.) She had obviously taken a hard fall in the manner she described, though not necessarily for the reasons she described. Photographs were taken of the bruising on her leg, shoulders, and arms. Full penetration had occurred, semen was present, and Willie later admitted that sex had taken place. It was unprotected, no effort having been made to use a condom.

There was also the emotional state observed by the detective questioning her. The report stated the observations: ''She [Bowman] was sitting on a couch with her legs drawn up to her chest, in a fetal position, and she would panic at any quick movement in the room. She appeared to be emotionally frightened, distraught, and in shock, she was physically shaking. The victim was also exhibiting pain when she would change position on the couch, and when walking she could only manage to walk at a very slow pace.'' The report also stated, ''During the physical examination the victim would become very withdrawn and frightened and would not permit the physician to touch her. She would then calm down, regain her composure and permit the physician to continue her examination.''

In other statements, additional facts were revealed. Bowman's judgment easily could have been impaired. She talked of having two glasses of wine, then, over dinner, splitting a bottle of chianti with Anne Mercer and Chuck Desiderio. She also took the muscle relaxant Carisoprodol at 8 o'clock because of the back pain she was enduring.

Michael O'Neil was also known to be an enemy of the Kennedys, dating back to business deals where he had been hurt by Joe Kennedy. O'Neil was active in the Republican Party in 1960 and had worked to assure the Kennedy loss in Ohio during the presidential election.

Author John H. Davis, when preparing to write about the allegations against Smith for the paperback update of his book *The Kennedys: Dynasty and Disaster,* interviewed his longtime friend Gino Desiderio, the uncle of Chuck. According to that interview, Chuck allegedly believed that Bowman was not physically injured or in pain when he picked her up. The suspicion was that Patty was trying to either win favor with her stepfather for hurting a Kennedy, or seeking money that would ultimately come her way.

Only Patty Bowman knows if she wanted to gain favor from her stepfather. But the money angle quickly proved false. In interviews with several tabloid journalists involved with trying to get Bowman's story, it was discovered that the price paid for a story is always based on the number of additional copies of the tabloid the story will sell. The exclusive story, which the tabloid would then syndicate to other publications internationally, was expected to arouse so much interest that $1 million was considered a fair high-end offer. But Patty refused all offers, quite literally the first such ''instant celebrity'' any of the journalists had encountered who declined.

Of equal importance was the fact that Bowman never returned

to the media to obtain money. She did not later try to sell her story, something she might have done if she was holding out for what she thought would be a larger offer. And when she went public, she did so on network television, again refusing any payment.

By contrast, Michele Cassone had remained at the compound for part of those early morning hours, though inside with Patrick. She claimed that when a drunken Ted came by wearing only a long shirt, she was so upset that she left. Patrick claims to have gone to bed and to have been asleep when the alleged rape occurred. However, once Michele learned what had happened, she used the incident as her ticket to fame and fortune. She gave interviews to anyone at any time, provided they paid her.

I was asked to be on the Sally Jesse Raphael television program to discuss the case, along with Patty Bowman's attorney, Michele Cassone, and others. I was probably the most knowledgeable of the guests, having learned about the case from Kennedy staff members even before the story was released to the media. I had known Willie Smith and Ted and Patrick Kennedy for more than a decade. I had worked in the home, knew the grounds, and knew Palm Beach, West Palm Beach, and Jupiter intimately.

Cassone, by contrast, could claim familiarity for a matter of only hours. Yet she obviously thought of herself as the star of the show. Either she or someone helping her had contacted the news media, assuring that she would be filmed, photographed, and interviewed when she arrived. Her clothing consisted of a short white skirt and a sleeveless blouse so casual she might have been going to a Palm Beach lunch counter rather than making a network television appearance. She sat apart from everyone else in the waiting area for guests. Her only concerns seemed to be her makeup and getting a copy of the videotape of the show and still photographs taken during the show. And when she spoke, it was obvious that she had almost no knowledge of the Kennedys, and no more knowledge of the allegations than anyone who read the daily newspaper. I also noticed that

Michele's description of the Kennedy house was frequently inaccurate, indicating that she had either not seen as much as she claimed, or had not paid very close attention.

Her stories varied at times, but always she demanded justice against the horrid Kennedy family. She was like a spiritual sister to the victim, a crusader for justice because the real victim could not appear. The trouble was that she looked and acted like an opportunist, someone who would say almost anything for money, and some members of the press decided to learn more about her.

The climax of her "career" came on what seemed at first to be a shocking segment of the television show *A Current Affair*. Later, when Cassone attempted a suicide, the pathetic nature of all the opportunists related to the case became apparent. But at the time it seemed that she had simply gotten her comeuppance.

At some time in the past, Michele, in love with a man she was dating, posed for sexually explicit photographs. Posing may have been stupid, but it was the act of a girl in love, wanting to please her boyfriend and not thinking about the consequences. Having broken up with Michele, the boyfriend thought mostly of the $16,000 he was allegedly paid by *Current Affair's* field producer, Malcolm Balfour.

Steve Dunleavy, the on-air reporter, took Michele, who was being paid $1,000 for her appearance, to lunch at New York's 21 Club. It was April 23, and the story of Willie Smith's Easter weekend was old news. Something more was needed, and Dunleavy felt he could seduce it from Michele.

Lunch included two $90 bottles of 1987 Pouilly-Fuisse from the club's extensive wine list. By the time Dunleavy, Michele, a girlfriend who accompanied her to lunch, and Balfour arrived at the studio at 3:15 that afternoon, Michele was coherent but not sober.

Dunleavy went right after Michele's opportunistic nature, setting her up by three times asking her if she would ever pose nude for *Penthouse*. She claimed that she would never do something like that, the response he wanted. Then he removed four color photos, holding them at such an angle that she could see them but the audience could not view the most explicit of them.

Michele gasped in horror. Two pictures showed her topless in a swimming pool, and the other two showed her engaging in a sex act. She tried to grab the pictures, and then attacked the much larger Dunleavy. She yanked his tie and kneed him in the groin. When he grabbed her wrists, she bit his hand. The power that her rage gave her meant that others had to come to Dunleavy's help. But by then the story was on tape.

Of course, the media was obviously more opportunistic than Michele. They knew from the start the depth of her knowledge, but because her lifestyle and the circumstances enabled them to portray her as a bimbo, they enjoyed paying her for appearances. The extremes they went through to hurt her in a manner unrelated to the case would prove typical in the coverage of what some reporters saw as the best Kennedy story since Chappaquiddick.

Everyone's credibility was questioned early in the case when the issues of the violence and the lack of a condom arose. Bowman's past was dredged up, too. On July 23, 1976, college student Mark Rodeman, then nineteen, picked up Patty, whom he thought was at least eighteen. She was actually underage, but had sneaked out of her house looking for a good time. Rodeman lost control of his car and smashed into an embankment. Patty, rushed to Children's Hospital Medical Center in Akron, had a broken neck. She had to be in traction, her neck in a brace, and extra support was later provided through surgery, which fused a piece of hip bone to a vertebra in her upper spine.

From that day forward, Patty Bowman was very careful to avoid hurting her neck. She knew that a harsh jolt could leave her paralyzed, and a more severe injury could cause her death.

Dr. William Smith, having completed his training in internal medicine, had to be keenly aware of sexually transmitted diseases, including AIDS. He knew that the use of a condom was critical for health. Yet he had unprotected sex.

Smith later claimed that the sex was voluntary. He had been rough with her because she wanted him to grab her, to forcefully pin her down. It was a game, he explained.

Certainly the lack of a condom and the nature of Bowman's past injuries substantiated the allegations to many people. However, both parties had been drinking and were not thinking clearly. Thus it would not have been unlikely for Willie Smith to think only of his sexual desire, not common sense protection. And it would not have been unlikely for Patty Bowman to fail to think about her neck during a moment of drunken lust on the grounds of one of the nation's most famous families.

So was Patty Bowman raped, or did she have consensual sex?

The Kennedy family may or may not have known but certainly did not seem to care. Maybe Willie raped the woman, in which case there was a disturbing violent streak that indicated a need for therapy. Rape is not a sex crime, though it utilizes a sex act. Rather it is a crime of violence, a means of hurting the victim in a way our society considers the most demeaning and painful possible.

Anger toward women was a common aspect among many of the Kennedy men. The abuse might have been verbal, psychological, or physical, but it was repeated frequently with any number of short-term relationships. There were allegations that rapes had been committed by the second-generation men, though never reported. Research into the Smith case, for example, resulted in more than a dozen women coming forward to testify that Willie had raped them and/or tried to physically force himself upon them against their will. One alleged victim was a friend of Willie's mother; others were women he had met at parties, in medical school, and elsewhere. There were stories in publications such as *Spy* magazine detailing past encounters.

But the initial problem the Kennedys faced was controlling the police, not the media, and from what they had learned through the Chappaquiddick experience, they were masters of the game.

First came avoidance. It was Easter Sunday, and the Kennedys, Smiths, and Barrys were preparing to eat when the police arrived. The officers asked a staff member to tell Ted and Willie that they were there to talk with them.

William Barry covered for the senator. He said that he thought Ted was out at the moment, and that Willie had left the area an hour earlier, though he wasn't certain. He promised to have Ted contact the officers in the next hour when he returned.

There was a second attempt to locate Smith and his uncle, this time by telephone an hour after the contact at the house. A housekeeper explained that Barry had just driven the senator and Willie to the airport to catch a 3:00 P.M. flight. He would be back sometime after the plane's departure, and he would call then, which he did. It was 3:20 P.M., and as Barry explained, the police had just missed the men they were seeking.

Barry lied. Ted and Willie hid from the police, then Willie fled the city, Barry and Jean Smith taking him to the airport to catch the flight out of town. Ted stayed in Palm Beach another day, returning to Washington on Monday. Yet later efforts to bring obstruction of justice charges against former FBI agent Barry, whose loyalty to the Kennedys was greater than his sense of responsibility to law enforcement, proved futile. He was not guilty of obstructing justice, and the two men were not guilty of a criminal act for leaving town. No one had as yet been criminally charged.

Ted Kennedy would later claim that he had misunderstood the allegations against his nephew. Since the term *sexual battery* was used (Florida legal terminology for *rape*), he claimed he thought that Willie was being investigated for sexual harassment. Yet because of the way he hid from the police, that statement seemed hollow.

There were other activities that weekend. Amanda Smith, Willie's younger sister, went to mass with Bill Barry, Jean Smith, and her brother Willie. It was a 10 o'clock mass, and at some time after that, Ted and Patrick Kennedy went to Chuck and Harold's Restaurant, another popular eating establishment in Palm Beach. Despite the early hour, both men drank, according to the deposition of bartender Tatianna Lee. The senator had two alcoholic beverages followed by Perrier water. Patrick had a mixed drink. The two men were allegedly overheard discussing the possible allegation of rape that might be made against Willie.

By Monday it was clear that the issue of Willie Smith's guilt or innocence did not matter to the Kennedy family, nor did it seem to matter to the Palm Beach Police Department. If anything could be done to avoid a conviction, it would be done. Truth was secondary. And as with Chappaquiddick, the family destroyed the person they were protecting.

First there was the police effort that has left the impression that it was meant to assure Willie would get off. Whether routine procedure was deliberately avoided for the Kennedys, or whether it was the result of a department whose priorities had become skewered through too many compromises over too many years, is unknown. All that is certain is that a crime of violence was reported by the person who claimed to be the victim and the police did not send a scientific investigation unit to check the grounds for possible physical evidence. No effort was made the day of the reporting, or the next day. In fact, the grounds were not checked for three weeks, during which rain storms and routine grounds maintenance occurred, predictably destroying that which might have convicted or cleared the accused.

Such a check might have resulted in the trial taking place exactly as it did—with each person stating a different story, the jury having to decide who was telling the truth. But what is important is that it is routine for the police to check for evidence before it can be lost or destroyed. The case might have been a relatively low priority on the day it was reported, but without incompetence or deliberate negligence on the part of the police, it seems highly irregular that the search would be delayed more than 24 hours.

If it is possible to come to the defense of the Palm Beach police investigators, perhaps they were convinced of Willie

Smith's innocence. Perhaps after taking the statement from the alleged victim, they decided she was not telling the truth. Yet their conclusions meant nothing. Their job was to investigate, to collect evidence, to obtain the statements of everyone involved in the allegations, including all witnesses. They were then to present that information to the prosecutor's office where it would be determined whether or not to bring charges. By doing anything less, they were derelict at best. At worst, they deliberately covered up for a rich, powerful family inclined to look favorably upon those who help them.

A second issue, one seldom addressed in the press, was the release of Willie Smith's name by either the defense team or law enforcement officers. Trying to investigate the release of his name has so far proven impossible, everyone blaming everyone else. What matters is that Willie Smith was named as the person suspected in a possible rape on the Kennedy grounds even before there was a criminal indictment.

The conflict between a free press and the right of a defendant to a fair trial has long been argued in the courts. This is especially true with a rape case. Although there are far more vicious crimes that occur, especially child molestation and the deliberate maiming of another person, most Americans are hostile to rapists. Some people ridicule the person who rapes, laughing at the person's inability to find a sex partner in a "normal" way. Others ridicule the victim. And still others recognize the crime for what it is, an angry act of violence acted out with sex but revealing a deeper, potentially dangerous motivation. They fear the anger remaining in the rapist, wondering when the person will go too far; when the violence will escalate to murder.

Technically, someone is innocent until proven guilty, and juries do find individuals innocent of crimes for which they are arrested. Yet the fact of being arrested implies probable guilt to the average person. When the person named is famous, there is an even greater presumption of guilt, because who would want to falsely accuse the rich and powerful?

The release of Willie Smith's name *before* he was charged

assured nationwide pretrial publicity that could only hurt his reputation. It had to have been done deliberately, and many insiders believe it was done to give Willie the chance to appeal if he was convicted. His lawyers could charge that the publicity he received before he was arrested made it impossible for him to have a fair trial. Any jurors selected would be biased. With luck, he would avoid jail entirely, even if guilty, based on the issue of fairness, a valid one that would not have arisen had his name not deliberately been leaked.

Thus, the headline on the front page of *The Palm Beach Post* for Wednesday, May 8, 1991, almost six weeks after the incident, read: "Police Want Smith Charged with Rape." And the article, written by Val Ellicott and Charles Homes, began this way:

PALM BEACH—Police said Tuesday that they will recommend that William Kennedy Smith be charged with raping a Jupiter woman at the Kennedy estate over Easter weekend. "We do know a crime occurred, and our recommendation (to prosecutors) will reflect that," police spokesman Craig Gunkel said Tuesday. "We're confident that a sexual battery did occur."

A week earlier, in what amounted to an attack against Palm Beach Police Chief Joseph Terlizzese and State Attorney David Bludworth, who was also talking about convening a grand jury to avoid making a decision to prosecute himself, the *Miami Herald* noted what happened with other sexual assault cases in Palm Beach. The paper's reporters reviewed rape allegation cases going back to 1987. The first incident mentioned occurred on February 18, 1989, when a woman first claimed that she was raped, then said that she wasn't.

The second rape allegation came on November 2, 1989, in what was an extremely sensitive case. A woman claimed that her father sexually assaulted his grandchildren in March 1987. Emotions were high, and the length of time that had passed required careful investigation into the allegations. However, by January 31, 1990, the police asked for an arrest warrant.

More typical was the first case to be similar to that of Patty Bowman in that the victim identified her assailant. It took twelve hours for the man to be arrested. On January 23, 1988, a man accused of attempted rape was arrested in two days. An October 14, 1990, rape resulted in an arrest four days later. A June 30, 1987, rape resulted in an August 24 arrest. But one on October 21, 1987, resulted in a same day arrest. Finally, on October 1, 1987, a man was arrested for allegedly forcing a woman to perform a sex act eleven days earlier. None of the cases required a grand jury. None of the cases had delays in a full-scale investigation. None of the cases involved a Kennedy.

A profile of Willie Smith that ran the same day as the story of the police recommendation to indict ironically mentioned that Stephen Smith was the man responsible for "damage control" after Mary Jo Kopechne was killed. It also portrayed Willie as the quiet Kennedy, someone who had majored in history, was interested in children, and worked for a year for the Wall Street investment banking firm of Rothschild, Unterberg and Towbin, the same type of business in which his father was skilled. However, Willie was uncomfortable with such work and traveled to both mainland China and Taiwan, eventually working as a volunteer laboratory assistant at a Seventh-Day Adventist Hospital in Taiwan. The travels lasted more than a year, from February 1984 to December 1985. He gained a working knowledge of Chinese, and the experience seemed to stimulate his interest in medicine, for he abandoned history and political science and enrolled in medical school in 1987.

The Kennedy damage control plan for Smith was a simple one. Before Willie had his day in court, it was necessary to destroy the credibility of Patty Bowman. If the case became a contest between the two parties, as seemed likely given the failure of the police to investigate in a timely manner, the Kennedy defense team wanted to be certain the jury liked Willie more than Patty.

At the same time, the news media decided to take on Willie's more sordid reputation. Later there would be reports of Patty Bowman's failings, but first it would be Willie's turn to take the heat. It was yet more motivation for the defense team to try to destroy the young doctor's accuser.

Rape is actually a simple charge no matter what term is used to describe it under the law. If one person has sex with another without consent, it is rape. A prostitute can have voluntary sex with a man 100 times, but if the 101st time he asks, she says, "no," and he forces himself upon her anyway, it is rape.

Without witnesses, the question becomes one of whether or not intercourse occurred with mutual consent. This is always true with unmarried adults. However, many juries are biased according to a victim's past. Thus a nun who says she refused a man's advances is more likely to be believed than is a woman who is notorious for spending her weekends in hotel bars, picking up men for sex. The law does not discriminate between virgin victims and those who have extensive sexual experience. If he asks, she refuses, and he does it anyway, it is rape. But the Kennedy defense team wanted to be certain the jury would see things their way.

Stories were planted with the media, including one in which the alleged victim supposedly returned to the mansion and kissed Willie good night after the rape supposedly occurred. Since Anne Mercer was directly involved with the aftermath, her credibility was challenged by reports of her father being in prison, as well as allegations that her father was in some way an associate of Nicodemo "Little Nicky" Scarfo, who was involved in organized crime in Philadelphia. Neither Scarfo, who was in jail at the time, nor Leonard Mercer had any connection with the case.

Witnesses were allegedly threatened with revelations of personal indiscretions. And newspapers were told that Patty Bowman was a thief who cried rape only after being caught stealing the valuable urn removed from the property, which she had taken to prove she had been there.

Later there would be stories that Patty had at least three abortions and a miscarriage, the pregnancies resulting from different fathers. One former boyfriend claimed that a Kennedy investigator told him that Patty was known to have had sex with a man, then call him and demand money. There was a report released that investigators had discovered the sperm of three different men in the woman's body, which was not true.

By June 1, Bowman fought back by allowing the release of a three-and-a half-hour polygraph exam she took on April 22. A polygraph is not admitted in evidence in Florida courts because of its potential for error. But what mattered with Bowman's exam was the degree of questioning. Palm Beach Police Sgt. Keith Robinson honed in on all the dirty little secrets Patty might try to hide during the test conducted by Warren Holmes of Holmes Polygraph Service of Miami.

Patty's story of being tackled, pinned to the ground, and forced to have sex were all considered truthful. But also considered truthful were her answers to embarrassingly intimate questions. In a report released to Val Ellicott of the *Palm Beach Post,* the young woman said that she began using marijuana when in her early teens, though stopped when she was fourteen. However, after that she used stimulants and depressants, mescaline, alcohol, and cocaine, the latter as often as once a week, during her early twenties. She claimed that she had not had cocaine since December 29, 1990. She said that while she was never a drug dealer, she was present when drug sales were being discussed.

Bowman's traffic tickets were discussed, and she said that she had at least seventeen, mostly for speeding. She also said she shoplifted when she was fourteen, the same year her neck was broken.

Her income included $1,700 per month from a trust fund established by her stepfather. Although not during the polygraph, she also discussed battering and other abuse she received from her father before her mother divorced the man. Others would relate her teenage wildness to an emotional reaction to the unresolved issues from that abuse.

The tabloids took whichever side sold publications. At first they went after Willie because of the Kennedy connection. Later they attacked everyone. Among the headlines of the various papers were the following:

KENNEDYS' NIGHT OF WINE, WOMEN AND WRONG DOING WITH THE SCOTCH-SWILLING SENATOR

BOOZY NIGHT AT PALM BEACH BAR ENDS WITH SOBBING WOMAN PLEADING TO BE RESCUED

DIRTY TRICKS AT PALM BEACH SMACK OF ONE MORE KENNEDY COVERUP

WILLY'S OWN STORY: SHE BEGGED ME FOR ROUGH SEX

THAT KENNEDY KID NEARLY KILLED HER, SAYS OUTRAGED DAD

KENNEDY RAPE VICTIM SNORTED COKE AND HAD THREE ABORTIONS

KENNEDY RAPE VICTIM'S SECRET TERROR: WILLIE MADE ME PREGNANT

RAPE GAL EXPOSED

BRITS UNMASK SECRET HEIRESS WHO CHARGED TED'S YOUNG NEPHEW WITH SHOCKING ATTACK

BLONDE BEHIND RAPE CHARGE IS AN UNWED MOM WITH POSH HOME

JOAN AND JACKIE BLAST TED FOR LEADING THEIR KIDS ON BOOZY, SKIRT-CHASING HUNTS

The last headline was especially confusing. Joan Kennedy, a recovering alcoholic, was the mother of Patrick, whose career as a Rhode Island state senator could have been jeopardized by his association with the rape charges. She had left Ted because of his unrepentant womanizing. She had tried to help their children grow up to be healthy, responsible individuals. She had gone through the emotional hell of seeing one son, Teddy Jr., lose a leg to cancer, then admit himself to treatment for what he stated was alcoholism. She also had suffered with

Patrick when he had a benign tumor pressing against his spinal cord, and while the removal was successful, the surgery could have caused paralysis. Thus Ted's actions were especially despicable to her, as well as adding stress beyond what she had long experienced.

By contrast, Jacqueline Kennedy had nothing to do with the situation. Her children were not in Palm Beach. No one ever alleged that her son, John Jr., was connected with the case. And though Caroline was intimately involved with the death of another Kennedy grandchild, she, too, had nothing to do with the case. However, as the editors and publishers of the various tabloids explained, they chose their headlines based on what would increase their sales. "Jackie" sold more papers than "Jean Smith," the mother of Willie, who was the key player in the story. And Joan Kennedy, the wife of the senator, had a higher name recognition and buyer interest than any of the other mothers except Jacqueline.

By the time of the December 1991 trial, postponed from August, no one other than partisans knew what to think. Other alleged victims of Willie's sexual aggression were revealed. Prosecutor Moira Lasch found three alleged victims who were willing to come forward and take the stand, though the judge did not allow them because an accused's past cannot be held against him. There were reports in the tabloids of Alexandra Marr, a twenty-eight-year-old London socialite having been beaten by Willie, though no criminal charges were filed.

Eventually the three women whose testimony was not heard discussed their stories with members of the press, though remaining anonymous. One of the women talked of being raped in Willie's Washington, D.C., apartment. A second woman, a medical student at the time, discussed being assaulted after a pool party in the Smith family's home, though he did not rape her. And the third was dating Willie's cousin, Max Kennedy. She was nineteen at the time, and accepted an invitation to spend the night of a party in a Kennedy family guest room. She claimed that a drunk Willie pushed her on the bed, tried to remove her clothing, and touched her in a sexual manner.

She said that she forced him from her body and escaped, after which he apologized. All the women had given sworn depositions, but none were called to testify, and thus none faced cross examination by Willie's defense attorneys.

The court presentation lasted ten days. The jury deliberated just seventy-seven minutes before reaching its decision to acquit Willie Smith. The ten days provided one of the greatest shows on television, and the cameras of Cable News Network (CNN) recorded the entire drama.

The ratings for the days-long soap opera were immense, CNN reporting that the 3.2 million Americans watching the proceedings were nine times their usual audience. Bowman's face was blocked with a blue dot during the broadcast in order to assure her privacy, though her name had been released by the tabloid *The Globe,* British newspapers, the *New York Times,* and other publications. Patty herself would not go public until she agreed to an interview with Diane Sawyer, a respected television journalist who did not pay Bowman for the appearance.

There was discussion of the underclothing the alleged victim had worn that night, including the tensile strength of her black bra. She was asked about how Willie forced her legs apart and whether or not penetration had been difficult or easy, implying she might have been sexually aroused. The questions were intimate, the attitude of Smith's defense attorney Roy Black one of mild condescension. He was respectful enough so that the jury did not turn against him or his client. However, he did his best to make her appear a liar. On Thursday, December 12, her eyes swollen from tears, she leaned forward and angrily scolded both Smith and his attorney. "What he did to me was wrong," she said. "I don't want to live for the rest of my life in fear of that man. I don't want to be responsible for him doing it to someone else."

Judge Mary Lupo was forced to order the jurors to disregard the statement, and Attorney Black dutifully objected to her statements. However, just before she left the stand and the courtroom, not talking to reporters, she said to Black, "Sir, your client raped me."

But the jury decided that there was a reasonable doubt.

Outside the courtroom was a show in itself. For years the Kennedy name had been used to sell newspapers and magazines. At first the focus had been Jacqueline Kennedy Onassis and her children, Caroline and John Jr. First she was the widow, and her suffering seemed to lead the nation in mourning. She was respected in much the manner of the mother of Christ, though she had been the wife, not the one who had given birth, and her picture did not hang in homes in the manner of the Madonna.

Ted Kennedy was also popular with the press, as was his wife, Joan, perhaps the most attractive of the Kennedy women. Rose Kennedy was still good for sales, but the rest of the family usually required one scandal or another to boost the circulation of a magazine that ran their pictures.

Someone who did not have the Kennedy name, who took a job, worked hard, and became a professional, as Maria Shriver did when she entered the world of television news, was of limited interest. The tabloids ran stories about Maria Shriver and Maria *Kennedy* Shriver, neither approach affecting circulation figures. Eventually, after she married the immensely popular Arnold Schwarzenegger, she was usually referred to as "Arnold Schwarzenegger's wife," an appellation that *did* boost sales.

The final sales tool is the Kennedy scandal. Ted Kennedy has often handled the honors in recent years, being photographed having sex with one woman, in drunken revelry with another, and generally carrying on in a manner disdained by most people after the age of twenty-five. Still, any time the name Kennedy can be linked to disreputable behavior, the media goes into a frenzy. People were delighted to read about the traumas, whether in the sensational though generally accurate *National Enquirer, Star, People, Us,* or *USA Today,* or in the more serious publications, such as *Newsweek, Time,* or *U.S.*

News & World Report. They wanted to hear about the case on network news shows, CNN, National Public Radio, and the entertainment/newsmagazine format shows such as *Hard Copy*. Readers in Canada, England, Australia, Germany, Japan, and elsewhere wanted information. Some overseas publications sent reporters, others relied upon syndicated material and satellite relays. Whatever the case, a Kennedy rape combined money, sex, power, and violence—all the things that make for great ratings and circulation boosters.

The trial was held in West Palm Beach, and that fact made the situation even nicer for the locals. The proper image of Palm Beach was not jeopardized, yet the courthouse was close enough so that a short drive might allow a glimpse of the reporters whose celebrity status was more of a curiosity than the trial. (More than five hundred came for the trial.) Everyone knew the Kennedys in Palm Beach, and few liked them. But there was an excitement about being able to see network anchors, top reporters, and whoever might show to support Willie in his time of trauma (Jackie? John Jr.? Arnold Schwarzenegger? Elvis? Marilyn? Anything was possible.)

To the embarrassment of civic leaders, some residents thought that the media presence was ideal for making money. Mansion owners delighted in renting their homes for from $25,000 to $40,000 for up to six weeks to groups of reporters and photographers. They could see how a real Palm Beach family lived (unless the family went north or south or anywhere but home), and they would be in the midst of the city where it all happened.

T-shirts were everywhere, and they ranged from the obscene to the nasty to the humorous. No one really cared who won or lost. What was important was meeting the taste of the buyers at an average $15 each. One of the most-seen T-shirts listed the eight most popular Palm Beach bars and the caption "The Kennedys Easter Tour 1991."

There were also instant experts on the trial. Attorneys from both sides were constrained from talking about the case by Judge Lupo. But the reporters could not go on the air with their own opinions about what was taking place, even if their opinions were as valid as those of the experts. Thus they would call local attorneys for an explanation of what was happening. The attorneys had little or no idea in most cases. They had read nothing more than the public, and often less than those reporters who had purchased public record legal documents. But they were in the right profession in the right location at the right time, and who knew what being shown on television might do for their careers? Thus they modestly agreed to talk with just about anyone about just about anything so long as their names were spelled correctly.

When it was over, everyone was muddied. Patty Bowman, if truly a victim, had been subjected to ridicule, humiliation, and an example of Kennedy-dominated injustice. Willie Smith, if truly innocent, may have had his career jeopardized. If guilty, an extremely disturbed young man was one step further away from seeking help, and could perhaps end up acting out a more violent version of the personal life of his Uncle Ted.

And what of the "tweenager," Ted Kennedy, the man who was never fully a part of the second generation, yet too old to be considered part of the third generation? He was criticized for his drinking, for his carousing, for a lifestyle that included womanizing, numerous incidents of skirting the law, and a generally disreputable personal life. He vowed to change, giving a dramatic speech that essentially claimed he had seen the light. He also began losing weight, aware that excess poundage made him look like the stereotyped fat, old, Irish laboring drunk. He even married again in 1992, to Victoria Reggie, having to go through a civil ceremony because the Catholic Church did not recognize his divorce from Joan.

But the difference between Ted and Willie is that Willie is starting his career, and the accusations, if true, certainly will come back to haunt him. Men who are routinely violent toward women do not change without some sort of reaching out for help, whether through counseling, a support group, or some combination of both. The skill of the coverup, if it occurred, may have simply established an even more tragic future.

Ted Kennedy, supposedly the instigator of the late night visit to Au Bar, has a professional life even he fails to understand. He has been a U.S. senator for more than thirty years. He has gained power, respect, and influence through his efforts in the Senate. He has accomplished more for both the state of Massachusetts and the people of the United States than his brothers ever did. Personal life aside, Ted Kennedy has risen to greater heights than his self-centered father, the relatively incompetent Jack, or the bullheaded Bob. It does not matter how they might have changed and grown had they lived. It does not matter where they were heading. Each time Ted Kennedy has to make reference to the ideals of his brothers, something he invokes frequently when speaking on the Senate floor and in public, he is belittling the one second generation Kennedy who accomplished what the others only talked about. If Ted Kennedy is ever able to break the mental constraints of his family, to look at himself objectively, to create a personal life as respectable as his professional life, he will become the patriarch Joe Kennedy could only fantasize being. And if he continues denying the truth, acting in a self-destructive manner, then the future will be filled with more stories of drunken revelry, accidents, humiliation, and possibly even more death.

There is a martyr image in the minds of many of the members of the insular Kennedy family. It is more than just the tragedies the family has endured, and the deaths of Jack, Bob, and Kathleen were certainly outside everyone's control. It is the fact that the Kennedys have an obsessive need to unite against anyone and anything, including the truth about one of their members if truth is less pleasant than the myth they created prior to 1960.

Ted Kennedy was responsible for a woman's death, but the family went about business as usual, and even Joan stood by her man until she did what any self-respecting person would do—she divorced the drunken womanizer. Jean Smith's son William was almost destroyed because of actions encouraged by her brother Ted, yet neither brother nor nephew was condemned. The family gathered at the compound and put on a stiff upper lip, got the best lawyers they could find, and attacked the accuser instead of looking at the actions of Ted and his nephew.

Jacqueline Kennedy raised her children to live a world apart from their cousins. They may have been spoiled and self-centered in many ways, but they seemed to have better judgment than to get themselves involved with too many scandals. Even when Caroline was caught growing marijuana at home, the reality was that she was acting no differently than many other teenagers who thought they wanted to rebel, to do something naughty that really shouldn't have been against the law in the first place.

Yet during the William Smith trial, even John Kennedy Jr., an assistant district attorney in New York, flew down to be photographed with his cousin. Kennedy was not working as a legal advocate. He was not an adviser on the case, nor was he using the knowledge he had gained prosecuting criminals in New York. He was there to be seen. The public so idolized the son of the great martyred president, his presence alone might vindicate Willie.

(Later it was learned that John Jr., who was acting as representative for his mother's family, had apparently been coerced. People close to the family allege that Jacqueline was warned that if her immensely popular son did not make an appearance, there would be no Kennedy family support for him if he ever decided to enter politics.)

During the same period, Caroline Kennedy made a speech, commenting that she loved Willie Smith and believed in him. The family was simply coming together to support a man who, at best, had acted without regard to health, safety, or propriety; at worst, was a rapist who would never have to face the consequences.

Thus the family continues to gather around its own, to protect uncivil behavior, to hide the dirty little secrets. And it would be the dirty little secrets when set up next to the Kennedy myth that would bring the third generation to its lowest point.

9

WANDERING IN THE WILDERNESS

It was in the early 1970s that the seemingly solid front the Kennedys had always shown to the public developed cracks. When Sargent Shriver ran for vice president in the disastrous McGovern campaign of 1972, and then tried for the presidential nomination in 1976, the family helped him not at all. The other members of the family were going their own way, addressing their own concerns. The discipline that had so effectively and foolishly molded the family was gone.

Perhaps the assassination of Bobby was the root of the problem. For some of the clan, Bob was the family patriarch. He was closest in temperament to the crippled Joe Sr. He was the one who would tell the third generation what his father had told him, that they should be up and doing things, anything, just so long as they were active. He wanted them outdoors rather than reading, competing rather than thinking. Action, competition, triumph—that was what mattered.

Bob was also patriarch by default, and bearer of the personal charisma that had been so effective for Jack. Small, strong, and wiry, better looking than his brother Ted, he cast a shadow over the others. They had looked to him to lead them to the future.

After Bobby Kennedy was shot in 1968, the Kennedy clan disintegrated. They had seen so much of death that they seemed no longer to be able to talk of it. Joe Jr. had committed suicide in 1944. Kathleen, the most vibrant of the second-generation women, had died in an airplane crash in 1948. Rosemary's life was a form of death, and Jack had been assassinated. Joe Sr. sat helpless and dying from his stroke and other health problems, and now Bob was gone. Each of the surviving first- and second-generation Kennedys coped in his or her own way, but no one reached out to the grandchildren, to try to understand their needs, to help them through the overwhelming turmoil.

Rose handled the situation through long walks, regular swimming, and solitude. She spent more and more time by herself, often engrossed in the religious ritual that had always given her solace.

Ted was thrust into the role of leader of the clan, a role he should not have had. The Kennedys were not one monolithic family. The Shrivers had their lives, the Smiths theirs. There was Jacqueline Onassis and her two children; Ethel Kennedy with her brood; Pat Lawford and her son and three daughters; and Ted, Joan, and their children. Ted could not be the guiding light to all the family members with their disparate lives and interests. He was an adult victim of child abuse who had never learned to respect himself. He was a senior senator, a father, a husband, and in his weaker moments, a drunk and a womanizer. He lacked the intense drive to dominate others that Joe Sr. had had. He tried to be strong—not grieving for Bob, not showing weakness. He tried to be as much like his father as Bob had been, which may have been his undoing. He was just not like Joe Kennedy.

Ethel Kennedy became America's most admired woman in the Gallup Poll (a distinction Jacqueline had once held), but she was increasingly hostile to her children during the first year after Bob's death. She became an angry mother, frustrated, turning away from her children, who seemed to remind her too much of her late husband.

And no one cared about the kids, all of whom were coming to feel abandoned. They desperately needed someone to talk to, to air their grief, to establish a new direction for them. But it seemed as if the adults had little time or patience for that. The kids grew wild and undisciplined, taking what they wanted, feeling above the moral bounds that held others who were not Kennedys. Whenever they came to visit at Hyannis Port or Palm Beach, it was as if a horde of rampaging Huns was descending on us.

When the grandchildren were coming, Rose would place signs on objects around her home saying, "Do Not Take." Even so, the grandchildren would take almost whatever they wanted. One summer at Hyannis Port, I happened to look out the window of my office and saw Joe II and some other cousins moving a mattress out of the house. He was going to use it in the apartment he was staying in. However, it was *my* mattress that he was taking. He never asked permission, and he showed no remorse when I stopped him.

Rose eventually warned me and her other staff people to not leave money or valuables where her grandchildren could get to them, because they would steal whatever was out. Chris Lawford once took the typewriter off of my desk in order to type a term paper, but he didn't return it. Rose had to call his mother, Pat, to make him bring it back. And the others were constantly taking supplies and money from my desk.

The maid at Rose's house informed me that she wanted to know when the Shrivers were coming so she could lock certain doors in the house to limit where both children and grandchildren could go and who they could harass. (One time, Ethel had the chauffeur drive her to the airport. Needing cash, she took it from the chauffeur's wallet, which for one reason or another was lying on the front seat of the car. When he caught her, she told him to contact the Park Agency in New York to be reimbursed. There was no thought to how she had violated the man's property, nor if he needed the money himself.)

The maid was even more hostile to the Lawford kids. She would always demand vacation time whenever they came to stay, and Rose had to agree with her. Among other complaints, the maid said that Christopher Lawford broke the window to the president's bedroom in order to sneak his girlfriend inside to spend the night. He didn't want to use the front door because Rose would hear him.

This disdain for the staff was not innate—it was learned. The Kennedy women were volatile, cheap, and domineering when it came to household help. They held their staffs in disdain, rewarded loyalty with low pay, and made unrealistic demands.

Eunice would come inside to use the bathroom, and leave the door wide open despite the fact that I was right across the hall, able to hear everything she did. Instead of being an exhibitionist, it was one of many ways Eunice liked to put down the help. The first day I worked for Rose, for example, when Eunice entered the room, she looked through me, at the same time scratching her crotch. She did not acknowledge me until forced to do so by her mother's belated introduction. It was as though engaging in this crude personal act was a way of showing the hired help what she thought of them. I and the rest of the staff were always angered by such insults.

The only time Eunice changed her treatment was when she realized Rose liked me and that I would be staying for months or years. Then she stopped giving me what the staff considered the Kennedy "I'm rich, you're poor, and I'm better" look.

Later, in Palm Beach, I was walking rapidly through the house when I encountered Sargent Shriver for the first time. He was alone, so I extended my hand and said, "Hi, I'm Barbara Gibson, Mrs. Kennedy's new secretary." Shriver looked at me with the disdainful look he may have learned from his wife, and said, "Well, la-de-da." Then he walked on.

* * *

Bobby Jr. did not see his father being shot, but he learned of it almost as abruptly as David had. He was back East, as were Joe II and Kathleen, and stayed awake only long enough to hear that his father had won the primary. The next morning, he went outside to get the newspaper and saw the awful headlines. Bobby had no idea whether his father would live or die, though something about the writing indicated there was no hope. Dazed, horrified, determined to slay the messenger that brought the bad tidings, he sat in the living room before a roaring fire, feeding the newspaper page by page to the flames.

Joe, who was at the Milton Academy, was at least told of his father's situation by his Uncle Ted. The senator either misunderstood the seriousness of the injury or did not want to terrify his nephew, telling him that the shooting was not so bad as the reports.

Kathleen, who was at the Putney Preparatory School in Vermont, was one month short of her seventeenth birthday when the headmaster awakened her in her dormitory. She immediately went to the family home in McLean, where she was joined by Bobby and Joe. The three took a private jet to California.

Their father's vital signs were gone as the children raced across the country. He was injected with adrenalin, and his heart began pumping once again. Then he was transported three blocks to Good Samaritan Hospital, which was better equipped for the delicate brain surgery required to attempt to save his life.

Joe, Bobby, and Kathleen arrived after the surgery was over. Their father was in an oxygen tent, the back of his head so shattered that survival seemed impossible. The hospital staff was unable to handle the crisis. They had never had to deal with the murder of a man so prominent as Kennedy. There was something almost personal about the death, and many of them lost their composure. And so, surrounded by hysterical adults, the children lost their father.

Something seemed to change with Bob Kennedy's children. Perhaps reflecting the attitudes of the second generation, they started to drift apart as well. When Joe was going through his trials, none of the other children reached out to him. Nor did they come to help Bobby Jr. when he was arrested for having drugs and as he dove deeper and deeper into the drug lifestyle. And only Kathleen tried to do anything to help David as he self-destructed.

During the year following Bob's death, everything seemed to fall apart for Ethel, and her children paid the price for her inattention to their needs. Instead of trying to be more nurturing and supportive of the family anguish and grieving process of her children, she became more self-centered. Bob had been the focus of her life, and without him, she could only fall back on the activities in which all Kennedys liked to engage. She became more competitive, playing intensely aggressive tennis games well into her pregnancy with Rory Elizabeth. Those around her remarked that she seemed to have a love/hate relationship with the idea that she was bearing the last of her late husband's children.

No one seemed to know how to help Ethel with her problems. And if anyone had some sense of how to help, no one reached out because the Kennedys had spent too many years making clear to outsiders, even close friends and sycophants, that ultimately Kennedys supported Kennedys. All others might face impregnable walls.

Ethel also began giving parties, as though gala events would help her forget or large numbers of people would protect her from her emotions. Every weekend she would have famous people coming to stay, filling the main house, the two-room apartment in which the Secret Service stayed, and even the Doll House. I remember coming to work one morning and finding David Hartman, former host of *Good Morning, America*, coming out of the Doll House, his tall frame looking somewhat cramped. Since Ethel had eleven bedrooms in the main house, the overflow was an indication of how many people she tried to cram into her life to help her emotional state.

Joe, despite his adolescent troubles, always felt the sense of purpose the the second generation had. There was always a drive—he knew he was going to follow the family road to political power. David had a sense of helplessness—he seemed to know his drug use was endangering his life, but he didn't have the will to stop himself. Bobby Jr., however, didn't seem to care about anything at this point except his animals. One summer he built a pen in his mother's backyard where he kept several unusual animals—an iguana and other reptiles so unfamiliar that they frightened the neighbors. During that time, he was never seen out walking without his pet falcon perched on his shoulder. Needless to say, he was an awesome sight with his lanky frame, shoulder-length black hair, and loping stride.

Young Bobby was living the adventurous life often attributed to his Uncle Jack. He was a charismatic leader to his friends, in both good and mischief. However, he lacked the drive for politics, preferring veterinary medicine or working with animals in some capacity. He was the type of boy in whom any family other than the Kennedys would have taken great pride, but the family pressure he endured—to win in life, to lead others, to gain power—resulted in antisocial, self-destructive behavior. One result was his first drug arrest, along with his cousin Bobby Shriver, in 1970 for possession of marijuana. Bobby was only sixteen, but since most of the third generation used marijuana, no one in the family was concerned with the incident. Tragically, this casual attitude prevented the family from taking a long look at where Bobby was heading, and he later plunged headlong into drug abuse.

As his troubles surfaced, the family encouraged Bobby to be more involved with animals, but the activities never seemed to allow Bobby to study animals for the sake of studying. Family friend Lem Billings took him to Africa on a photographic safari that became a television special. As his uncles before him had done, Bobby kept a diary that Lem, true to the Kennedy tradition of exploiting writing for future success, thought Bobby Jr. might get published.

Bobby was expelled from Millbrook prep school in March 1969. Ethel wanted to ignore the situation, letting him be home so long as he didn't trouble her. Family friends helped Bobby spend a few weeks in Colombia where he was able to study the animals, roam the rain forest, and live with the laborers. The trip was good for him, related to his interests, and kept him away from his mother's anger, his siblings' problems, and his friends' delinquency. But when he returned, he started sneaking out at night again, this time to be with a girlfriend, Kim Kelley, a fact that caused Ethel to throw him out of the house. Rather than trying to reconcile with his mother, he simply camped out on the property of a friend's family, allegedly entering area homes to take food from their refrigerators as he needed it.

Certain of the third generation took Bobby as their leader: David, Bobby Shriver, and Christopher Lawford. While staying in Hyannis, this group would sneak out at night, joining other friends from the area, and then engage in whatever mischief they could do. Sometimes they would untie boats during high tide so the vessels would be beached when the owners came to sail the next morning. Or they would toss firecrackers at passing cars.

Soon, they became more and more a destructive gang. The boys were using LSD and amphetamines, and police reports, neighbor complaints, and their own bragging to various writers over the years reveal a litany of pranks both benign and dangerous. They monitored police frequencies with radios, wore dark clothing, and blackened their faces. Then they went out, their actions ranging from shooting water balloons at police cars to sending one of their members into the street to allegedly look for a lost contact lens. When a car stopped to avoid hitting him, one of the others would shove a potato in the tailpipe. The pressure would build, the potato would be expelled, and the resulting noise would cause great merriment among the youths.

It was not that the boys were trying to be like a rich version of an inner-city street gang. Rather, it was that their dysfunctional extended family had led them to act out their anger, frustration, and confusion about life. Their parents were generally taking no responsibility for their children, shipping them off to one boarding school or another, one trip or another. And there was no sense of group purpose as there had been when Jack and Bob were still alive. The grandchildren still talked avidly about politics, and everyone knew that eventually Ted would make his bid for the presidency, yet there was no shared experience. No one really cared, not even Ted. The Kennedys were alive, they were special, they were privileged, but emotionally, many of them were dying.

Peter Lawford had little interest in his children, and had no ability to reach out to them. He abandoned them to their mother, his contacts infrequent. They were always welcome to visit him, and he seemed to care about them as much as he cared about anyone. But Lawford was in neither the physical nor emotional condition to guide impressionable children and young adults.

Unfortunately for Chris Lawford, his mother, Pat, seemingly had no interest in dealing with her children's troubles after Bob's death. She took her daughters and moved to Paris, leaving fifteen-year-old Chris to attend Middlesex boarding school.

Thus cast adrift, Chris, along with Bobby and David Kennedy, began traveling. They hitchhiked to New York, then panhandled at Grand Central Station for money to buy drugs in Central Park. This time they tried heroin, which they snorted like cocaine. Their crash pad was the Sutton Place duplex of Chris's mother, where they would stay with the girls they picked up and the assorted street people they encountered. The neighbors in the luxury apartment building quickly demanded that the boys get rid of the disreputable characters staying there.

Ironically, there would have been fewer problems had Pat not been so cheap. Each time she went away for a week or two, she would tell her live-in Scottish cook to leave the apartment. She would not pay her for the time the family was away, and the cook, having no other place to call home, had to move in with her married sister on Long Island. Had she let the cook remain as caretaker for the apartment, Chris probably would have been somewhat more discrete.

Lem Billings finally took control of Bobby during his senior year. He couldn't influence Bobby's self-destructive behavior, but he did change his environment. This time Bobby was enrolled in the Palfrey School in Watertown, Massachusetts. He boarded off campus with a family Lem knew, and Lem called the boy almost daily. It was as close to a normal, caring home life Bobby had known since his father died.

Billings was an odd, rather tragic figure in the later years of his life. He had experienced vicarious fame, power, and glory by working with Jack and Bob Kennedy. He had been to the White House—Jack even maintained a bedroom for him there. He had heard the cheering crowds. He had been an intimate of men who were intimates with heads of state, the wealthy, and the powerful.

Some say he was one of the most sensitive of the hangers-on. He allegedly recognized how the children, especially Bob's children, had been traumatized by the murders. He reached out to Bobby, primarily, and later to Chris, in order to give them what they had lost.

Others say that Lem wanted to restore himself to past glory. Unwilling to seek a life of his own, Billings saw in Bobby the combination of drive, intelligence, animal cunning, occasional amorality, and charisma that could take him to the White House. It did not matter what ambitions Bobby may have had for himself. He was a Kennedy, his career would be in politics, and he could be Lem's ticket back into the insider world of power.

Whatever the case, eventually Lem would go from surrogate father to drug using friend to jealous lover—not a sexual relationship, but rather one in which he would be jealous of anyone else who came into Bobby's life, who could influence him or reduce his dependence on Billings.

Ethel refused to get directly involved with her children. She thought it was better to keep them apart and to keep them distant from her. David went off to La Paz, Mexico, to work in the lettuce fields with Cesar Chavez. However, he actually did menial work at the United Farm Workers headquarters rather than being nurtured by the labor leader or anyone else. And when, at the end of the summer, he went to his Uncle Peter Lawford's house where Chris was visiting, both boys were provided with hashish by the irresponsible Lawford.

In 1972, Bobby followed family tradition by going to Harvard. He was more controlled than Chris and David due to the stabilizing influence of Billings. The nurturing of the older male, one of the closest friends of his late uncle Jack, was probably the greatest outside influence in Bobby's young life. Certainly it kept him moving forward faster than his self-destructive actions dragged him backward.

The early 1970s was a difficult time for a family without direction, without purpose, with limited moral values, intense competitiveness, and yet with such a mythic aura to them, the public was shocked by their humanness. Steve Smith and Sarge Shriver both explored political careers, and both found that they lacked both a base of support and the skills necessary to succeed. Smith, the consummate behind-the-scenes politician, was a power broker, not a hand-shaker. Shriver, the man with vision and compassion for the average person, was unable to relate to the political leadership. And Ted Kennedy was torn by the ghost of Chappaquiddick, as well as the political reality that he had been reelected in Massachusetts because he had claimed he would not seek the presidency in 1972. It was obvious that his Senate seat was safe, and he seemed to genuinely love that position. Running for president would deny his promise to the voters, jeopardizing the one thing he valued.

Politics was the focus for the third generation's discussions, yet they were growing further and further from a time when politics was a viable option. They were living through a period when the world was changing rapidly, something neither they nor most people understood. By the time they would be in position to make dramatic moves, winning votes was no longer simplistic. Jack, Bob, and Ted had gotten to power on a combination of machine politics and emotional issues such as the Communist menace, the involvement of organized crime in the leadership of the labor movement, and, to a degree, the civil rights movement. But the third generation was facing a time of change among the power blocs in Europe. The possibility of Cuban aggression was not a consideration. Fear of war had faded from the American scene, the public far more concerned with the economy.

While some elements in the media still focused on glamor over substance, politicians were finding campaigns built on image less and less successful. It was not enough for the Kennedy grandchildren to mouth the platitudes about public service with which they were raised, but which they were frequently not shown. No longer would Rose's quoting of the statement from Luke that to whom much is given, much is expected, seem meaningful without substantive action. There had to be both substance and vision; a plan, not just a famous name. It was all right for Ted to continue in his Senate seat, in part because of his development as a statesman, in part because he was the last link to Jack and Bob. It was all right for Joe II to buy his way into Congress in a safe seat and to be marked as the next Kennedy hope. But lip service was no longer the same as public service. The public wanted leadership, ideas, alternative answers. No longer could there be a political dynasty where any of the third generation could be elected to any office because of a name and a lot of money.

Without an assured future, the family floundered. They were undisciplined, unprepared for real life, without direction, seemingly unloved, and abusers of both prescription and nonprescription drugs. Jack Kennedy had won by invoking the image of a generation born in the twentieth century, tempered by war, heralding the fresh breeze of change. Bob Kennedy had boyish good looks, a pugnacious attitude, and a personal drive that appealed to youth seeking to make their mark by stopping the

Vietnam War, returning to the cities, and helping the disenfranchised. The third generation did not know how to call upon
image, to give the illusion of substance, or to position themselves in a manner where others would see them as the leaders
they fancied themselves to be.

The third generation was paying the price of weak parents,
unable to examine the child abuse they had endured from Joe
and Rose, unwilling to heal so that they could be the loving
adults the Kennedy grandchildren so desperately needed.

Peter Lawford was probably the most destructive of the
males, even more so than Ted, though since he wasn't a real
Kennedy (only the Lawford children were "real" Kennedys),
his influence was limited. There were times when Christopher
would go to his father, and together they would talk seriously
about their lives and their troubles. Their closeness would be
fueled by drugs, because the two men never could talk without
at least Peter being on pills, powders, or excessive alcohol. And
when the talks were over, when father and son had embraced,
declaring their love, coming down from the mellow high, Peter
turned viciously against his son. Sober, Peter rejected Christopher in a manner that was verbally vicious. Peter could not
handle intimacy, fatherhood, or being vulnerable to the child
he sired. And each rejection played havoc with Chris's sense
of self-worth, throwing the son into the same pattern as the
father.

Lawford was also becoming increasingly impotent. The
intense drug abuse affected him sexually. He turned to multiple
partners, youthful partners, more drugs, and even an electrified
mechanical device to try to restore his sexual prowess. But he
was losing everything he had wanted, everything he enjoyed,
everything he knew how to do. And while he would not die
until Christmas Eve 1985, he could only destroy, not nurture
the child in whom he should have taken pride.

Lem Billings tried to reach out to Chris Lawford, nurturing
him almost as much as he did Bobby. He tried to counter the
negatives in Chris's life by telling him about the good in his
parents. He told Chris about his parents when they were dating,

when they were newly married, when each loved the other as much as they were capable of doing. He did not talk of the womanizing. He did not speak of the drugs. He spoke of a time when the Lawfords genuinely cared for one another, who gave parties people enjoyed, who led lives of glamor and fun, and who had friends like Judy Garland who cared only for the couple, not the fact that they were part of the Kennedy family.

The summer of 1974 was a great one for Bobby, who, with Chris, David, Lem, Doug Spooner, and journalist Harvey Fleetwood, decided to travel the Apurimac River at the headwaters of the Amazon. White men had never succeeded in traveling and exploring the waterway, so Bobby convinced the others that they should be the first. Bobby, at twenty, was the leader of the group.

The trip was an adventure others had tried and failed. Some had died. Others had been forced to stop part way along. Bobby was determined to succeed for the sake of success, the group using rafts they built, equipping themselves with medicine, canned goods, three sticks of dynamite, live chickens they could kill and eat along the way, and similar necessities. It was a wilderness trip, and any serious injuries would put their lives in jeopardy.

The group made it all the way down the river. There were problems—Lem injured his ankle, David developed strep throat, and Bobby had severe dysentery. Their guides were drunk through much of the trip, and Indians who were hostile to their presence on the river almost drove them off. But they had won; they were the first to accomplish the trip.

When Bobby went back to Harvard for the fall semester, he saw himself as having surpassed the Kennedy legend in many ways. Already he had conquered a river no one else in his family had even considered attempting. He had reached his full height of six feet, two inches and was strong and athletic. He saw himself, not Joe, as the next Kennedy in the White House. Chris Lawford, who had impressed his cousins with tabloid headlines indicating he had had sex with Elizabeth Taylor, would be second in command.

But by the time Bobby was a senior, he wasn't attempting to deal with the demons that were leading him into such serious addiction that, by 1981, his heroin habit alone would cost him $1,000 a week. Since his inheritance more than covered the cost without his having to sacrifice in other areas of his life, it was easy for everyone to ignore what was happening to him.

This was the hidden side of Uncle Jack's legacy haunting Bobby. Neither he nor those around him comprehended how incongruous it was to talk about heavy drug use and a run for the presidency. Kennedys were leaders. Kennedys were presidents. Kennedys were better than everybody else. There could be no limits to ambition, to a vision for success. Whatever they wanted, they would have, regardless of what it took to do it.

There was also genuine personal tragedy within the family. Teddy Jr. was twelve years old when he learned that he had bone cancer. By December 1973, the only way to save his life was to amputate his leg. Then there was a course of chemotherapy, with the attendant pain, nausea, and emotional trauma.

Once again the family could not help the third generation. Teddy's younger brother Patrick and older sister Kara had their own crises. No one wanted to talk about the cancer, what it meant, the risks, and how it spread, all information Kara desperately needed. At fourteen, impressionable, unsure of herself, overweight in the manner of her father when he was growing up, not particularly attractive to teenage boys as yet, and the subject of ridicule by other girls, she fled. She tried drugs, and periodically ran away, the family having to bring her home from halfway houses.

Kara's life was always difficult. Her father was nearly killed in a plane crash in 1964, and though she was too young to understand about her uncle's assassination or the meaning of her father's time in traction, life was hard. Then, when she was nine years old and able to understand what was taking place, her father was in the headlines because of the death of Mary Jo Kopechne.

Kara reacted to Teddy Jr.'s cancer in typical fashion for a young teenager. Too young to fully understand medicine, she became convinced that the disease was contagious. She was certain she would die from it and went through several months of personal trauma. Rather than seeking counseling to help her through the period, an action no second-generation Kennedy is ever comfortable with, her father insisted she become part of the caretaking process. She eventually stopped fearing her own mortality, but she was caught in the midst of a family where everyone was sick. Teddy had cancer, since successfully cured. Patrick developed severe asthma requiring close attention by the parents. And her parents were alcoholics.

Kara had the courage to attend Alcoholics Anonymous meetings with her mother during visits to her mother's home in Boston. She came to understand both the disease and her own problems that stemmed from it. Ironically, she also sensed her father's alcohol abuse and reached out to him by creating a wall hanging of the serenity prayer utilized by many recovering alcoholics to keep them focused on sobriety. It reads: "God grant me the serenity to accept the things I cannot change, the courage to change the things I can, and the wisdom to know the difference."

It has been said that the family participated in a private program created for them because they were uncertain their anonymity would be preserved in AA and the family support group, Al-Anon. This story reflects only the failings of other family members to be honest with themselves. Joan's alcoholism was well publicized, and after she had been sober for a year, she told of her experiences in a national women's magazine. Since large cities have meetings literally around the clock, and since Ted's personal reputation at that time could hardly have been made worse by the admission of his weakness, the family's avoidance of successful programs was another denial. Fortunately Kara had the courage to do what the others did not.

Eventually Kara entered Tufts University to study public affairs. She took a job with Metromedia Television in New York, then worked as co-chairman of her father's 1988 reelection campaign. Now married to Michael Allen, she is media director of the Very Special Arts Program in Washington, D.C.

Teddy Jr. has suffered beyond his cancer. I think it was equally difficult to deal with the way his father handled his recovery after his leg was amputated. The boy had been fitted with an artificial leg, but he was still emotionally adjusting to the physical loss. There seemed little question that all danger had been removed and that he could lead a normal life. But he was twelve years old, coming into the adolescence when he would be both self-conscious about his appearance and his involvement with the opposite sex.

I remember overhearing the senator calling Teddy on the telephone right after the prosthesis had been fitted. Instead of giving loving encouragement and support, Teddy ordered him to go play tennis, an activity Teddy was reluctant to try. The senator insisted that the boy use physical activity to heal when a more loving response seemed appropriate. Still, Ted was doing the best he could for his son. It was just not what the boy needed.

Teddy desperately tried to please his father. His life had been saved from the chondrosarcoma that had cost him his leg, but he needed time to grieve, to get angry, to heal both emotionally and physically, something his father refused to consider. So Teddy went skiing in Vail, Colorado, four months after the operation. He used special poles for support and just a single ski, his prosthesis not ready for such action. And everyone applauded his courage.

Teddy *was* courageous, and those who know him today reveal that he has finally gained the strength to follow his own desires, not the demands of his family. He has a strong interest in the environment and has received a degree that will enable him to work in some aspect of ecology. But before he had the strength to turn his back on the destructive side of his parents and siblings, he experimented with drugs, and was arrested in New

Jersey in 1980, at the age of nineteen, for possession of marijuana. Then, in 1991, Teddy announced to the press that he was an alcoholic, strongly denounced the pressures his father had forced him to endure, and entered a rehabilitation program in Hartford, Connecticut.

According to hospital sources, Teddy felt that he had never been able to lead a normal life. He understood that the senator was a national laughingstock, and he was angry that the man could decide to go drinking in Palm Beach, grab his son and nephew, and then end with the tragedy of the Patty Bowman scandal.

One of the saddest stories about Teddy's earlier relationship with his father came when Nellie, the cook, told me about Teddy's effort to give his father a Christmas present that would make him happy. Teddy wanted to give his father something that could not help but bring him pleasure. He could think of nothing better than a bottle of champagne. It was another tragic symbol of the problems both the senator and his namesake would face.

Patrick Kennedy, who overcame severe asthma as a child, also became a drug addict. He quit earlier than most of the other cousins, entering a New Hampshire rehabilitation program while in his senior year at Phillips Academy in Andover, Massachusetts.

When Patrick Kennedy was a junior at Providence College, he became interested enough in politics that he decided to run for state representative in Rhode Island. Patrick won the election in 1988, becoming the youngest Kennedy to hold office. He also did it the old-fashioned way—spending sums of money disproportionate to the rewards. He spent $30,000 during his campaign for the part-time position. The annual pay for the office is $300.

But Patrick, who seems to be following the Kennedy pattern of image over substance, is in trouble in Rhode Island politics. Rather than building a power base by serving his constituents, he has switched districts. The people he represents are resentful of the fact that he seems to be using them for his own ends instead of being a public servant. His father has helped him raise large sums of money from the family home in McLean, but he is expected to be the first Kennedy to go down to defeat for failure to understand the electorate.

Most of the other grandchildren had their own troubles. Both Caroline and John Kennedy were involved with drugs, and Caroline was even caught growing marijuana in the backyard of her mother's home in Hyannis Port. The officer who discovered this fact brought it to Jacqueline's attention rather than running Caroline in, and so the incident was not publicized. Sydney Lawford was caught with drugs while speeding in Rose's car in Florida.

Both Bobby Kennedy and Chris Lawford fell apart during these years. For a time, Bob served as an assistant in the office of New York District Attorney Robert Morgenthau, the same post his cousin John would hold. He was ironically moving into a position where he theoretically might have to fight his wife, attorney Emily Ruth Black, a public defender, in court. They were both in the same law school, but unlike any of the Kennedys, she had a brilliant undergraduate career. She became a member of academic honorary Phi Beta Kappa while at the University of Indiana, and later joined the Legal Aid Society in New York.

Bobby's troubled past caught up with him fairly quickly. He had gained positive attention when, at twenty-four, he authored a book on Alabama Judge Frank Johnson Jr., a man who had fought the Ku Klux Klan and was in line for the job of FBI director under President Jimmy Carter. As with other Kennedy books, it read like a padded college thesis, which is what it essentially was. But instead of realizing a promising legal future, his heavy drug use dragged him down. He failed the New York bar exam in July 1982, then walked out of the exam in February 1983, when he made his second attempt to pass.

His 1982 marriage may have been a positive step, but it did not prevent the drugs from briefly destroying his life. He nodded off in the midst of prosecuting an assault case, and eventually resigned from his $20,000-a-year position. Then, on August 3, 1983, Bobby was arrested on a flight to Rapid City, South Dakota. He had apparently overdosed on heroin, went into the bathroom, and sat down, incoherent. He had not bothered to lock the door, and was discovered by a passenger who had not realized the room was occupied. The pilot was alerted by the flight attendants, and an ambulance was waiting for him when the plane landed, by which time he was able to walk and talk with clarity. He did not wish to go to the hospital, a fact which made the police curious. They confiscated his luggage and found two-tenths of a gram of heroin inside. He was criminally charged, prosecuted, convicted, and received two years' probation.

It was only then, when he should have had everything to live for, that Bobby truly hit bottom and was willing to seek help. Information was revealed that he went from one drug to another. He would get high on cocaine one night, alcohol another, and heroin a third. Sometimes, when the stimulants were too great, he would also use Valium to try to calm himself.

The drugs were usually offered by friends who wanted to ingratiate themselves. However, he often traveled to Harlem in the same manner as David, seeking drugs sold on street corners. Ironically, he liked to work with some of the street kids, though obviously never admitting that he was destroying his own life. He was also destroying his marriage, Emily deeply troubled by Bobby's lack of control and her inability to help him.

Christopher was also caught with heroin, though in his case it occurred in December 1980 in Boston. He was caught making a buy outside a bar, and he, too, received probation. Earlier that year, in Aspen, Colorado, he attempted to obtain Darvon from a pharmacist. The pharmacist refused to sell him the prescription painkiller, then called the police. Charges were later dropped.

* * *

Ted Kennedy ran for the Democratic presidential nomination in 1980, but he was defeated by the incumbent, President Carter. After his defeat, the third generation did not know what to do. They were mostly involved with drugs at the same time that they were starting their own careers. The second-generation leader had gone down in disgrace. The women were never role models, never allowed to be anything other than support figures for the men or to do "good works" that would perpetuate the family name in ways that would help one of the men get elected.

When it came time for a decision about a 1984 Ted Kennedy campaign, the family members closest to Ted had no heart for it. They told him it was time to stop, to stay in the Senate, to end the dream of a Kennedy White House that was proving a nightmare even in the pursuit. Finally, the third generation would have time to heal, time to create their own lives, time to remake the Kennedy legend in their own way.

* * *

Ted Kennedy ran for the Democratic presidential nomination in 1980, but he was defeated by the incumbent, President Carter. After his defeat, the third generation did not know what to do. They were mostly involved with things at the same time that they were starting their own careers. The grandchildren had gunned down in the race. The women were never role models, never allowed to be anything other than homemakers figures for the next or the next good works. The result is that none the family felt it was that would sweep one or the next generation, when it came time for a decision about a 1988 Ted Kennedy campaign, the family members chose to try. Ted had no heart for it. They told him it was time to stay to stay in the Senate, to end his dream of a Kennedy White House that was proving a mountain even in the present. Finally, the third generation would have little to look upon to order to create an even higher time to restore the Kennedy record to their own way.

10

THE DYNASTY: DEATH AND REDEMPTION

Shortly after 1982, the third generation began exploring their roles for the future. Some, like Joe Kennedy II and Patrick Kennedy, followed the traditional Kennedy path to power—politics. Others, like Bobby Kennedy Jr. and Michael Kennedy, went into business. But more and more, as the first and second generations faded into memory, the third generation Kennedys found their own ways in life. Sometimes this meant constructive action and social concern. At other times it meant a reckless disregard for others, arrogance, bravado, and stupidity.

Jacqueline Kennedy wanted to keep her children from engaging in the same type of lifestyle as their cousins. She was emotionally overwrought by the assassination of Bobby. According to author Lester David—*(Jacqueline Kennedy Onassis: A Portrait of Her Private Years)*—she arrived in Los Angeles ". . . in a confused, disoriented state. The shooting of Bobby in the hotel pantry became mixed up in her mind with the tragedy in Dallas five years earlier. She rambled disjointedly, making little sense. She talked of Jack Kennedy as though he were still alive, and she was still first lady."

Aristotle Onassis flew to the United States to take care of

Jacqueline, accompanying her to the funeral. He was a man with a disreputable past, including an arrest by U.S. Marshals for using dummy corporations to buy surplus U.S. ships designated for sale solely to U.S. companies. Although criminal charges were dropped, he did pay a $7-million fine. In the world of Onassis, the fine was the price of doing business.

No matter what his history, what mattered was that he could provide emotional and financial security for Jacqueline and her children. She was quoted by numerous sources as saying, "I hate this country. I despise America, and I don't want my children to live here any more. If they're killing Kennedys, my kids are number one targets. I want to get out of this country."

No matter what else Bobby may have been—and his womanizing, though less blatant than Jack's, has been amply documented by newly declassified FBI records—he was a close friend of his sister-in-law. It was Bobby who provided the emotional support Jack's children needed, and it was Bobby who supported Jacqueline through the turmoil of a murdered husband and the effort of raising two children endlessly pursued by reporters. It was also Bobby who was the mainstay of his brother's children, and the best family influence on Caroline and John. So long as Bobby was alive, Jacqueline's children were taken to his Hickory Hill estate, which they loved. However, the feelings for her brother-in-law, with whom some say she had a brief sexual affair, were not matched by her feelings for Ethel. She held Ethel in disdain, calling her ". . . the baby-making machine—wind her up and she becomes pregnant." That was why Bobby's death left her with no one who could bring some semblance of rational existence into her life as a Kennedy in-law. She needed to escape entirely.

John Jr. was Jacqueline's primary concern. Many of the journalists writing about the family history talk of his being unfocused as a child. When they first lived in New York, Jacqueline sent him to Saint David's Catholic elementary school for boys. Later she transferred him to the Collegiate School on West 77th Street. Whether this was because she preferred the nonreligious curriculum or because he was going to be asked to repeat the second grade is not known. Certainly he was only an average student, much like his father, though always popular.

He also was frequently in trouble for his practical jokes. As early as the age of six, John was caught trying to coax ponies into the tent set up for the wedding reception of his aunt. He managed to get the ponies from the Newport estate to nearby Bailey's Beach, where the tent was located.

Despite Jacqueline's hatred and fears, she kept John and Caroline in New York area schools, trusting in their Secret Service agents even as she lived on board the Onassis yacht. Later, when John had a tendency to have to repeat courses because of low academic standing, she switched him to Phillips Academy in Andover, Massachusetts, to try to improve his grades. He graduated from Phillips in 1979.

Much to Jacqueline's disappointment and concern, John had a natural ability as an actor. This went beyond his handsome physical appearance. After playing Fagin in a production of *Oliver* at age eleven, John became seriously involved with acting at Phillips Academy and later at Brown University.

At fifteen John appeared in a Phillips Academy production of *Petticoats and Union Suits,* which was reviewed in the *New York Times,* a paper normally not known to take an interest in high school plays. Two years later, he and his girlfriend, Jenny Christian, costarred in another school play, *Comings and Goings.* By the time he was nineteen he had appeared in *A Comedy of Errors* and *One Flew Over The Cuckoo's Nest.* Then, at Brown, he became extremely active in the theater productions, appearing in everything from Shakespeare's *The Tempest* to *Short Eyes,* a play in which he was cast as a child molester.

Caroline was old enough to remember her father, but John knew only his uncles, Secret Service agents, and Onassis. To remedy this, he majored in history at Brown, taking courses about the Vietnam War and other aspects of his father's presidency. It was during those undergraduate days that he also began developing his body, playing rugby and lifting weights.

It was the acting, not the other activities, that resulted in a period of estrangement from Jacqueline. She did not see John going into the Kennedy family business—politics. She had lost a husband and brother-in-law to the to political power. Instead, she saw her son involving himself in public service—such work fit within that portion of the family's tradition she thought should be sustained. However, nothing could detract him from his love of the theater, a fact that became most blatant in 1985, when he was twenty-four years old. The Irish Arts Center had him star in a revival of the play *Winners*. The play, held in a small West 51st Street theater, also starred Christina Haag, his actress girlfriend since he graduated from Brown. It ran only six performances, and was not considered a professional acting debut. Christina is now an established professional actress.

It was *Winners,* a Brian Friel story about an Irish Catholic man and his pregnant girlfriend (both of whom die in the end) that forced John away from a theatrical career. That his mother hated the idea of his becoming an actor was not so much of a concern to him as the reaction of his older sister. Caroline joined her mother in refusing to attend any of his performances. She also stood by her mother's ordering the production not to allow reviewers to attend.

I never did learn whether this was because she was afraid her son would be hurt or if she feared he would be encouraged. Whatever the case, with John's looks, interests, and abilities, he might have earned his living on the stage and in films had Jacqueline not been so hostile to the entertainment world.

I believed so at the time. Kennedy disputed my conclusions after the run of the show, though. When he met with reporters outside the theater, he commented, "This is not a professional acting debut. It's just a hobby." As if to underscore that statement, the other actors in the workshop production were friends from Brown.

The only other acting he would do would be in film, something he had wanted to try while still at Brown. His first opportunity was a major one. Producer Robert Stigwood was planning a feature film based on John's father's early years. He wanted the son to play the father, but Jacqueline said there would be no such work until he finished college. She added that while he could do almost anything he wanted after graduation, the one exception was acting.

When he did break into the movies, it was with a bit part in a film called *A Matter of Degree,* produced by Randy Poster, a friend from Brown University. Christina Haag was also involved. He had two lines, and was listed in the credits as "Guitar Playing Romeo." The movie played in Europe but had no U.S. distribution when first completed. Because it was done with friends and was essentially an art house film, Kennedy's role was never exploited or widely mentioned, even when the film began playing smaller locations in this country.

Haag, like all of Kennedy's friends, will not talk about him or their relationship, the longest one of his young adult life. She has never tried to use John for publicity, and a number of people in the industry have commented that, if anything, she was more hurt than helped by her ongoing friendship with him.

Jacqueline's hostility toward her son's acting interests probably came from her own awareness of Hollywood and the morality that had caused her so much pain. Her brother-in-law and former close friend, actor Peter Lawford, had also been the procurer for her husband. He had been the middle man for actress Marilyn Monroe during her affair with the president, and he had also provided starlets and prostitutes.

There were also the other entertainers in her late first husband's life, such as Frank Sinatra, Sammy Davis Jr., and the other members of what the press dubbed the Rat Pack. They were "swingers" at the time she encountered them. Casual sex was a way of relaxing. Commitment to one woman was a quaint idea none of them followed.

Although she enjoyed the arts, Jacqueline's exposure to the men who lived in that world had not been a positive experience. They were philanderers, drug and alcohol abusers, and generally unstable. She may also have feared that young John would be exploited because of his looks and famous name. Even American politics, which she had come to loathe, would have been preferable to her as a career for her son.

John's social conscience, like that of many of the third generation, is hard to interpret. He was involved with a number of
activities meant to make him more sensitive to others. During
the time between high school and college, he went to the
National Outdoor Leadership School. Students from the United
States and Africa studied mountaineering and environmental
issues 17,000 feet up Mount Kenya. The following summer he
again went to Africa, this time meeting with government and
student leaders in Zimbabwe. Through the intervention of a
close friend of his mother's, Maurice Tempelsman, who had
mining and manufacturing interests in Johannesburg, South
Africa, he had a chance to work in a mine. While the sights
he encountered shocked him and seemed to sensitize him a
bit, the trip was carefully controlled. Tempelsman assigned an
executive from one of his businesses to accompany the youth.

Despite the controlled visit, the reality of apartheid, the back-
breaking, underpaid labor involved with the exploitation of the
black majority, and other factors were vivid for him. Upon his
return to Brown, he started a study group called the South
African Group for Education (SAGE). It was an objective program, something that seemed out of character at a time when
the world was increasingly hostile to apartheid in South Africa.

The summer following John's sophomore year, he worked for
Ted Van Dyk at the Center for Democratic Policy, a Washington
think tank. He had a student internship and lived with the
Shrivers. He was involved with research, fund-raising, and
similar tasks, discovering his unusual celebrity power for the
first time. When he made appearances, women clutched at him,
trying to touch him. Their screams and emotional displays
unnerved him. He was aware, for the first time, that he was a
celebrity. The attention paid to him while growing up had been
just normal childhood experience. Now he understood, perhaps
also for the first time, that he was considered special, not for
who he was or what he did, but because of a father he never
really knew and certainly did not remember.

During John's junior year, he and his cousin Tim Shriver
tutored underprivileged children in English, working through

a University of Connecticut program. John took nine months during 1983 to study at the University of New Delhi, India. His courses were in public health and education, but the real reason he was there was because of his mother's fears. It had been twenty years since Jack Kennedy was assassinated. The news media was planning endless features, including some on the children. She was still nervous about nuts seeking to kill Kennedys, and she wanted her son to avoid the spotlight. Caroline, she knew, would get less attention. John would be mobbed, a situation she wanted to avoid. Having him out of the country would be a constructive way to let him avoid the media circus. In 1984, he continued his work with Van Dyk, going to the Democratic National Convention in San Francisco to help raise money.

There were other jobs to follow. He took a $20,000-per-year job with the New York Office of Business Development, working on programs meant to keep business in the city. While he never held a major position, despite or perhaps because his mother had founded the group, he worked hard. If anyone noticed anything unusual about him, it was that he was less sophisticated than other workers his own age. He had traveled the world and met prominent people, but he had done so only within controlled circumstances. The problems of the business world, the concerns of corporations, and such issues as worker availability, taxes, cost factors, and the like were foreign to him. He was a rich kid who had led a life of insulated sophistication. The others had a better understanding of the streets and the real world.

Many people believe that when someone is wealthy and has a social conscience they should work full time in a field that might not otherwise be able to pay them for their skills. John Kennedy and the others are not necessarily expected to donate money, though that issue periodically arises. Rather, they are expected to lead lives of selfless giving, as a way of paying society back for their privilege.

Before anything else, John needed the opportunity to grow up, and that included adolescent rebellion. He was always close to his mother, but she did not see him as being as mature as Caroline had been. Caroline was the brighter of the two, the more studious, the one who had been more aware of the nightmare of their father's assassination. There was a maturity about Caroline that John did not achieve at the same age—or perhaps he did, but his interests were so at odds with his mother's that she refused to respect them. Whatever the case, he was rebellious.

For John's eighteenth birthday, Jacqueline, John, and some of John's friends from Phillips Academy went to New York's Le Club. Several of them brought marijuana, which they proceeded to smoke after Jacqueline left them on their own. They also drank tequila.

John would later try cocaine, as well, though his use was not abusive like his cousins'. Whether this moderation showed maturity or pure luck is hard to say.

Pornography allegedly became another interest. John was reportedly seen from time to time in the Times Square area where live sex shows were common. In addition, one video store owner reported that John owed more than a thousand dollars in late fees for X-rated videos he rented. Again, this seemed to be a period of rebellion and curiosity rather than some obsessive degeneracy revealing itself. It was also behavior that did not continue as he grew older.

Jacqueline had long taken care to limit John's contacts when he was living at home. She checked to see who was calling her son on the telephone, screening those she felt were undesirable. She did this with his early girlfriends, as well, delighting in his first serious relationship with Jenny Christian, whom he began dating at sixteen. The two stayed together for four years, while he went to Brown and she went to Harvard to major in psychology.

Jacqueline also delighted in Christina Haag. That relationship had the advantage of having nothing to do with competition for wealth or prestige. Her father was a successful marketing executive, and she had attended the exclusive Brearley School. Although he dated many girls, the two were essentially an item from the time he stopped dating Jenny until he started dating actress Daryl Hannah.

Prior to John's decision to become a lawyer, a career that would last less than his years as a sometime actor, there were questions raised in the press. Should John Kennedy open a legal clinic in Harlem? Should he work on Indian reservations? How could he prove that he was truly compassionate and concerned? And if he did take such action, would he be equally criticized for trying to use the poor as a stepping-stone to public office?

John was quoted at the time as saying that he was thinking about working with blacks. Certainly a genuine commitment to social issues on his part would gain far greater attention than might be achieved by anyone else in his family. Those who bought the myth of Camelot would say he was following in his father's footsteps. And those who knew that his father failed to fulfill campaign promises would feel that the son was at last doing what the father had only talked about. Either way, he would have an impact greater than his work. However, such interests or actions have not revealed themselves so far.

John's decision to become a lawyer was made to please his mother. He was not intensely motivated by the law, nor was he a particularly good student. The law was essentially the family profession, acceptable, and a good background for a politician. He graduated in 1989 and quickly obtained a job as an assistant district attorney in Manhattan.

The assistant district attorney's position is initially a combination of postgraduate training and intense real world experience. Most assistants are hired in August, shortly after the bar exam. They must pass the exam within three attempts in order to stay with the DA's office, and the exams are given only twice a year. The results may take five to six months to be known, so none of the new assistants coming fresh from law school are able to go into court to prosecute. Instead, they receive orientation and training, write complaints coming in, and handle arraignments. They are always supervised, their work subject to constant scrutiny by more experienced attorneys.

An assistant district attorney signs a three-year contract that allows for extensive training. He or she will focus primarily on misdemeanors (a case load of approximately two hundred at any given time, including court activity, grand jury appearances, motions, and the like) until sometime in the second year of the contract. Then the attorney graduates to felonies, and may appear before the state Supreme Court. Most spend five years as assistant district attorneys, then go out on their own. However, the initial three-year commitment assures that they receive adequate training and provide the city with a fair return on the investment that training represents.

John had almost no problem getting hired. He was adequately qualified, and the Manhattan DA's office made no effort to publicize his hiring. He was just another working attorney on the staff. The biggest concern, other than his being a part of that minority of graduates who failed to pass the New York State Bar Exam, was his parking tickets. John did not feel that Manhattan's traffic and parking laws applied to him. Every time he received a ticket, he ignored it. He had to pay $2,300 in back fines in 1988 in order to have the completely clean record expected of each new assistant.

John failed both his first and second tries at the test, not passing until his third attempt. Of the sixty-four men and women who joined Manhattan District Attorney Robert Morgenthau's staff at the time, only seven, including Kennedy, failed. When the seven made their second attempt, John was one of only three who failed to pass. Even more frustrating, his score was 649—eleven points short of passing and just one point lower than the level where an appeal of the grade could be made.

While Kennedy's hiring by Morgenthau's office was not news, his failings became headlines. My favorite was "The Hunk Flunks." He was chastised by newsstand dealers and strangers passing him on the street. The most humorous story, which may be apocryphal, was of him walking in his West Side neighborhood. A homeless man was lying on the sidewalk, watching the passersby. When he recognized Kennedy, he raised his head and said, "You should be home studying." According to the story, John admitted, "You're right."

There were moves into the public eye during this time, though what they have meant in hindsight is less than what they implied at the time. First there was the 1988 Democratic Convention. Ted Kennedy, despite his personal reputation as a philanderer and heavy drinker, was one of the most powerful politicians in both the nation and the Democratic Party. He arranged for his nephew, John, to make a speech presenting him. It was an obvious first step on Ted's part toward an implied passing of power and a way of bringing John more fully into the political arena. It went nowhere. The moment was not particularly meaningful, and John did not follow it with any political activities. He would support his uncle, but he would not use the action as a stepping-stone to anything more.

John lent support in a very different way during the William Smith trial. That time it was more like a cameo appearance in a continuing soap opera. He was not present as legal counsel or consultant to his cousin, though being an assistant district attorney in New York would give him reason to be there. In fact, because he just showed up in order to be photographed, he was barred from the courtroom.

How much John knew about Willie's past is not known. Family members had long talked about Willie's overly aggressive attitude toward women. There were two who gave sworn statements to the Palm Beach County State's Attorney's Office. One had been dating Max Kennedy back in 1983, met Willie, and became interested in him. She was a guest in his parents' home when he allegedly forced her onto the bed, holding her down, trying to get her to agree to sex with him. She was able to flee the house, and he later apologized for making a "pass." She told Max what happened, and she was willing to go to court in the Patty Bowman trial to at least add credibility to the allegations.

The other woman was a year ahead of Willie in Georgetown Medical School. The incident occurred in the spring of 1988, and was somewhat similar. In this instance it occurred in his apartment. Again he apologized, trying to convince her he had done nothing wrong, even though she felt she had fought off a potential rapist. The stories were not permitted in court because Willie's past could not be held against him.

There seemed to be no question that John's presence was intended to connect his untainted image with his cousin's very damaged one. "How could the son of John Kennedy be with William Smith unless young Smith was innocent, his accuser a vicious liar?" seemed to be the message meant to be conveyed. Yet I have been told that the real reason John was present was because his mother, who claimed to hate politics, made him go there. She had allegedly been told, during a family conference, that if he did not show up the family would never support him should he run for the presidency. Politics may be the furthest thing from his interest, but no member of the third generation can escape the family enthusiasm for elected power. Tragically, the incident came as close to tarnishing him as anything in his life, because he obviously had no place being with Smith. Still, a media event is a media event, and the picture of John alongside his cousin appeared in papers coast-to-coast.

Close family friends often looked to John to go into politics. Retired Senator George Smathers, a close friend of the late president and usher at Jack and Jacqueline's wedding, was interviewed about the younger Kennedy's chances. Even he saw superficial over substance as he commented, "John would make a marvelous candidate. He is far and away the best looking of all the Kennedy kids, and has all the other attributes that can take him a long, long way—even to the White House."

Part of the appeal was sexual. *People* magazine, the nation's reflector of popular culture, named Kennedy "America's Most Eligible Bachelor"; in 1988, he was declared "The Sexiest Man Alive"; two years later, he was named as one of the world's fifty most beautiful people. Such accolades are of no value on one's resumé, but they do show how he has been viewed.

Most of John's affairs, unlike those of his father, have been of relatively long duration, and intense. He has dated women in the entertainment field for the most part, yet the more serious romances, such as with Daryl Hannah, Sally Munro (not an actress, a classmate at Brown), and Christina Haag, have not been publicized. The women are intensely protective of his privacy. He did not treat them as his father treated women, and he would never have made the comment that Jack allegedly made to Peter Lawford: ''I want my women three different ways, and then I am done with them.''

The public also has had trouble taking him seriously on issues rather than substance. Back in November 1988, Bloomingdale's, New York City's favorite department store, agreed to have a sales display of boxed Christmas ornaments. These were all created by retarded individuals living in Third World countries. The ornaments were being sold to benefit the charity Very Special Arts, and it was hoped that an appearance by John would add some solemnity to the occasion.

John was not the only family member present. His aunt, Jean Smith, and cousin, Willie Smith, were also there. Actress Lauren Bacall was present, as well. However, all anyone cared about was seeing John, and his presence resulted in a mob scene. He autographed boxes of the ornaments, and almost $50,000 worth were sold that day. In addition, national programs such as *Entertainment Tonight* covered the event, as did seven local news shows. John became the focus, not the charity. No matter how well the sales went, the charity probably would have done better with retaining its name recognition and gained more publicity for itself without him.

John was apparently a willing victim of another type of promotion, this one by the singer/actress Madonna. She met John through Bobby Shriver, who was having a number of popular singers contribute their efforts to a record album being made to benefit Special Olympics. Madonna invited John to hear a concert she gave at Madison Square Garden. She also began using the same athletic trainer as Kennedy. Numerous press reports indicated that Madonna also seduced John—a way of better relating to one of her idols, Marilyn Monroe, who had been seduced by Jack Kennedy. More reports say there was a brief sexual liaison, though friends of the actress maintain the relationship never went that far. Friends of Kennedy say that he has always been uncomfortable with aggressive women, and would not have responded if her private moves were as blatant as the act she used in public. Some reports went so far as to say they had sex, but that Madonna's tastes were too wild for the sexually conservative Kennedy.

What is more likely is that Jacqueline was not pleased with any aspect of this relationship. One report had her meeting Madonna and being livid about the idea. Another report indicated that though she was upset, there was enough of a groupie about her that she reached John at 2 A.M. when he came in from a date with Madonna. The singer/actress was by his side as he talked on the telephone to his mother, being questioned about his date.

The tolerance ended when Jacqueline discovered that Madonna had posed for a photograph carefully made up to look exactly like Monroe. Her husband's infidelity was thrown in her face through her son's liaison, and that she could not tolerate.

Madonna understood what she was doing, whether to the former first lady or anyone else. "If I weren't as talented as I am ambitious, I'd be a gross monstrosity. I've been called a tramp, a harlot, a slut, and the kind of girl who always winds up in the backseat of a car. If people can't get past that superficial level of what I'm about, fine," Madonna has been quoted as saying.

What Madonna did not say was that she did not want people to get past the superficial. She made her fortune on creating and recreating an image that ranged from materialistic to sexual without any hint of sensuality or romance. Her book, *Sex,* is a series of pictures of herself nude in public places, with other women, and in bondage. Rather than the types of images meant to arouse desire, it is as though each photograph, no matter what is shown, is her way of saying, "I'm naked. Look at me." It uses nudity and sex acts for attention, not eroticism. Even the text is little more than foul language, much of which reads like dirty words spray-painted on a school building wall by teenagers who think they discovered them.

It is true that Madonna has been credited with a genius-level intelligence. Certainly she is esteemed as one of the most brilliant businesswomen in the entertainment field. At one time she was considered by *Forbes* magazine to be worth $39 million, and by now has certainly surpassed that figure.

Most reports of the short affair give both parties credit for keeping much of the relationship private. John and Madonna attended plays and various gatherings separately, then sneaked off together. Still they were caught, even by Madonna's husband, Sean Penn.

No matter what happened during the brief affair, the ongoing saga of Madonna's life, including her adultery with John and her decision to have a baby out of wedlock with her personal trainer, indicate that publicity may have been a part of the would-be seduction. The result for John was amusing to the public, and helped keep him in the image of the male bimbo, all through no fault of his own.

It might be said that John Kennedy became the living equivalent of a Ken Doll during this period. His athleticism was well known and he frequently Roller-Bladed through Central Park. Photographs occasionally showed him without his shirt, his body one that could have been used for workout equipment advertisements. *People* declared him the "sexiest man alive" for no reason other than the editors thought him handsome and his pictures would sell magazines. Other than being aware that he was not setting the legal world on fire, people knew little about him. They simply mentally dressed him in whatever clothes they desired, created a fantasy existence for him, then placed him with the latest Barbie of the moment. The fact that his long term relationships, such as the one with actress Christina Haag, were with women who were bright, professional, and pursuing serious career and life goals, was irrelevant. If John could be Ken, then his girls had to be variations of Barbie and her friends.

Among the women who tried to use Kennedy was the Brazilian television and movie star Xuxa. The actress was an extremely beautiful woman, and her interest in John Kennedy seemed quite genuine when she aggressively pursued him for a date. She was financially successful and famous in her own right, and he thought that having lunch with her would be enjoyable. When he was picked up in a stretch limousine she provided, it seemed as though he was enjoying one of the prerequisites of being a rich, eligible, handsome bachelor.

The couple lunched at the Tribeca Grill, owned by actor Robert De Niro. Then they walked the neighborhood surrounding the restaurant as he showed her that part of the city with what amounted to a native's eye.

There was no big romance, no sex. Whether or not he enjoyed himself is unknown, and he soon discovered that the entire date was a publicity stunt. Still photographs turned up in a March 1992 copy of *National Enquirer,* which revealed that the date had been secretly filmed for *A Current Affair.* The tabloid television program could not be stopped, but both Kennedy and the show's viewers had been misled by a woman seeking to become better known in the United States. It was another instance where the Kennedy name and fame became a detriment to his trying to lead a normal, though admittedly glamorous life.

If there was a romance that seemed to indicate John's future life, it was the one with actress Daryl Hannah, a tall blond who had experienced her own childhood traumas. First there was the divorce of her parents. Almost all children of divorce go through a period in their lives when they feel responsible for what has taken place. They believe that somehow their behavior led to the end of their parents' marriage, and that if they could just do something different, everything would be all right. Hannah was seven years old when her parents divorced, and she was devastated by the experience. Shy, a loner, she began to feel that she had to somehow help her brother, Don, and sister, Page, both of whom were younger. She decided that they could eat at McDonald's, then determined the cost. Later she tried to list jobs she could get, at seven years of age, that would pay the bills for all the McDonald's food.

Daryl's beliefs, though unrealistic, were not all that unusual for a child trying to find a way to cope with the turmoil of divorce. As with many other actors and actresses with difficult childhoods, Hannah immersed herself in films. She frequently had insomnia, and used old movies on television to put herself to sleep. The few interviews she gave during the time she was dating John often mentioned films such as *Singin' in the Rain*.

Several years later Daryl tried professional dancing herself. She became a student of Maria Tallchief, a former ballet star and onetime wife of George Balanchine. Tallchief felt that Hannah could easily have become a star, though Daryl did not wish to put the time and discipline into her training to make that happen. Her lifestyle was, and is, too casual for the intensity of training necessary for ballet.

The change in Hannah's life, though apparently not her attitude toward herself, came six years after her mother's divorce. When Daryl was thirteen, her mother married Jerry Wexler, changing all their lives.

Wexler was important in two ways. As the chairman of Jupiter Industries, he was a Chicago industrialist of great wealth and power. Wexler was also the brother of cinematographer Haskell Wexler, one of the most respected cameramen in Hollywood.

The first year of the marriage was an odd one. Wexler had four children soon on their way to college. Daryl's mother had three much younger children. It seemed to make the most sense to them for Wexler to stay with his family and Sue Hannah Wexler to live with her children in a suite in one of the hotels her new husband owned.

The living arrangement seemed uncomfortable for Daryl. She withdrew still more, so her mother took her out of school, then to the Bahamas for a break. Later, when Daryl was more outgoing and relaxed, they returned to Chicago, where Hannah was enrolled in the Francis W. Parker School for theater and dramatics. It was there that she worked with Tallchief, and after that experience switched to acting. She took classes at the Goodman Theater, the only teenager doing so. And she soon became obsessed with acting.

Hannah's first role was as a bit player in the movie *The Fury*. Brian De Palma's horror story was filmed in Chicago, and the new actress said one word—"Creep"—while spilling her milk. Later, after moving to Los Angeles when she was seventeen, Hannah began playing a variety of parts, most worth forgetting.

It was 1984 when Daryl Hannah made her breakthrough film. She had tried two years of college at the University of Southern California, found formal education stifling, and focused solely on her career. That paid off when Ron Howard asked her to read for the starring part of Madison, the mermaid of his box office success *Splash*. She worked opposite Tom Hanks, who was rapidly rising to a level where he was considered one of the great actors of his generation, and the critics loved the film.

Splash brought Hannah instant fame. She was on the talk shows. She was on the cover of *Vanity Fair*. She was on the cover of *Life*. She had become an ideal of beauty and sensuality, neither of which related to her negative self-image. Her figure had not developed until she was eighteen, and that sort of "late blooming" had led to much teasing during her school years.

Numerous other films followed, one of the more important being *Steel Magnolias*, in which she played opposite Dolly Parton, Sally Field, Shirley MacLaine, Olympia Dukakis, and Julia Roberts. Her work had become so varied and respected that she was repeatedly asked to be a presenter at the Academy Awards ceremony.

John Kennedy first met Daryl in the early 1980s, when both their families were vacationing in St. Martin in the Caribbean. In 1988 they were both invited to the wedding of his aunt, Lee Radziwill, who was marrying Daryl's *Steel Magnolias* director, Herbert Ross.

John and Daryl were seen together, though there seemed nothing romantic about their friendship. For almost a decade she had been living with singer Jackson Browne, whom she had met as a teenager. She was a fan attending one of his Chicago concerts when he spotted her in the audience and had her come up on stage. They became lovers when he left his second wife, Lynne Sweeney. They lived together on and off for nine years. The relationship was continuous, though not so intense as the duration seemed. Frequently he was touring and giving concerts, and she was off on movie locations. Neither exploited the relationship, which would end in 1992. Friends alleged that he had become repeatedly physically abusive.

It was in September 1988 that John and Daryl first became an "item." *People* magazine reported that friends of Daryl said that Browne had given her a black eye, a broken finger, and numerous bruises. She went to the hospital and then called John, who flew out to get her, bringing her back to New York.

Exactly what happened after that was the subject of intense media speculation but little substance. Both had extremely troubled, privileged, and somewhat public childhoods. Both understood loss. Both delighted in casual dress to such a degree that many of Daryl's high school friends thought she was the janitor's daughter when they first went to see her in the luxury apartment owned by her stepfather. While John had greater formal education, Hannah was an avid reader with great intelligence.

Daryl eventually traveled with John to Providence for his tenth reunion at Brown, and he traveled to Los Angeles when she was starring in a remake of *Attack of the 50-Foot Woman* for HBO. Eventually he moved from his downtown penthouse to her Upper West Side apartment.

Daryl remained with John through the last great crisis he faced in his immediate family. On May 18, 1994, Jacqueline Kennedy Onassis lay dying in the Cornell Medical Center in New York City. She had an unusually aggressive form of non-Hodgkin's lymphoma. Normally doctors expect four out of every ten sufferers to survive five years or more following chemotherapy. Jacqueline did not respond.

Next came steroids, used in conjunction with the chemotherapy, and finally the Stich Radiation Therapy Center was utilized for a special new form of therapy that could pinpoint radiation to areas such as her brain. Instead of helping, the combination of tumors having permeated her body and the debilitating effects of the treatment led to a severely weakened immune system. The cancer spread to her liver. She developed pneumonia. Her body was irreversibly failing, and earlier, in February, she had signed a living will to ensure that no heroic or experimental methods would be used to prolong her life.

Once Jacqueline learned her condition was terminal, she insisted on going home to die. It was a decision that assured her both family and privacy. Any Kennedy event—birth, marriage, divorce, or death—was a major media concern. Hospital personnel were too numerous to avoid the risk of someone giving a photographer or reporter inappropriate access. At home she could die in peace.

Family and the closest of friends began to gather at 1040 Fifth Avenue on that May afternoon. Her sister, Lee Radziwill Ross, flew in from California. Monsignor George Bardes of St. Thomas More Church on East 89th Street heard Jacqueline's last confession, and gave her communion. Then he administered the sacrament the Catholic Church now calls Anointing the Sick. Non-Catholics remember the older term—the quite appropriate "last rites."

Entertainer Carly Simon, a longtime friend who had also produced a book for Doubleday that Jacqueline edited, came by. There were Joe Armstrong, former publisher of *Rolling Stone,* Rachel "Bunny" Mellon, wife of the wealthy Paul Mellon, and others. Some lived in Manhattan. Some came from Palm Beach or California. They all came to say good-bye. And in the midst of the others, Daryl Hannah arrived to spend some time with her boyfriend's mother.

Daryl's arrival was seen as proof that John Kennedy would marry the actress. She would not have come without Jacqueline liking her. She would not have been permitted into the apartment. However, it gradually became obvious, though, that as strong as Daryl's relationship may have been with Jacqueline, the relationship with John was fading. They would soon go their separate ways.

On May 19, 1994, at 9 P.M., Jacqueline Kennedy Onassis slipped into a coma. An hour and fifteen minutes later she was dead. The next morning, John went to the door of his mother's apartment and met the press, saying:

"Last night, at around ten-fifteen, my mother passed on. She was surrounded by her friends and her family and her books and the people and things that she loved.

"And she did it in her own way and in her own terms, and we all feel lucky for that, and now she's in God's hands.

"There has been an enormous outpouring of good wishes from everyone, both in New York and beyond. And I speak for all of my family when we say we're extremely grateful. Everyone's been very generous. And I hope now that, you know, we can just have these next couple of days in relative peace."

There would be more than just peace for John Kennedy. With his mother dead, he was free to choose the direction of his own life. He no longer had to be bored with law. He no longer had to worry about his mother's reaction to his workaday life, his personal interests, his girlfriends, or anyone else. He had always been close to Jacqueline, and he mourned her loss, yet she had been his albatross as well. For all her own indiscretions and moral failings—including spending the last years of her life with her still married lover, Maurice Tempelsman—she tried to force John into a mold from which she, herself, had declared her independence.

At first John spent his days doing little other than working out and, when the weather cooperated, making certain he could be photographed bare-chested as he Roller-Bladed through Central Park. He was simultaneously shy and an exhibitionist, ironically much like his mother. She publicly decried photographers like Ron Galella, who followed her everywhere, yet when she sued Galella she insisted upon keeping hundreds of his images for her personal collection. When she knew there were photographers in the area of the Onassis yacht, she stripped to the waist, showing off a chest as impressive for a woman as her son's was for a man. So John sought attention for his physical appearance at the same time that he tried to keep a quiet private life.

Friends claim that John considered acting after his mother's death. Certainly he still loved show business and the people who earned their living as performers. However, he was in his mid-thirties, old for a male to break into pictures. He had little experience and no training, and while there might be a following for any movie in which John had a role, the novelty of seeing John Kennedy would not last. Worse, if he started studying seriously for the profession, he would be merely competent at an age where actors of far greater experience are usually coming at the height of their skills. He could not compete.

The answer for John was to create *George,* a magazine dedicated to politics, theater, irreverence, celebrity, investigative articles, and selling advertising in the name of John Kennedy. If this sounds unfocused, it was, and, to a degree, remains so. The only exception is the last point, selling advertising in the name of John.

There was a logic to the magazine, John explained after its launch. "My mother knew something about politics. It was said she was the only person in the administration who could get along with de Gaulle. And my father knew something about journalism. Fifty years ago he was a working reporter covering the United Nations in San Francisco. For me, the marriage of publishing and politics simply weaves together the two family businesses."

John also explained, "One of our premises is that politics and culture are not two separate worlds sealed off from one another, but each helps shape the other. I was a little young in nineteen sixty to notice the sea change then, but in my own life, I think nineteen sixty-two was a similar benchmark in our understanding the opportunities that were created by this new way of covering politics."

John also began talking with the press more than he had in the past, a necessity for the magazine's launch. For one of the first times in his relationship with the press, he showed a humorous side only his close friends knew. For example, he offered the answers to the most frequently asked personal questions he regularly faced. He said they were: "Yes. No. We're merely good friends. None of your business. Honest, she's my cousin from Rhode Island. I've worn both. Maybe someday, but not in New Jersey."

George made its debut in September 1995. The cover pictured model Cindy Crawford dressed to look like George Washington, though with enough bare flesh to show she was a great looking woman. The idea was partially repeated in the second issue, with actor Robert De Niro also posing as Washington. Advertising sales were massive, with John fronting for the magazine. The advertisers were more seduced by his name's potential than by the planned content. As a result, advertising declined by the third issue.

The magazine was not John's alone, though he is in the top editorial position. Hachette Filipacchi Magazines, a respected French giant in the periodical industry, provided $29 million in underwriting, counting on staying for the long haul.

The magazine was supposed to have a political focus, a cross between *Vanity Fair* and *People* though concentrating on national politicians. However, the first issue contained an article by Madonna, and the second had John providing a personal interview with actor Warren Beatty, rumored to have been, briefly, a lover of his mother.

The bi-monthly went monthly in August 1996, one month before John and a woman named Carolyn Bessette flew to Georgia, where they traveled to Cumberland Island near Hilton Head. Freed slaves had built a wooden chapel that came to be known as the First African Baptist Church. It was small, containing just eight pews, though adequate for forty guests. Father Charles O'Byrne, a Jesuit deacon from the Church of St. Ignatius Loyola in Manhattan, officiated. Tony Radziwill, John's cousin, served as best man. John's sister, Caroline Kennedy Schlossberg, was matron of honor. And Caroline's children—eight-year-old Rose, six-year-old Tatiana, and three-

and-a-half-year-old Jack—acted as flower girls and ring bearer, respectively.

Carolyn was the wild card in John's history of relationships. She wasn't in show business, had no aspirations to be on the stage. At the same time, she had done just enough modeling to gain a photo portfolio that made her image as intriguing as her future husband's.

Carolyn, born in 1967, was named "The Ultimate Beautiful Person" when she attended St. Mary's High School in Green-wich, Connecticut. She went to Boston University, graduating in 1988 with a degree in elementary education. While she seemed not to be interested in teaching, her mother was a public school administrator. Of greater interest to Kennedy watchers was the fact that she modeled for a calendar titled "B.U.'s Most Beautiful Women."

More serious modeling came in 1990, two years after graduating from Boston University. She posed for Bobby DiMarzo, a Boston-based fashion photographer whose quite sexy images of Carolyn made their biggest impact when he sold them to *The Globe* in 1996. At the same time that DiMarzo was cashing in on his images, another photographer who had worked with Carolyn during the same period was quoted by the *New York Post* as saying that she was the most beautiful girl he had ever photographed. "She could have modeled full time, but she wasn't interested. She couldn't sit still long enough. I think she's so smart, she wanted a better job."

Her looks and intelligence gained her a number of high profile companions even as she began doing marketing and public relations work for the Lyons Group. Her responsibilities involved booking for two nightclubs, something she hated, quickly switching to jobs at Calvin Klein's stores, first in Chestnut Hill in Massachusetts, then in New York. At the same time she was dating men ranging from professional hockey player John Cullen to Alessandro Benetton, heir to the Benetton fashion fortune.

No one is certain where she and John met. One story has them coming together by chance in Central Park. Another has her assigned as his personal shopper during a visit to the Manhattan Calvin Klein store. Whatever the case, they began living together in 1995.

The engagement of the couple made national news—not in the announcement, but in the near break up. Despite the photographers always present in their lives, the couple managed to carry over a fight concerning the wedding ceremony from their apartment into Central Park. John wanted a small ceremony. Carolyn wanted a big one. Their arguing led to John pulling off the engagement ring, and to a series of emotionally charged pictures that made the tabloid and mainstream press. Ultimately there was a compromise involving a small wedding and two massive parties, one by the Schlossbergs and one by the Schwarzeneggers.

The wedding brought other strains. Though Carolyn had last worked for Calvin Klein, her wedding dress designer was the Paris-based Narcisco Rodriguez, who created her $40,000 pearl-colored, silk crepe gown. In her hair was a comb that had previously belonged to Jacqueline, while John wore a watch that had been his father's.

John's blue wool suit was designed by Gordon Henderson. He also wore a pale blue silk tie and white piquè vest.

The cost of the quiet, private wedding was enormous because John insisted on total control. He did not want a media circus. He did not want his tendency toward exhibitionism to carry over into the first serious commitment he had ever made. There were fifty armed security guards. Private jets brought the guests to and from the island. The hotel accommodations and all other aspects of the wedding were all paid by John for those in attendance. Including the honeymoon in Istanbul, Turkey, the cost was estimated at more than $600,000. Had Carolyn gotten her way about having a much larger ceremony, the cost would easily have exceeded a million dollars.

The only public part of the event came when John released the statement, "It was important for us to be able to conduct this in a private, prayerful, and meaningful way with the people we love."

Since the marriage there have been numerous rumors of all sorts about the Kennedys: Carolyn signed a prenuptial agreement with a $10-million cap. Carolyn was pregnant when she married. Carolyn was pregnant later. Carolyn can't get pregnant because John can't get her pregnant. Carolyn and John are fighting. Carolyn and John are getting a divorce. Carolyn and John are happily married, and find the rumors of their discord to be humorous. Carolyn and John are—

At this writing, the marriage is still working, and if there are problems the press is not privy to them. The couple is intensely private in many ways, though John has become more outgoing due to his work with *George*. He has also taken up flying, and flew his own plane to the traditional Cape Cod Kennedy Thanksgiving celebration in 1998.

As for the magazine, it still seems to be floundering. It is still a mix of fluff and serious journalism, though the serious journalism seems to be increasing. There are many questions as to whether or not it will survive, and if it does, in what form.

Some feel that John is a front man, a puppet for the real editorial personnel, perhaps based in France. Others are convinced that John is in charge, a bright, quick study of the industry in which he now earns his money. They say that his reputation for not being particularly intelligent was based on his feeling forced to study for a profession in which he had no interest, that his failings in law school were not based on an inability to do the work but rather with boredom.

Whatever the case, his marriage has decreased his role as America's Ken doll. He is still a major celebrity. He can still talk his way into commercial appearances lesser individuals with better products can not attain. For example, he appeared on the then popular Candace Bergen comedy series *Murphy Brown* plugging *George*. However, his marriage has made him less of an attainable fantasy, a fact that has cost him some of his appeal to women, something Carolyn Bessette Kennedy undoubtedly finds a relief. He does remain an almost mythological figure, and if *George* should fold or stop being his primary

interest, it will be interesting to see in which direction he decides
to go.

CAROLINE

Caroline Kennedy has had fewer pressures than her younger
brother. The Kennedy women of the third generation have
been allowed to live relatively normal lives within the family.
Caroline evoked images of a little girl riding her pony, Maca-
roni, on the White House grounds. She did not evoke the image
of a future president.

Joe and Rose were focused on their sons, a not unusual
circumstance for their generation. Eunice was probably the
strongest and most aggressive of all the second generation, yet
her political activities have remained behind the scenes.

The men of the second generation put pressure on the males
of the third, which is probably why Joe II, Robert Kennedy's
oldest son, went into politics. After Jack's death, Robert made
it clear that Joe was next in line to carry on what was viewed
as the family tradition. The other sons, under similar pressures
to one degree or another, turned to drugs and alcohol, sometimes
triumphing over the stress, sometimes continuing their fight
against their inner demons.

Kathleen Kennedy Townsend, now the lieutenant governor
of Maryland, was little more than a "hippie" in appearance
when she married. Maria Shriver avoided the family political
pressures entirely by moving into television journalism. The
names of Sydney and Victoria, the daughters of Peter and Pat
Kennedy Lawford, might as well be trivia question answers to
outsiders. Caroline, though, still has the slight aura of being a
Kennedy, a connection with the White House. She has been
followed, photographed, and even suffered a bombing during
her early years.

The death of Jack Kennedy was probably harder on Caroline
than it was on her brother. She was older, had greater understanding of the confusion all around her, and retained memories
of living in the White House. However, according to her writing

years later, she did not remember her father in any significant way, learning about him from family, friends, and school courses.

If Caroline had problems during the first few years after her father's death, it was because she was thrown into public circumstances that were extremely uncomfortable for her. In 1965, when her mother took the children to visit England, there was an entourage that included the nanny and two Secret Service agents. Two years later, the children and their mother had to christen the aircraft carrier John F. Kennedy. There were always reporters, always photographers, and Caroline was not yet a teenager.

It was Caroline who was most keenly aware of her uncle Bob's murder. Bob had become a surrogate parent for several months after the assassination. Jacqueline later commented that Caroline thought of Hickory Hill, her uncle Bob's estate, as her own home. "Anything that comes up involving a father, like Father's Day at school, I always mention Bobby's name," Jacqueline said later. "Caroline shows him her report cards. She makes drawings at school marked *To Uncle Bobby.*"

Jacqueline and Jack had thought that of all the Kennedys, they most wanted Bob and Ethel to take care of John and Caroline. Later, after Bob's death, that changed. Jacqueline was horrified by the lack of discipline, the seeming lack of caring by Ethel.

Caroline was very sensitive to her mother's anger, fear, and grief in the aftermath of uncle Bob's assassination. She was also one of the brightest of the third generation, and unlike her brother, earned high grades.

Caroline never grew close to Aristotle Onassis when her mother remarried. She had an established life that involved her uncle Ted, family friends, and children her own age. Her needs and desires were different from those of her brother.

Although Caroline, like John, admitted that she had learned most of what she knew about her father since his death, she tried to establish some sort of connection. She collected the stamp bearing his portrait issued by the various countries that honored him in that manner. She collected coins bearing his image. Her room was filled with memorabilia of Jack.

In 1970, twelve-year-old Caroline was transferred to the Brearley School in Manhattan from the Convent of the Sacred Heart. Jacqueline feared her daughter would be too socially isolated in the Catholic school. She had thrived intellectually, but Brearley, a school for the academically elite, offered a greater challenge for Caroline. She received high marks on her entrance exams, and continued to thrive in the school's rich intellectual program.

Although Caroline was not the Kennedy child of choice for the media, she did suffer from inappropriate attention, which became obvious when she was fifteen. Jacqueline wanted her daughter to have a measure of freedom not possible in a school in the midst of Manhattan. She chose Concord Academy in Concord, Massachusetts, near Boston. The school was on thirty-two acres of land, affording great privacy. Most of the children in attendance had prominent, wealthy parents, a fact that made them security-conscious for everyone.

Oddly, in the effort to give Caroline privacy, some of the community leaders in Concord used their weekly paper, *The Concord Journal,* to do the opposite of what Jacqueline wanted. In a well meaning editorial, the paper assured that everyone would be on the lookout for Caroline.

A LITTLE GIRL IS COMING TO VISIT
As the daughter of Camelot's prince and his ethereal princess, she was marked for mass adulation too early in life. Events not of her making or choosing have crept up and around her to make her a sometimes frightened child denied the pleasures of childhood in an American town, the heritage guaranteed by the country her father headed to millions of kids.

The editorial attempted to give her freedom when she moved about the community, though it probably resulted in neighborhood watch groups seeking Caroline as birders might search for a rare ornithological specimen.

> Please treat her as you would any other Concord kid. Ignore her as you do your neighbor's kids, except for the occasional circumstance when a cheery word or two might be indicated . . . Remember, she's only a kid.

To be fair, some of the precautions were necessary. While the school was isolated, the dormitories were not. They were in seven homes that had been privately owned a hundred years earlier.

Caroline seemed to blossom at the Concord school. Classes were small—twelve to fourteen students on average, with a total enrollment of 265, fifty of whom were boys. Dress was casual, and no one cared about her background. These children of privilege barely remembered the Kennedy presidency. If they were impressed with anything, it was her tendency to play practical jokes. She baked a laxative into brownies meant for a bake sale, and she put bubble bath in the water-holding tank of a drinking fountain.

Though Secret Service agents were constantly present until Caroline turned sixteen, she came to see them as a challenge, not an albatross. She delighted in slipping away from them, sometimes going into town, once even traveling the seventeen miles into Boston where, unguarded, she heard a speech by her uncle Ted. Her greatest prank was an imitation of a classic motion picture ploy. She boarded a bus the agents were following in a car, then slipped out the rear door before the bus was rolling. The agents never saw her do it.

Caroline had the usual adolescent preoccupation with herself. She was not certain her features were right, and she worried that her face was unattractive. She also worried that people would think her arrogant, snobbish, and self-centered. She wanted to be liked for herself, not adored for her family. While both John and Jacqueline often cultivated attention even as they sought privacy, Caroline just wanted to be another kid, liked or disliked for her own actions.

There was political involvement during Caroline's teen years. She rang doorbells in Concord for John Kerry, an antiwar candidate for Congress. She traveled a bit for George McGovern's senatorial campaign. She worked on her uncle Ted's campaigns.

At sixteen, Caroline traveled to the eastern Tennessee hill country to help make a documentary about the lives of miners. The project was done under the auspices of the Federation of Communities in Service. She received no special attention, no publicity. She was simply another teenager helping on a project that would enable her to assist with interviews, camera work, and film processing in the Appalachian town of Clairfield.

Some publicity came out, especially when the Knoxville, Tennessee, *Sentinel* interviewed some of the miners' families concerning the documentary. They found that she was living with one of the families, and seemed no different from the teenagers who lived in the area.

Caroline's activities were usually quiet ones, even when adventurous. In 1974 she expressed an interest in learning to fly. She took fifteen lessons in a Cessna 150, a small, single-engine, two-person airplane frequently used for basic flight training. However, her schedule caused her to decide to stop just short of being eligible to solo.

There were negative stories about Caroline during this period, as well. There were times when the girl, usually so concerned with how others might see her, also acted like a spoiled brat. She tried to see how far her name would get her, and there were occasional newspaper stories about her trying to get service ahead of others. While a teenager, she was reported by the press to try to obtain ice cream immediately from a busy vendor in New York. She announced that she was Caroline Kennedy, and when the vendor was more concerned with the customers who had been waiting ahead of her, she stormed out. In another incident, when she first was enrolled in college, she went to the Harvard Trust Company on a busy Friday.

There was a line, but she cut in front and was promptly told by the teller that she would have to wait. Caroline, not about to be forced to act like normal people, demanded to see the person in charge. The teller then informed her that she, the teller, was in charge.

Caroline also seemed to come to love the press far more than many members of her family. I remember one time when she was in her bikini, talking with reporters gathered outside the family compound. There were also times when she willingly posed for photographs.

Some of Caroline's actions with the press may have been the result of her grandmother's admonitions. Rose dictated a letter to me in which she explained to her granddaughter that it was important to allow press photographers to take her picture. She said that they had jobs to do. If they returned without photographs, they would have trouble with their employers. She explained that she had found that if she stopped, posed for them, and let them take the picture, they were pleased, their jobs were secure, and often they would not be pests. Although Caroline's mother hated the press, Caroline seemed ambivalent at times, a willing victim at others.

What did matter to Caroline, and what would be a major part of her life before her marriage to Edwin Schlossberg, was photography. Concord Academy had a program that encouraged the students to involve themselves with off-campus learning experiences. Caroline was given six weeks to handle a project for credit in her filmmaking class. Working without pay, she was a volunteer assistant for the NBC feature *Weekend.* She worked during February and March of 1975, acting as a gofer. She helped carry equipment, ran errands, and did anything else necessary both on location and during a trip through several major areas of the Middle East.

Caroline spent her time learning, observing, and taking still pictures. She was involved with the post-production editing and preparation, fascinated by the field.

When the work was finished, Jacqueline flew to New York from Europe to be with her daughter. It was a time when her husband, Onassis, was suffering from Lou Gehrig's disease. Onassis died in a Paris hospital while Jacqueline was in Manhattan, a fact that resulted in extremely harsh feelings on the part of Onassis's daughter, Christina.

Fears about Caroline's safety proved justified in 1975, after Caroline graduated from Concord. A boyfriend at the time was Mark Shand, a London youth who met Caroline when she was a teenager vacationing in the Bahamas. He was just enough older so that by the time Caroline finished her high school education, Mark was a graduate of an art course given by the London art dealer and auction house, Sotheby's.

Shand, though extremely young, was a successful dealer in international art. He was reunited by chance with Caroline in New York. Caroline was going through a period of rebellion, rejecting all formality in her life. She refused to come out as a debutante, and she refused to dress in an appropriate manner when going to expensive restaurants with her mother or others. She was trying to find her own way, breaking from her mother and her mother's values. In that regard she was no different from other girls experiencing adolescent rebellion. She was just more noticeable.

When I was with Caroline, I watched the reactions of passersby. She was not a beautiful woman. She did not have striking features that would cause someone to more than glance her way. The attention she received only occurred when her casual dress was a radical contrast to those around her. Any other time she seemed to disappear in the crowd.

Caroline decided to travel to London to take the art course at Sotheby's. The class in 1975 was limited to fifty people, was inexpensive, and an interest of Caroline's her mother approved.

Caroline found herself in the midst of a scandal when she arrived in England. Jacqueline had contacted family friend Hugh Fraser, a member of Parliament, to arrange for Caroline to stay with him. This delighted the British press because Fraser's wife, the highly respected historian Lady Antonia Fraser, was the mistress of playwright Harold Pinter. The Frasers had separated because of the affair, and the Pinters were in the midst of a divorce.

The work was more intense than Caroline had anticipated, though, unlike her brother, she was a good student. There was extensive reading expected of the participants, in addition to studying art, watching auctions, and generally learning the business of buying and selling paintings, sculpture, and other art objects.

Fraser lived in a home in Campden Hill Square, far enough from Sotheby's so that Caroline had to be driven or take the tube. Fraser routinely either took her to work or drove her to the Holland Park Underground Station, always leaving at the same time each day.

On October 24, 1975, Fraser's Jaguar XJ6 was parked in front of his house. He was planning to take Caroline to the subway as usual, but a telephone call from a fellow member of Parliament prevented their leaving as planned. The trains ran with such frequency that Caroline could still get to Sotheby's if they waited, so Fraser talked, delaying their departure.

Also a creature of habit, Dr. Gordon Hamilton walked his poodle past Fraser's home at 8:30 that morning. It was unusual for the Jaguar to still be parked by the curb, and it was also odd that a package of some sort was under the car. Hamilton went closer to look just as a bomb exploded, destroying the Jaguar and dismembering the doctor, a respected cancer specialist.

For Caroline, the bomb was not the personal threat it seemed for her mother. Jacqueline had experienced the murders of her husband and brother-in-law. She was aware of a number of potentially violent incidents that had been defused by the presence of the Secret Service anticipating trouble. In her mind, Caroline was another target, and the thought terrified her. It was a great act of courage on Jacqueline's part to let her daughter stay in England.

I don't know if Caroline appreciates her mother's courage at that time. Perhaps she will not understand until her own children are preparing to go out on their own. John Jr. was called a mama's boy by his cousins, and certainly their mother tried to be protective, but no matter what tension existed between mother and daughter, Caroline was living in the midst of adults who would help Jacqueline with whatever she desired. The compromise she and Caroline reached, allowing Caroline to stay in England until September, at which time she would enroll in Radcliffe, was an act of selfless love on her mother's part.

Caroline's work at Radcliffe, part of the same Harvard University her grandfather, father, three uncles, and several cousins had attended, was always good. She roomed at Winthrop House, the same house where her father and uncle Bob had lived. I was surprised that they made no effort to treat her differently from any of the others. The only privilege she had was a room to herself. It was so small that it held only a bed and a sink. Caroline told me that there was so little space that when she wanted to comb her hair she had to step outside in the hall. She often travelled to Manhattan to dance at Studio 54 with one or another boyfriend.

Caroline was interested enough in the media to take a summer job as a copy girl at the New York *Daily News,* eventually traveling to Memphis to cover Elvis Presley's death. She went in the company of columnist Pete Hamill, her mother's boyfriend at the time.

Caroline's life was relatively unremarkable. The press kept trying to get stories from her. She continued to be observed, though as a sloppy teenager without a sex scandal for the news, she seemed rather boring compared to her brother. He was not more accessible, but he was the heir apparent, something Caroline could never be.

Public attention did affect Caroline's life, during her relationship with Thomas R. Carney, a freelance writer and novelist who was ten years older. He was Irish Catholic, a Yale graduate, and had worked as a copywriter at Doubleday for a time. Jacqueline knew him and approved of his relationship with her daughter, and the couple allegedly became rather serious. They vacationed together in the Caribbean, and he took her home to

Wyoming, where his family had a ranch. She also brought him to Palm Beach to meet her grandmother and to hang around the kitchen with Nellie, who teased him that he was really there to one day write a book about the family.

Carney claimed that he broke off with Caroline because he could not stand the constant publicity. He did not want to spend his life being followed by photographers and reporters. Whether or not the age difference, a large one considering her youth at the time, was more of a factor is not known. Certainly, for all their international experiences, neither Caroline nor John was particularly streetwise.

As a side note, it is interesting to see what happened to Carney. In 1981 he married another woman interested in photography, a professional in the field named Maureen Lambrey.

Caroline's life became the most stable after college. She worked in the Film and Television Development Office of the Metropolitan Museum of Art, coordinating media projects both within and outside the museum. She began as a researcher, then rose to be manager and coordinating producer. It was a job that was occasionally demeaned at first by the New York press, which delighted in detailing embarrassing moments. However, she had the background and the skills for the work, and she was extremely effective. She might have stayed in that field had she not decided to go to law school in 1985.

Caroline's decision was unexpected by the public, but not by her closest friends. They knew she was becoming bored with museum work. Her position was exciting, but only as far as it went. She had reached a level where the next years would see her doing similar tasks. She wanted a new challenge. Quietly, without publicity, she enrolled in the Columbia University School of Law. There she was quiet, studious, at once dedicated and torn. During times of exhaustion following intense study she confided to classmates that she could not understand why she had chosen such pressure, that all she really wanted to do was stay at home and have babies. She stayed with it, though, earning high marks and passing the bar exam on the first try.

It was earlier, in the fall of 1981, that Caroline moved into an apartment with two men and another woman. This was not a wild sex scene in which the late president's daughter could run rampant behind closed doors. Instead, it was a practical decision based on her income and the type of apartments available.

Caroline is rich, as are all the Kennedy children. They were millionaires at birth, and their incomes have increased year after year. In addition, Caroline gained income from the Onassis estate, adding to her wealth. She and John were willed an additional $500,000 each at his death.

Caroline was not inclined to flaunt what she had. She could afford to go anywhere, buy anything, dress in the finest clothes. Instead, she chose to dress almost as casually as her brother, John, avoiding makeup and keeping a low profile. The apartment she rented in 1981 was a massive three-bedroom triplex with library on the Upper West Side of Manhattan. The area was more trendy than expensive. Her suite cost $2,000 a month, a modest figure for that location, affordable when the rent was shared four ways. The males were friends, not lovers. The apartment was so large that each was afforded complete privacy. The men added a certain amount of security for Caroline.

Caroline's problems with strangers were mostly minor, though there were some potentially dangerous incidents in those years. The most serious was in 1984 when she was working at the Metropolitan Museum of Art in New York City. Randall Gefvert, a former mental patient, decided that it was necessary to kill her and blow up the museum. He sent messages that she would be killed by twenty hit men. He was the only one involved, and he was arrested before any violence could take place.

Three years earlier, California lawyer Kevin King decided that he wanted to marry her. He began sending Caroline love letters that eventually became both obscene and threatening. When she failed to respond, he traveled to New York and tried to break into her apartment building. He was arrested, and was so hurt by so blatant a rejection that he renounced his desire to marry her when given a chance to speak in court. Then, because obsessive love conquers all, he apparently forgave her for having him arrested and said he would marry her, after all. Instead, the judge fined him $1,000 and sentenced him to a year in jail.

During the year that Caroline was living on her own and working for the museum, she met Edwin Arthur Schlossberg, a man friends jokingly said was still trying to figure out what he wanted to be when he grew up. He had been called a Renaissance man—an author, a designer, and a consultant, among other things. In reality, he was that rare individual who combined great intellect with skill in a wide variety of areas.

Alfred Schlossberg, Ed's father, was a self-made multimillionaire who began in the textile business in Manhattan, then bought a vacation home in Palm Beach. He was an Orthodox Jew, a financial supporter of causes related to his religion and to the state of Israel. He was also president of Congregation Rodeph Sholom.

Ed was raised on Park Avenue and attended Birch Wathen School where he captained the soccer team and headed the social committee. He then went on to Columbia University, where his interests were too broad for a normal degree program. He ended his academic years by taking two Ph.D.s, one in science and one in literature. For his thesis, he combined the arts and sciences in a dialogue between Samuel Beckett and Albert Einstein.

At first Schlossberg did whatever seemed to be enjoyable following his 1971 graduation. He tried teaching at Southern Illinois University, then began making money with an eclectic mix of oddball projects. Pocket calculators were still new enough so that inexpensive ones were novelty items. Schlossberg wrote *The Kids Pocket Calculator Games Book,* meant to teach mastery of this new tool, as well as providing fun. Later, as computers became less expensive, he also wrote *The Home Computer Handbook.*

Schlossberg was also an early leader in the craze to place slogans on T-shirts. He worked with designer Willi Smith, combining his skills to produce poetic slogans that were produced with a special paint. Each time the wearer's body temperature changed, the color of the paint was likewise altered.

His greatest notoriety came from his work with museums. Ed designed exhibits for numerous museums and organizations, including one for the Massachusetts Society for the Prevention of Cruelty to Animals. That exhibit allowed visitors to see what life was like through the eyes of a pig. Some of his work has been praised. Some was not liked by clients, who had other designers take over. Such successes and problems are normal in the design business, and Schlossberg was able to earn fees of $500 a day just for sharing ideas with clients.

Caroline met Ed at a dinner party in 1981, then invited him to her mother's Christmas party that year. Jacqueline liked him immediately because he was everything the Kennedys were not. He was not really athletic, being somewhat stocky, and with his prematurely gray hair he seemed the kind of man who could be viewed as comfortable, dependable, and honest. He was also thirteen years older than Caroline, a man who was no longer trying to prove anything to others through sex, drugs, and drinking.

Caroline had moved from her large apartment to a small one on East 78th Street. She was obviously in love with Schlossberg. Most of her time was spent in Ed's Wooster Street loft. On weekends they frequently escaped Manhattan by driving to Ed's parents' "barn" in Chester, Massachusetts. This was actually a barn converted into an expensively furnished home where members of the family get away from New York.

Perhaps the most important part of the relationship was that Schlossberg loved Caroline for herself, not because she was a Kennedy. He was not impressed with her family. He did not feel the need to compete with her cousins. And when there was the crisis of David Kennedy's death, it was Ed who provided Caroline with emotional support. She was in the midst of the biggest personal scandal she might ever encounter, and he was constantly helping her. Yet despite his closeness, both physically and emotionally, his name was not in the press coverage. He did not need to enhance his own image, something that cannot be said for many of the other men and women in the lives of the Kennedys.

The possibility of a Schlossberg-Kennedy marriage surfaced in 1984, before Caroline went to law school. Arguments for and against such a union abounded. The Catholic-Jewish relationship was raised, especially since the Kennedys were notoriously anti-Semitic. Joe Kennedy had gone so far as to say that he thought National Socialism (Nazism) was destined to be England's ruling political ideology at the start of the Blitz. Bobby Kennedy, so long the support of Jacqueline, had frequently spoken of "Jew bastards." Jacqueline, though, was quietly dating the Orthodox Jew Maurice Tempelsman, a man who was also committing adultery with her.

Then there was the question of money, and Ed supposedly refused to sign a prenuptial agreement relating to Caroline's wealth. There were two factors at play in that consideration. The first, and probably most important for the couple, was that Ed loved Caroline and had no interest in her money or her fame. The second, though possibly unknown to the couple, was the issue raised by several divorce lawyers at the time. They claimed that they had never written a prenuptial agreement for a couple marrying without a divorce looming in the distance. They felt that starting a marriage with a prenuptial agreement is starting with an air of mistrust, with a sense that the relationship is doomed to failure. Schlossberg may have instinctively understood this.

The official announcement of the wedding was made in March 1986, with the wedding scheduled for Hyannisport on July 19. Caroline had been obsessed with the event, according to fellow students at Columbia.. She was frequently seen playing with her engagement ring, and during one law school class she carefully sketched the design for her wedding dress, showing the paper to friends as soon as class was over.

That year, 1986 proved the year for Kennedy weddings. Maria Shriver was marrying Arnold Schwarzenegger on April 26. Her brother, Timothy Shriver, was marrying Linda Potter on May 31. Nothing mattered to the press except Caroline.

If there was anything unusual about the Kennedy-Schlossberg wedding, it was the intense bitchiness of the press. Ed had twenty-one guests while Caroline had 404, a point carefully noted by reporters, though they never explained why that fact might be significant. (There were also 2,500 spectators, more than 100 people handling security, and enough photographers and members of the press to outnumber the invited guests). The Jesuit priest Reverend Donald A. McMillan officiated at the Our Lady of Victory Catholic Church. It was a traditional Catholic service without the mass. No rabbi was present, though it would not have been out of line for the couple to request one. Mixed Catholic-Jewish ceremonies, with a rabbi and priest sharing the service, had taken place in the church. Many in the media tried to vie with one another to say something memorable and often unkind about the day.

There was a certain amount of tension for Alfred and Mae Schlossberg, though little was said by the parents. Orthodox Jews feel that the religion is carried through the mother, not the father. Having a male Jew marry a female Catholic was as difficult for a devout family as for a devout Catholic family to know that one of their children was marrying a Jew.

This did not mean that the marriage was considered wrong. Caroline was twenty-eight. Ed was forty-one. The Schlossbergs liked Caroline, and Jacqueline and John liked Ed. They understood that they would all make accommodations for each other because there was no question in any of their minds that the couple genuinely loved each other.

The honeymoon was a quiet one in Hawaii, not the media circus the wedding had been. They then left their respective apartments, obtaining a $2.5-million, twelve-room apartment on the eleventh floor of an older building at 888 Park Avenue. The suite would be decorated with modern furniture Ed had designed, as well as various objects he collected during his travels.

Caroline was not finished with law school when she got married. She interned in the law firm of Paul, Weiss, Rifkind, Wharton, and Garrison, and in her third year, though pregnant, she graduated in the top ten percent of her class of 346 students. She was named a Stone Scholar in honor of the late United States Supreme Court Chief Justice Harlan Fiske Stone, who was a law professor and dean at the university in the 1930s.

Caroline also traveled monthly to Boston because she was on the board of trustees of the John Fitzgerald Kennedy Library.

On June 24, 1988, Caroline gave birth to her first child, Rose Kennedy Schlossberg. Because of Caroline's activities, a nanny was hired, though Jacqueline frequently handled sitting chores.

The Schlossbergs began living the good life of a wealthy couple interested in family and community. Ed wrote a children's story called *Hiccup's Tale* when Rose was five months old. They also spent time in Ed's summer home in Chester, Massachusetts. It was on several acres of land, and Ed had long been involved with the Citizens' Cooperating Group, a volunteer organization that maintains the homes of residents who can not afford such necessities as painting their houses. He was also on the hamlet's 1976 Bicentennial celebration committee.

The marriage meant little to the fewer than a thousand people in the small town. The only outstanding factor was Ed's shopping, since he is a gourmet chef who delights in preparing elaborate meals. Caroline's skills were limited to knowing that a can had to be opened before its contents could be heated.

On May 5, 1990, Caroline and Ed had a second child, Tatiana Celia Kennedy Schlossberg. John Bouvier Kennedy Schlossberg was born on January 19, 1993. However, because of the nanny, Caroline was able to attend regular workouts at the Trainer's Edge on Third Avenue, and to write books.

Caroline's first book—*In Our Defense: The Bill of Rights in Action,* written with Ellen Alderman—was based on a good idea, but an odd presentation given her personal history. The book detailed ten cases, each of which related to one of the first ten amendments to the Constitution.

There was nothing dramatic or personally revealing about the book, though there easily could have been. Caroline had been hounded by the news media all her life. There were a number of issues about press freedom she could have raised when it came to people in the public eye. However, she chose to avoid anything that might link her personal life with the material under discussion. As a result, although the family has many issues relative to the media that would make fascinating reading and directly relate to the Bill of Rights, none are present. Instead, the book reads like an extremely well-written research project that could have been handled by anyone.

The Kennedy name (Caroline did not use Schlossberg) helped assure sales. The two women were sent on a media tour during which they discussed the issues covered in the book, not what it was like to be a Kennedy or where she bought her clothing. However, the sales were boosted beyond what would otherwise have been expected for the book because of the Kennedy name. Many people sought her autograph when they bought books wherever the two women were speaking.

The two women followed up with a second book in 1995. Titled *The Right to Privacy*, it was a more thorough exploration of a single Constitutional issue, though still avoiding the personal.

Today Caroline has achieved a lifestyle that would delight her mother. She handles her celebrity well, keeping a quiet profile focused on her family and various activities related to the Kennedy Library and museum. She seems the most stable of the Kennedy women, leading a life of luxury and privilege without arrogance or an expectation of special favors.

KATHLEEN

Perhaps the most dramatically successful of Bob Kennedy's children is not the high-profile first son, Joseph II, or the namesake, Bobby Jr. Rather, it is the oldest child, Kathleen Hartington Kennedy Townsend.

There is a concept in the Judeo-Christian tradition that seems to fit the majority of the third generation of the Kennedy family. This is the idea of the unlikely vessel.

Bible stories are filled with instances of the unlikely vessel, the person who seems the wrong one to deliver God's message. The prophets were lowly individuals, probably illiterate, certainly with little or no access to the ruling class. They were the people most likely to be overlooked by others, most likely to be "invisible" as they walked the streets. Even the story of Jesus begins with a teenage mother who was pregnant out of wedlock.

The majority of the members of the third generation were a reverse of the unlikely vessel concept. Instead of being separated from the elite, they were rich, well connected, and isolated from the needs and concerns of society. Worse, they were often alcoholics, drug addicts, arrogant, and self-centered. Yet even if they, personally, were putting on a show for the public at large, the social programs they created and/or supported, such as Special Olympics, were of great value to others. Hundreds of thousands of individuals have benefited in ways that might otherwise have never happened.

Kathleen Kennedy Townsend was different. She had the money and the privilege, but her concerns for others have been genuine. She has been doing work in which she believes, which has justly elevated her to a position of power and influence unheard of for a Kennedy woman. Instead of being the loyal follower and supporter of whichever Kennedy male was in need of political support at the moment, she was the leader—the politician whose power drive was based on what she could accomplish for others, not on what she could gain for herself.

Kathleen is a feminist in a family where the role of women was always subjugated to the perceived needs of the men. Equally ironic is the fact that the only second-generation rebel had been her aunt, Kathleen Kennedy, who had married an English lord during World War II and adopted England as her home. That Kennedy, widowed during the war, was killed with her boyfriend when flying to France to see her father in 1948. She had abandoned her Catholic upbringing, had an affair with a married man, and generally lived a life that caused great discomfort to her mother.

Third-generation Kathleen was raised much like her father

had been raised. Joe and Rose tried to make each child responsible for the younger ones, the firstborn being given the greatest responsibility. Joe Jr. had been abusive and resentful of his role, the stories of his constant berating of Jack being a part of the lore of the second generation. But Kathleen was more sensitive, and no matter what her feelings about the responsibility in a home where there was little discipline, she was the one who reached out to David when he turned to drugs. She was the one who seemed to care most about the future of the brothers, and her eventual work in Maryland is proof of that caring.

Kathleen was never concerned with the family's wealth except for the attitude toward money taught in the New Testament. She has been quoted as saying, ''You're taught that it's easier for a camel to go through the eye of a needle than it is for a rich man to get to Heaven. That had an impact on me.''

Kathleen and her siblings were raised in chaos that revolved around their father. There were dogs and children everywhere, a fact that Rose Kennedy always hated. The animals were fine on her son's estate at Hickory Hill, but she resented the damage the dogs did when they came to visit the compound. She prohibited Ethel from bringing them after Bob's murder, and eventually it seemed a family game as to how many could be sneaked onto the grounds before Rose noticed. Fortunately, the children left their horses, ponies, donkey, squirrels, birds, fish, snakes, and other pets at home. Bobby, especially, loved any creature that moved, and all the children delighted in a massive assortment of animals.

Kathleen had nothing to prove in her early years, and her personality developed in a manner as close to normal as can happen with a wealthy child. She was not groomed for the presidency. She was not forced into competition with her cousins. The growing number of third-generation Kennedys were always too young to interest or influence her, as the oldest. She rebelled against a strict Catholic upbringing, and was allowed to attend the Putney School in Vermont. And when, on a family vacation in the Southwest in 1966, her father took her to an Indian reservation, she discovered that her world was not a common one. She saw abject poverty for the first time, and while she might have dismissed it as an anomaly of the area, she was no longer naive.

Kathleen's rebellion came as a surprise to the family. They had originally enrolled her in the Stone Ridge Country Day School of the Sacred Heart in Bethesda, Maryland. She has been quoted as describing the Catholic Church's doctrines toward women as being "suffocating." Even as a girl, she constantly argued with her teachers in religion class. She was never happy, finding the church inflexible. She longed to be with other rebels, capable of challenging all ideas. Eventually her parents agreed, allowing her to transfer to the Putney School.

She seemed to change at Putney. All the normal outdoor activities were available, including skiing and horseback riding, but the curriculum was more progressive than in parochial schools, and the admissions program allowed low-income children to attend. Kathleen mingled with millionaires and working-class children. The location kept her isolated from urban America, but the diversity of the students assured that she would be socially challenged as she had never been before.

One of the activities Bob Kennedy forced upon his children was the writing of papers each week about different important persons in American history. It was his way of adding to his children's education. While some hated it, Kathleen developed a strong interest in writing. When, in 1970, she obtained a job working in an Alaska day care center designed for working mothers, she began a newsletter to educate and unite the parents.

Kathleen, like Caroline, attended Radcliffe College. She took advantage of the semester abroad program, living with a mechanic and his family in Italy, learning the language, working in a pottery studio, and otherwise becoming familiar with the tradespeople.

Although she missed the hippie movement of the 1960s, Kathleen became what had earlier been called a "flower child." Her clothing was seldom more formal than blue jeans and floppy hats. She traveled with a backpack, even when visiting her grandmother in an expensive hotel in Paris. The fact that her grandmother, as well as her mother and aunts, preferred designer clothing made her "Salvation Army Chic" a shock for them.

Robert Kennedy was especially fond of Kathleen, and their closeness became obvious when she was competing in a horse show in August 1965. Kathleen was an extremely skilled rider who had won four blue ribbons for excellence. However, during the competition at Sea Flash Farms in West Barnstable, Massachusetts, she was thrown from a horse named Attorney General. The accident occurred when her horse tripped during a jump, causing her to land on her head, being knocked unconscious. She was immediately rushed to Cape Cod Hospital, where she was found to have possible kidney damage and internal bleeding.

Robert, Ethel, and other members of the family were not attending the competition that day. Instead, they were out on a boat, The Neris. The Coast Guard was notified, and alerted the family that Kathleen was in trouble. However, the alert came when the sea was so rough that any effort to get back to shore would be hampered in their craft. Kathleen's father realized that he could swim easier and faster than he could maneuver the boat. Since Ethel and the others could handle bringing the boat safely back to harbor, he leaped over the side, swam to shore, and rushed to his daughter's side at the hospital.

Kathleen was not in serious danger, but she did have a contusion of the bladder, internal bleeding, and a mild concussion. While she was recovering, President Lyndon Johnson sent her a bouquet of Texas yellow roses, along with a note in which he recalled his own experience. He wrote, in part, "It's no fun to part company with a horse, especially in mid-air, and I speak from experience."

It was during her student years that Kathleen seemed to be the typical rich liberal kid who wanted to revel in comfort without giving up the good life. She was determined to help the poor, though not to the extent of using her inheritance. She identified with the masses by staying in cheap lodgings and wearing old clothing. When she traveled, her suitcase was liable to be a box tied with string. She did volunteer work in low-income areas and became involved with the antiwar movement. Then she worked on the George McGovern presidential campaign in 1972.

Kathleen met her future husband that year. David Lee Townsend, four years older and finishing his doctorate, was six-foot four inches, red-haired, bearded, and as casual in his lifestyle as Kathleen. They were concerned with the environment, avoided "proper" dress for conservative Boston, liked the simple life, and were both interested in American literature. (David's doctoral thesis was on American visionary poetry.)

The couple married on November 17, 1973. The date produced a minor crisis, for Ted Jr. was in Georgetown University Hospital at that time. His cancer-ridden right leg had to be amputated, the surgery scheduled for a time that proved to be one hour before the Kennedy-Townsend nuptials were to begin. However, the senator gave Kathleen away. Singer Andy Williams provided the music. Townsend made the gold rings the couple exchanged. Kathleen had her hair parted down the center, then flowers intertwined in proper "hippie" fashion. They recited poetry to each other, and the ceremony generally seemed like a throwback to the counterculture lifestyles of a decade earlier. The only differences were the fact that they were married in Holy Trinity Church, and that among the 160 guests were family friends ranging from politicians to syndicated humor columnist Art Buchwald. Perhaps the most interesting guest was actress Angie Dickinson, one of her uncle Jack's more serious girlfriends during the time he was running for the presidency.

Kathleen and David stayed in Cambridge while she finished her senior year, then moved to Santa Fe, New Mexico. There he had a teaching job, and she found work with the Human Rights Commission. They lived in a rural area, burned wood for heat, and tried to live in harmony with their desert surroundings.

Restless to do more, Kathleen began seeking a law degree from the University of New Mexico and worked part time on a Santa Fe newspaper during the summer. She also became pregnant in the summer of 1977, and began preparing herself for childbirth by walking several miles a day. When her daughter, Meaghan Townsend, was born on November 8, she became the first child of the fourth generation. Two years later, on November 1, 1979, the couple had their second child, Maeve Townsend, though that birth took place in the home of David's parents. Four years after that, Rose Katherine was born.

The Townsends returned to the East so that both could earn law degrees from Yale University. They worked together on Ted Kennedy's 1980 presidential campaign, and Kathleen headed her uncle's 1982 Senate reelection committee.

In 1984, David accepted a teaching position at St. John's College in Annapolis. Eight years later, Kathleen gave birth to their fourth daughter, Kerry Sophia.

Kathleen, the idealist, began writing articles for publications such as the *Washington Monthly* and the *New York Times*. She began discussing the need for private citizens and public officials to do what is right, regardless of risks. She expressed a firm belief that religion is a major help in developing a moral framework in life, and she attacked the religious right because it used the Bible to justify increasing stockpiles of nuclear weapons while ignoring the poor, the sick, women's rights, the elderly, and public resources.

Kathleen focused regularly on the need for Americans to be involved with the political process, and to demand politicians who were concerned with the public good. She wanted to see a nation in which people were aware of past history, ethics, and the need to prevent officials from deviating from what is right.

Kathleen Townsend became more and more interested in the philosophy of integrity in politics, and also in practicing that philosophy herself. In 1986, established in Maryland, she decided to seek public office. She ran for the House of Representatives in Maryland's 2nd Congressional District.

"It was never expected that I would go into politics," Kathleen explained later. "It was not even dreamed about, talked about, thought of. It wasn't in the realm of possibility."

There was no appeal to glamour. Kathleen campaigned in the same manner she lived, rather conservative in dress and conversation. She had short hair, large glasses, and wore business suits. She was a liberal, deeply concerned with the issues affecting her constituents, and pro-choice, a surprising stand for a Catholic. She was not a particularly effective speaker, not dynamic. She did not evoke images of her father or uncle. She was only a solid candidate, and that was not enough to beat a more familiar candidate.

From politics, Kathleen entered into a career that has changed education in Maryland and is now doing the same for the nation.

Townsend lost the election to freshman Representative Helen Delich Bentley, 94,404 to 66,943. Although Kennedy family members supported her, Kathleen ran as a Townsend. She did not try to use her maiden name to give herself an edge. It was a mistake she would not make twice, having learned that without winning an election, social changes could not be instituted.

Her seriousness has long brought ridicule rather than admiration in the male-centered family. Her brothers delighted in calling her "the nun." She also has a serious interest in religion, her faith having a depth that seems greater even than her grandmother's.

In 1985, the Maryland State Board of Education passed a bylaw requiring that every high school introduce community service into its curriculum. The idea was to make the students more aware of the world around them and more sensitive to the needs of others. Everyone applauded the concept, yet no one did anything about it.

In 1987, Kathleen talked with the head of the state board about allowing her to open an office that would make the law a reality. She was given the opportunity the following January, and became the head of the Maryland Student Service Alliance (MSSA). She pursued several goals successfully, working with a small budget, almost no assistance, and within a state where many of the schools were still resisting the mandated effort.

Kathleen had been concerned with the fact that American children were raised with great freedom but little opportunity to participate in any form of service. They had little sense of value and responsibility. It is only during the high school years that outsiders have a chance of reaching them in order to instill such values.

Kathleen's programs fell loosely into three categories. One involved students in the greater community. They might volunteer in soup kitchens, provide support care for the elderly, tutor younger children, or otherwise help with needs that affect everyone.

The second category was one that involved students within their schools or immediate neighborhood. For example, Suitland High School had a high absentee rate. There were many reasons, most of them seeming to relate to families that had no one at home to see that the teenagers went to classes.

MSSA devised a program wherein high school students telephoned each other to make certain they were awake. It was a little like the programs in some churches and community groups where shut-ins and the elderly are telephoned each day to make certain they are all right. In this case the students motivate one another, making certain they are out of bed in time to be ready for classes. The first year that the program was in effect, attendance improved a reported 87 percent.

The third category involved cross-cultural experiences. Students came into direct contact with the wealthy and the poor, with different races, ethnic backgrounds, and religions. They experienced young, old, and in-between. They dealt with the disabled, and with the emotionally disturbed. Their experiences sensitized them to those who lived differently than they did, whose lives might be richer or poorer, easier or harder.

Kathleen's efforts were so successful at so little cost to the state that other school systems in different states began adopting the concept. A set number of volunteer hours are required for graduation. The students are forced to confront life away from their homes, their immediate neighborhoods, and all that is familiar. The time may be limited—thirty hours total in one system, seventy-five hours total in another. And it may be all required in one year, for each of three years, or spread over two or three years. It offers an alternative experience that should ultimately have an influence on how young people interact when on their own in society.

Kathleen moved into the position of deputy assistant attorney general for the Clinton Justice Department. It was a job for which she was qualified, yet it was almost certainly one given for political reasons. However, she resigned from the job in 1994 in order to run for lieutenant governor of Maryland. This time she ran as Kathleen *Kennedy* Townsend, involving her husband and children as well. She won easily.

Today Kathleen Townsend is living the ideal ascribed to her father and uncle. The second generation Kennedy men so admired in myth were always flawed. Their accomplishments have been minimal, having been credited for the work of others. Their writings have been primarily the handiwork of ''ghosts'' and ''research assistants.'' Their religious faith has been a convenience, something familiar, to be honored through ritual, breached for convenience, and manipulated for such sticky matters as adultery, divorce, and remarriage.

It is impossible to predict how far Kathleen will go in politics. Unlike her brother Joe, she does not view high office as a goal for its own sake. Instead, politics is a vehicle for positive change, and she will fight for whatever position she feels will allow for that change. As she explained in the June 1996 issue of *The Washington Monthly,* one of many publications for which she is a freelance writer, ''The challenge now is to return to the original Jeffersonian ideal, in which everybody—not just the experts, not just the wealthy—can participate in government. For too long, Republicans have simply knocked national government and looked only to voluntary local solutions. For too long, Democrats have thought that the national government had to solve every problem on its own, meanwhile forgetting the need for local participation. Clearly we need both. If we really hope to restore a sense of the rewards of citizenship, we have to stop treating people like customers and start treating them like Americans.''

Kathleen Kennedy Townsend is the embodiment of what others in the family have only talked about as an ideal.

BOBBY KENNEDY

Just as Kathleen Townsend made a change in education, so Robert Kennedy Jr. is truly involved in issues of the environment. His long bout with drugs never dampened his fascination with animals. Bobby traveled the world with family members and friends. He visited the Serengeti National Park in Tanzania, he observed lions in Nairobi, and—in 1974, when he was twenty—worked with television producer Roger Ailes on a multipart series filming the story of an American in the wilds of Africa. The program, *The Last Frontier,* was aired on Sunday evening, September 7, 1975, on ABC. Bobby was paid several hundred thousand dollars for his work, including acting as host for the series, as the voice-over narrator, and as consultant on the wild animals he had been studying since he was a small child.

Bobby's wildlife education was largely obtained through personal study or family friends who took an interest in a boy with unusual problems. Despite his frequent use of drugs and, his difficulty maintaining a relationship—like most of the third-generation males—he gained an education that would lead him to a highly successful, behind-the-scenes career. His Harvard bachelor's degree was in history, and he took his law degree at the University of Virginia Law School. He also trained at the London School of Economics.

Bobby has applied the intensity that almost killed him as a drug addict to his work. He teaches at Pace University in White Plains, New York, where, in 1987, he earned his master's degree in environmental law, and runs the Pace University Environmental Law Clinic. He also became an attorney for the National Resources Defense Council, specializing in issues involving water, international, and nuclear issues.

The low profile Bobby now maintains has nothing to do with the quality of his work. For example, New York City's drinking water has improved dramatically in recent years partially because of Kennedy's actions in protecting the upstate New York reservoir system. He helped arrange the use of $47 million for land conservation, and was instrumental in the preservation of the watershed.

Kennedy has been actively involved in fighting a Canadian project—the James Bay Wilderness Area dams—that flooded 4,000 square miles of forest during the first phase of the massive project. Wildlife habitats were altered, and the native population, mostly Cree Indians, was seriously endangered. While the first phase of the project could not be stopped, Kennedy was able to cripple plans for a second stage by convincing New York State to cancel a $13 billion contract for power from the project. He then helped a team of experts assure that energy could be obtained from other resources in a manner that would be gentler on the environment and actually save the state money.

In another energy-related situation, Kennedy worked in Chile with the Grupo de Accion por el Bio-Bio to try to halt a dam on the Bio-Bio River. The dam would destroy the land that is home to 9,000 natives. It would cause massive damage to forests and greatly endanger the territory. He tried to obstruct the dam, and to help the Chilean government find more efficient means of power generation so the hydroelectric dam would not have to be used.

Kennedy devised ways to hold municipal and state governments responsible for environmental problems. He has helped maintain public landholdings, and has stopped municipalities from operating sewage treatment plants that violate the Clean Water Act.

Some of Kennedy's causes seem so boring at first glance that the news media largely ignores them. For example, he fought the shooting of guns into Long Island Sound, an action that resulted in the closing of the Remington Gun Club. He was able to prove that the deposit of lead from the ammunition fired into the water was causing serious pollution no different from toxic dumping. The Clean Water Act had never before been used in such a manner, but Kennedy won and the fishermen's association was thrilled.

Bobby's love of animals has not diminished, though his skills have increased. He is a licensed wildlife rehabilitator. He has also been president of the New York Falconry Association, working with his own Harris's hawk.

Bobby has supported some local politicians, but it is doubtful that he will run for office unless he needs the power to advance causes that matter to him. There have been rumors he is considering running for the Senate from New York, a state where Kennedys have done well in the past. Certainly he has stronger ties than his father did when he won that Senate seat, but Bobby's father was perceived as a man with broad experience in the urban, national, and international problems facing the nation. Bobby himself is limited to a famous name and his solid track record with the environment, an area that may not be as important as other concerns in the densely populated urban regions.

What matters for Bobby is that he has not only overcome his self-destructive past—a way of life that could have made him a victim like his brother David—but he has quietly established a career of great importance to the nation. Unlike many in his family, he has done so quietly, for personal beliefs, not because he wants attention.

MARY COURTNEY

Mary Courtney Kennedy is a rebel compared to Kathleen. She had the typical Kennedy education. There were private schools—Our Lady of Victory in Washington and the Potomac School near her Hickory Hill home. And there were good works—caring for inner-city youth who were visiting the family compound, working one summer at a Utah ranch, helping her uncle Ted's campaign, and working in the campaigns of both Joe and Kathleen.

What has set Courtney apart is her interest in her Irish heritage, something that Joe and Rose did their best to run away from. In addition to studying at the University of California, she took history and literature courses at Trinity College in Dublin, Ireland.

In 1980, while a production assistant for the Children's Television Workshop, Courtney married Jeff Ruhe, then an assistant to Roone Arledge, the president of ABC-TV News and Sports as well as a longtime friend of the Kennedy family. The couple frequently traveled together for Jeff's work, especially during the Olympics.

The marriage lasted ten years. It was low profile, most of Courtney's work being volunteer for groups such as Head Start and Very Special Arts, the program in which artists work with the retarded. She was never career-driven, never found an area to pursue full time, and never sustained the marriage.

The one interest Courtney maintained was in international human rights issues. She was working for a Rome-based AIDS foundation when her marriage failed and her mother arranged for her to meet a man named Paul Hill.

According to the press at the time, Hill, a member of the Irish Republican Army, was a murdering terrorist. What was little known was the full story behind his imprisonment in 1974.

The facts are that a pub in Great Britain was bombed in 1974, killing seven people and maiming several others. Because the attack was in England, the police were under intense pressure to find the terrorists. Four known members of the Irish Republican Army, later called the "Guildford Four" by the press, were arrested. A decision was made that they were guilty, and it became the interrogators' job to get them to confess no matter what evidence might exist. By the time the men had experienced many hours of sleep deprivation, food deprivation, and intense abuse, Paul Hill "confessed" and was imprisoned for life. Fifteen years later, the convictions were overturned.

Paul wrote the book *Stolen Years* about his experiences. That book was turned into the 1993 film *In The Name of the Father*.

Ethel Kennedy had known Paul Hill and when Courtney was recovering from a skiing accident, she arranged for him to meet her daughter. They related instantly, marrying the same year as the film was broadcast. This resulted in negative headlines because Hill, though cleared of the pub bombing, was under indictment for another murder. This was the kidnapping and killing of former British soldier, Brian Shaw, who had been taken from another pub the same year as the bombing. He had been convicted of the crime earlier, confessing at the same time that he confessed to the pub bombing, but this was a case that had to be retried. Unlike the pub bombing, there was still some suspicion that he was guilty despite the fact that he did not have a fair trial the first time.

In a move that was the first known involvement of any Kennedys in Irish nationalist politics, Courtney attended Paul's 1994 trial in the company of her mother, Kathleen, Rory, Kerry, and Joe II. Joe was still a congressional representative, so his presence and his statement to the press had greater weight than might otherwise have been the case. He commented, "We just hope that Paul—an Irish Catholic—can get justice in Northern Ireland. Our Irishness is fundamental and instinctive. It is not something we were taught."

Joe's comments may have been accurate. However, if they were, it was the first time anyone in the family had ever publicly expressed such thoughts.

Paul was acquitted.

The couple spent the first year of their marriage living in County Clare, Ireland, then moved to the United States, where Courtney has a Fifth Avenue apartment in Manhattan. She remains involved in human rights issues, though she maintains an extremely low profile. Her husband, a man many would like to see killed, remains entangled in the struggles of Northern Ireland. The fact that he is married to a Kennedy makes his profile higher, his death assuring greater headlines. In addition, the couple have a child—Saoirse Roisin Hill. Her name is Gaelic for "Freedom Rose."

MICHAEL

To the American public, Michael LeMoyne Kennedy, like his brother Bobby, seemed to be a survivor. His public image was that of a man who had triumphed over the drug abuse and self-destructive behavior of his earlier years. He married Victoria Gifford, the daughter of sportscaster and former professional football player Frank Gifford, who at one time dated his mother, Ethel. Michael became an attorney, a graduate of the University of Virginia Law School, and had three children, Michael Jr., Kyle, and Rory.

Michael looked much like his father, but his career was quite different. He was chairman of the Citizens Energy Corporation, the organization once headed by his brother Joe II. Although Joe helped start the corporation, it was Michael who was the true businessman. If the attainment of wealth were his priority, he could perhaps have surpassed even his grandfather's success. Instead, he was using business as a form of public service, something previous Kennedy generations never considered. (Not that he was totally altruistic. In recent years he added highly profitable business ventures as an adjunct to his work.)

With the help of others, Joe conceived of a simple idea that would allow Massachusetts residents to lower their fuel bills. The program began with a relationship with Humberto Calderon Berti, the energy minister of Venezuela. Joe purchased two million barrels of crude oil for thirty-one dollars a barrel. This was $12 million less than he would have had to pay under the prevailing OPEC rates. Kennedy's company refined the oil, then resold it, the profits being used to subsidize the energy bills of the poor in Massachusetts.

The arrangement worked for everyone. The money was modest by comparison with larger companies, but it still totaled $26 million over a ten-year period. Venezuela used the program for public relations, and the sale was so modest by OPEC standards that there was no hostility.

Essentially what was done was to take corporate profits out of the retail equation and charge the price that would be possible without such profits. Since the oil companies make a substantial return from what they sell, Joe's first year saw him arranging for low-income Massachusetts residents to buy heating oil for fifty-seven cents a gallon. The prevailing rate was eighty-two cents a gallon. And while the costs varied from year to year, the price of oil from Citizens Energy was always substantially lower than from other sources.

The program began to broaden. Joe set aside cash from the company for a loan program. Landlords who rented to low-income tenants and met state requirements were given loans to pay for insulation and other energy-saving measures in their buildings. The original amount set aside, used strictly for collateral so that any defaults would not be a problem, was $450,000. Heating costs were usually reduced by a third, a substantial dollar savings in the cold New England winters. Then the repayment was designed so that the money saved was divided in half. One portion was used to repay the loan, and the other portion was meant to allow landlords to keep their rents low. The landlords' payments remained what they had always been for a fairly short period of time, then dropped drastically after the repayment period. Fuel was conserved and low-income tenants saw one of their biggest winter expenses reduced.

Another project that was soon developed with Michael's help was buying leftover heating oil from families switching to natural gas. The corporation took the leftover oil that would have been wasted and sold it to state governments at below-market rates. Again the benefits all went to the needy.

Next came reinvestment and alternative energy programs, not only with OPEC countries but also with non-oil-producing third world companies. The program involved countries that sold crude oil and those that did not. Citizen's Energy arranged for twenty-five percent of corporate profits to be reinvested in alternative energy measures, such as a solar hot water system for a hospital and a fish-drying project in Angola. And the company keeps adding projects, including foreign oil exploration. It is very much a major business, but it is not pushing solely for profits.

How far the corporation will expand is unknown. One of the reasons for Michael's success was the fact that he had a degree of congressional access through his older brother, his uncle, and family friends. Some of the oil-producing countries were anxious for this sort of access, and they had felt encouraged with Michael's corporation because he could conceivably smooth the way for them.

There had been less pressure on Michael than on some of the other males in the family. While Joe actively pursued Congress, *People* magazine and the tabloids actively pursued John, and narcotics investigators actively pursued Bobby Jr. For a while, Michael was left alone.

Oddly, Michael was perhaps the most likely political comer among the sons who had not explored politics. He was a Harvard graduate, worked for a while at the law firm of Hogan and Hartson in Washington, D.C., and then went full time with Citizens. Profit margins had been extremely small, even though the dollar volume had been extremely high. Subsidiary companies were so successful that Citizens Gas Supply Corporation is one of the top ten marketers of natural gas in the nation. Michael also added such diverse services as pharmaceuticals by mail and a for-profit operation called Citizens Housing Access, which helps low- and moderate-income individuals buy foreclosed buildings that can be made viable.

Michael developed skills in international diplomacy, made liaisons with emerging and oil-producing nations, developed multinational business arrangements, and became sensitive to the needs of both urban and rural individuals. With this quasi-diplomatic background, he was perhaps better equipped for government leadership than his volatile brother Joe, who at one time made the transition to congressional representative.

The trouble with Michael was the trouble with so many of the Kennedy third-generation males. He was a "jerk," and his family encouraged his behavior by apologizing for it. Some blamed it on alcoholism, and he would be treated for a drinking problem. Others, oddly including his mother-in-law, the television personality Kathie Lee Gifford, tried to put a nice "spin" on his inexcusable behavior. None of them wanted to admit the truth—that Michael was an adulterer, a philanderer, and the seducer of a child who should have had the right to have his trust.

Michael Kennedy's betrayal of trust was not interesting enough to be part of a bad novel. The girl was not some Lolita-like nymphet. He was not trying to regain his youth through the seduction of a virgin stranger in a new town where he had come to stay. Instead, he was nothing more than a sleaze, a man who watched the daughter of close friends reach physical maturity, then had a longterm affair with her.

No one knows who started the rumors that led to the discovery of the affair. Paul and June Verrochi thought they had achieved the idyllic life in Cohasset, Massachusetts, a seaside community where the wealthy enjoy the fruits of their labors. Paul had started simply, establishing a cleaning company that, through his skills and hard work, led to the family's becoming quite wealthy. That company was sold to a British corporation, following which he formed the American Environmental Group. Selling that at a large profit, he ultimately founded American Medical Response, a company consolidating ambulance services nationwide. Not needing to work, though a brilliant businesswoman who helped her husband plan his companies, June Verrochi became a successful volunteer. In fact, it was in November 1996, about the time that the story of Michael was being whispered, that she and Paul were to be honored for their fund-raising on behalf of the Crohn's and Colitis Foundation of America.

The Verrochis had achieved another aspect of the American dream in the community where they were living. Their daughter and two sons would have contact with powerful families they would never have met anywhere else. That their daughter was a baby-sitter for Michael and Victoria Kennedy, a couple who were also considered friends, added to the delight.

Close friends finally forced the confrontation between June and her daughter. They had noticed that the relationship she shared with Michael Kennedy did not seem quite right. However, when June confronted her daughter, the first response was denial. Only the next day did the girl admit something was going on. By December Michael felt the need to hire a criminal defense attorney to advise him.

The story broke in the April 25, 1997, edition of the *Boston Globe* and the April 26 edition of the *Boston Herald*. There was no doubt as to the affair, the girl admitting to sleeping with Michael from the time she was sixteen.

This time, for seemingly everyone except the immediate family, a Kennedy had gone too far. This was not Joe Kennedy Sr. moving an endless array of movie stars in and out of his bedroom, then squiring his mistress of the moment, Gloria Swanson, to England on the same boat as he was taking his wife, Rose. This was not John Kennedy Sr. having a woman in the morning, a woman in the evening, and bragging that he had each woman three different ways before he was finished with her. This was not even the routine adultery of the Kennedy men, leading them to change from first wife to adult girlfriend to second wife in a round robin of casual commitments and dishonored wedding vows. This was a grown man seducing a child. And while sixteen may be the age of consent, every parent of a teenager knows that sixteen is a time when there is as much little girl as adult in that nubile body.

Michael never denied the affair. Yes, he was thirty-six and she was sixteen, yes, he was married, but she was a willing participant and there was no crime because she was of legal age when they had their affair. Besides, to bring charges would be emotionally upsetting for the girl. Besides . . . Well, Michael was a Kennedy.

The response to the child seduction (not molestation and not child abuse because she was, after all, sixteen years old) was swift. *Life* magazine proudly hailed the Kennedys on their cover. *Vanity Fair* featured "Bobby's Kids" as a major photo article. No one mentioned Michael's "messing around." No one mentioned that there was a serious concern about bringing criminal charges, though too many factors concerning who did what to whom, when, and why ultimately prevented that scenario.

It was not the story itself that was troublesome, even though the affair had gone on for several years. It was the response to it all. The average man on the street might have opted for jail, public condemnation, or castration had his own daughter been involved. Certainly the tabloids reported the scandal with the outrage they knew that their readers felt. Yet beyond ignoring the issue, as *Life* and *Vanity Fair* chose to do, the harshest condemnation came from cousin John Kennedy on the editorial page of *George*.

If any other writer had written what John did, it would have been so mild and meaningless as to get nowhere. In fact, it was within an issue (September 1997) that had a naked Kate Moss on the cover ("Kate Moss As Eve" read the small caption). Among the stories featured on the cover were "20 Most Fascinating Women in Politics" and "Sex Wars: A National Poll."

The editorial showed a naked John Kennedy sitting with his arms wrapped around his knees (plenty of muscle but keeping what some thought was his best part in shadow), looking up as though contemplating an apple. In the text that accompanied the image, he wrote, "I've learned a lot about temptation recently. But that doesn't make me desire any less. If anything, to be reminded of the possible perils of succumbing to what's forbidden only makes it more alluring." He then went on to discuss his cousin Joe's adultery and public divorce, to be discussed shortly, and his cousin Michael's scandal, never mentioning their names. He wrote, "Two members of my family chased an idealized alternative to their life. One left behind an embittered wife, and another, in what looked to be a hedge against mortality, fell in love with youth and surrendered his judgment in the process. Both became poster boys for bad behavior. Perhaps they deserved it. Perhaps they should have known better. To whom much is given, much is expected, right? The interesting thing was the ferocious condemnation of their excursions beyond the bounds of acceptable behavior. Since when does someone need to apologize on television for getting divorced?''

Even John was limited in the outrage he could muster, though his mild statement was enough to raise the ire of the family. Michael was handling the affair as any true Kennedy would. He admitted it like a man, then checked into alcohol rehabilitation therapy. He was an alcoholic. The whiskey made him do it. He was going to kick the habit of that old demon rum, and everything would be fine.

The problem was that this was not some drunken grope he could not remember the morning after the night before. This was not a one-shot or a short-term relationship caused by a mind clouded by alcohol. Michael Kennedy had been bedding the baby-sitter for at least four years. And not even his greatest apologist dared claim he was in a constant fog during a four-year bender.

Victoria Gifford Kennedy separated from her husband in April 1997, but she refused to comment beyond that. Only her mother would weigh in with a certain amount of support, ironically for Michael, several months later when the family received a second shock.

Michael was always considered the most athletic of Bobby's kids, the one who would take the greatest risks in the name of athleticism. Friends and apologists like to say that his strength was his willingness to "push the envelope," but the reality was he used little judgment. He dove seventy-five feet off Maine's Moxie Falls in 1979, and some of his most daring actions were taken when alcohol had dulled his senses and quite possibly his reflexes. While he was a brilliant natural skier, he and his family devised games to play on the slopes that were stupid rather than proof of athletic prowess. One of these games involved playing football—actually tossing a toy football or other object from player to player while skiing down the slopes. The Aspen, Colorado, ski patrol had repeatedly warned the family not to play the game. It was unsafe, keeping them from having full control of their movements on the slopes. They warned them that one of them would be hurt or killed.

Kennedys see such warnings as challenges—at least, Michael did on December 31, 1997, when out skiing with his son and daughters, other family members, and friends.

The game they played had already brought a formal complaint to Ethel Kennedy the day before. The ski patrol was adamant that the family not play the game. If they didn't hurt some other skier, they were likely to lose control themselves.

If anything, the warning meant they had to play the game. Even worse, Michael was not on drugs or alcohol. His bad judgment and immature behavior were the products of a sound mind.

Michael looked toward the football being tossed to him late the following afternoon. And just as a car driver will crash if looking away from a winding road, so Michael smashed into a tree he would have avoided had he not been playing a game.

Rory rushed to her brother's side, administering CPR. The ski patrol was called, and Michael was rushed to a hospital, but there was no hope. Three days later he was laid to rest following a service at Our Lady of Victory Church in Centerville, Massachusetts. His brilliant business sense had never been matched by good judgment about his own life. He died a foolish adulterer, the seducer of his best friend's child, a man who shattered the lives of his children for the sake of a game he had been warned not to play.

Two days later, Kathie Lee Gifford, wife of Michael's father-in-law, expressed her outrage at the media for daring to imply that Michael's affair with the girl had started at the age of fourteen. He may have behaved inappropriately when she was fourteen, but Michael passed three polygraph tests prior to his death, each one proving that he had waited until she was sixteen, the Massachusetts legal age of consent, to take her to bed with him. Even in death, the extended Kennedy family had to apologize for one of its fools.

JOE II

The arrogance Michael showed on the mountain was mirrored by Congressional Representative Joe Kennedy. The only difference was that instead of the death of the body, he experienced the death of his career.

Joe claimed that his decision not to seek reelection to Congress was the result of Michael's affair with his baby-sitter. Michael had helped run Joe's campaign, and the two were quite close. However, the idea that anyone held Joe responsible for Michael's actions was probably not shared by anyone else. The truth was that Joe did not have the fire, the skill, and the personal life for hardball politics.

The classic example of political survival in the face of inappropriate actions was Joe's uncle Ted. The senator's drunken night of what has been assumed might have been a brief affair with Mary Jo Kopechne led to her death in Chappaquiddick. Because of his refusal to make self-incriminating statements and the skills of the professional handlers and spin doctors, he went on to be reelected to the Senate five times.

Joe's problems went much deeper than just Michael's actions. First was his temper. He was always the family bully when growing up, not unlike his namesake, Uncle Joe Jr., who had been killed in World War II. Joe Jr. was the bane of his brother Jack's existence, especially since Jack was sickly as a child. Joe II taunted his siblings in much the same manner.

Interviews conducted with high state Republican figures when Joe was thinking of making a bid for governor of Massachusetts revealed part of their campaign strategy. They planned to goad Joe into losing his temper before the press. His volatility was well known by family, friends, and congressional opponents, but rarely was seen by the public.

Even Joe's grandmother recognized her grandson's limitations. I can remember sitting on the porch one day, talking about Joe. She commented, "Too bad he is not smart. He is so good looking!"

Second, Joe was not a politician in the sense his uncle Ted

was. Neither Joe nor Ted are intellectual giants, but Ted has been famous for assembling one of the best staffs in the Senate. They help him find the issues his constituents feel are important, and they help draft both legislation and position papers that give confidence to the voters. They may find his personal life—filled with womanizing, overeating and overindulgence in general—rather unpleasant, but they feel he represents their interests.

Joe has not engendered such loyalty. The staff did not do a good job with crisis management or preparing Joe for public appearances. As a result, his less than skilled handling of personal problems made him look foolish.

The third issue was his biggest personal problem, his divorce from his first wife.

Sheila Rauch Kennedy was never a vindictive woman. She loved her husband passionately when they married. She was an Episcopalian who agreed to a Catholic service because such a service was important to her husband. By the time he was having an affair with Beth Kelly, his assistant in Washington, Sheila recognized that the marriage was over, that Beth was good for Joe at this time in his life. Her only objection was that the two of them moved in together in Brighton, Massachusetts, before he married her. Sheila felt that it was not good for their sons to be going to see their father, a man who claimed to be a devout Catholic, and have him not married to the woman who shared his bed.

The divorce created a furor for Joe because he decided to show typical Kennedy arrogance for social conventions. Sheila Rauch was an Episcopalian when she married Joe. Had she not agreed to marry Joe in the Catholic Church, as he requested, raising their children as Catholic, the marriage would not have been recognized under Catholic canon law. This would mean, in effect, that it never took place.

Catholic canon law is controversial for many because it does not allow the divorce of couples married as Catholics in the Catholic Church. Instead, there are grounds for annulment that allow the marriage to end by showing there are reasons it was never valid. For example, since marriage is for procreation in the Catholic Church, if either party insists upon refraining from sex the marriage will be annulled. Likewise if a spouse lies about a previous marriage or some other serious problem is discovered, the marriage can be ended. Just falling out of love with the person to whom you made a commitment is not grounds for ending a Catholic marriage. Thus, when there is a divorce without an annulment the couple is still married in the eyes of the church and neither party can remarry within the church, though they can still be married to others in a civil ceremony and in the churches of most other faiths. But Joe Kennedy was a Catholic who only wanted to be married in the Catholic Church, so he requested an annulment and expected Sheila to go along.

Instead, Sheila Rauch Kennedy rebelled. She and Joe had been deeply in love. She had extensive letters he had written to her describing his love. They had committed to each other in the church, and meant that commitment. And their union had brought them twin sons. If the marriage was annulled, the love, the wife, and the children would be denied. In the eyes of the church, those very wanted, very legitimate sons would be declared bastards. Sheila would not tolerate such seeming insanity.

The American Catholic Church does not reflect the attitude of the church throughout the world. Many within the Catholic Church feel that the United States is to annulment of Catholic marriage what Las Vegas is to divorce. It is a place where morals, ethics, and the intent of canon law do not matter. You want a divorce, go to Las Vegas. You want an annulment, come to the United States. And if you are a Kennedy, there is a good chance that there is a cardinal or other high church official quite willing to earn your favor by granting what others might see as inappropriate at best.

It was *Time* magazine that first broke the story of the annulment scandal and the issues surrounding it, including Joe Kennedy's decision to seek such an annulment after a dozen years of marriage. Sheila immediately responded, her slightly edited letter being published in the September 6, 1993, issue of *Time*. She wrote, "Your article 'Till Annulment Do Us Part,' [which] the editors quoted, erroneously states that Joseph P. Kennedy II divorced me. I fact, I was the plaintiff in our 1990 civil divorce case, which became final in January of 1991. Second, while you note that we have twin sons, you fail to mention the impact of the possible ruling on them or on children of annulment in general. If our marriage were deemed never to have existed in the eyes of the Church, then our children, like others of annulled marriages, would have been neither conceived nor born to a sanctified union. I find this contention untrue, abhorrent, and contrary to the Church's teachings that such a union is a desirable prerequisite for bearing children. I am, of course, grateful the U.S. law will continue to protect my children's legal rights. But should an annulment be granted, such protection does nothing to fill the spiritual void left by the claim that my sons are 'issue' of an unsanctified union. Thus, even though the odds of my prevailing in resisting an annulment are bleak, I will continue to defend the bond that brought my children into the world. I know of few mothers who would do any less. Sheila Kennedy Cambridge, MA.''

Sheila's letter and the *Time* story brought the annulment issue before the public, but not to the degree that she would shortly openly explore it. Losing her first go-round against the area diocese while determined to preserve the integrity of her marriage and the family of that union, she wrote a book about her experience, updating it in 1998 for Owl Books of Henry Holt. On pages ten and eleven of her book *Shattered Faith: A Woman's Struggle to Stop the Catholic Church from Annulling Her Marriage,* Sheila wrote about Joe saying: " 'Look, Sheila, get yourself under control. Of course I took our marriage and the children seriously. And of course I think we had a true marriage. But that doesn't matter now. I don't believe this stuff. Nobody actually believes it. It's just Catholic gobbledygook, Sheila. But you just have to say it this way because, well, because that's the way the Church is.'

" 'I'm sorry Joe, but I believe it,' I replied, my entire body shaking with anger,'' Sheila wrote. ''I couldn't believe that he would ask for an annulment when even he didn't think our marriage was invalid.''

Sheila continued, '' 'We both wanted the divorce, Joe,' I tried to answer more calmly. 'Our marriage became unworkable and intolerable, not just for us, but even for the kids. We certainly had irreconcilable differences. But there is a big difference between saying that the marriage doesn't work anymore and saying that, in the eyes of God, it never existed.' ''

In October, 1996, the Catholic Church granted the annulment of Joe and Sheila's marriage so Beth and Joe could be married in the church. At this writing that annulment is on appeal, Sheila refusing to stop her fight. And for many of Joe's former constituents, as well as for many Catholics throughout the nation, the annulment was too easily given. It was also given for reasons that were seemingly outrageous.

The hypocrisy of the Catholic Church in Boston, which seemed to be playing Joe's game, and of Joe himself, shocked many of Joe's constituents. His willingness to effectively separate himself from his children, to pursue a mistress to the exclusion of his family in order to have his second marriage be declared his first, was a shock. While the dialogue in Sheila's book might not be exact because she probably was not making notes in the heat of so emotional an exchange, certainly the attitude was seen as accurate.

Sheila also refrained from attacking Joe concerning their time together. It had been good at the start. They had drifted apart. It was time to end the relationship, and she had done just that.

Suddenly Joe, a thrice-elected congressional representative and probably candidate for the 1998 Massachusetts governor's race, was forced to drop out of politics. His career was momentarily as dead as his brother Michael. And again, it was because a Kennedy could not imagine that the public would be hostile to anything he might do, no matter how outrageous or wrong.

MARY KERRY

Early on, Mary Kerry Kennedy seemed to be one of the Kennedys who would lend only her name to charity work, developing image over substance. Her earliest memories were of playing on the furniture in her father's office when she was three and he was attorney general of the United States. The press's earliest memories were of her partying in New York discos, often in the company of a celebrity such as Andy Warhol. She could be seen attending important benefits, such as the Kennedy celebrity tennis tournaments or a museum opening. She also managed to crash her car into a snowplow in the winter of 1976-77 while attending Brown University, again resulting in newspaper stories.

But Mary Kerry's early activities held only a slight hint of her future. Her sister Kathleen acted as her mentor in the way of all the Kennedy older children. That may be one of the reasons she became a volunteer for Amnesty International after her 1982 graduation from Brown and briefly worked for a news photography agency.

Mary Kerry's work included visiting other countries to document human rights violations. This work threw her into the midst of the problems of Salvadoran refugees. After she returned, she enrolled at Boston College Law School, passing the Massachusetts Bar without difficulty after graduation.

Mary Kerry became involved with one of the family organizations that sometimes seemed more a project to beatify the Kennedy dead than to do good work. This was the Robert F. Kennedy Memorial, which in its early years was more mythmaker than substantial foundation. The memorial was established in 1968, and much of its early efforts involved annual awards. For example, there was the Robert F. Kennedy Journalism Award, which honored print and broadcast media that most effectively covered the problems of the disadvantaged. A few years later, the book award was given to authors who reflected

Kennedy's dedication to justice, especially for the poor and powerless.

It was easy to be cynical about the awards. Bob Kennedy was notorious for bending or breaking the law in pursuit of those he hated when he was at the Justice Department. The idea of due process in many of the cases he handled seemed foreign to him. It was as though his actions did not matter so long as the men he went against had long criminal histories (usually in organized crime). That was how he managed to deport Mafia leader Carlos Marcello to a country with which he had no connection.

But Kerry, like Bob Kennedy, seemed to be evolving during that period. Unlike her late father, she lived to achieve her promise. She became the memorial's legal counsel and began focusing on human rights issues. There was an annual Human Rights Award presented in the name of the center every year around the time of her father's birthday. Rather than letting it just be another way to show the world that her father must have been great because of the award in his honor, Kerry began following up on the issues for which the award was given. She traveled the world, using her skills as a writer, a lobbyist, and anything else that needed to be done to bring genuine change in various areas of the world. She worked with limited funding, limited staff, and constant drive.

Mary Kerry's marriage reflected her values. In 1990 she married Andrew Cuomo, son of New York's ex-governor and now assistant secretary of Housing and Urban Development in the Clinton administration. The marriage between Kennedy and Cuomo was touted as a politician's dream. Mario Cuomo, Andrew's father, is one of the most respected Democratic leaders in the nation, a senior statesman following his term as governor of New York. Brilliant, articulate, his life lived with dedication to both the state and his family, the older Cuomo was long considered a possible presidential candidate. He was also enough of a legal scholar to have been considered for the United States Supreme Court. However, he felt dedicated to resolving the severe financial and social problems in New York State, and declined all other opportunities.

The idea that the son of such a man could marry a Kennedy woman sent the same Democrats who delight in the superficial coverage John Kennedy receives into ecstasy. They saw the image of a political dynasty. They did not see the substance. (And in a humorous aside, they did not see Kerry's relief that once she was married to Andrew the press stopped asking her about any of her Kennedy brothers, sisters, or cousins and started only asking about her husband.)

Andrew Cuomo has never been a politician, though he thought about politics as a career in the manner of any son of a major political figure. His love has always been in creating solutions to the most basic of community needs—housing. He was the founder of Housing Enterprise for the Less Privileged (HELP). The original idea was a simple one. The group wanted to find immediate housing for the homeless, then work them into permanent homes. It is the same quest to which others regularly pay lip service in cities throughout the nation. The difference was that Andrew understood the realities of the problem, not the media image.

Andrew Cuomo took a look at the homeless and recognized that there were many reasons why families found themselves in such a crisis. These included limited education for the existing job market in any given area and also such difficulties as substance abuse and mental illness. There were teenage mothers trying to do right by the children they had too young. There were young men who found themselves fathers without being men themselves. There was no specific profile, no single solution, yet all the people shared the same streets. As a result, part of Cuomo's program involved drug treatment and an ongoing commitment to stay drug-free. His program required the active participation of the people he helped while providing them with the services so they could participate. He did not just announce that they had to get sober and get a job, then sit back and watch individuals, who had no idea how to do otherwise, fail miserably. Instead, he addressed every issue of their lives, starting with the most immediate needs in order to change, then build on each new skill they gained.

For example, HELP created Genesis Homes in Brooklyn. The project, which looks like any quality apartment complex you might find in an upscale neighborhood, provides transitional, low-income, and special needs housing. There are 150 permanent homes and the tenants were made partners in management, upkeep, security, and repairs. The tenants also established the rules and regulations that govern the facility. The complex was designed to protect the residents without being the kind of fortress that is sometimes used for low-income areas. There is an internal courtyard where children can play, where the surface has been designed to prevent or reduce injury on playground equipment. There are no elevators and open interiors; thus, criminals cannot hide or take advantage of areas difficult to see. Equally important, the facility is part of the neighborhood. This means that the day care for children, youth activities, job training programs, drug and alcohol education, and health services are available for everyone. This assures full utilization and an impact that helps a community beyond the narrow confines of the structure in which it is all housed.

Cuomo has repeatedly stated that the homeless are not hard luck versions of the average person. They may have drug and/ or alcohol dependency problems. They may be undereducated, or need special counseling. They may not know how to read or write. As he explained, ''All homeless people need housing. But for some, that's only the beginning. And it doesn't make the homeless bad people that they have drug problems and/or other disabilities. But they are people in need, products of a failed system.''

Cuomo's HELP program does not coddle the homeless or express compassion for their addictions. Instead, there is an ongoing demand that they work to change their lives, not live off the compassion of well-meaning liberals. At the same time, no matter what steps must be taken to effect those changes, the support system is available. There is no excuse for failure because there is no need that will go unmet during the period when the person involved with HELP is working to change his or her life for the better. It is a liberal-created program meeting the goals of the most conservative critics of the welfare system, and that combination intrigues political kingmakers.

Critics of Cuomo and Kennedy claim that they are simply trading on the value of their names. But between his success with an initiative that was unique in the nation coupled with his work at HUD, and Mary Kerry's increasing involvement with human rights, they are accomplishing work that is making a major change in the nation. Mary Kerry, like Kathleen and Bobby, is giving substance to what had been only image with the second generation.

The Cuomos have three children at this writing, including twins Cara Kennedy Cuomo and Mariah Kennedy Cuomo.

CHRISTOPHER, MAXWELL, AND DOUGLAS

The youngest sons of Bob and Ethel—Christopher, Maxwell, and Douglas—are in the earliest stages of carving out their careers and their lives. Christopher Kennedy was born the year his father died. He was raised by a single mother and her staff, having none of the memories of his much older siblings. There were no sycophants trying to take advantage of him, no politicians trying to relive past glories through the children of Jack or Bob. He was an infant allowed to grow to manhood without any of the emotional baggage, or foolish reactions, of the other. The closest he came to discussing his late father came when he was five and explained that his father was in Heaven in the morning and went to his office in the afternoon.

Chris's interest, unlike the rest of the family's, is in money. He is not competitive on the slopes and playing fields, but in the marketplace. He understands his grandfather's belief that it is only in business that you know how you stand in life. At the end of a day, you have either made or lost money. It is an instant scorecard in a game he loves. At this writing he is vice president of marketing for the Chicago Merchandise Mart, a furniture and trade center that was one of the major legitimate sources for Joe Kennedy Sr.'s wealth. Although it was sold in 1998, Chris remains with the company.

Chris has long recognized his family's tendency to abuse drugs. He jokingly has said. "It's easier to get an AA meeting together [for the family members] than [to organize] a touch football team."

Christopher is married to attorney Sheila Sinclair Berner. They are the parents of three children—Katherine, Christopher Jr., and Sarah.

Douglas Harriman Kennedy's childhood was not all that different from Michael's in that he was barely a toddler when Bob Kennedy was shot. However, unlike Christopher, Douglas has explored his father's history to learn more about the man, much as Caroline did for Douglas's uncle Jack.

Douglas's interest is in media, and he is currently building a career with Fox Television. He graduated from Brown University in 1990, then worked for the *Santa Monica News* in California before taking a law degree at the University of Virginia. From there he joined the *New York Post,* an experience that left him outraged. He discovered that the news business was not about its employees' sensitivities but about covering the stories of the day. He resigned when the paper ran a story claiming that Jacqueline Kennedy Onassis briefly had an affair with Bob Kennedy. His cousin, Maria Shriver, has always been more realistic about the news business, but Douglas got lucky. His current job with Fox News has some executives willing to keep him happy. They did not include a story on Michael Kennedy's death when Douglas was anchoring a broadcast at a time when every other national news organization felt the Michael Kennedy death was worth airing.

Douglas married in July 1997, leaving only his younger sister Rory unmarried at this writing.

Matthew Maxwell T. Kennedy would probably have been almost unknown to Americans had it not been for his cousin William Kennedy Smith. After Patty Bowman came forward with her rape charges against Smith, one of Max's girlfriends came forward to say that the story sounded truthful to her. She had been with Smith and he had attacked her. She had not reported the crime, had not discussed the matter with Max. She just felt that she could no longer remain silent when a second alleged victim came forward.

Max has had a varied career before going back to school for a business degree that will probably either lead him in a pursuit of money not unlike his brother Christopher's or into environmental causes like his brother Bobby. When he was majoring in history at Harvard (he graduated in 1987) he was quoted as saying, "The environmental problem is not caused by people hunting but by business polluting, and they are the most powerful. In order to have any kind of effect on them, you have to know how they work."

Max earned a law degree at Harvard, becoming both a law clerk and then an assistant district attorney in Philadelphia. He went on to work for both the Citizens Energy Corporation and Citizens Conservation. At this writing he is in the UCLA business school, married to Victoria Strauss, who teaches at Harvard, and is the father of Matthew Jr. and Caroline.

STEVE SMITH JR.

Steve Smith Jr. thought it would be fun to work behind the scenes, to help with the election campaigns of family members as his father had. He liked the idea of being a quiet mover and shaker. But there was no one to help. The members of the third generation no longer saw politics as a family business, though most had no sense of what they wanted to do or where they wanted to be.

Steve is old enough to have memories of his uncle Jack in the White House. He graduated from Harvard and Columbia Law School, then returned to Harvard to teach political ethics and international relations.

Today Steve Smith, like his brother William Kennedy Smith and his sister Amanda Mary Smith, is unmarried. He works for the Conflict Management Group teaching negotiating skills to groups as diverse as diplomats and gang members.

AMANDA SMITH

Amanda, one of the two adopted daughters, earned her Ph.D. in special education at Harvard. She lives and works in Boston, where she is also writing a book on her late grandfather, Joe Kennedy Sr.

KYM MARIA SMITH

Kym Maria Smith, the Vietnamese child who was one of the last children airlifted out of her native country, was adopted as a toddler. She was also intensely disliked by Rose, who used to speak harshly to her. I remember being shocked when Rose looked at the baby Kym, a toddler still in diapers, and said, "Be nice to me, child. One day you'll inherit my money."

The hurt Kym experienced is reflected in her attitude toward being a Kennedy. She attended every day of her brother's rape trial, though she never spoke with reporters. However, she has refused to pose for magazine photos with the other Kennedys. Kym married Alfie Tucker in 1995, and the two lived for a period of time in Dublin, Ireland. Later he managed a pub and she stayed at home. At this writing she is divorced.

MARIA SHRIVER SCHWARZENEGGER

If Kennedys can escape relatively unscathed from a family that had been morally corrupt, intensely aggressive, and dedicated to power, then the Shriver children have done so.

The Shrivers ultimately proved to be the most devoted parents among the Kennedys; their children, along with those raised by Jacqueline, have been the most consistently successful in their chosen fields. Later problems in their personal life caused such an estrangement between Eunice and Sargent Shriver that when they traveled to Palm Beach together she stayed at the family compound and he often stayed at the Breakers Hotel. In the early years, however, Sargent was the most respected of the outsiders who married into the family, and Eunice was the strongest of the surviving sisters.

It is Maria Shriver Schwarzenegger who gains the most attention of the five Shriver children, though she is the second oldest. It was her decision to enter the world of broadcast journalism, making her a celebrity involved with the same medium with which her family is often so frustrated. When she married the even higher profile bodybuilder/actor/investor Arnold Schwarzenegger, public interest in her dropped. She does not use the Kennedy connection in her profession, and his muscles, accent, and flamboyant career make him the more watched celebrity of the two.

Maria Shriver was the willful child of the Kennedy cousins. She also was among the most sophisticated in terms of experiencing a broad range of life without being victimized by it. Though John and Caroline Kennedy traveled to different parts of the world, they did not experience the intense international upbringing Maria enjoyed as daughter to the ambassador to France. The fact that Sarge was also Peace Corps director and one-time vice-presidential candidate also helped. Although Eunice has long been as bullheaded as any of the Kennedy women, Sarge is an intellectual whose interest in literature is quite different from most of the second generation of Kennedys.

Maria was raised differently from the others of the third generation. She was sent to Israel to live on a kibbutz during part of the time when her father was ambassador to France. Sargent brought home all types of people when he was with the Peace Corps. He refused to let her use her name or her looks, refused to tolerate the type of bigotry that was acceptable to most of the Kennedys. Sargent had no need for the family, in that he was comfortable working for a living. (Rose derisively commented about him, "Blue blood but no money.") He participated when he felt they were doing something morally right, such as when Jack created the Peace Corps, but he went over to "the enemy," becoming Lyndon Johnson's ambassador to France when he thought that was where he could best serve. During the brief period when he held political ambitions, he had social concerns that defied the parameters of what he would do if he achieved office. The idea of winning for the sake of winning, the typical motivation for Jack and Bob in the early years of their careers, was foreign to him.

Maria had been interested in journalism since she was sixteen and her father was running for the vice presidency. Maria understood the appeal of journalism that most people do not think about. A reporter is in the midst of the most dramatic events taking place each day, high profile, noticed, glamorous by being present where the average person is excluded, yet a reporter as a person is almost anonymous. The reporter asks the questions. The reporter reveals the sins, the triumphs, the humor, and the sadness in the lives of people who make the news. Millions of Americans recognize Dan Rather, Jane Pauley, Tom Brokaw, and Diane Sawyer, yet almost no one knows anything about their personal lives.

Maria graduated from Georgetown, a competent student majoring in American studies. Her thesis was on Jack Kennedy and the role of religion in politics. Then, determined to become successful in television, the medium she felt would dominate the future, she went to New York to look for a job.

Maria was different from the other Kennedys. She did not try to capitalize on her name and family connections by seeking a make-work job from someone such as Roone Arledge at ABC, a close Kennedy friend who over the years controlled unfavorable news about the family that might go on the air. However, the reaction she received as she knocked on doors was not what she expected. She became the first Kennedy whom nobody wanted.

To outsiders, Maria had less of the Kennedy arrogance then most of the family. However, I found her to be a spoiled brat. For example, Maria once asked my permission to take Rose's car to a party in Miami when she was in college. I refused because the car was not running well enough for long trips. It was fine for Rose to use it to go to church—part of Rose's ritual and the reason it had not been repaired—but it could not make the ninety-minute trip to Miami without breaking down, stranding both Maria on the road and her grandmother in the house.

Maria refused to listen to reason. She announced that if I would not turn over the keys she would "call Mummy" who, she presumed, would order me to do what Maria demanded. Angered, I said that she could call Eunice, but that I would talk with her mother as well, telling my side of the story. Not even a Kennedy had the power to keep a broken car from completely falling apart.

Defeated, Maria angrily announced that she would never ask me for another favor, as though the hired help was only blessed when they could make a Kennedy happy. "Would you put that promise in writing?" I asked her.

When Maria went to New York, she arrogantly thought she could get work immediately. However, like other college graduates who come to the media capital of the country and think that they will instantly parlay their educations into fame and fortune, she didn't realize that she was seen as inexperienced, potentially incompetent, and too great a risk to hire for the type of work she desired. Maria announced her presence to New York television and New York television said, "So what?"

Family connections did help Maria to learn why no one wanted to hire her. Successful television journalists such as Barbara Walters explained that, now that she had her degree, it was time to get her education. She needed to gain experience, to both learn the business and to prove that she had the ability to cope with its demands.

Maria did pay her dues, working at KYW-TV in Philadelphia and at WJZ-TV in Baltimore. She did a little of everything, starting as a gofer and moving up to producing at KYW. The move to WJZ allowed her to produce the station's *Evening Magazine* program. It was also while in Baltimore that she realized that if she was writing the questions for on-air personnel, she might as well ask them herself. However, it would take time before she was given such an opportunity. She was the newest, least experienced person, so she was given the holidays and other odd times when the more established professionals were home with their families.

Once Maria decided that she had the competence and experience to try for a major market again, she went to Los Angeles. It was the start of her rise on network television.

Los Angeles proved another shock. Maria needed an agent for on-air work, and she discovered just how far her family name would take her. Nowhere. She was overweight. Her voice not only had a Boston accent, considered unpleasant by many Americans, but she also had a tendency to talk too fast and to use her hands too much, distracting the viewers. She had to change to go on in television.

Shriver spent two months improving herself. She hired a voice coach, began studying successful interviewers, and dieted. She was one of the more attractive of the third generation women, and with the weight loss and makeup her face became striking before the camera. The only parts of her body she could not change were her thighs. Rose, looking at the massive thighs of her granddaughters Maria, Caroline, Kara, and Victoria Lawford, commented that they inherited their heavy thighs from Joe's side of the family. As a result, photographs of the girls tend to be from the waist up. Arnold Schwarzenegger once said that Maria should wear skirts because she looked better than when she wore pants.

Maria's first job after her transformation was a Special Olympics winter special for WTBS. The Turner station used her as a cohost, and while she may have been hired because of her name (Eunice created the Special Olympics program that enables the physically and mentally disabled to compete in athletic events designed around their abilities), her work was professional enough for the show to win two Emmys. And unlike with many other Kennedys, no rich and powerful relative was lurking in the background to assure her success.

In 1981, Maria worked as a national correspondent on *PM Magazine*. That job lasted into 1983, and involved both profile pieces and stories about the entertainment industry. It gave her more experience in planning segments, being on air, writing, timing, and the other skills she needed, as well as exposing her nationally. Eventually she found it boring, and turned to family friend Tom Brokaw for help. Brokaw was anchorman for the NBC evening news and knowledgeable about the industry. He felt that she needed a different level of representation and got her a new agent. From that person, she learned that the *CBS Morning News* needed someone to work as West Coast reporter, and her audition earned her the job.

The news business was becoming more of an entertainment medium, and discrimination against women was high. Physical appearance had become more important than news-gathering abilities for some executives, so while men were able to continue on television regardless of age, many women were learning that somewhere in their mid-forties they were being taken off camera. They were "too old" or "too ugly." It was a viciously sexist situation, and few women were able to overcome it.

At the same time, the *CBS Morning News* was a different type of show. Its competition included *Today* and *Good Morning America,* both of which combined news, celebrity interviews, and entertainment. The CBS programming was harder-edged, mostly news, and closer to the soon-to-be-developed Cable News Network (CNN). Looks might have been important, but either you were effective both on and off camera, or you did not survive. When she moved into a position of regular co-anchor, her life was determined by the ratings, and the ratings were determined, in part, by her willingness to work thirteen hour days.

Socially, Maria was already known in Hollywood because of Arnold Schwarzenegger, to whom she had been introduced by her brother Bobby back in 1977, when she was twenty-one. Bobby had seen the documentary *Pumping Iron,* which told the story of a pair of bodybuilders preparing for the Mr. Olympia contest. It was a low-budget film, well produced, that introduced Schwarzenegger to the world at large. He was an Austrian who knew he needed a gimmick to leave his homeland and succeed in America. Bodybuilding competition gave him that opportunity, and his intelligence and articulate nature carried him the rest of the way.

Arnold's interests were in business, not bodybuilding or even acting, though he would become famous as the star of such films as *Conan the Barbarian, Conan the Destroyer, Raw Deal, Twins, Kindergarten Cop, The Terminator,* and others. While still a bodybuilder he had begun investing in Southern California real estate, amassing a fortune that is currently between at least $50 million and $75 million or more. There has also been a serious belief that Schwarzenegger, a staunch Republican, has political ambitions. Living in California, a state where actors have turned to politics and achieved all levels of high office, there is a chance that he will one day run for Congress.

When Schwarzenegger was introduced to Maria at the annual RFK tennis tournament in New York in 1977, there was no love at first sight. Arnold, not one for monogamy, was living in an open relationship with a woman in Los Angeles. They were devoted to each other while in the same city, living together and sharing a life, but able to date others when traveling, which he did frequently.

Over the next few years, Arnold traveled to wherever Maria was working. She was becoming increasingly independent of her family, and it was thought by others that she saw in Arnold a man who could be her physical protector, who was not part of the East Coast big money scene, and who could be mentally dominated. In truth, they were quite similar in temperament.

Schwarzenegger came from poverty in Austria, his father a police officer. He had the intense ambition that Maria could easily find in her Irish ancestors. Even his politics, which included a close friendship with Kurt Waldheim, who had been secretary-general of the United Nations and was active in Austrian politics, were not unlike those of Ambassador Joe Kennedy. Waldheim was a former Nazi, a fact he kept well hidden for many years. When the facts were revealed, just before the Schwarzenegger-Shriver marriage in 1986, Arnold continued to give Waldheim his full support. Arnold may or may not have approved of Waldheim's past, but it did not affect his friendship.

Eventually Maria became the permanent coanchor for the *CBS Morning News,* moving to New York City. Schwarzenegger had no intention of joining her, for his home, his office, and his work are all based on the West Coast. She proved herself to be an excellent on-air interviewer. Because of her father, she had witnessed more of the realities of politics and government than her cousins, and she used the situation to advantage. However, she still had occasional lapses into the Kennedy arrogance that she grew up with.

On July 5, 1988, Maria interviewed Mark and LaVonne McKee, parents of a boy who had been shot by his friend, who was playing with the friend's father's gun. The interview was for a TV special titled "Guns, Guns, Guns." The couple thought she was hostile to them because, despite their tragedy, they were gun people who thought that guns were safe in homes with adequate safeguards. Besides that, the McKees found Maria unconcerned with them:

"Maria's concern that day was not with us," said LaVonne McKee. "While she was in our home, she telephoned to be certain a limousine would be available to pick her up, since she apparently was not returning with the crew. Then she called her mother, Eunice Kennedy Shriver, who was in Los Angeles, apparently so that she could attend the premiere [of Schwarzenegger's movie *Red Heat*]. Maria wanted to be certain that her mother called to get an appointment with a beauty shop. Finally there was an effort to learn how to get to Bakersfield, where she apparently had another appointment, whether for an interview or yet another personal matter we never knew. It all seemed to us to be very unprofessional."

Although close to her family, Maria became one of the few women among the Kennedys to have a career drive, ambition for herself, and a future involving life where she was not the center of attention. The press accepted her as one of their own, a fact that meant she was increasingly ignored by the tabloids except when she was with Arnold Schwarzenegger.

The one exception was her wedding, which took place in Hyannisport on April 27, 1986. There were five hundred guests, ranging from Austrian Ambassador Thomas Klestil, to longtime family friends such as Andy Williams, columnist Abigail Van Buren, actress Susan St. James, Tom Brokaw, Barbara Walters, and, of course, numerous Kennedys. There were also more exotic guests such as actress Grace Jones, who wore a clinging green dress and black fur, and her escort Andy Warhol.

The crowds of watchers began gathering outside the Church of St. Francis Xavier at 6:00 A.M., slightly more than four hours before the first guests arrived. Reporters could not be discouraged, so arrangements were made to have them stay on a viewing stand across the street. They were at a distance, yet they could still film everything that happened outside. Extensive police and private security protection was in evidence, and even air security was assured. Knowing that helicopters and small planes would be chartered by some of the news media, the family used their political clout and their money to arrange to have all air traffic banned within a radius of two miles around the family compound. The ban was in effect from ten in the morning until six at night, assuring as much privacy as they could control.

When Arnold arrived he played to the crowd, starting as he approached in his limousine, slowing outside the church, opening the window, and smiling for the public and the photographers. Maria, a few minutes late for the ceremony, moved quickly inside. Her wedding gown was from Dior and was designed by Marc Bohan. Eunice also wore a Dior.

The ceremony was handled more simply than the usual Kennedy rites, with only the Reverend Edward Duffy and the Reverend John Baptist Riordan, no cardinals, officiating. Among those assisting with various readings during the service was fellow Baltimore television employee Oprah Winfrey, whose star would soon eclipse Maria's. Winfrey read "How Do I Love Thee?" by Elizabeth Barrett Browning. Finally, after the couple left the church to the song "Maria," they posed for reporters before moving on to the reception.

The reception was a delight for gluttons. The list of food and drink was seemingly endless. There was lobster, chicken breasts in champagne sauce, shrimp, asparagus over pasta shells, julienne vegetables. Viennese pastries, strawberries, and chocolates filled with marzipan, an Austrian specialty known as Mozart Kgeln. Ultimately there was the wedding cake, created by Stephen Hesnan. Seven feet high, containing eight tiers of carrot and pound cake iced with butter cream frosting, the masterpiece weighed 425 pounds and was adorned with flowers, white sugar bells, replicas of the bride and groom, pink ribbons, and lace.

The following year, Maria left CBS when NBC offered her the chance to anchor the Sunday version of *Today*. Next she took on the anchor spot of the Saturday edition of the *NBC Nightly News,* the show anchored by Tom Brokaw during the week. In addition, she was cohost of a newsmagazine show called *Yesterday, Today and Tomorrow,* a program that did not do well. Her salary came close to $500,000 a year, and she was obviously being groomed to be a major figure in the news division.

Critics became more aggressive as they watched Maria move up. One story in *TV Guide* referred to her as "Maria Striver." She was attacked for being both worldly and naive, traits the article claimed were common to children born of privilege. And while the criticism was accurate to a degree, the truth about the professional life of Maria Shriver was that she was willing to put the effort into a longterm goal, not just try to be an instant success, gain a few headlines, and get on with some other "good work."

Maria became pregnant three years after the marriage, giving birth on December 13, 1989, to Katherine Eunice Schwarzenegger. A second child, Christina Maria Aurelia Schwarzenegger, followed not long after. And in September 1993 she gave birth to the couple's first son, Patrick. Their fourth child and second son, Christopher Sargent Shriver Schwarzenegger, was born on September 27, 1997. Her pregnancy was difficult because she developed hyperemesis, a condition that prevented her from retaining food or liquids. She had to be fed intravenously for the sake of herself and her baby toward the end of her first trimester. Fortunately the hospitalization and a leave of absence from work assured that the birth was without complications.

At this writing, Maria and NBC have an excellent working relationship. Having the four children has changed her priorities, but not her ambition. She and Arnold are both devoted to the children and their careers, and are never in competition. The only problem in their lives may be a serious one. Arnold has long admitted that he took steroids when actively competing as a bodybuilder. It was a standard method for bulking up the body in those days—so common that some high schools had local doctors supply them to the football team and to some students involved with track and field if their parents agreed. Since then we have learned that steroids in the wrong quantities will cause serious problems. Frequently these effect the liver, and numerous deaths have been attributed to the use of steroids ten and twenty years earlier.

It has been alleged that Schwarzenegger has occasionally been on dialysis for his problems. He also has apparently lost some of the size of his body. However, the latter may also have to do with his working out less now that he is earning his money with both business investments and movies that do not require him to be so visibly bulked up with muscles. What any of this will mean for the quality of his life has yet to be determined.

BOBBY SHRIVER

Robert "Bobby" Sargent Shriver III became involved with venture capital and invested in the Baltimore Orioles, living quietly as an attorney-turned-businessman-turned-producer. Despite his early troubles, he managed to escape the influence of Bob and Ethel's kids. His father did not want his son to be a stoic who could not cry when hurt, could not reveal emotion. Sargent wanted his children to be whole people, not restricted by an image created by someone else. When his son was arrested, he did not try to hide the fact, nor did he berate him. He made it clear that he would stand by Bobby, and that he expected Bobby would never repeat his mistake. Unlike many of his cousins who were repeatedly in trouble, Bobby immediately straightened himself out.

Bobby followed the family path and got his law degree from Yale, but thereafter he diverged into his own pattern. He was a writer, and got several jobs on newspapers, including a small newspaper in Annapolis, Maryland, the *Chicago Daily News,* and the *Los Angeles Herald Examiner.* He chose to live on his salary, which, when he started, was $125 a week. Stories about Bobby pictured him as a character from the more aggressive newspaper days of the 1930s, when a reporter would do anything to get a story before a rival, but he was certainly a professional writer. He had the sensitivity of New York columnist Jimmy Breslin, who—when sent on his first assignment to cover Jack Kennedy's funeral—avoided the crowds, the dignitaries, and the other personalities around whom other reporters converged. He focused solely on one forgotten man, the individual whose job it was to dig the president's grave. Thus, when the *Herald Examiner* sent Bobby to cover a local visit by the Rolling Stones, Bobby looked to the people around the group, not just the singers.

Though talented and with an excellent future ahead of him, he lacked both the seasoning and the drive that would keep him successful throughout a writing career. He commented to friends that he lacked the anger needed to sustain impact. He pointed to Mike Royko, then a columnist for the *Chicago Sun-Times* and a man who was angry about incompetence, injustice, and the closed circle of men and women who ran the country. Bobby was raised in the midst of that power structure, lacked the anger, and did not see himself sustaining the career where he showed so much promise.

Sargent Shriver never pushed his son to be involved with politics. In 1972 Bobby had a job working as a truck driver in Israel for the film company producing the movie version of *Jesus Christ, Superstar.* It was at the same time that his father was running for U.S. vice president. Other Kennedy family members would have insisted that their children be involved with the campaign, taking a leading role from the time of the nominating convention. Sargent was so convinced that his children should lead independent lives, pursuing their own interests, that Bobby only learned about his father's campaign when a tourist mentioned it to him.

Later, upon reflection, he commented: "We have to measure what we are by what our parents were. Grandpa had things completely wired—Massachusetts, the whole of the East Coast. He had it under control. He was a political consultant, a political action committee, and a media consultant all rolled into one. His only client was his family. He was fanatically dedicated to making it happen. Nobody in this family is ever again going to decide that it's a life-or-death matter whether or not a Kennedy gets elected to something. Even if they did, they can't make it happen anymore. That's what's changed, and we might as well admit it."

Eventually Bobby moved to Los Angeles to work both with Special Olympics and to earn his living as a movie producer. He is best known for developing the story that became the script for *True Lies,* starring his friend Arnold Schwarzenegger. It was Bobby who introduced his sister, Maria, to Arnold, the friend eventually becoming the brother-in-law.

TIMOTHY SHRIVER

Timothy Perry Shriver, a man with the seriousness of purpose of his father and commitment to religious action as deep as his grandmother's commitment to religious ritual, received his master's degree in spirituality and education at Catholic University. He then got a job in the New Haven, Connecticut, school system working with abused children. While his own life was one of nurturing, he is acutely sensitive to the emotional abuse in his own extended family.

Tim's work has always been quiet. He taught high school equivalency classes at the Lorton Prison near Washington because he believed in giving the inmates the education they would need when they returned to society. He has also developed special academic programs for gifted children, who are at risk of dropping out from lack of stimulation. He has worked to involve the families of at-risk children with the education of their sons and daughters. His world is that of teacher and counselor. He works with individuals who might otherwise become involved with drugs or early pregnancy. For a while he was the one Kennedy who was considered a candidate for the priesthood, but his marriage to attorney Linda Potter in 1986 and his growing family ended that speculation. Their children now include Rose, Timothy, Samuel, and Kathleen. Still, his life reflects religious theology rather than the religious ritual to which his grandmother escaped over the years. And today he runs the Special Olympics organization founded by his mother, though unlike her, he remains low-profile.

MARK SHRIVER

Mark Kennedy Shriver, born in 1964, created CHOICE, a program designed to tutor and mentor Baltimore's inner-city children. It was one of the first in the nation rather than being imitative of what already existed. Currently he is a member of the Maryland General Assembly and a telephone company executive. His wife, Jeanne Ripp, works for American Express.

ANTHONY SHRIVER

Anthony Paul Shriver, who was born in 1965 and graduated from Georgetown University, is still finding his path in life relative to his driven, directed siblings. He is also sometimes victimized by their antics.

Anthony founded and maintains an active role in Best Buddies, a program that teams college students with the mentally retarded in order to give both a broader life experience. In February 1965, he was quoted in *People* magazine as saying, "Part of our position is to make it so people won't stare. So when you go downtown or into church, they're used to having people with mental retardation in there."

Anthony is the one Kennedy family member who truly cares for his elderly aunt Rosemary. He regularly visits her and planned his home in Miami Beach, to which he has relocated, so that she would be able to visit.

Anthony has also decided to make a move into politics. Unfortunately he decided to start with a run for mayor of Miami Beach at the same time the scandals involving Joe and Michael broke—Joe's adultery, divorce, and effort to gain an annulment, coupled with Michael's affair with his baby-sitter—tainted Anthony. He had nothing to do with either crisis, but the family was ridiculed by members of the press. In addition, since he was relatively new to Miami Beach, which he seems to love, he was considered a carpetbagger for running for mayor so soon.

Anthony, who heads a pharmaceutical delivery firm, is married to art gallery director Alina Mojica. Their three children include Teddy, by her previous marriage, Eunice, and Francesca.

KARA

Ted Kennedy's children have, in many ways, experienced a life more difficult than any of the other Kennedy children except Christopher Lawford's. Kara Kennedy, the oldest, was three when uncle Jack was killed, four when her father had a near fatal plane crash, and in elementary school when uncle Bob was shot. The following year, when Kara was nine, Chappaquiddick occurred. While other children did not understand the affair her father was probably having or about to have with Mary Jo Kopechne, they did understand that her death was his fault. They began teasing Kara in ways that were extremely hurtful.

As with all children, the loss of attention (when her younger brother, Teddy, got cancer) was difficult for Kara. She feared the disease was contagious. She also was upset because her parents had to be focused on Teddy when he was undergoing treatments that would mean the difference between life or death. It wasn't a case of wanting her brother to die. Like all siblings in such circumstances, she was hurt that she was no longer receiving the attention that had been hers in the past.

All of this was compounded by family difficulties. Her mother, Joan, was an alcoholic trapped in a marriage with a womanizing husband. Her youngest brother, Patrick, had asthma, a condition that could cause the family to radically shift plans when he had a severe attack.

Some of these experiences caused Kara to close down and live quietly. She graduated from the National Cathedral School in Washington in 1978, then went on to Trinity College in Dublin and, finally, Tufts University in New York. She attended Alcoholics Anonymous meetings with her mother, determined to help her defeat her drinking problem. She also had to experience her second year at Trinity protected by a pair of bodyguards. Her father hired them after his office staff was confronted by a knife-wielding woman determined to kill the senator.

Eventually Kara took a job with Metromedia Television in Washington, then briefly became producer for *Evening Magazine* on Boston's WBZ-TV. From there she became media director for the Washington, D.C., Very Special Arts Program.

In 1990, Kara married architect Michael Allen. She quit work to stay at home with their children, Grace and Max Allen.

TEDDY

Edward "Teddy" Moore Kennedy Jr. has always been troubled by media attention, especially when, at the age of twelve, he had to have his right leg amputated as a result of cancer of the cartilage (chrondosarcoma). In November 1986, his life became part of the network sweeps efforts, a movie titled *The Teddy Kennedy Story* used to help boost ratings. The film covered the cancer operation of November 17, 1973, through to a trip to Ireland the following summer.

The story was an emotional one. Teddy's father has never

been a man of strength. Over the years he has overindulged in food, drink, and women. With Teddy becoming an amputee, the senator grew unrealistically cautious, demanding his son do nothing that might prove too difficult or dangerous, including playing soccer, which the boy loved. As the movie showed, Ted watched from his hotel room as his son was on the lawn down below, playing soccer and successfully making a save the senator would have thought impossible.

Teddy was against the movie, but realized that it was going to be made whether he agreed or not. He decided to cooperate, earning almost $100,000, which he donated to Facing the Challenge, a Boston organization working with the handicapped to get them mainstreamed in businesses, schools, and universities.

Teddy's popularity with his cousins became obvious when all twenty-nine of the third-generation family members came to Georgetown where the surgery took place. The amputation took place on Saturday, November 17, 1973, so unexpectedly that it came at the same time as Kathleen Kennedy's wedding to David Townsend.

Senator Kennedy has a well-deserved reputation for being self-centered and self-indulgent, but after the amputation he rarely left his son's side. He arranged to be at the Senate no more than two or three hours a day. He took every meal with Teddy, and helped him through both the psychological and physical rehabilitation. He also had the good sense to pull away and let him face the stares and occasional ridicule, including some from within his own family. Kara and Patrick, for example, made bets as to how far he would get walking on the above-the-knee prosthesis before he fell flat on his face.

Eventually Teddy developed a bravado about the leg. He would wear shorts, making no attempt to hide it. And at one party, when a woman stared, he explained to her that it made a great chopping block. Then he proceeded to place a hunk of cheese against his artificial leg and cut it into pieces.

That there was pain was evident in Teddy's use of drugs. He enrolled in Wesleyan University and began using marijuana. Then he seemed to switch to his parents' drug of choice—

alcohol. He managed to earn a master's degree from the Yale University School of Forestry and Environmental Studies, then gradually became more and more troubled. In 1992 he admitted his alcoholism and enrolled in the Hartford, Connecticut, Institute for Living, in an alcohol and drug rehab program.

On October 10, 1993, Teddy married Katherine "Kiki" Gershman, a psychiatrist. Then he began attending law school at night, completed his degree, then working as director of community projects for the lead-detection program of the Yale Medical School's department of pediatrics. He is now a lawyer and the father of Kiley Kennedy.

PATRICK

Patrick Kennedy, the youngest of Ted Kennedy's children, is perhaps the most politically aggressive without having the ego and temper problems that eventually cost Joe his congressional seat. He has been aggressive in other ways, as well. He has had severe problems with bronchial asthma, yet while attending Boston's Fessenden School as a teenager he played on the football team and was a competitive wrestler. He was equally active when he transferred to Phillips Academy in Andover, Massachusetts.

Patrick's drug problems were faced earlier than those of many in the Kennedy third generation. He was nineteen when he admitted a cocaine addiction and checked into the rehab facility Spofford Hall in New Hampshire. He later explained to a reporter that he thought experimenting with drugs and alcohol could alleviate the stress in the family.

By 1986, Patrick had moved to Rhode Island and enrolled in Providence College, majoring in philosophy. He then took a degree in social science, becoming fascinated with politics. He worked on his cousin Joe's congressional campaign, then ran for Rhode Island state representative, a position that paid only $300 per year. So determined was he to beat five-year incumbent John Skeffington that he spent $87,500 on the campaign. He also brought his cousin John to campaign for him, a major draw.

Patrick held his own, serving six years in the Rhode Island House of Representatives before being elected to Congress in 1994, 1996, and 1998. His focus has been in maintaining jobs, and such benefits as nutrition and food programs for the elderly in his district. They feel he serves them well, his popularity far greater than his cousin Joe achieved. He also admits to using the Kennedy name to open doors, believing in his projects so much that he feels justified in using whatever advantage he can gain.

CHRISTOPHER LAWFORD

The Lawfords and the Smiths are an odd mix. Best known among those who have kept out of the news of late is Christopher Lawford. His troubled childhood, including his being given drugs as a birthday present by his father, Peter, led to a troubled adulthood with periodic times of success. He was extremely close to David, and his cousin's death remains an emotional experience for him.

Chris's drug use, which seemed to end in 1985 with the support of Jeannie Olsson, a fellow drug addict who was working for *New York* magazine when they met. Together they completed the Addictive Behavior Course in Massachusetts' Cambridge Hospital. They married and have three children—David, Savannah, and Matthew.

Chris tried to study law, graduating from Boston College Law School in 1983 and then abandoning the idea of such a career when he failed the bar exam. He then went on to become an actor in movies such as *Run, Pulp Fiction, Mr. North,* and numerous others. He has begun to do television work, ranging from the movie *The Abduction* to an episode of *Tales from the Crypt* directed by Arnold Schwarzenegger. He also appeared in the soap opera *All My Children* for a while, though of late he has moved into producing, including the film *Kiss Me, Guido.*

Chris has not been a major success as either actor or producer.

It is hard to know his ambitions, and some of the people with whom he has worked find him still reacting to the stress of his troubled early years. However, given his upbringing, each day sober, working, and involved with his family is a triumph his own father never achieved.

SYDNEY AND VICTORIA LAWFORD

Both Sydney Lawford, a former model, and Victoria Lawford have married, choosing to stay home with their children. Their youngest sister, Robin Lawford, followed a different course, becoming a Marine biologist. Prior to that time, she worked as a stage manager for off-off Broadway theater productions.

For many of the third generation, life is the sort of transition that their great-grandparents experienced when striving to find their way in nineteenth-century Boston. They have far greater wealth, of course. All are millionaires. They have never known tenement houses and slums except during those periods of drug abuse when the more self-destructive among them passed out in areas they would never have approached sober. Few have been involved longterm with any lifestyle other than that of privilege. Yet in their frustration, confusion, and sense of isolation, they are no different from their immigrant ancestors, fighting all but immediate family in a desperate attempt to establish a personal identity in a strange land.

As I watched them grow into adulthood, I found that many of them shared Christopher Lawford's attitude that it did not matter if the Kennedys tried in school and in life. When they were twenty-one they would come into their inheritances, and then they would never have to work again. What mattered was filling eight or nine hours a day with personal pleasure, then seeing what excitement could be enjoyed after midnight. The problem was that they all grew up, and what seems a perfect lifestyle as a teenager can quickly become boring or deadly as an adult. What is fun, albeit a little scandalous, to outsiders when you are a rich, famous teenager, becomes juvenile, irresponsible, and worth criticizing, not applauding, when you are over thirty. A teenage Willie Smith could walk away unscathed after being acquitted of rape. The adult Dr. William Smith may find that the life he might have led had he not gone to Au Bar will forever be denied him.

Many of the names of the third generation are unfamiliar because the family members are as yet too young to have made an impact on society. Perhaps many of the names will never be familiar, and the third generation will develop lives that fit their interests, their goals, and not the egocentric family's master political plan. Camelot never existed, yet like so many legends the public's fantasy has been slow to die. The sins of the grandfather have passed on to the third generation. With luck, at least some of them will have the courage to lead their own lives, to break free of the stranglehold of fear, self-adulation, and knee-jerk mutual support, regardless of circumstances, that earlier led them to alcohol, drugs, disease, and early death.

EPILOGUE

If there is one remarkable fact that stands out about the third generation of Kennedys, it is that any of them survived at all. David is dead. Michael is dead. And now, John is dead. Dr. William Kennedy Smith lives under a shadow that no amount of good works is ever likely to eradicate. Joe II has learned that many, perhaps most, Catholics and Protestants look upon marriage vows as sacred. They are not to be treated casually, and when children are involved, the denial of their existence by requesting an annulment is met with moral outrage that can shatter a promising career.

Marital estrangement and divorce are seemingly common-place for them, their difficulties with emotional commitments a mirror of the problems of their parents' generation. Even the wealth that so obsessed Joe Kennedy Sr. is fading rapidly compared with that of such families as the Rockefellers, the Fords, and others who made their wealth in Joe Sr.'s generation.

Joe Kennedy was unique among the robber barons, bootleg-gers, stock manipulators, and investors in not teaching any of his children the businesses that supplied the family wealth. He used partners from both the conventional world and the underworld, keeping the minimum necessary records. He established the Park Agency in New York as a conduit for many of his financial ventures, though none of his sons, daughters, or grandchildren ever worked there. He kept his children beholden to him for every dollar they spent instead of showing them how to preserve and enlarge the family fortune. As a result, though the third generation is wealthy by the standards of the average American, the fortune is being spent. The only new money being added seems to come from the Chicago Merchandise Mart, and that is only a few million dollars a year. By contrast, no matter how philanthropic the lives of the other third-generation families whose backgrounds include great wealth, they have always had one or more of the children working to preserve and enlarge their family's holdings.

Joe and Rose wanted acceptance in a society where one's ancestry and the age of one's money were more important than one's character. Failing to find such acceptance in Boston, Joe relocated his family, then began a quest for power that almost caused him to challenge Franklin Roosevelt for the presidency in 1940. When that failed, he transferred his plans to his sons, losing one to war and two to assassins' bullets. The remaining son, the youngest and least secure, eventually rose to the highest level of power the family has yet reached, but in the process almost destroyed himself through alcoholism and philandering.

At first, it seemed that most of the third generation would be lost to the same afflictions as their parents. Most lacked direction in their lives. Almost all experimented with drugs and alcohol, several to such excess that they earned arrest records and frequent stays in rehab centers. Joe Kennedy II, the most publicly ambitious of the third generation, caused an accident that left a young woman paralyzed, then had a failed marriage while trying to build a career in Congress. Christopher Lawford's father encouraged his drug abuse, yet Christopher, unlike his father, had the courage to stop using drugs and become a professional actor and producer. Today his career may not be considered brilliant by many industry observers, but it is still slowly rising at the same age in life when his father's was beginning to decline due to substance abuse.

A few of the third generation are remarkable for their accomplishments. Lieutenant Governor Kathleen Kennedy Townsend has helped a generation of Americans understand that they are part of a greater community than their immediate neighborhoods, the four walls of their high school rooms. Her volunteer service program has spread from her home state of Maryland and reversed the selfish isolation of previous generations of teenagers.

Robert Kennedy Jr. has stopped overdosing his body and become an expert advocate in the field of environmental law. He is responsible for international changes in the field of conservation of natural resources. Maria Shriver made perhaps the most impressive career move. Instead of being a professional Kennedy, she has established such a presence for herself in the television industry that many people do not realize that she is related to the family.

Some of the grandchildren have even achieved what passes for normalcy for the Kennedy clan. Caroline Kennedy, though a law school graduate and published author, spends most of her time being a wife and mother. John Kennedy Jr., seen by many as the great Kennedy hope, stopped living for the ambitions of others when he married Carolyn Bessette. The relationship was based on shared interests rather than because it might somehow have furthered any political ambitions John might have had.

If the third generation continues as in the past, and if their children begin to go their separate ways, the family will likely blend into the mainstream society toward which Joe and Rose were so hostile. There is no longer a great family purpose, as there was when brothers and sisters united to try to elect each male in turn to the White House. There is no effort to create vast family wealth, property, or businesses. And there is no longer a need to divert attention from the dark side of the family's history by doing "good works."

Camelot was a myth, as were the stories of King Arthur and

the Kennedy White House. Both were destroyed by greed, lust, and man's inhumanity toward man. Yet from the ashes of their parents' losses, failings, and tragedies have come a surprising number of individuals who are making a more positive impact on society than the myth makers of the first and second generation could have ever imagined.

ADDENDUM: ANOTHER TRAGIC ENDING

"It's hard for me to talk about a legacy or a mystique," John Kennedy, Jr., commented in 1993. "It's my family. The fact that there have been difficulties and hardships or obstacles makes us closer."

John Kennedy, Jr., was America's Ken doll—an appellation that amused him. (We mentioned it when requesting a series of in-depth interviews for this book.) People liked to dress him up and pretend they knew him, the life he led, and the future that was his destiny. The truth was both less and more than outsiders desired, and therein was the biggest story of all.

Kennedy barely knew the father whose fame and good looks set an orgy of media attention in motion following his assassination on November 22, 1963. John, Jr., was born November 25, 1960, just two-and-a-half weeks after his father had been elected the 35th President of the United States. Millions of Americans watched the toddler playing hide-and-seek under his father's desk. They saw a now famous picture of the most powerful government leader in the world looking out the Oval Office window at his little boy at play.

The press called him John-John because they mistakenly believed it was his beloved father's pet name for his son. In truth, his father only called him John, though one fateful day, when the recalcitrant child did not respond, his father repeated the name a second time to get the boy's attention. "John!" he shouted. "John!" Misunderstanding what they were hearing, the press began referring to the child as John-John, a name he would always hate and one that was never used by his family.

Ultimately there was the touching picture of a little boy saluting the caisson on which his father's body was being carried through the streets of Washington, D.C. The salute had been taught to John by a Secret Service agent whom he adored and who was a surrogate parent for a few difficult weeks. It had nothing to do with John's understanding of death, the funeral, and the loss of a father, but the image touched the hearts of hundreds of millions of people throughout the world.

Ironically, when John, Jr., met his own untimely end in the ocean waters off Martha's Vineyard, the majority of the reporters, researchers, and technical support people in the media covering the frantic search operation knew of President Kennedy only from history books. Both the authors of this book were inundated with calls for stories about John on Saturday, July 17, 1999, the day after his plane disappeared. In every case, with the exception of such veterans as ABC's Ted Koppel, the people asking the questions were in diapers or kindergarten when President Kennedy was killed. Their fascination was with a 38-year-old man whose image was honed by *People* magazine and the *National Enquirer,* not by history books and politics.

John Kennedy, Jr., was the media's darling, but he held no love for the media. He was a quiet man, a gentle man, a youth with ambitions more like the handsome, friendly boy next door than an international celebrity. That he was wealthy was a fact of his life. He was a millionaire at birth because of trust funds. His millions increased as part of a prenuptial arrangement between Jacqueline and her second husband, Aristotle Onassis, the only real father John knew. And there was still more wealth through inheritance upon the deaths of his stepfather and mother.

The money brought John a degree of privacy, and he handled the funds with maturity. His lifestyle was not as lavish as his wealth would allow. His indulgences were not self-destructive in the manner of his cousins, some of whom abused drugs, alcohol, and the privilege afforded them by adoring sycophants, often to their detriment. For John, Jr., there were no stories of near death from drug overdose, as with his cousin Bobby. There was no tragic, lonely decline into death, such as his cousin David's. There was no headline-grabbing, high living, destructive behavior, as his cousin Chris Lawford experienced.

Instead John walked a fine line between pursuing his dreams and trying to keep his mother happy. He was an inherently skilled actor with a deep love of theater. Producers sought him, sometimes for his name and sometimes for his quiet good looks. Many of his girlfriends, such as Sarah Jessica Parker, were actors, and through them, as well as friends from Brown University, he appeared in film and in theater. The roles were never big. Jacqueline often prevented reviewers from attending. But he held his own, friends said, as accomplished in his performances as those with whom he appeared.

Jacqueline's fears of a theatrical career for her son were based on the life and untimely death of John's uncle, Peter Lawford. Lawford, whose first of four wives was Pat Kennedy, lived a life of self-destructive, hedonistic indulgence. Sex of all types, prescription drugs, recreational drugs, and alcohol fueled his behavior and ultimately destroyed his body. Uncle Peter was so out of control that when he wanted to bring someone a special birthday present, he brought cocaine. Uncle Peter also "pimped" for John's father, including arranging the famous trysts with actress Marilyn Monroe.

To Jacqueline, men in show business were scoundrels at best—her father-in-law, Joseph P. Kennedy, was a movie producer who brought his most famous mistress, actress Gloria Swanson, home to HyannisPort to live under the same roof as his wife. At worst, they destroyed themselves and those who loved them.

If there had been any chance of John being allowed a show business career, it was ended when he briefly dated Madonna. The reminder of his father's affair with actress Marilyn Monroe was too great for Jacqueline.

John's cousins frequently called him a "mama's boy" for considering Jacqueline's wishes when conducting his life. More accurate would be the idea of respect and sensitivity for what she had endured. Acting was one of several interests, and as long as he could pursue others with at least equal happiness, he was pleased to respect her wishes. That was why, after her death, John pursued the literary field, an area dear to his mother's heart and a separate longtime interest of both John and his sister Caroline, a published author.

It was the accessibility of John Jr., the ordinariness of the man, that made him so beloved. You could picture him at a backyard barbecue or bowling a few lanes over on your league night. Sure, he was so good-looking every woman in the place would be staring at him, but you didn't feel he was a predator. He had his girl and you had yours, and he'd never make the move on someone else's woman. That moral earthiness, that sense of his being a good guy and an "average Joe," affected ex-lovers as well as strangers.

In interview after interview with women who had dated John, sometimes quite intimately, the reaction was always the same. "Don't tell John I'm talking with you. He'd be embarrassed. But you have to understand how nice he is. He's a good friend. He's loyal. He treats you with respect. He's someone you can count on. He's nothing like the stories about his father." And such comments often came from women who had lived with him, who thought they might marry him, but ultimately went their separate ways. In such circumstances, a hint of bitterness would be expected, but there was none.

John had trouble with his bar exam. Attending law school was almost a Kennedy rite of passage he endured without enthusiasm. He was ridiculed by the press—"The Hunk

Flunks'' read one tabloid's headline—and the New York public took his failure to heart. After he failed the second time (he passed on the third try), he was walking past a homeless man who was sitting in a doorway. The man recognized the famous Kennedy profile, looked up, and, as he might to a friend, remonstrated, ''You should be home studying.'' John, embarrassed, looked down at a man most people would have ignored and said, ''I know. I know.''

The creation of the magazine *George,* a hybrid of political commentary, satire, interviews, and serious investigative journalism, represented the fulfillment of a dream his mother would have approved. She had been ridiculed by the family's enemies for capitalizing on her looks and marital position. What they did not know was that Jacqueline Bouvier went from newspaper reporting to being the Inquiring Photographer for *Vogue* magazine. She wrote articles and took pictures, including one of a young senator named Jack Kennedy. Until her death, she worked as a senior editor at Doubleday, respected by the editorial staff who saw her as one of them. Ted Schwarz remembered being in Doubleday to see a different editor and, while walking down the hall to get to the editor's office, passing the copy machine. A young woman in her early twenties was finishing copying a stack of papers. Behind her was a young man who was an editorial assistant. Behind him was a department secretary. And behind her, holding a handful of papers she needed duplicated, was Jacqueline. There was no deference asked or offered. She was one of them, an editor handling her own drudge work like everyone else.

It was this professionalism that John, Jr., knew, and it was this attitude he took to the French publishing giant Hachette, which invested millions of dollars and valuable knowledge in his magazine. He became a hands-on editor, conducting major interviews with such controversial and prominent figures as the Dalai Lama, former governor George Wallace, evangelist Billy Graham, and boxer Mike Tyson. At the same time he showed his sense of humor by dressing actress Drew Barrymore the way Marilyn Monroe had appeared when she sang to his father the most sensual version of "Happy Birthday" ever rendered.

John also could be objective about his own family. When Michael Kennedy was caught in a romance with his children's baby-sitter, and Congressman Joseph Kennedy II tried to annul a marriage that had lasted many years and resulted in sons, John editorialized that they were "poster boys for bad behavior."

The skill with which John handled his private life was so great that he became a role model for Princess Diana of England. She used John as an example for her son William, hoping he would learn to handle the celebrity thrust upon him in so humble a way.

Because of the Kennedy image in charity, John's name was used in ways he did not always like. He attended social events for various charities, and was involved to some degree in the family project of Special Olympics, but he was aware that he had not as yet accomplished great achievements on behalf of the unfortunate.

In the spring of 1999, John was asked to address the 200 graduating seniors at Washington College in the small town of Chestertown, Maryland. His fame would bring the school attention. His work as founder and editor of *George* was a valid reason for his appearance. But the school felt the need to give him an honorary degree based on public service work he had promoted.

John believed in public service and had been involved, though not nearly to the degree of his cousin, Maryland Lt. Governor Kathleen Kennedy Townsend. Certainly he felt that his involvement did not warrant an honor. And so, while John made his speech and thrilled the graduates with his presence, he went home without the degree. Later, longtime friend and associate editor of *George* Douglas Brinkley said that he thought John was nuts to turn down the degree. Brinkley pointed out that such honors are given out routinely and for even fewer reasons than why it was offered to John. Kennedy's reply, according to Brinkley, was, "I don't think I've done anything to deserve it."

The marriage to Carolyn Bessette came as a surprise, perhaps because she was so different from the image expected of John Kennedy. She was born to wealth and privilege, the stepdaughter of a successful Greenwich, Connecticut, orthopedic surgeon. Her mother, Ann Freeman, worked as a teacher and administrator in the New York public school system. Carolyn's high school classmates dubbed her "The Ultimate Beautiful Person," and no one was surprised when she majored in elementary education at Boston University. She had money, looks, and a personality that was so caring everyone who knew her seemed to like her. She could do anything she wanted. Teaching children seemed as appropriate as any other career, though it was not to be.

Carolyn's first job was with a Calvin Klein store in Boston. She never applied for it. The manager saw her walking down the street and realized her inherent slender good looks, her aura of class, and her openness made her a natural to represent the designer's clothing line. From that first job, she became Klein's publicist in his New York office.

Neither Carolyn nor John ever discussed exactly how they met. One story has her helping him to buy suits when he was shopping in the men's wear division of a Klein store. Another story has him spotting her jogging in Central Park, tracking her down after becoming instantly fascinated. Whatever the case, he had been living with actress Daryl Hannah, a woman who had so ingratiated herself with the Kennedys that she was one of the few outsiders visiting Jacqueline the day she died of cancer.

From the time John saw Carolyn, the actress and all former lovers were history. Carolyn Bessette was the woman he intended to wed, and she adjusted to his world with ease.

Not that there weren't problems. The couple fought like anyone else. There was even a tabloid "scoop" when a photographer caught John taking the engagement ring back from Carolyn during an argument in Central Park. The anger was human and not a major crisis. They worked through it all, then quietly wed in a private ceremony on Cumberland Island, just off the Georgia coast. The wedding was kept secret; not all the family members were invited.

It was in character for Kennedy to be helping a friend, in this case his sister-in-law Lauren Bessette, the evening of his death. John and Carolyn were going to attend his cousin Rory's wedding. Lauren just wanted to go to her parents' home for a visit.

Rory Kennedy, Bobby's youngest daughter, who was born after his death, was a filmmaker. Her media interest was behind the scenes, and she had fallen in love with kindred spirit and fellow filmmaker Mark Bailey. The family was gathering at the HyannisPort, Massachusetts, family compound off Nantucket Sound for what would have been a Saturday wedding. (It was postponed.) John and Carolyn were flying in their new Piper Saratoga II, a single engine turbo-prop. (Ironically the registration number was N529JK, the "529" representing his father's May 29 birth date.) As a favor they gave Lauren, Carolyn's older sister (by 18 months), a ride to the airport and on to New England.

The Kennedys and Lauren Bessette, 33, an investment banker at Morgan Stanley Dean Witter in New York City, flew from Fairfield, New Jersey. Carolyn's other sister, Lauren's twin Lisa, was in Munich, Germany, working on her doctorate in Renaissance studies, which she is earning through the University of Michigan.

The weather was excellent for line-of-sight flying except when approaching the airport on Martha's Vineyard. A mist had created a dangerously disorienting effect, which made it impossible to see where the sky ended and the water began. Pilots who were instrument trained could easily handle the confusing approach. John was not instrument trained.

The cause of the crash is not certain at this writing. It is believed that John became disoriented by the mist. It is presumed that he confused sky and water, making the wrong corrections and dropping into the ocean. However, there is also a possible contributing cause. The plane had two fuel tanks and a pilot had to switch from one to other to keep flying.

Because John would have been preparing his approach for landing, and because he could have been disoriented, it is possible that he forgot to make the switch, running out of fuel even as he fought to find his equilibrium.

Whatever the details prove to be, the crash was an accident that could not have been anticipated by someone with John's experience. Unlike the senseless death of his cousin Michael, who slammed into a tree while trying to play football, take videos, and ski on an advanced slope simultaneously, John's was a true tragedy. He was a man on his way to a wedding, helping his sister-in-law return home, and flying on a day when he thought the weather matched his skills. He could not have anticipated the visual effect of the mist, something he had never encountered. He could not have imagined he had a destiny with death at so young an age. John was just being "Joe average," a nice guy whose tragic accident could as easily have happened in a minivan had he truly been the man next door.

In what may be the ultimate irony, four months prior to John's death, his cousin Maria Shriver published her first children's book. Entitled *What's Heaven?,* it is an illustrated volume meant to answer children's questions about death.

John Kennedy, Jr., never tried to be famous. He never thought fame mattered. He never wanted adoration or unearned respect. He had no intention of fulfilling the Ken doll fantasies of politicians, movie stars, or even some of his family members. In the end, he was just plain John, and in his ordinariness, he will be missed.

ADDENDUM: KENNEDY CRASH UPDATE

For a while there was hope. There had to be hope. For Richard and Ann Freeman, the idea of the loss of two of their three daughters meant unspeakable agony. For the Kennedy family, there was prayer that somehow John, Jr., would be as fortunate as his Uncle Ted, who had survived a plane crash when he was in his thirties.

There was a difference, though. Uncle Ted had crashed on land. John and Carolyn Kennedy and Lauren Bessette were over the Atlantic Ocean. The water temperature where they went down was 68 degrees. If they lived, and if they had been able to free themselves from the aircraft, they would have had to be located within 12 to 14 hours. Anything longer would have resulted in hypothermia and death.

Still, as the hours turned to days, as the search and rescue teams switched from looking for survivors to seeking corpses, the families had only prayer. Caroline Schlossberg stayed in seclusion with her husband and children, the only immediate family she had left. The rest of the Kennedys were in Hyannis Port, where they had gathered for the joyous marriage of Bobby's youngest child. The Freemans were in seclusion, waiting for Lauren's twin sister to return from Germany. And all of them wanted a miracle.

What little hope existed was lost on Wednesday, 21 July 1999. The wreckage was found buried in the Atlantic Ocean with the body of John Kennedy, Jr., still in the cockpit.

At the same time, evidence from radar and other sources revealed the technical details of what had happened. John, Carolyn, and Lauren were 34 miles away from the Martha's Vineyard airport, traveling at 5,600 feet, just over a mile in the air. It was time to prepare for landing, so John began descending at a rate of 700 feet a minute, gradually reaching an altitude of 2,300 feet after five minutes. By then he was just 20 miles from the airport.

John turned the plane to the right, ascending to 2,600 feet, where he stayed for the next sixty seconds, still on a southeasterly heading. And that was where disorientation occurred. The mist, the water, and the sky blended into one seamless condition where sideways seemed right side up, right side up seemed upside down, and only the instruments he could not yet use could help him retain control.

In seconds John had to decide which way to turn the plane. If he guessed correctly, they would land and have a harrowing tale of near tragedy to tell their friends. If he guessed incorrectly . . .

"We call this getting yourself in a square corner, when you run out of ideas and experience at the same time," said Michael Barr, a former Vietnam War fighter pilot and the director of the Aviation Safety Program of the University of Southern California, a leading training center for accident investigators.

"He would have been looking straight out at the dark ocean on a nearly moonless night. He probably looked over his right shoulder for lights. Then when he started to sink, he would have been trying to get the nose back to the horizon, get the wings level, and find where he was—all at the same time. Even for a good pilot, that could produce a death spiral."

John turned to the right, then began descending at what may have been greater than 5,000 feet per minute. The plane was

16 miles from the airport when it reached 1,100 feet, the lowest point recorded by the radar before it dropped off the screen.

The families undoubtedly knew the outcome of the search. With each passing day their prayers were for three adult children who were already in the loving hands of God. Yet there must have been a glimmer of hope, because that's the way we are. They were too young, too bright, too beautiful, and too full of promise unfulfilled. And now they belong to history. Now the families have buried their children at sea and begun the long, slow process of recovery that will bring what healing can occur after so tragic a series of losses.

John, his wife Carolyn, and his sister-in-law Lauren will be dearly missed.

BIBLIOGRAPHY

American Medical Association. "Example of a Patient with Adrenal Insufficiency Due to Addison's Disease Requiring Elective Surgery." *Archive of Surgery,* November 1955.

Beschloss, Michael. *Kennedy and Roosevelt: The Uneasy Alliance.* New York: HarperCollins, 1991.

Brown, Peter, and Patte Barham. *Marilyn: The Last Take.* New York: Dutton, 1992.

Bryant, Traphes, with Frances Leighton. *Dog Days at the White House.* New York: Macmillan, 1975.

Bullitt, Orville, ed. *For the President, Personal and Secret: Correspondence Between Franklin D. Roosevelt and William C. Bullitt.* Boston: Houghton Mifflin, 1972.

Burke, Richard, with William and Marilyn Hoffer. *The Senator: My Ten Years with Ted Kennedy.* New York: St. Martin's Press, 1992.

Cameron, Gail. *Rose: A Biography of Rose Fitzgerald Kennedy.* New York: Putnam, 1971.

Clifford, Clark, with Richard Holbrooke. *Counsel to the President*. New York: Random House, 1991.

Collier, Peter, and David Horowitz. *The Kennedys: An American Drama*. New York: Simon & Schuster, 1984.

Costello, John. *Ten Days to Destiny*. New York: William Morrow, 1991.

Cutler, John. *"Honey Fitz": Three Steps to the White House*. New York: Bobbs-Merrill, 1962.

Damore, Leo. *The Cape Cod Years of John Fitzgerald Kennedy*. Englewood Cliffs, N.J.: Prentice-Hall, 1967.

———. *Senatorial Privilege: The Chappaquiddick Cover-up*. Washington, D.C.: Regnery Gateway, 1988.

David, Lester. *Ethel: The Story of Mrs. Robert F. Kennedy*. New York: World, 1971.

———. *Ted Kennedy: Triumphs and Tragedies*. New York: Grosset & Dunlap, 1971.

Davis, John. *The Kennedys: Dynasty and Disaster, 1848-1984*. New York: McGraw-Hill, 1984.

De Toledano, Ralph. *R.F.K.: The Man Who Would Be President*. New York: Putnam, 1967.

Dineen, Joseph. *The Kennedy Family*. Boston: Little, Brown, 1959.

Dorman, Michael. *We Shall Overcome*. New York: Delacorte, 1964.

Everson, William. *American Silent Film*. New York: Oxford University Press, 1978.

Farley, James. *Behind the Ballots: The Personal History of a Politician*. New York: Harcourt, 1938.

Gallagher, Mary Barelli. *My Life with Jacqueline Kennedy*. New York: David McKay, 1969.

Gentry, Curt. *J. Edgar Hoover: The Man and the Secrets*. New York: Norton, 1991.

Giancana, Sam and Chuck. *Double Cross*. New York: Warner, 1992.

Goodwin, Doris Kearns. *The Fitzgeralds and the Kennedys: An American Saga*. New York: St. Martin's Press, 1987.

Hamilton, Nigel. *J.F.K.: Reckless Youth.* New York: Random House, 1992.

Handlin, Oscar. *The Uprooted: The Epic Story of the Great Migrations That Made the American People.* Boston: Little, Brown, 1951.

Heymann, C. David. *A Woman Named Jackie.* New York: Carol Communications, 1989.

James, Ann. *The Kennedy Scandals & Tragedies.* Lincolnwood, Ill.: Publications International, 1991.

James, Ralph and Esther. *Hoffa and the Teamsters.* Princeton: Van Nostrand, 1965.

Kelley, Kitty. *Jackie Oh!* Secaucus, N.J.: Lyle Stuart, 1978.

————. *His Way: The Unauthorized Biography of Frank Sinatra.* New York: Bantam, 1986.

Kennedy, John F., ed. *As We Remember Joe.* Cambridge: Cambridge University Press, 1945.

————. Personal Papers. Correspondence, 1933-1950 (Box 4A): Inga Arvad letters January 27, 1942; February 14, 1942; March 11, 1942.

Kennedy, Joseph P., ed. *The Story of the Films.* Chicago: A.W. Shaw, 1927.

————. *I'm for Roosevelt.* New York: Reynal and Hitchcock, 1936.

Kennedy Library. Scott Rafferty papers: Interviews, correspondence, and FBI documents, 1938-1949.

Kennedy, Rose. *Times to Remember.* New York: Doubleday, 1974.

Koskoff, David. *Joseph P. Kennedy: A Life and Times.* Englewood, N.J.: Prentice-Hall, 1974.

Krock, Arthur. *Memoirs.* New York: Funk & Wagnalls, 1968.

Lasky, Jesse. *Whatever Happened to Hollywood.* New York: Funk & Wagnalls, 1968.

Lasky, Victor. *J.F.K.: The Man and the Myth.* New York: Macmillan, 1963.

Latham, Caroline, and Jeannie Sakol. *The Kennedy Encyclopedia.* New York: New American Library, 1989.

Lawford, Patricia Seaton, with Ted Schwarz. *The Peter Lawford Story*. New York: Carroll & Graf, 1988.

————. *Peter Lawford*. London: Sidgwick & Jackson, 1988.

Leigh, Wendy. *Arnold*. Chicago: Congdon & Weed, 1990.

Lippman, Theo. *Senator Ted Kennedy: The Career Behind the Image*. New York: Norton, 1976.

Madsen, Axel. *Gloria & Joe*. New York: William Morrow, 1988.

Manchester, William. *Portrait of a President: John F. Kennedy in Profile*. Boston: Little, Brown, 1962.

Martin, Ralph. *A Hero for Our Times: An Intimate Story of the Kennedy Years*. New York: Macmillan, 1983.

Martin, Ralph, and Ed Plaut. *Front Runner, Dark Horse*. New York: Doubleday, 1960.

McCarthy, Joe. *The Remarkable Kennedys*. New York: Dial, 1960.

Miller, Hope. *Scandals in the Highest Office*. New York: Random House, 1973.

Moley, Raymond. *After Seven Years*. New York: Harper, 1939.

————. *The First New Deal*. New York: Harcourt, 1966.

Navasky, Victor. *Kennedy Justice*. New York: Atheneum, 1971.

Newfield, Jack. *Robert Kennedy: A Memoir*. New York: NAL, 1988.

Olsen, Jack. *The Bridge at Chappaquiddick*. Boston: Little, Brown, 1970.

Otash, Fred, and Ted Schwarz. *Marilyn, The Kennedys, and Me*. Unpublished manuscript, 1992.

Parmet, Herbert. *Jack: The Struggles of John F. Kennedy*. New York: Dial, 1980.

Rainie, Harrison and John Quinn. *Growing Up Kennedy*. New York: Berkley, 1985.

Reeves, Thomas. *A Question of Character: A Life of John F. Kennedy*. New York: Free Press, 1991.

Roosevelt, Elliott, ed. *F.D.R.: His Personal Letters, 1928-1945*. New York: Duell, Sloan & Pearce, 1950.

Rust, Zad. *Teddy Bare*. Boston: Western Islands, 1971.

Saunders, Frank, with James Southwood. *Torn Lace Curtain:*

Life with the Kennedys Recalled by Their Personal Chauffeur. New York: Holt, Rinehart, 1982.

Schlesinger, Arthur. *A Thousand Days: John F. Kennedy in the White House.* Boston: Houghton Mifflin, 1965.

————. *Robert F. Kennedy and His Times.* Boston: Houghton Mifflin, 1978.

Schoor, Gene. *Young John Kennedy.* New York: Harcourt, 1963.

Searls, Hank. *The Lost Prince: Young Joe, The Forgotten Kennedy.* Cleveland: World, 1969.

Shannon, William. *The Heir Apparent: Robert Kennedy and the Struggle for Power.* New York: Macmillan, 1967.

Shriver, Eunice Kennedy. "Hope for Retarded Children." *The Saturday Evening Post,* September 22, 1962.

Slevin, Jonathan, and Maureen Spagnolo. *Kennedys: The Next Generation.* New York: St. Martin's Press, 1992.

Sorensen, Theodore, ed. *The Speeches, Statements, and Writings of John F. Kennedy: 1947-1963.* New York: Dell, 1988.

Spada, James. *Peter Lawford: The Man Who Kept the Secrets.* New York: Bantam, 1991.

Swanson, Gloria. *Swanson on Swanson.* New York: Random House, 1980.

Tedrow, Richard and Thomas. *Death at Chappaquiddick.* Ottawa, Ill.: Caroline House, 1976.

Thimmesch, Nick, and William Johnson. *Robert Kennedy at 40.* New York: Norton, 1965.

Thompson, Robert, and Hortense Myers. *Robert F. Kennedy: The Brother Within.* New York: Dell, 1962.

U.S. Department of State. *Foreign Relations of the United States,* III, 1940.

Whalen, Richard. *The Founding Father: The Story of Joseph P. Kennedy.* New York: New American Library, 1964.

White, Theodore. *The Making of the President 1960.* New York: Atheneum, 1961.

————. *The Making of the President 1968.* New York: Atheneum, 1969.

Wills, Garry. *The Kennedy Imprisonment.* Boston: Little, Brown, 1982.

Wolf, George, and Joseph DiMona. *Frank Costello: Prime Minister of the Underworld.* New York: William Morrow, 1974.

Woodham-Smith, Cecil. *The Great Hunger: Ireland 1845-1849.* New York: Harper & Row, 1963.

New Perspectives in Health Care
from Kensington Books

__Cancer Cure $12.00US/$15.00CAN

The Complete Guide to Finding and Getting the Best Care There is
by Gary L. Schine with Ellen Berlinsky, Ph.D.   0-8217-024-5
Diagnosed with incurable cancer, author Gary L. Schine found the
treatment that led him back to full recovery and perfect health. Now,
in this inspiring and invaluable guide, he shows you how to take
charge of your illness, your treatment, and your recovery. Includes
a complete glossary of terms and a comprehensive resource guide.

__Health and Fitness in Plain English $14.00US/$19.00CAN
by Jolie Bookspan, Ph.D.   1-57566-288-4
If you care about keeping fit, you've been bombarded with exercise
and nutrition advice. This powerful guide cuts through the hype and
brings you the truth about top nutrition plans, permanent weight loss,
osteoporosis prevention, the biggest health food store rip-offs, and so
much more.

__The Brain Wellness Plan $14.00US/$19.00CAN
by Dr. Jay Lombard and Carl Germano, RD, CNS 1-57566-293-0
Now, a leading neurologist and renowned nutritional scientist bring
you the latest developments in brain research, as well as a comprehensive plan for building brain health. In fascinating, easy-to-under-
stand detail, this innovative bestseller guides readers through proven
medical, hormonal, and nutritional therapies that will help prevent
and treat disease.

Call toll free **1-888-345-BOOK** to order by phone or use this
coupon to order by mail.
Name _____
Address _____
City _____ State _____ Zip _____
Please send me the books I have checked above.
I am enclosing $_____
Plus postage and handling* $_____
Sales tax (in New York and Tennessee) $_____
Total amount enclosed $_____
*Add $2.50 for the first book and $.50 for each additional book.
Send check or money order (no cash or CODs) to:
Kensington Publishing Corp., 850 Third Avenue, New York, NY 10022
Prices and Numbers subject to change without notice.
All orders subject to availability.
Check out our website at **www.kensingtonbooks.com**

More Novels by
Jane Heller

__Cha Cha Cha $5.99US/$7.50CAN
   0-8217-5895-0

__The Club $4.99US/$5.99CAN
   1-57566-038-5

__Crystal Clear $5.99US/$7.50CAN
   1-57566-388-0

__Infernal Affairs $5.99US/$7.50CAN
   1-57566-154-3

__Princess Charming $5.99US/$7.50CAN
   1-57566-261-2

Call toll free **1-888-345-BOOK** to order by phone or use this coupon to order by mail.

Name _____
Addres s_____
City _____ State _____ Zip _____
Please send me the books I have checked above.
I am enclosing $_____
Plus postage and handling* $_____
Sales tax (in New York and Tennessee only) $_____
Total amount enclosed $_____
*Add $2.50 for the first book and $.50 for each additional book.
Send check or money order (no cash or CODs) to:
Kensington Publishing Corp., 850 Third Avenue, New York, NY 10022
Prices and Numbers subject to change without notice.
All orders subject to availability.
Check out our website at **www.kensingtonbooks.com**

A World of Eerie Suspense
Awaits in Novels by Noel Hynd

__**Cemetery of Angels**   0-7860-0261-1 $5.99US/$6.99CAN
Starting a new life in Southern California, Bill and Rebecca Moore
believe they've found a modern paradise. The bizarre old tale about
their house doesn't bother them, nor does their proximity to a graveyard
filled with Hollywood legends. Life is idyllic...until their beloved son
and daughter vanish without a trace.

__**Rage of Spirits**   0-7860-0470-3 $5.99US/$7.50CAN
A mind-bending terrorist has the power to change the course of world
history. With the President in a coma, it's fallen to hardboiled White
House press aide William Cochrane to unearth the old secrets that can
prevent catastrophe. After an encounter with a New England psychic,
he finds himself descending deeper into the shadowy world between
this life and the next...

__**A Room for the Dead**   0-7860-0089-9 $5.99US/$6.99CAN
With only a few months to go before his retirement, Detective Sgt. Frank
O'Hara faces the most impossible challenge of his career: tracking
down a killer who can't possibly exist—not in this world, anyway. Could
it be the murderous psychopath he sent to the chair years before? But
how? A hair-raising journey into the darkest recesses of the soul.

Call toll free **1-888-345-BOOK** to order by phone or use this
coupon to order by mail.
Name _____
Address _____
City _____ State _____Zip _____
Please send me the books I have checked above.
I am enclosing $_____
Plus postage and handling* $_____
Sales tax (in New York and Tennessee only) $_____
Total amount enclosed $_____
*Add $2.50 for the first book and $.50 for each additional book.
Send check or money order (no cash or CODs) to:
Kensington Publishing Corp., 850 Third Avenue, New York, NY 10022
Prices and Numbers subject to change without notice.
All orders subject to availability.
Check out our website at **www.kensingtonbooks.com**

"Book 'em!"
Legal Thrillers from Kensington

___**Character Witness** by R.A. Forster $5.99US/$7.50CAN
      0-7860-0378-2

___**Keeping Counsel** by R. A. Forster $5.99US/$6.99CAN
      0-8217-5281-2

___**The Mentor** by R.A. Forster $5.99US/$7.50CAN
      0-7860-0488-6

___**Presumption of Guilt** by Leila Kelly $5.99US/$7.50CAN
      0-7860-0584-X

Call toll free **1-888-345-BOOK** to order by phone or use this coupon to order by mail.

Name _____

Address _____

City _____ State _____ Zip _____

Please send me the books I have checked above.

I am enclosing	$_____
Plus postage and handling*	$_____
Sales tax (in New York and Tennessee only)	$_____
Total amount enclosed	$_____

*Add $2.50 for the first book and $.50 for each additional book.

Send check or money order (no cash or CODs) to:

Kensington Publishing Corp., 850 Third Avenue, New York, NY 10022

Prices and Numbers subject to change without notice.

All orders subject to availability.

Check out our website at **www.kensingtonbooks.com**

Your Favorite Mystery Authors Are Now Just A Phone Call Away

__Buried Lies   1-57566-168-3 $5.50US/$7.00CAN
 by Conor Daly

__Skin Deep, Blood Red 1-57566-254-X $5.99US/$7.50CAN
 by Robert Skinner

__Shattered Vows 0-8217-4943-9 $4.99US/$5.99CAN
 by Pat Warren

__Murder by Tarot 0-8217-3637-X $3.99US/$4.99CAN
 by Al Guthrie

__The Murder Game 1-57566-321-X $5.99US/$7.50CAN
 by Steve Allen

__Twister   1-57566-062-8 $4.99US/$5.99CAN
 by Barbara Block

__Dead Men Don't Dance 1-57566-318-X $5.99US/$7.50CAN
 by Margaret Chittenden

__Country Comes To Town 1-57566-244-2 $5.99US/$7.50CAN
 by Toni L. P. Kelner

__Just Desserts 1-57566-037-7 $4.99US/$5.99CAN
 by G. A. McKevett

Call toll free **1-888-345-BOOK** to order by phone or use this coupon to order by mail.

Name _____

Address _____

City _____ State _____ Zip _____

Please send me the books I have checked above.

I am enclosing $_____

Plus postage and handling* $_____

Sales tax (in NY and TN only) $_____

Total amount enclosed $_____

*Add $2.50 for the first book and $.50 for each additional book.

Send check or money order (no cash or CODs) to:

Kensington Publishing Corp., 850 Third Avenue, New York, NY 10022

Prices and numbers subject to change without notice.

All orders subject to availability.

Check out our website at **www.kensingtonbooks.com**

Get Hooked on the
Mysteries of
Jonnie Jacobs

__Evidence of Guilt $5.99US/$7.50CAN
   1-57566-279-5

__Murder Among Friends $4.99US/$6.50CAN
   1-57566-089-X

__Murder Among Neighbors $5.99US/$7.50CAN
   0-8217-275-2

__Murder Among Us $5.99US/$7.50CAN
   1-57566-398-8

__Shadow of Doubt $5.50US/$7.00CAN
   1-57566-146-2

Call toll free **1-888-345-BOOK** to order by phone or use this coupon to order by mail.

Name _____

Address _____

City _____ State _____ Zip _____

Please send me the books I have checked above.

I am enclosing $_____

Plus postage and handling* $_____

Sales tax (NY and TN residents only) $_____

Total amount enclosed $_____

*Add $2.50 for the first book and $.50 for each additional book.

Send check or money order (no cash or CODs) to:

Kensington Publishing Corp., 850 Third Avenue, New York, NY 10022

Prices and Numbers subject to change without notice.

All orders subject to availability.

Check out our website at **www.kensingtonbooks.com**